GW00992283

THE THIRSTY SWORD

Early twentieth-century folk print of ʿAntar, ʿAbla, and Shaibūb. *Courtesy of the Egyptian Ethnographical Society, Cairo.*

THE THIRSTY SWORD

Sīrat 'Antar and the Arabic Popular Epic

PETER HEATH

University of Utah Press
Salt Lake City

©1996 by the University of Utah Press
All rights reserved
∞ Printed on acid-free paper

Library of Congress Cataloging-in-Publication Data

Heath, Peter, 1949–
The thirsty sword : Sīrat ‘Antar and the Arabic popular epic / Peter Heath.
p. cm.
Includes bibliographical references (p. 288–316) and index.
ISBN 0-87480-515-5 (alk. paper)
1. ‘Antar. 2. ‘Antarah ibn Shaddād, 6th cent.—Legends.
I. Title.
PJ7702.H43 1996
892'.73—dc20 96-22394

For Marianne

Contents

A Note on Transliteration and Dates

TRANSLITERATION

1. Consonants (in the order of the Arabic alphabet):
’ b t th j ḥ kh d dh r z s sh ṣ ḍ ṭ ẓ ‘ gh f q k l m n h w y

2. Vowels: short, *a i u*; long, *ā ī ū*

3. Diphthongs: *au ai*

4. *Hamza*: within or at the end of words as above (’); word-initial *hamza* is not expressed. Immediately preceding *hamzat al-waṣl* (prosthetic *hamza*) long vowels become short and the following *hamza* is represented by ‘.

5. *Tā marbuṭa*: *-a* in final pausal form, *-at* in construct form.

6. Definite article: normally *al-*, but when the article is prefixed to words beginning with Sun Letters (*t, th, d, dh, r, z, s, sh, ṣ, ḍ, ṭ, ẓ, l, n*) the *-l-* changes for reasons of euphony. Following words ending in a vowel the definite article gains *hamzat al-waṣl* (as in 4 above) and becomes *’l-*.

7. Proper nouns are transliterated, with the exception of a few that have standard English spellings, such as Abraham and Nimrod. Place names that are common in modern English are given in their familiar forms (Sudan and Oman instead of as-Sūdān and ‘Umān). Less familiar names (such as al-Madā’in), however, are transliterated. The Arabic word for tribe is put in the oblique case when referring to tribes in the *Sīra* (hence *banī* instead of *banū*, although the latter is sometimes used when referring to historical units).

DATES

Dates are generally given according to the Gregorian calendar. When further precision is required, the Hijrī date precedes the Gregorian date, separated by a slash.

Note on Transliteration and Dates

Acknowledgments

I first began my study of *Sīrat ʿAntar* and the fascinating field of Arabic and Islamic popular literatures twenty years ago. My research began as a dissertation, which was accepted by Harvard University in 1981. It continued in the form of independent studies on various aspects of Arabic popular literature that appeared in print or were presented as conference papers in the years that followed. It now attains some temporary sense of culmination with the appearance of the present monograph. This area of research is daunting in regard to the amount of materials available and challenging in the scope of its intellectual complexity. Yet it is also very rewarding. It has taught me much about how literature functions in its aesthetic, cultural, and social dimensions. I will be gratified if this study clarifies some of the questions that it raises; I will be even happier if it encourages other scholars to enter this engaging field of research.

Over the years, my project has been aided and facilitated by many institutions and individuals, and it gives me great pleasure to acknowledge their help and support here.

In the course of my research, I have relied on the help and efficiency of the staffs of the libraries at Harvard University, Princeton University, the American University in Cairo, the National Library of Egypt (Dār al-Kutub), the Topkapı Saray Museum Library in Istanbul, the Kongelige Bibliotek in Copenhagen, the British Library in London, the John Rylands Library in Manchester, England, and the Staatsbibliothek in Berlin. I was also given research access to the Semitic Institute of the University of Copenhagen and to the Ethnological Museum of the Egyptian Geographical Society in Cairo. To each of these institutions and to the courteous and friendly individuals who work in them, I owe my thanks.

My study was significantly aided by a year-long grant for dissertation research from the American Research Center in Egypt in 1976–77 and by a summer research grant awarded to me by Birzeit University in 1984. This support was essential, and I am grateful to these institutions for their help.

Parts of this volume have appeared in earlier forms. A version of chapter 1 appeared as "A Critical Review of Scholarship on *Sīrat ʿAntar ibn Shaddād* and the Popular *Sīra*," *Journal of Arabic Literature* 15 (1984): 19–44 (E. J. Brill, Leiden). Part of chapter 7 appeared as "Lord and Parry, *Sīrat ʿAntar*, Lions," *Edebiyāt* n.s. 2, nos. 1 and 2 (1988): 149–66 (Middle East Center, University of Pennsylvania). Part of chapter 4 appeared in my article "Arabische Volksliteratur im Mittelalter," in *Neues Handbuch der Literaturwissenschaft*, vol. 5: *Orientalisches Mittelalter*, ed. Wolfhart P. Heinrichs (Wiesbaden: AULA-Verlag, 1990), 423–39. I thank these publishers for granting me permission to reprint portions of these articles in this new and revised form. I am especially grateful to the Ethnological Museum of the Egyptian Geographical Society for permission to use a picture of one of their ʿAntar folk prints as a frontispiece.

I also wish to acknowledge the work of my colleagues in the field of Arabic and Islamic popular literatures. This still-nascent field requires enormous investments of time, energy, and thought from anyone who enters it. As I have worked with the sources, my admiration for the essential foundational contributions of earlier generations of scholars, such as Victor Chauvin, Wilhelm Ahlwardt, and Rudi Paret, has grown more profound. As someone who works primarily with written sources, my gratitude for the intelligent and groundbreaking research of my contemporary folklorist colleagues is also profound. I hope that they benefit from my forays into the manuscript and print traditions of Arabic popular epics as much as I have profited from their fieldwork and scholarly analyses.

It is a great pleasure to acknowledge the contributions of individual colleagues who have directly helped to improve this study. Professors Muhsin S. Mahdi, Albert B. Lord, and Wolfhart P. Heinrichs oversaw the completion of this work in dissertation form. I thank them for their personal wisdom, intellectual stimulation, and infinite patience. Professor Ahmet T. Karamustafa, my valued colleague and friend at Washington University, checked my translation of the introduction of the Ottoman Turkish translation of *Sīrat ʿAntar* that appears in appendix III and saved me from numerous errors. Professors Pierre Cachia and Susan Slyomovics examined this monograph at a late stage and provided useful comments and suggestions. Each of these scholars has my deep gratitude; I alone am responsible for any errors of detail or analysis that remain.

Finally, I wish to thank the editor and the staff of the University of Utah Press for their interest in this study and for the friendly and efficient way in which they have brought it to print. I am gratified that this volume has joined their growing and impressive list of books on premodern Islamic civilization.

Introduction

The study of epic has undergone enormous transformations in the past century. In the nineteenth century, literary scholars developed a genealogy of epic that concentrated on the Western literary tradition. This genealogy began with Homer and Virgil, continued with such medieval works as *Roland* and *Beowulf*, and culminated with such complex literary works as John Milton's *Paradise Lost*. While some scholars still explore this intracultural literary tradition, most have opened to the world. Researchers continue to focus on individual linguistic and literary traditions (as indeed they must), but many have become increasingly aware that traditions of epic have flourished throughout the globe in diverse cultural, social, and historical settings. The implications of this diversity and of the wealth of the newly discovered epic traditions throughout the world have increasingly directed scholarly research as the century has progressed.[1]

The recognition of the copious fecundity of epic has influenced modern study in two ways. First, it has encouraged comparativist study of the genre. Few scholars now focus only on the epic production of one culture or period. Even as they specialize, researchers keep in mind the international and cross-cultural context of their efforts. Classicists cannot ignore the Serbo-Croatian storytelling tradition that Milman Parry and Albert Lord brought to their attention. Africanists must be ready to take into consideration Turkic, Chinese, Arabic, Persian, or Middle English traditions. No one scholar can claim mastery over all of the world's epic traditions, but neither can he or she ignore their existence and their possible relevance to immediate and more circumscribed research interests.

Second, the study of epic is no longer confined to investigation of literate, elite bodies of literature. The recognition that many of the epics that nineteenth-century scholars viewed as literary masterpieces, from Homer to *Beowulf* to *Roland*, probably emerged (in different ways) from the contexts of oral and folk storytelling has widened the attention of scholars to include these arenas of artistic creation—with enormously productive results. Scholars' understanding of the cultural and historical complexity of the settings within which epics are produced has been enriched. This in turn has led them to explore such issues as the tension between orality and writing, on the one hand, and the relations between popular and elite literatures, on the other. Having opened to the world, researchers have discovered how complex, but also how fruitful and beneficial, its investigation can be.[2]

The present study draws from and builds on the modern study of epic. It focuses on a popular epic from the Arabic storytelling tradition, the account of the adventures and achievements of the pre-Islamic Arab poet ʿAntara ibn Shaddād. *Sīrat ʿAntar* (The Life Story of ʿAntar) is one point of culmination in the rich tradition of the premodern Arabic popular epic.[3] These popular epics (usually termed in Arabic *sīra shaʿbiyya*) are works of battle and romance, primarily concerned with depicting the personal prowess and military exploits of their heroes.[4] Pseudo-historical in tone and setting, they base many of their central characters on actual historical figures. Details of history are quickly transcended by the imaginative improvements of fiction, with the result that historical features usually reflect only general setting, atmosphere, and tone. The creators of *sīra*s may not have intended to contradict history, but they were quite willing to refashion it for their own purposes.[5]

Sīrat ʿAntar purports to recount the life story of the famous pre-Islamic Arab poet and warrior ʿAntara ibn Shaddād. The historical ʿAntara was a half-caste slave (his father was Arab and his mother black African) who won freedom and fame through his poetic and martial abilities and ended life as a respected member of the northern Arabian tribe of ʿAbs.[6] The *Sīra* builds upon the framework of ʿAntara's life to construct its own pseudo-historical account. As the protagonist of the *Sīra*, ʿAntar is black and begins life as a slave. Like his prototype, he achieves fame as a warrior and poet. And just as the historical ʿAntara addressed some of his poems to his beloved, ʿAbla, some of the most beautiful poems in the *Sīra* are those that ʿAntar composes to express his passion for his beautiful cousin ʿAbla, for whose sake he undergoes countless trials and performs numerous exploits. Indeed, the love affair between the two in *Sīrat ʿAntar* has become one of the most famous love stories of Arabic popular culture.

Like most Arabic popular epics, *Sīrat ʿAntar* is composed in rhymed prose (*sajʿ*) frequently interspersed with poetry. The work is exceedingly long; in its various manuscript and printed versions, it runs between three and eight thousand pages, depending upon page and script size. The formulaic character of its rhymed prose, the episodic structure of its story-line, the continual repetition of a limited number of narrative patterns and motifs, the lack of any identifiable author, and its great length all indicate that the narrative originated and developed within a flourishing tradition of oral, public storytelling.

To be understood and appreciated fully, *Sīrat ʿAntar* must be viewed within the overall context of the particular genre of Arabic literature to which it belongs. It should also be considered from the perspective of its relations with flourishing popular literatures that existed contemporaneously in Arabic- and non-Arabic-speaking areas of the Islamic world. The most important such corollaries are found in Persian and Turkish literatures, but others exist in Swahili and other sub-Saharan African languages, in North African Berber dialects, in Southeast Asian languages such as Malay, and in Caucasian tongues such as Armenian and Georgian. Finally, instances of direct or indirect mutual influence of Western epics of the medieval or Renaissance periods and comparison with epic traditions from all parts of the world should not be ignored.

THE ARABIC POPULAR EPIC

Arabic popular literature produced a rich harvest of heroic cycles that, taken together, cover almost all of recorded pre-Islamic and Islamic history.[7] Early Persian history is represented by *Sīrat Fīrūz Shāh*, whose protagonist is the son of the Achaemenid King Darius II; the Sassanid dynasty figures in the *Story of Bahrām Gūr*; and in between falls *Sīrat Iskandar*, the *geste* of Alexander the Great.[8]

Pre-Islamic South Arabian history forms the backdrop for *Sīrat al-Malik Saif ibn Dhī Yazan*, while pre-Islamic North Arabian history is dealt with in *Sīrat ʿAntar*, as well as in the story of *az-Zīr Sālim* and other accounts of the war of Basūs between the tribes of Bakr and Taghlib. Early Islamic history is broached in *Sīrat Amīr Ḥamza*, which narrates the adventures of Ḥamza ibn ʿAbd al-Muṭallib, uncle to the Prophet Muḥammad. *Dhāt al-Himma*, *Ghazwat al-Arqaṭ*, and *al-Badr-Nār* deal with the tribal feuds and holy wars (*al-jihād*) of the Umayyad and ʿAbbasid caliphates; while Fatimid and Mamluk history are treated in *Sīrat al-Ḥākim bi-Amr Allāh* and *Sīrat al-Malik aẓ-Ẓāhir Baibars*.[9]

The protagonists of the cycles of *Aḥmad ad-Danaf* and *ʿAlī Zaibaq* are not martial heroes but *ayyārūn* (rogues), who rely on craft and guile to achieve their aims.[10] Finally, there is *Sīrat Banī Hilāl*, with *Sīrat ʿAntar* the most famous and beloved cycle of this genre, a legendary account of the history of the tribe of the Banī Hilāl from their pre-Islamic days until their conquest of much of North Africa in the fifth/eleventh century.[11]

Although the genre of the Arabic popular epic probably began to develop in the early period of the Islamic empire, references to written examples appear only in the early sixth/twelfth century, while the earliest manuscripts date from the early ninth/fifteenth century. The tradition continued to flourish in oral form until the middle part of this century, and written versions of the narratives are continually reprinted.

There are significant differences in style, content, and historical origin among works of the genre. *Sīrat Fīrūz Shāh*, for example, is Persian in origin, while *Sīrat az-Zīr Sālim* is based on pre-Islamic *Ayyām al-'Arab* (Battle Days of the Arabs) sources. *Sīrat al-Malik Saif ibn Dhī Yazan* is full of sorcery and demons, while *Sīrat 'Antar* is practically devoid of magic. *Sīrat al-Malik aẓ-Ẓāhir Baibars* is cast mainly in unadorned prose, while other *sīras* use rhymed prose (*saj'*) and poetry. Nevertheless, these works form a cohesive genre by reason of their shared emphasis on heroes and heroic deeds of battle, their pseudo-historical tone and setting, and their indefatigable drive toward cyclic expansion: one event leads to another, one battle to another, one war to another, and so on for hundreds and thousands of pages.

ISLAMIC POPULAR LITERATURE

Viewed from a wider cultural perspective, these popular epics are Arabic examples of a larger body of vibrant popular literature that existed in most parts of the Islamic world. Premodern Persian and Turkish literatures also developed strong traditions of popular epic, and there is convincing evidence that despite their linguistic differences neighboring traditions of popular storytelling borrowed and translated from and mutually influenced one another. *Sīrat 'Antar* exists in a Turkish translation (see chapter 4 below), and many of these epics exist in multiple versions across disparate linguistic borders. Renditions of *Sīrat Amīr Ḥamza*, for example, exist in Arabic, Persian, Turkish, Georgian, Urdu, and Malay, while versions of *Sīrat Iskandar* are even more widely disseminated.

Furthermore, Arabic and other Islamic popular epics constitute only one portion of a vast tradition of multilingual Islamic popular literatures that also encompasses nonepic pseudo-historical narratives, religious literature of various types (stories about Muḥammad and his companions, saints' legends, accounts of miracles, etc.), numerous genres of popular poetry, songs, proverbs, and humor, and tales of wonder and fantasy, the best known of which is *The Thousand and One Nights* (*The Arabian Nights*).[12] The history and nature of this body of literature are still largely unexplored, as are the ways in which different genres, within single linguistic traditions or across them, influenced one another. Nevertheless, no single example of these popular literatures should be considered without at least an awareness of the existence of this larger literary context.

A similar situation holds for the field of comparative epic. Muslim heroes appear in European epics, and Crusaders and other Western heroes appear in Arabic *sīras*. Yet questions of mutual influence, direct or indirect (such as the use of similar narrative patterns), have not yet been seriously broached. In critical discussions of world epic traditions, Arabic or Islamic epics are perhaps most noted for their lack of scholarly representation.

ISSUES OF THEORY AND METHOD

Since investigation of Arabic popular epic (and of Islamic popular literatures as a whole) is still in its infancy, some general remarks regarding the practical and methodological challenges involved are warranted.

In general, literary works are considered from three perspectives. *External historical research* traces the historical background of texts, authors, and audience response to particular works or genres; *internal critical inquiry* examines the technical aspects of literary creation to elucidate the ways in which authors use style, structure, convention, and creativity to achieve their literary effects; and *aesthetic evaluation* raises the issue of how particular works or types of literature should be judged as well as exploring the nature of the individual emotional and psychological effects and the broadly cultural responses that literary works evoke.

Underlying all of these perspectives is the larger issue of *hermeneutical context*, the "horizon of expectations" that determines a particular culture, period, or critic's understanding of what literature is, which facets of it deserve attention and are awarded priority, and what ways of studying or evaluating literary artistry are best. In this regard, the three perspectives of literary study referred to above merely reflect the hermeneutic context that participants in modern Western literary study have constructed for themselves. They involve expectations and parameters that, we must recognize, are not necessarily shared by practitioners of literary study in other historical periods or in non-Western cultures, whether past or contemporary.

Explicit awareness of the issue of assumptions of hermeneutical context is necessary for the study of *Sīrat ʿAntar* and other examples of Arabic and Islamic popular literatures because many obstacles stand in the way of placing such works in their proper interpretive contexts and thus impede their study and evaluation. These obstacles are both practical and methodological.

Practical Obstacles

1. Few scholars in the West or the East have devoted attention to premodern Arabic and Islamic popular literatures. As a result, substantial areas of basic

research concerning the external circumstances or the history of these works' textual and oral transmission remain untouched. Manuscripts are unpublished and even unexamined, rapidly disappearing traditions of public performance fade away unrecorded, and the many secondary sources that contain references to this body of literature and its performance are still largely unexplored.

2. The extreme length of *Sīrat 'Antar* and its companion works makes the study of even one epic or popular narrative a daunting task. Investigation of the full manuscript traditions of even so well known an example of popular literature as *The Thousand and One Nights* is still in its early stages. The vast geographical and linguistic ranges of the public performance traditions complicate investigation of so widespread an epic as *Sīrat Banī Hilāl*, despite the praiseworthy recent efforts of a number of dedicated scholars.[13]

3. Increasingly few of the limited number of researchers who address themselves to the study of premodern Islamic popular epics are linguistically prepared to investigate more than one literary tradition. As a result, studies of the Arabic tradition are carried out in isolation from those in the Persian, Turkish, Urdu, Swahili, and Malay traditions, not to mention examination of possible corollaries with premodern Western or Asian literatures.[14]

4. Even those few scholars who do extend their gaze to multiple linguistic traditions tend to focus on a single genre—epic or tale, for example—without placing these works in the broader context of the full range of premodern Islamic popular literatures.

Methodological Obstacles

1. Many scholars of literature (in both the West and the East) are uninterested in the study of popular literature. Some are sympathetic but unconcerned; others passively or actively disdain the academic study of popular literature or popular culture.

2. Those who are interested in popular culture—folklorists, anthropologists, ethnomusicologists, and scholars of cultural studies—are usually untrained in literary study. Moreover, they tend to concentrate on contemporary culture and are thus methodologically ill equipped for the historical investigation that the study of premodern literatures requires. For their part, literary scholars have only recently begun to avail themselves of the methodological insights of students of oral literature, popular culture, and anthropology.

3. Premodern popular Arabic and Islamic literatures are mixed media. They are performed and transmitted both orally and through writing, and they usually combine prose, rhymed prose, and various types of poetry and song. Specialists of oral or written traditions or of narrative or verse tend to focus on their preferred modes of transmission and literary media. The necessity

for such specialization is understandable, but it can also result in an uneven or distorted picture of popular works and traditions in which all were common.[15]

Each of these obstacles is understandable. Academic disciplines and fields have—and must have—their own histories, self-defined boundaries, and frameworks of inquiry. Mentioning these obstacles is less a complaint than a realistic assessment of the existing impediments to the study of premodern Islamic popular literatures, as well as an explanation of the course that this study of *Sīrat ʿAntar* will pursue.

IMMEDIATE GOALS OF THIS STUDY

This book has two parts.

Part I elucidates the general hermeneutic and historical context within which, I believe, the study of a narrative such as *Sīrat ʿAntar* should take place. Chapter 1 explores the history of previous studies on the *Sīra* and similar works to evaluate their contributions and oversights. Chapter 2 examines the history of the narrative's development, while chapter 3 investigates the performance context of the professional storytellers who created the work. Finally, chapter 4 discusses the concept of "popular literature" as understood in this monograph, concluding with a brief historical overview of premodern Arabic and Islamic popular literatures.

Part II concentrates on internal literary scrutiny of the narrative. Chapters 5 through 8 delineate structural, thematic, and stylistic components of the epic in order to reveal how the storytellers who created *Sīrat ʿAntar* used these building blocks to create the exciting, suspenseful, and romantic plots and descriptions that lie at the heart of the audience's enjoyment. Chapter 9 explores the nature and rationale of the epic's pseudo-historical framework and tone. Chapter 10 offers some final remarks on fruitful directions for future research.

BROADER GOALS OF THIS STUDY

A single monograph cannot surmount all of the obstacles to the study of premodern Islamic and Arabic popular literatures. It cannot even address all the pertinent questions that must be answered concerning a single narrative such as *Sīrat ʿAntar*. Nevertheless, one goal here is to broaden the interpretive framework within which future studies of such texts are conducted. Focusing on individual works is necessary, but I hope that this monograph convinces readers that ignoring the full literary context of individual examples of premodern Arabic and Islamic popular literatures only serves to distort our overall understanding and appreciation of these works.

A second goal is to emphasize that the study of Islamic popular literatures is necessary for an understanding of elite literatures as well. The two traditions have been in continuous interaction, both drawing from and playing off one another. One can seriously argue, in fact, that the dynamics, trends, fashions, and histories of either are only incompletely understood if one fails to take into account the contours and internal operations of the other. It is essential for scholars of Islamic literatures to realize this. Focusing on the magnificent achievements of Arabic and Islamic elite literatures while neglecting their constant interaction with their popular literature analogues can only lead one to misconstrue and misrepresent the concerns and accomplishments of elite authors and their works.

Third, this description of the narrative structure and compositional dynamics of *Sīrat ʿAntar*, limited as it must perforce be, aims at providing criteria for contrast and comparison that allow it to serve as a case study upon which future examinations of other premodern Arabic and Islamic popular epics can rest.

Finally, I hope that this study serves to bring this body of literature to the attention of two groups of scholars who could enormously benefit from its acquaintance: Islamic historians and specialists of the epic in other literary traditions.

For specialists in Islamic history, popular epics are superb sources for the study of the social and cultural history of the premodern populace of the Islamic world. Aside from the empirical historical data they provide, they are, when used wisely, an extremely valuable reflection of the ideals, aspirations, and concerns of ordinary individuals in these societies.

For scholars of epic and popular literatures from cultures beyond the Islamic world, the huge masses of material that have been preserved from the tradition of premodern Arabic and Islamic popular literatures provide instructive analogues for the study of other major epic and narrative traditions, such as the medieval Western or premodern Chinese. Their examination can contribute to the creation of a truly global conception of comparative and world literature.

PART I

History and Context

CHAPTER 1

The Modern "Discovery" of *Sīrat ʿAntar*

NINETEENTH-CENTURY EUROPEAN SCHOLARSHIP

IN 1799 Baron Joseph von Hammer-Purgstall—Austrian Orientalist, diplomat, and man of letters—set out for a sojourn in Istanbul. Before his departure his friend Baron Thugut, then minister for foreign affairs for the imperial Austrian government, asked Von Hammer to obtain for him "at whatever price" a manuscript of *The Thousand and One Nights* in the original Arabic. This request, coming from a diplomat, might seem surprising, but it was not so unusual. Ever since its first translation into French almost a century before, *The Thousand and One Nights* had enjoyed spectacular popularity in Europe; hence, it was natural that persons of culture and education such as Baron Thugut—even those who might not ordinarily have taken an interest in "Oriental" literatures—might desire an Arabic copy of the *Nights* for their libraries.[1] Whatever the motive behind this request, it proved impossible to fulfill. Baron von Hammer searched dutifully among the bookstalls and storytellers of Istanbul, but although the *Nights* was well known, no copy was to be found. In the course of his inquiries, however, the baron came across another work that was, like *The Thousand and One Nights*, a part of the standard repertoire of Arab storytellers: *Sīrat ʿAntar.*

Von Hammer found only a small fragment, but he was excited by his discovery. ʿAntara ibn Shaddād was already known to European Orientalists as a famous pre-Islamic warrior and poet, the composer of one of the long poems of the famous *Muʿallaqāt* anthology, and Von Hammer recalled that the prominent English Orientalist Sir William Jones had seen a fragment of *Sīrat ʿAntar* and had declared that "it comprises all that is elegant and noble in composition. So lofty, so various, and so bold is its style, that I do not hesitate to rank it among the most finished poems."[2]

In general, three areas of study dominated the interest of European students of Arabic during Von Hammer's time: *The Thousand and One Nights*, the early history of the Arabs, and the study of pre-Islamic poetry. Here was a work that encompassed all these interests. Like *The Thousand and One Nights*, it was a standard narrative of the popular storytellers of the time; it was set in the historical period of pre-Islamic Arabia; and it not only had as its protagonist a famous pre-Islamic poet, but also contained a great number of poems attributed to him. One can understand Von Hammer's excitement and imagine how avidly he must have searched Istanbul for other parts of the work. His efforts proved fruitless; but he was told that the epic was popular in Syria and Egypt and was advised to continue his search there.

Two years later, Von Hammer's travels took him to an Egypt recently evacuated by Napoleon's French expeditionary forces. The baron had not forgotten *Sīrat ʿAntar* and had, in fact, procured several more portions during a short visit to Jaffa. Now his hopes were high that he would obtain a complete copy in Egypt. At first, he was again unsuccessful. In Alexandria the coffeehouse storytellers and bedouins he inquired among brought him different fragments of several popular narratives—*Sīrat Iskandar, Sīrat Banī Hilāl, Sīrat Dhāt al-Himma*—but apparently no one possessed, or at any rate was willing to part with, a complete copy of *Sīrat ʿAntar*. Not until he arrived in Cairo did the energetic baron finally meet success. Upon the offer of a purse of gold, the sheikh of the Cairene storytellers produced a complete text bound in six large volumes, which, Von Hammer tells us, were parts of two different copies. The first three volumes dated from the fifteenth century, while the last three, although complementary to the first part, were of quite modern date.[3] Von Hammer shipped the manuscripts back to the Imperial Library in Vienna and in the following year, 1802, announced his discovery in print.

> This work, which must be reckoned as very instrumental towards learning the manners, dispositions, and habits of the Arabs, seems to us more interesting than the celebrated "Thousand and One Nights"; not indeed with respect to the fictions, in which this work almost entirely fails; but as a picture of true history. There is nothing about genii, magicians, or talismans, or fabulous animals; and if, indeed, the bravery of the hero, who, unwounded, slays hundreds and thousands of the foe, or the swiftness of his generous steed, that outstrips the wind, appear incredible; these are rather the results of a hyperbolic style, than to be considered fabulous figures, which never, in the opinion

> of orientals, invalidates the truth of history. The whole of this work may be esteemed as a faithful account of the principal tribes of the Arabs, and particularly of the tribe of Abs, from which sprung Antar, in the time of Nushirvan, King of Persia, more faithful in painting manners than in describing events.
>
> The style is often flowery and beautiful, mixed with poetry, frequently in a common diction, and sometimes the augmentations and more recent interpolations plainly prove the adulterations of the copyist. (What would that light of oriental literature, Sir William Jones, have thought of the style and merits of this work, who only treated the fourteenth volume, in his *Commentaries on Asiatic Poetry.*) It chiefly treats of the love of Antar and Abla, and also of their family, down to the death of the hero.
>
> This work, which is generally called a romance of chivalry, though impossible to be translated, owing to the number of volumes, may be gleaned; every part appertaining to history, should be carefully collected, and nothing relative to manners omitted. Such, with God's help, we intend to publish.
>
> The author, from beginning to end, appears to be Asmaee, a famous philologist and poet at the court of Harun Rasheed; but sometimes other authors and sources are mentioned, who according to our opinion, appear to have been inserted by the story-teller in the coffee-houses. This is the work, and not, as is generally supposed, the *Thousand and One Nights,* which is the source of the stories which fill the tents and cottages of Arabia and Egypt; though materials are often supplied from other works of the same kind.[4]

Such was the formal introduction of *Sīrat ʿAntar* to the West. Von Hammer's notice deserves full quotation because it contains perspectives that have, in one way or another, continued to preoccupy scholars up to our times.

First of all, Von Hammer appears to value *Sīrat ʿAntar* most as a potential historical source, a *Sittenbild*, an excellent picture of the manners and mores of the pre-Islamic Arabs. He admits that the work is not a historical account in the exact sense of the term, but it is a "picture of true history . . . faithful in painting manners." Because of this, he judges the *Sīra* to be superior in every sense to *The Thousand and One Nights,* which is quite unreliable in this regard. Although *Sīrat ʿAntar* might possess a "hyperbolic style," it is happily free of "fabulous figures" of any kind. As such, the work should be "gleaned; every part appertaining to history . . . carefully collected, and nothing relative to manners omitted."

Along with its merits as a historical source, Von Hammer considers the *Sīra* a fine piece of literature: a "romance of chivalry" with a style "often flowery and beautiful." If it also contains what appear to be unfortunate lapses into "common diction" as well as other "augmentations," these should be considered the recent "interpolations" or "adulterations" of later copyists or storytellers.

Third, Von Hammer is anxious to determine the epic's author and date of composition. He has no doubts that *Sīrat 'Antar* was originally composed by the famous Arab philologist and collector of early poetry 'Abd al-Malik ibn Quraib al-Aṣma'ī, who died around 208/823.[5]

Finally, the baron offers his opinion on the advisability of attempting to translate the epic. He deems it too voluminous to be translated in full, but he announces his intention to publish an extract from it; thus, as A. J. Arberry has noted, "In this time-honoured fashion Hammer-Purgstall staked out his claim."[6] In spite of this stated intention, the energetic Austrian soon became involved in a host of other projects. Almost twenty years were to pass before more was heard about *Sīrat 'Antar*—from Baron von Hammer-Purgstall or anyone else.

In 1819 the first volume of a projected full translation of *Sīrat 'Antar* into English appeared in London. This volume, the work of Terrick Hamilton—at that time the British Oriental secretary in Istanbul—had been rushed into print by an impatient publisher without even the benefit of the translator's introduction.[7] One may describe its reception by the public as marked more by tentative interest than by spectacular enthusiasm, but it is safe to say that the book's appearance did not please one party at all.

This incursion into his scholarly territory rekindled the banked fires of Baron von Hammer-Purgstall's interest in the *Sīra.* He promptly fired off an article in which he described the great pains he had undergone to obtain "his" copy for the Imperial Library in Vienna; taking advantage of the English translation's lack of introduction, he generously proceeded to offer his own account of the work's origin and nature.[8] This article is much longer than his 1802 notice, but Von Hammer's opinions remain essentially the same. He contrasts the "virile" *Sīrat 'Antar* with the "effeminate" *Thousand and One Nights* and restates his belief that it was al-Aṣma'ī who originally composed the work. Furthermore, he introduces the hypothesis that al-Aṣma'ī wrote it for the subtly panegyrical purpose of currying favor with Caliph al-Ma'mūn, whose mother, like 'Antar's, had been a black slave.[9]

Von Hammer also criticizes Hamilton, who based his translation on an abridged version of *Sīrat 'Antar* that he had obtained in Aleppo. Von Hammer remarks, on the one hand, that the Englishman should have abridged his translation even further, noting that "the whole, if continued in the same manner, would make eighteen or twenty similar octavo volumes, the perusal of which is more than can be fairly expected from the patience of the most intrepid romance reader." On the other hand, he criticizes Hamilton for leaving out "many historically and ethnographically remarkable circumstances" that appear in the full version of the work.[10]

In 1820 Hamilton published a full edition of the first four volumes of his translation (about one-third of the Arabic text of his abridged manuscript) and his own preface.[11] In general, he echoes the opinions voiced by Von Hammer concerning the *Sīra*'s nature, authorship, and time of composition. Hamilton judges the work to be "a most faithful narrative of that mode of life in all its variety . . . which prevailed among the Arabs in that 'period of ignorance.' " But he also admits that al-Aṣmaʿī had not intended "to compose a faithful history of those times: his view seems rather to comprise in a pleasing tale, numerous isolated facts, and the most striking traits of the manners and usages prevalent in that period."[12]

Hamilton concludes that it is "one of the most ancient books of Arabian literature" and is surprised at the purity of its language, considering that it "has for a thousand years been transcribed chiefly for the use of the Bedoweens, and often by persons who probably did not comprehend one word they were writing." He agrees with J. L. Burkhardt's view that *Sīrat 'Antar* is "in every respect superior" to *The Thousand and One Nights.*[13] Hamilton also notes the popularity that the work enjoyed in the deserts and coffee shops of Syria and, like Von Hammer, explains the colloquialisms of the text as the interpolations of storytellers, mentioning that "it is given to children, who are obliged to copy it out, and thus acquire the habit of speaking elegantly and correctly: and it may be attributed to this cause, that the copies of Antar are generally found written most execrably ill, and abounding in errors of every kind."[14]

In spite of some of the vagaries of critical opinion that exist in his preface, Hamilton's translation of the first part of *Sīrat 'Antar* is a fine piece of early-nineteenth-century prose. Unfortunately for Hamilton, Von Hammer's unfriendly article had appeared in English by this time; influenced by so prestigious an authority, English reviewers were less than kind.[15] Disheartened, Hamilton relinquished any hope he may have cherished of becoming a second A. Galland and never completed his translation. But partial though it was, his effort did serve to reawaken the interest of European scholars in the *Sīra.*

For the next few decades *Sīrat 'Antar* became an object of scholarly interest among Orientalists, the main arena of debate being the pages of *Journal Asiatique.*[16] In 1833 A. Caussin de Perceval published a translation of the episode that describes the death of 'Antar, accompanied with a short notice about the work as a whole. In this note he ascribes to the *Sīra* "a style, various and elegant, reaching sometimes to the sublime; characters drawn with force and skillfully sustained, render this work eminently remarkable; it may be termed the *Iliad* of the Arabians."[17]

Caussin de Perceval agrees with Von Hammer, Burkhardt, and Hamilton that the *Sīra* is a much finer work than *The Thousand and One Nights*, quoting the Prophet Muḥammad's remark to the effect that the only Arab of the past he wished he had met was 'Antar.[18] He also shares the opinion that the colloquialisms of the text were due to interpolations on the part of the storytellers, but suggests that they changed the wording on purpose so that their audience could better understand the narrative. Nevertheless, Caussin de Perceval does not agree with his predecessors on the question of who authored the work. He disputes the notion that al-Aṣmaʿī was its true author, observing that one manuscript attributes the epic to one Sayyid Yūsuf ibn Ismāʿīl, who, he supposes, might have collected materials gathered by al-Aṣmaʿī and other early philologists to create the *Sīra.* Finally the Frenchman, judging from the style of rhymed prose in the narrative, conjectures that it was written sometime in the fifteenth century.[19]

The next person to enter the discussion was Fulgence Fresnel. In one of his "highly curious letters from Jiddah, on the history of the Arabs prior to Islam," Fresnel—in contrast to the scholars encountered so far—has some rather harsh words concerning *Sīrat ʿAntar.*[20] He remarks that the work was proscribed by the Islamic "clergy" and adds that "as the style is flat, and the poetry homely, the literati of the country do not include it amongst the works which compose the literature of Arabia."[21]

In the face of this attack, Von Hammer rushed once again to defend his discovery. In his reply to Fresnel he presumes that the latter has not seen an original copy of the *Sīra* but only a "disfigured" version from the hand of some common storyteller. He goes on to say that "if the Ulemas of Cairo depreciate at the present day this chief of Arabian romances, as Mr. Lane tells us they do, it tends to prove the decay of Arabian literature."[22] Even as he counterattacks, however, the baron retreats. He no longer asserts that al-Aṣmaʿī is the *Sīra*'s author; now he places the date of the work's composition in the twelfth century and announces that he has discovered its real author in an article of Ibn Abī Uṣaibiʿa's biographical dictionary of famous physicians. One entry concerns Ibn aṣ-Ṣāʾigh al-ʿAntarī who, Ibn Abī Uṣaibiʿa says, obtained his nickname because in his youth he had written stories (*ahādīth*) about ʿAntar al-ʿAbsī. This Ibn aṣ-Ṣāʾigh, Von Hammer decides, must be *Sīrat ʿAntar*'s true author. In spite of this retreat, Von Hammer still declares the *Sīra* to be a masterpiece of Arabic literature, subsequently surpassed in rhetorical brilliance only by the works of Ibn ʿArabshāh. He concludes his article with the remark that since he had the privilege of bringing the first complete manuscript of the epic to Europe thirty-six years before, it was only fitting that he also uncovered the identity of its true author.[23]

Despite Von Hammer's protestations, scholarly opinions regarding the literary merits of *Sīrat ʿAntar* were metamorphosing. By the middle of the nineteenth century enthusiasm had notably declined. As more was learned about the *Sīra* and Arabic literature in general, the European Orientalist community began to feel that perhaps Fresnel's estimation was closer than Von Hammer's to the truth. The shift in attitude may be clearly seen in H. Thorbecke's study of the life of the historical figure 'Antara ibn Shaddād, published in 1868.[24] A. Perron had published a translation of the biographical account of 'Antara in *Kitāb al-aghānī* as early as 1840.[25] Thorbecke published the text itself and added a full analysis of the information in it and in other early sources concerning the life of 'Antara. At the end of his monograph, he offered a short description of the *Sīra.*

It is obvious from this account that *Sīrat 'Antar*'s reputation as the *Iliad* of the Arabs has completely evaporated. Thorbecke harbors no doubts that the narrative is a piece of popular literature rather than an exemplar of belles-lettres. He cites Lane's description of recitation of romances in Egypt, lists other works that also refer to popular storytelling in the Middle East, and reviews the various theories concerning the identity of the *Sīra*'s author, ending with Von Hammer's final proposal of the twelfth-century Ibn aṣ-Ṣā'igh. He concludes: "Is he really the author? More probably only an arranger, revisor, editor."[26] Thorbecke ends his description with the following words:

> But for one reason is it an important piece of literature for us, deserving thorough consideration: it is the national and therefore authentic representation of that bedouin life that has remained the same through the centuries . . . the knowledge of which is a necessary key for the understanding of ancient Arabian poetry. *Sīrat 'Antar* is the best means of obtaining this knowledge.[27]

In other words, *Sīrat 'Antar* is only interesting on the level that had particularly excited Von Hammer and Hamilton in the first place: it is a historical source that "must be reckoned as very instrumental towards learning the manners, dispositions, and habits of the Arabs." And, Thorbecke adds, for understanding their ancient poetry.

Thorbecke's matter-of-fact tone in discussing *Sīrat 'Antar* is not a voice in the wilderness. It is echoed by other Orientalists who discuss the narrative throughout the remainder of the nineteenth century and, indeed, to this very day. What happened to the enthusiasm that typified the earlier discussions? Did Fresnel's opinion carry such weight that it alone had won the day? In fact, this change of attitude can be attributed to the authority of one scholar, but it was not Fresnel. It was not even someone who had a particular axe to grind.

In 1836 Edward William Lane's account of the *Manners and Customs of the Modern Egyptians* first appeared in print. The result of years of residence in Cairo, this book is still a classic of sociological observation. Balancing a mass of detailed information with an evenhanded perception, Lane's book provided detailed points of information concerning everyday life in Cairo that were revelations, not only for scholars who had never visited Egypt, but even for many who had. He devoted several chapters to a type of event that was still a commonplace of everyday life but had never been described in any detail: the public recitation of romances.[28]

We shall discuss the details of Lane's remarks in chapter 3. It suffices to note here that Lane gave European scholars a much fuller picture of the social context of *Sīrat ʿAntar* than that to which they had previously been exposed. His account of *sīra* recitation in Egypt, combined with a rapidly increasing level of sophistication that study of other types of Arabic literature was evoking, made it clear that the *Sīra* was truly a piece of popular literature and not a masterpiece of belles-lettres fallen upon hard times. Lane revealed that it was only one of several romances publicly recited in Cairo—and not even the most popular one at that! Preceded as it was by the consensus that the *Sīra* was not the composition of the ninth-century al-Aṣmaʿī but originated from a much later time, Lane's description of the epic's common nature dampened scholarly interest considerably.

This was perhaps a natural reaction. After all, Orientalism was still very much in the exploratory stage of its development; there were many other literary masterpieces waiting to be "discovered" and investigated. One may doubt whether much more attention would have been lavished on *Sīrat ʿAntar* even if Lane's study had not appeared. As it was, the topic of its literary greatness was quietly dropped; such interest as the narrative inspired returned to the dimension that had interested scholars in the first place. If it had been proven that *Sīrat ʿAntar* was not a lofty epic masterpiece of classical Arabic literature, if it had been shown that it was not of early date or famous authorship, if it had not achieved even a faint shadow of the enormous popularity that *The Thousand and One Nights* enjoyed in Europe and had even ceased to be compared to it, at the very least the *Sīra* could still be considered a reliable picture of the life and ideals of the bedouin Arab, whether of pre-Islamic or later times. It was this aspect that drew scholars to read the work during the next half-century—to the extent that they read it at all.

The last nineteenth-century Orientalist who paid significant attention to *Sīrat ʿAntar* used it for exactly this purpose. Ignaz Goldziher turned the epic to philological ends. For the most part, he did not address himself to the problems of the narrative itself but used it as a secondary source in order to obtain a picture of the ideals and values of the pre-Islamic Arabs. The *Sīra* may thus be used to good effect in careful hands, as revealed by the frequent references to it in Goldziher's masterly essays on Islamic culture in the two volumes of *Muslim Studies.*[29]

Ironically, the myth of *Sīrat ʿAntar*'s literary greatness, created by Orientalists in the first decades of the nineteenth century and then quietly abandoned, continued to live outside the scholarly circles that had originated it. After all, the *Cantar de mío Cid* had first been published in 1799, *Beowulf* in 1815, and the Oxford manuscript of *Chanson de Roland* in 1837. Excited by these discoveries, scholars of European literature were more than happy to have an Arabic epic join the company. Moreover, the first part of the nineteenth century saw the high-water mark of the Romantic movement, and at least one prominent Romantic, the French writer and poet Alphonse de Lamartine, found in the figure of 'Antar an ideal of nomadic chivalry. Here, proclaimed Lamartine, was a hero completely free of the social bonds that an increasingly mechanized and regimented European society was creating.[30] As late as 1903, Hippolyte Taine continued to rank 'Antar as one of high epic literature's greatest heroes, placing him alongside Roland, the Cid, Rustam, and Achilles.[31]

The educated classes of the Arabs themselves were also influenced by the early Orientalists' effusions over *Sīrat 'Antar.* Arab writers, from medieval times on, rarely deigned to mention such works as *Sīrat 'Antar* or *The Thousand and One Nights*; the few opinions they did express indicate that they considered such works to be, at best, low forms of crude entertainment and, at worst, dangerous distortions of historical fact that misinformed and misled society's ignorant and unsophisticated masses.[32] One can only imagine the surprise members of the educated and cultured classes of eighteenth- and nineteenth-century Arab society must have felt when they were informed by European acquaintances that *The Thousand and One Nights* was considered a masterpiece of world literature in Europe; they must have viewed this as only one more telltale sign of the cultural inferiority of the West. Be that as it may, in the first part of the twentieth century several noted Arab writers composed works based upon the story of 'Antar, a change of critical opinion that can be at least partly attributed to the acclaim that Von Hammer and his contemporaries had lavished on the *Sīra.*[33]

REMARKS ON THE NINETEENTH-CENTURY SCHOLARSHIP

The studies mentioned here are generally out of date; nevertheless, reviewing them is still profitable because they offer prototypes of many of the misconceptions and methodological confusions that have, until recently, continued to mark studies of the Arabic popular *sīra.*

Early discussions of *Sīrat 'Antar* revolved around four main points: (1) the *Sīra* was valued as a masterpiece of "high" art, (2) the identity of its author and the date of its composition were discussed, (3) the *Sīra* was deemed a valuable historical source because of its realism, and (4) it was felt that the epic should be translated at least in part (because of point 1) and that it should be studied and analyzed (because of point 3).

By the end of the century, however, attitudes had changed. Point 1 was quietly dropped when it became clear that *Sīrat ʿAntar* was not the work of the famous early philologist al-Aṣmaʿī but the product of ordinary storytellers. Point 2, identifying the *Sīra*'s author and the date of composition, was still open to research, but one senses that little hope for success in this area was entertained. All that remained of earlier interests and aspirations concerning the epic, therefore, were investigations centering upon points 3 and 4: using *Sīrat ʿAntar* as a kind of historical document and translating those parts of it relevant to that purpose.

This brief description of the general direction of early research is incomplete, however, unless the underlying assumptions and methodological principles that guided it are examined as well. Appreciating the excitement that early scholars felt about *Sīrat ʿAntar* is difficult unless one views it in the context of the enormous success of *The Thousand and One Nights* in Europe. From the early years of the eighteenth century when A. Galland first translated the *Nights* into French, this story collection has enjoyed a popularity in the West unrivaled by any other work of Islamic literature. Indeed, *The Thousand and One Nights* is more than a literary success; it has become a living part of Western culture, a complex of ideas and associations that even now continues to regenerate itself in a multitude of forms: from children's storybooks to popular motion pictures, from erotic imitations in glossy magazines to the literary experiments of gifted authors.[34] It would have been impossible for such early scholars as Von Hammer, as much an enthusiast and popularizer of Islamic studies as a scholar, not to have been influenced by the popularity of the *Nights* during the course of his explorations into the largely unmapped (in Europe, that is) territories of Islamic literature.[35] There is no doubt that it was the enticement of discovering a new *Thousand and One Nights* that made Von Hammer persist in his pursuit of a complete manuscript of *Sīrat ʿAntar*. Once he found it, comparison with the *Nights* became a constant theme in the early studies of the *Sīra*. *Sīrat ʿAntar* is "more interesting than the *Thousand and One Nights*," proclaims Von Hammer. It is "in every respect superior to the *Thousand and One Nights*," says Hamilton, repeating the opinion of the famous Arabian explorer Burkhardt. "*Sīrat ʿAntar* is the *Iliad* of the Arabians," asserts Caussin de Perceval.

Are not these accolades founded to a large degree upon the hope and expectations that *Sīrat ʿAntar* would equal—if not surpass—the success *The Thousand and One Nights* had enjoyed? Is there not more than a hint of disappointment in Von Hammer's early admission that the *Sīra* was "impossible to translate," owing to its great size? Would Hamilton even have considered his ambitious translation attempt if he had not been enticed by the popular success of the *Nights*? Finally, would Von Hammer have responded so quickly to the appearance of Hamilton's translation with a "feline review, remarkable for its blend of insinuation and special knowledge" if he had not been panicked by the thought that this poaching in what he had marked out as his own special territory might result in a popular success?[36]

The instincts of these early scholars were not at fault when they compared *Sīrat 'Antar* to *The Thousand and One Nights.* Although there are significant differences between the two, both are products of the Arabic tradition of popular storytelling. Unfortunately, early European critics were praising the *Sīra* precisely because they thought that it was not a product of popular storytellers, but rather an example of early classical Arabic literature that had somehow become incorporated into the storytelling repertoire. By the time of Lane's description, however, the West had learned enough about Arabic literature to have some awareness of the *Sīra*'s popular provenance and literary context. And with Lane's own remarks about the public recitations of romances he had witnessed in Cairo, it seems that European students of the *Sīra* finally came to realize that it was not the belletristic masterpiece they had assumed it to be. Suddenly it became clear to them that the "augmentations and interpolations" of the storytellers that they had formerly complained of were not just a few colloquialisms or grammatical mistakes or a few blatant hyperboles in the work's narrative action but the work as a whole. Once they recognized and admitted this, they lost interest in the *Sīra* or at least relegated it to a compartment of literature that they considered much less deserving of critical attention: folklore.

Several factors precipitated this loss of interest. First, there is the prejudice educated people traditionally harbor against popular literature. Individuals who devote themselves to appreciating the merits of "high" literature often deem examples of popular literature unworthy of notice. *The Thousand and One Nights* escaped this fate because of its immediate popular success. When *Sīrat 'Antar* enjoyed no such response in Europe, Orientalists put it aside.

Another, perhaps more important, reason that scholars neglected the *Sīra* was that once they discovered it to be a popular work they had no methodology with which to study it. After all, even European folk narrative did not attract scholarly attention until the Grimms published their collection of *Kinder- und Hausmärchen* in 1812. Early students of *Sīrat 'Antar* were scholars, men of letters steeped in the literary traditions of their time. For them works of literature were written artifacts composed by single authors who worked within specific literary genres for the private edification of their circles of readers. These men had little knowledge of, and probably less interest in, the traditions of popular or oral narrative that existed in their own countries; it would be unreasonable to expect that they would understand the conditions and dynamics of such traditions in a foreign culture. Also, in this age of print it is easy enough to forget the differences of attitude and approach toward literature in those who lived and wrote in the age of manuscript; it requires an even greater leap of critical imagination to do justice to narratives that are the products of popular traditions, in which processes of oral composition often play a large role. Nineteenth-century students of *Sīrat 'Antar* had no folkloristic methodology or populist scholarly tradition to help them make such a leap.[37]

If nineteenth-century Orientalists were hampered in their study of *Sīrat 'Antar* by the lack of methodologies not yet developed, they were also ill served by the one they had. The dominant methodology of almost all Orientalist research (as well as a great part of all literary, religious, and linguistic research) of that century was a complex of ideas and methods commonly termed historical philology.

The development of historical philology was one of the great scholarly achievements of the nineteenth century. Most of the modern scholarly disciplines of linguistics, folklore, history, anthropology, archaeology, comparative religion, and comparative literature are founded upon the techniques of this methodology. Nineteenth-century humanists were obsessed with the idea of tracing the genesis and historical development of ideas, languages, religions, cultures, and types of literature. To a large extent this was due to the fact that with colonial conquests and ever-increasing links with foreign cultures Europe rediscovered its own history in the new context of world history. Of course, its historical viewpoint was highly ethnocentric (and still is, for that matter), but with the "discovery" of Sanskrit and the idea of the Indo-European language group, Europe suddenly perceived previously unknown or unrecognized links with Eastern cultures. Scholars eagerly began the task of examining and comparing languages, ideas, and literary motifs to build up a picture of the original state of things—whether it was the original Indo-European language, sets of "racially typical" religious ideas or worldviews, or even original versions and places of origin of folktales.[38]

Philology is also founded on the idea of discovering original form, in this case the original form of a text. And since nineteenth-century scholars often had to depend on defective or suspect texts for their new lines of research, it was natural that they also became philologists: masters of the techniques of textual criticism that had been developed in Europe since the Renaissance. Besides pure textual criticism—the comparison of manuscripts—diachronic concerns are also an integral part of philology. Beyond establishing the text, the conscientious philologist attempts to construct a picture of its history, both in the sense of reconstructing probable manuscript stemmata and by collecting exterior information concerning the text's author and time of composition.

Inspired, but also enthralled, by the methodology of historical philology—which developed and became more and more dominant as the century went on—nineteenth-century Orientalists really had no methodological base from which to study a popular work such as the *Sīra.* Their approach was based upon historicism: the study of objects, events, or trends in the realm of time. Their object was to cut away the encrustment of time in order to get back to the "original," to examine the influence of time upon certain ideas and trends, to compare the development of ideas, historical forces, or literary movements at different points in time. And the foundation stone of this brand of hermeneutics was philology: the study, comparison, and evaluation of texts through which time was defeated, the layers of history peeled, onionlike, away, and the original state of affairs (whatever that may mean) revealed in all its pristine glory.

Needless to say, historical philology, used in a careful way for the right purposes, is an essential scholarly tool. In areas where it was applicable, nineteenth-century scholars made valuable contributions to the study of Arabic popular epics. They sought out manuscripts, compiled bibliographies, and combed sources to trace the history of *sīra*s.[39]

Having done this, however, scholars had little idea of what to do with popular epics such as *Sīrat ʿAntar.* For a narrative stemming from a folk tradition based on anonymous composition and performance, no one author could be identified, nor were there very many external references from which to construct a picture of historical development. Scholars could not even establish an original text, since in folk performance one version is just as original and authoritative as any other.

What early scholars did not and, as I have tried to show, could not do was to think about *Sīrat ʿAntar* on its own terms. Absorbed in exterior concerns, they inquired into the narrative's authorship and history; they remarked on its usefulness as a historical or ethnological source; they compared it to *The Thousand and One Nights*; and, in accord with the nineteenth-century preference for realistic literary portrayal, they found the *Sīra*'s "true picture of history" superior to the *Nights*' "fabulous figures." They never thought to examine the *Sīra* as a work of imaginative literature with its own social contexts and its own aesthetic purposes.

TWENTIETH-CENTURY SCHOLARSHIP

Understanding the concerns and methodological underpinnings of early scholarship facilitates evaluation of the path that research on *Sīrat ʿAntar* and other Arabic popular epics has followed until recent years.

The first twentieth-century scholar to approach *Sīrat ʿAntar* was Bernhard Heller. A student of Ignaz Goldziher and no doubt prompted by his teacher's interest in the *Sīra,* Heller published three studies concerning the work. They all run along similar lines, well summarized in Heller's article "Sīrat 'Antar" in the *Encyclopedia of Islam.*[40]

Heller's inquiries take two directions. First, he studies the *Sīra's* history. He is unable to uncover much new external evidence regarding this subject, but by relying on interior philological and literary evidence he delineates four main thematic levels that he believes contributed to the epic's composition. One is the pre-Islamic level, from which comes the figure of 'Antar, the bedouin setting of the narrative, and many of its main characters.[41] Next are the Islamic contributions: the story of the prophet Abraham that serves as a prologue in many versions of the *Sīra,* the repeated references to Muḥammad and Islam, and the way that the narrative continues after 'Antar's death until the time of Muḥammad's preaching, ending with the conversion to Islam of 'Antar's children and companions.[42] The third influence is Persian history and saga, with its concomitant ideal of kingship "by the grace of God," typified in the *Sīra* by the representation of the court of Shah Anūshirwān. Finally, there is the European influence: the intrusion of Crusaders into the narrative and the representation of the Byzantine court, along with references to monks and the trappings of Christianity.

Heller's second interest is what he terms comparative literature. Here he compares incidents and motifs from other heroic works, mostly medieval European epics and romances, with the *Sīra.* Thus he points out that the incident in the *Chanson de Roland* where the dying Roland tries to break his sword so that no one will use it after him also appears in *Sīrat 'Antar,* where the dying warrior al-Ḥārith ibn Ẓālim tries to break his sword.[43] Considering the length of the *Sīra* and the number of works that Heller uses as a base of comparison—ranging from Shakespeare to the *Shāhnāma* and from Icelandic sagas to the Bible—it is not surprising that he succeeds in identifying numerous common motifs and incidents.

The problem with Heller's first line of research is that his four sets of thematic elements are based less upon internal analysis of the *Sīra* than upon externally imposed criteria. One cannot dispute that there are ingredients in the *Sīra* that might be termed pre-Islamic, Islamic, Persian, and Byzantine, and Western, but do they really represent chronological strata or individual thematic levels? Islamic civilization was full of pre-Islamic, Islamic, Persian, and Greek influences; it would be somewhat surprising if a long pseudo-historical narrative such as *Sīrat 'Antar* did not reveal some trace of them. Moreover, studying cultural influences is important only to the extent that it throws light upon the synthesis that emerges. Heller looks only for external influences, not for their synthesis within the epic itself.

For example, 'Antar's opponents are identified by nationality and/or religion. In their battle cries, the Arab warrior swears by the tribe (or sometimes, anachronistically, by Muḥammad), the Persian by fire, the Byzantine or Frank by the cross. Does this show the influence of these different culture groups?—one wonders. The code of action for each warrior is essentially the same, the descriptions of the ensuing battles are similar, and 'Antar's attitude toward his opponents is depicted uniformly, no matter who they are. Furthermore, although racial and religious differences are noted, there are no particular overtones of deep-rooted antagonisms. 'Antar willingly helps Arabs against Persians, Persians against Byzantines, Byzantines against Persians, Byzantines against Franks, Franks against Franks, Persians and Arabs against Indians, Arabs against Sudanese and Abyssinians (why has Heller no Indian or African thematic levels?), and of course Arabs against Arabs. The point is less which thematic elements appear than how the *Sīra* uses them to create its story.

Heller's second concern, comparing incidents and motifs from *Sīrat 'Antar* with those of other narratives, is equally problematic. Nothing elucidates literary study more than apt comparison, which can offer insight into the literary processes and conventions of both individual works and the genres to which they belong. Heller, however, compares the *Sīra* without regard to generic, chronological, or cultural differences. Despite casting his net so wide, the conclusions he draws are negative. It is extremely unlikely, he concludes, that *Sīrat 'Antar* and the examples of European epic or romance that he examined exerted any mutual influence. Any similarities of motif or outlook are merely the result of the use of folk motifs and literary themes and structures common to both cultures.[44] The only narratives to which Heller does not compare *Sīrat 'Antar*, however, are those with which comparison might have been beneficial: other Arabic *sīra*s and popular narratives or the epics of the popular traditions of such culturally related groups as the Persians and the Turks.

Heller is unsophisticated in regard to folklore methodology. For him folklore is not a literary or social process but a set of concrete thematic elements; thus he says at one point, "There is remarkably little folk-lore in *Sīrat 'Antar*."[45] He also shares the empirical prejudices of his predecessors, mentioning that Theodor Nöldeke saw a "decline" in *Sīrat 'Antar* in comparison to earlier accounts of pre-Islamic Arabia: "We see once again how little the *Romance of 'Antar*, the *Banī Hilāl*, and so forth have in common with the authentic *akhbār al-'Arab*."[46] Here is the philologist's preference for the "original," the oldest version of any phenomenon. Heller's defense is just as telling as Nöldeke's criticism: "Yet there is unjustness in this comparison of the *'Antarroman* with the *Banī Hilāl*. The *'Antarroman* stands higher than the *Banī Hilāl* or the *Romance of Saif ibn Dhī Yazan*, with its endless wonder stories."[47]

This defense reveals how little both scholars perceived such works as imaginative fiction operating, for all of their pseudo-historicity of tone and atmosphere, on a nonhistorical and nonempirical plane. This is similar to reacting to criticism that *Chanson de Roland* is poor literature because it does not portray a close picture of historical events by claiming that *Roland* is at least better than *Hamlet* because it does not have ghosts.

In accord with dictates of their inherited methodology of historical philology, much of the energy of *sīra* scholars has until recently been directed toward historical pursuits. Their studies are most successful when they put this methodology to its proper ends. Hence, the most useful parts of Heller's studies on *Sīrat 'Antar*, Rudi Paret's study of *Saif ibn Dhī Yazan*, or—to include a closely related genre, the legendary *maghāzi* literature—Henri Grégoire and Marius Canard's studies of *Dhāt al-Himma*, Helmut Wangelin's study of *Sīrat Baibars*, and Udo Steinbach's analysis of *Dhāt al-Himma* investigate the problem of the history and development of the narrative involved.[48]

Similarly, the use of *sīras* as historical sources has been fruitful to a certain degree. Orientalists from Von Hammer's time on have valued *Sīrat 'Antar* as a potential historical source from which to gain an idea of the ideals and manners of desert Arabs, and we have seen that Goldziher, in his careful manner, used the work to good effect in this regard. In the earlier part of this century Paret again pointed out the usefulness of *sīras* as sources from which scholars could detect the attitudes and historical perceptions of the masses in premodern Arab society.[49] Paret himself later analyzed the legendary *maghāzī* literature from this perspective, while a large part of Steinbach's work on *Dhāt al-Himma* is devoted to similar ends. This type of study is beneficial as long as one is aware that studying epics in terms of their representation of preselected categories (such as Christianity, Islam, *jihād*, or the caliphate) poses certain dangers unless one first has a firm grasp on the generic conventions and artistic ideals of the literature involved.[50]

The further scholars have moved from purely historical questions, the less fruitful their research. Scholars have recognized the need for extensive internal analyses of popular *sīras* and have at times even promised them; nevertheless, the few resultant efforts have usually been reduced to heavy-handed comparativism. One favorite strategy is to compare the *sīra* narratives to the historical events they purport to portray. Unfortunately, this line of research usually only reaffirms that *sīras* make for woefully imprecise history.

Alternatively, attempts at literary comparison are rarely more successful than Heller's. In her study of *Arabische Bahrām-Roman*, for example, M. Pantke compares the Arabic popular version of the story to historical accounts of the Bahrām story, to a Persian folk version, and to Niẓāmī Ganjavī's elite literary version of the story in his *Haft Paikar*. This is an interesting and ambitious project, yet because Pantke fails to establish a firm methodological framework she is reduced to concluding that these different versions sometimes agree in certain points and sometimes do not. Similarly, when Nabīla Ibrāhīm compared the history and contents of *Dhāt al-Himma* and the Byzantine epic *Digenis Akritas*, she concluded that apart from their common concern with the Arab-Byzantine wars, the narratives have little in common.[51]

The drawback of Pantke and Ibrāhīm's approaches is that they conceive of discovering similarities or links among different works as an end in itself rather than as a process of illuminating the narratives under study. J. Oliverius, for example, used both comparative and motif analysis techniques in his studies of *az-Zīr Sālim* to excellent effect because his purpose is to cast light upon the epic itself rather than to pursue external concerns. Similarly, ʿAbd al-Ḥamīd Yūnis investigated historical sources in order to illuminate the background of the *Banī Hilāl* cycle, but he kept these researches separate from the literary and folkloristic inquiries of the second part of his study. Yūnis's research was pioneering. Although now somewhat dated, his book was the first to study a *sīra* from the general perspective of modern folklore.[52] Another groundbreaking study is Mūsā Sulaimān's *al-Adab al-qaṣaṣī ʿind al-ʿArab* (Narrative Literature among the Arabs).[53] Sulaimān's division of Arabic imaginative narrative into five categories, of which the second, the heroic, is typified by such works as *Sīrat ʿAntar*, is tentative, but it at least attempts to view prose literature in a comprehensive fashion.

Two other noteworthy introductory studies on *Sīrat ʿAntar* and the *sīra shaʿbiyya* were carried out by the well-known Egyptian scholar Fārūq Khūrshīd. The first, *Fann kitābat as-sīra ʾsh-shaʿbiyya* (The Art of Writing Arabic Popular Epic), written with Maḥmūd Dhihnī, was an experiment in what the authors termed "applied" (*taṭbīqī*) criticism. Here they sought to explore the parameters of the genre, using *Sīrat ʿAntar* as their basis of analysis. The other, *Aḍwāʾ ʿala ʾs-siyar ash-shaʿbiyya* (Lights cast on the Arabic Popular Epic), is a brief general survey and summary of the main printed examples of the *sīra* genre as a whole. Both of these studies, written in the 1960s, were conducted without the benefit of the historical and manuscript information or the theoretical framework for understanding oral literature and performance that we now possess. Moreover, their vision of the *sīra*s tends to be preconditioned and influenced by the Arab nationalist ideology of the time. Nevertheless, these studies were groundbreaking and deserve to be better known among scholars of *sīra*s than they generally are.[54]

Despite these forays from the fields of folklore and literary analysis, students of Arabic literature in general and of Arabic *sīra*s in particular have only recently escaped the philological and historicist influences of their Orientalist predecessors (this is one reason I have examined this body of scholarship in such detail). Twenty-five years ago, at an international conference on epic literature, A. Abel delivered a paper on *Sīrat ʿAntar* that was based upon and included all of the methodological misapprehensions of Heller's studies of a half-century before.[55] Some years later G. E. von Grunebaum, one of the most prestigious modern Western authorities on Arabic literature of our time, described Arabic epics as follows:

> There are popular epics and they are in prose, so these would fall under the specifications of this paper. But I am afraid I shall have to take the point of view of the medieval Arab *littérateur*, which is another way of saying that those lengthy and repetitious tales lack the dignity that would qualify them for my notice, the Arabic being overly simple, not to say defective, their images vulgar, and their composition disheveled.[56]

The most recent study that focuses on *Sīrat ʿAntar* is H. T. Norris's *The Adventures of Antar*. This work offers a translation (about 100 pages long) of the part of the *Sīra* that describes ʿAntar's campaign into the Yemen and Africa and a general introduction to the history of the *Sīra* and commentary and analysis of various parts of it (another 150 pages).

Norris's study has several strengths. It reveals a general awareness of the literary context of *Sīrat ʿAntar* (i.e., Arabic popular narrative); it provides a measure of literary analysis by tentatively delineating some aspects of narrative structure shared by various *sīra*s (see Norris, *Antar*, 29–35); and, perhaps not least importantly, it views *Sīrat ʿAntar* from a perspective of genuine appreciation and affection. Unlike Von Grunebaum, Norris is willing to read and enjoy the *Sīra* on its own terms.

Yet Norris mainly studies the *Sīra* from the general methodological perspective of historical philology and ends up demonstrating once again this scholarly tradition's limitation in regard to works stemming from largely anonymous traditions of popular narration. Norris apprehends the *Sīra* almost solely in terms of external connections and criteria. He examines possible sources, medieval African history, possible connections with European romances and *chansons de geste*, and other *sīra*s. While these are all topics of potential interest, their investigation faces two problems. First, since Norris uncovers little definite evidence, much of his analysis ends up being highly speculative. Some of his speculations seem likely, some less so; many are thought-provoking—but speculations they remain. The second problem is an extension of the first. When one removes everything from Norris's work that relates to questions of genesis and linkage, little remains. The context of the *Sīra* is examined, but the work itself remains practically unexplored.

This is the danger of relying exclusively or overmuch on historical philological techniques to study such works as *Sīrat ʿAntar*. Too often the hope of identifying sources and proving connections turns out to be a mirage. Enticed by externalities—the mirage of the other, the far-off, the possible, the potential—one ends by neglecting what lies immediately before oneself, the literary work itself.

CONCLUSIONS

Two main conclusions emerge from this discussion. The first is that although much important groundwork has been done, serious study of *Sīrat ʿAntar* and other Arabic popular *sīra*s has barely begun. If the present discussion helps to draw scholars' attention to this literature, then its purpose will have been amply served.

The second is that at the present stage it does not appear appropriate to rely exclusively—or even mainly—on a historically grounded methodology such as historical philology to study this literature. This is not a criticism of the methodology itself. Although recent scholars have sometimes used it in a clumsy or mechanical fashion, historical philology itself remains a valuable scholarly tool that will doubtless make useful contributions to the study of *sīra*s in the future. At the moment, however, it does not seem that the particular questions it asks are those most in need of an answer. In this regard, the questions posed by other methodologies, such as literary criticism or folklore, for example, appear far more pertinent.

Fortunately, the last two decades have witnessed a dramatic change in the methodologies used to investigate Arabic popular epic. Trained folklorists and ethnomusicologists have undertaken the study of this genre, focusing particularly on the one example of it that is still widely publicly recited, *Sīrat Banī Hilāl.* Giovanni Canova, Bridget Connelly, Susan Slyomovics, Dwight Reynolds, and other scholars have produced important studies of how and by whom this popular epic is recited. These and similar studies do much to fill in our picture of the immediate human and aesthetic contexts of *sīra* recitation.[57] This study continues this line of inquiry, focusing on *Sīrat ʿAntar.* It also expands its horizons in two ways. First, it offers a picture of the broader literary and historical context in which *Sīrat ʿAntar* and other *sīra*s have operated. Second, it considers in greater detail *Sīrat ʿAntar*'s literary dimensions: its compositional structures, narrative strategies, pseudo-historiographical rhetoric, and aesthetic goals.

CHAPTER 2

The History of 'Antara, 'Antar, and *Sīrat 'Antar*

Discussion of the phenomenon of 'Antar in Arabic literature and culture must distinguish among three aspects of the figure: the historical 'Antara ibn Shaddād, the legendary 'Antar, and the representations this legendary figure assumes in particular fictional realizations.

THE HISTORICAL 'ANTARA IBN SHADDĀD

Little is known concerning the historical figure 'Antara ibn Shaddād. The few surviving fragments of information are contained in two major medieval anthologies of Arabic poetry: *Kitāb ash-shi'r wa-'sh-shu'arā'* (The Book of Poetry and Poets) by Ibn Qutaiba (d. 276/889) and *Kitāb al-aghānī* (The Book of Songs) by Abu 'l-Faraj al-Iṣfahānī (d. 356/967).[1] These two authors, for their part, base their accounts on reports (*akhbār*) collected by earlier philologists and transmitters of Arabic literature. Any attempt to obtain an impression of the historical 'Antara must be based on these materials.

The two individual transmitters who supply the most information are Ibn al-Kalbī (d. 204–6/819–21) and Abū 'Ubaida (d. 209/824–25). Ibn Qutaiba relies completely on their reports, while Abu 'l-Faraj al-Iṣfahānī, whose article on 'Antara repeats most of the material found in Ibn Qutaiba, also relies heavily on them, although he also draws on information offered by such other early transmitters as Abū 'Amr ash-Shaibānī (d. 206–13/821–28), 'Umar ibn Shabba (d. 263/876), and al-Haitham ibn 'Adī (d. 206–9/821–24). The information that all these scholars provide is anecdotal rather than schematic; unfortunately, their accounts tend to disagree as often as they concur. Still, it is useful to examine their more significant details, if only for the purpose of obtaining some idea of the impressions of later Arab scholars and critics.

The sources offer no exact dates for 'Antara's birth and death, but he appears to have flourished during the second half of the sixth century A.D., lived into old age, and died early in the seventh/first century.[2] His father (or perhaps his grandfather or his uncle) was Shaddād, a member of the clan of Qurād, a subunit of the northern Arabian tribe of the Banī 'Abs.[3] His mother was a black slave named Zabība. Since it was the custom among the Arabs of that time for the children of slave-women to remain enslaved unless they earned their freedom by distinguishing themselves in some way, 'Antara (like Zabība's other children) grew up as a slave. All the sources agree that the youth won his freedom through his skill in battle; they disagree, however, as to how exactly he managed this.

Ibn al-Kalbī provides the most famous version of how 'Antara won his freedom. Once when the Banī 'Abs were attacked by a group of raiders, 'Antara's father ordered him to join the fighting. The youth replied, "A slave is not fit to charge; he is only fit for milking and packing." Upon hearing this, 'Antara's father said, "Charge and you are free!" So 'Antara rushed into battle and thus won his freedom.[4] An anonymous source relates a different version. 'Antara joined an 'Abs raiding party. After the successful completion of the raid, however, the other participants refused him a full share of the booty, saying that he was only a slave and thus not entitled. As they argued about the matter, they were attacked by a group from the Banī Ṭayyi'. 'Antara refused to fight unless he was freed and thus forced his father to liberate him.[5]

Despite differences in detail, these reports agree that 'Antara won freedom and renown through his skills as a warrior. He participated in the war of Dāḥis and al-Ghabrā' between 'Abs and its sister tribe of Dhubyān and through this and other conflicts became one of the great warriors of his tribe.[6] He was also numbered among the "Ravens of the Arabs," the great black warriors of pre-Islamic Arabia.[7] His fame was such that it was said that the Prophet Muḥammad once remarked, "No bedouin was ever described to me whom I would have loved to see except 'Antara."[8]

Sources disagree as to the manner of 'Antara's death. Ibn al-Kalbī maintains that he was fatally wounded by Zirr ibn Jābir an-Nabhānī during an 'Abs raid upon the Banī Nabhān. Abū 'Amr ash-Shaibānī relates that he was killed as an old man in a raid against the Banī Ṭayyi'. Perhaps the most believable version, because it is the least spectacular, is that of Abū 'Ubaida, who reports that an aged 'Antara went out riding one day and fell victim to a windstorm.[9]

Little seems conclusive regarding 'Antara's life except that he was born of a black mother and Arab father, lived his early life as a slave, and won freedom and a degree of fame through his martial prowess. The report about 'Antara that seems most probable, again because of its realistic tone, is related by al-Haitham ibn 'Adī.

> It was said to 'Antara, "Are you the bravest and mightiest of the Arabs?" He said, "No." It was said, "Then how have you become famous for this?" He said, "[In battle] I would advance boldly when I saw boldness [among my companions], and refrain discreetly when I saw restraint. I would only enter a place for which I saw an exit. And I would head for the weakling, the coward, and strike him a fearful blow that made the heart of the courageous man fly, then I would turn upon *him* and kill him."[10]

If strength in battle gained 'Antara his freedom, poetic ability won him lasting renown. His best-known poem is a a long *qaṣīda* (ode) rhyming in *mim* great enough to warrant inclusion in the famous collection of *mu'allaqāt* (literally, hanging or suspended) poems.[11] Moreover, his presence in such prominent medieval anthologies as the *Kitāb ash-shi'r wa-'sh-shu'arā'* and *Kitāb al-aghānī* attests to the continued regard for his poetry. Despite such admiration, few of the poems ascribed to 'Antara may be considered authentic. *Sīrat 'Antar* puts thousands of verses into the mouth of its hero, and modern editors have not always resisted the temptation to enlarge their editions of 'Antara's *diwān* by delving into the *Sīra*'s pages. The most critical edition of his *diwān* contains little more than three hundred lines, and even these poems are not completely beyond suspicion. Ascertaining which poems were truly composed by the historical 'Antara may well be an impossible task at this late stage.[12]

Despite the passionate love that 'Antar and 'Abla share in *Sīrat 'Antar*, there is little mention of 'Abla or any other beloved in the historical 'Antara's biographical material. Neither Ibn Qutaiba nor Abu 'l-Faraj al-Iṣfahānī refers to 'Antara's love life. However, since 'Abla is named in a short anecdote concerning 'Antara in al-Hamdānī's (d. 333–34/945) *Kitāb al-Iklīl*, and since 'Antara addresses her in several of his poems, it seems possible that this famous love affair has some historical basis.[13]

THE LEGENDARY 'ANTAR

The story of how a black slave won fame and freedom in the closed tribal society of pre-Islamic Arabia was the stuff of legend. And the speed with which the historical 'Antara entered the realm of legend doubtless accounts for the later scarcity of concrete information concerning him. If the historical 'Antara has disappeared within the fictions of the legendary 'Antar, the resulting story has for centuries been an important part of Arabic popular culture. Nevertheless, care is needed in handling this legend. The dangers of confusing the historical 'Antara with the fictional character that grew out of—one might even say supplanted—him should be obvious. It is equally important to maintain a distinction between the general, archetypical figure of the legendary 'Antar and the specific artistic manifestations this character assumes.[14]

Each representation of 'Antar draws upon an abstract conception of the hero that rests upon a few core attributes and events. 'Antar is a black slave-warrior-poet-lover who wins freedom by refusing to fight an attacking enemy unless he is freed, who woos and weds his cousin 'Abla, and who composes a famous *mu'allaqa* poem. But although each manifestation of the story is based upon and envelops this associative core, each historical period, artistic medium, and particular artist-audience relationship produces, in the end, a different version of the story. If the core of the legend of 'Antar is relatively stable, the forms it assumes in any place or time are quite varied.

An example will clarify this point. The story of 'Antar continues to be popular to this day; the black warrior is still one prototype of the heroic ideal in the Arab world. However, it would be incorrect to assume that the immense prose and verse narrative that is the subject of this study is the only, or even the most important, current manifestation of 'Antar. Diverse reflections of the 'Antar legend exist in the Arab world. Film and television versions of the story have been produced in Egypt and Syria. Aḥmad al-Jindī's existential play *'Antar* was produced at the Zākī Ẓulaimat theater in Cairo in 1977. In Syria, one can purchase Abū Ṣubḥi 't-Tināwī's cloth block prints of 'Antar and 'Abla and even plastic shopping bags imprinted with the same picture; under-glass paintings, oil paintings, and embroideries also depict this scene. Children's versions of the 'Antar story exist, as well as a four-volume comic book edition, a synopsis of the *Sīra* in a first-year high school Arabic literature textbook, and a modernized edition of the story in two volumes intended for adults. The phrase *Yā 'Antar* is a common Arabic exclamation for an act of heroism (sometimes intended sarcastically). And, of course, the traditional narrative version of *Sīrat 'Antar* is regularly reprinted in Cairo and Beirut.

These examples, in no way exceptional, reflect the extent to which the 'Antar legend continues to flourish in the Arab world. They also suggest how methodologically dangerous it is to equate the popularity of the legend as a whole with the popularity of any single version of it. Although millions know the 'Antar story from television, film, or storybook, relatively few currently read *Sīrat 'Antar*. The *Sīra* is popular enough to be continuously reprinted, but it is hardly a modern bestseller. In fact, although I have never met anyone from any part of the Arab world who has not heard of 'Antar, I have met few who have ever actually read more than small parts of the *Sīra*. A similar state of affairs doubtless existed in the past. Several manifestations of the legend were present simultaneously, but not all of them were equally popular—or popular in the same way.

When studying the history of the development of the ʿAntar legend, therefore, clear distinctions among the different forms—literary or otherwise—of the legend must be maintained. One cannot assume the existence or popularity of one form from that of another. When confronted with a reference to ʿAntar, one must ascertain which manifestation of the legend is being referred to.[15]

The earliest versions of the ʿAntar legend were oral anecdotes concerning the hero's deeds. Although this level of material is lost, its form and nature are still recognizable in the strata of the legend's next manifestation, the *akhbār* (sing. *khabar*, report) concerning ʿAntara contained in *adab* (belles-lettres) works, such as the poetic anthologies of Ibn Qutaiba and Abu 'l-Faraj al-Iṣfahānī referred to above. The anecdotes and remarks contained in these works are, in fact, double-edged. On the one hand, they offer a picture of ʿAntara that, when critically examined, is as close to the historical figure as we are ever likely to get. On the other hand, the discrepancies and contradictions in different versions of individual incidents make it obvious that the process of fictionalization was already well advanced. The more significant aspects of the contents of these early reports have already been discussed, but it will be helpful to add a few observations concerning their literary form.

Although we lack a complete picture of the profane literary life of the early (sixth and seventh century A.D.) Arabs, it appears that by and large their literary activities, which were almost completely oral at this time, were dominated by three concerns: genealogy (*nasab*), poetry (*shiʿr*), and the individual report or anecdote (*khabar*, pl. *akhbār*). People entered literature because of who they were, what they said, or something notable they did. Early accounts of the life/legend of ʿAntara (as with almost all the surviving examples of early Arabic prose narration) fall into the domain of the last literary type, *khabar*. In regard to content, *akhbār* present a combination of anecdote, history, and pure gossip.[16] To a great degree, their literary form reflects the nature of their contents. The typical *khabar* is topical in intent and short and structurally independent in configuration. Hence, the reports concerning ʿAntara discussed above do not purport to tell the complete story of his life, but offer more or less fragmented pieces of information classifiable under such topical tags as "How ʿAntara was born," "How ʿAntara won his freedom," "Why ʿAntara recited such-and-such a poem," and "How ʿAntara died." Information is attached to a particular incident, not synthesized into a broader, sequentially organized narrative structure. Even the longest surviving early Arabic narratives, the accounts of the intertribal battles of pre-Islamic Arabia commonly termed the *Ayyām al-ʿArab* (Battle Days of the Arabs), only portray individual incidents, making little attempt to place events within a larger context. Prior knowledge is assumed.[17]

What is missing from these anecdotes—and from the whole system of conglomerative reporting that provides their structural basis—is a sense of, or interest in, large-scale, unified, sequential, causal narrative relationships. This lack is significant, for it separates anecdote from story. More specifically, it is the respective lack or presence of this general sense of narrative cohesion that most sharply distinguishes these early *akhbār* manifestations of the legend of 'Antar from the next version to appear on the scene: the huge epic cycle of *Sīrat 'Antar.*

THE HISTORY OF SĪRAT 'ANTAR

Sīrat 'Antar is one of the longest works of Arabic fiction. The version upon which this study is based runs over fifty-six hundred pages; the only Arabic fictional narratives that rival its length are other popular epics.[18] Judged by the criterion of size alone, *khabar* and popular *sīra* lie at opposite ends of the spectrum of literary form. *Khabar* is short, glancing, independent, and finite; *sīra* is long, cyclic, integrative, and (potentially, at least) infinite. Thus, although *Sīrat 'Antar* absorbed many *akhbār* concerning pre-Islamic Arabia, the differences that separate the two make it unlikely that the *sīra* evolved from the *khabar.* When and how, therefore, did *Sīrat 'Antar* originate and develop?

We know, in reality, as little about the early history of *Sīrat 'Antar* (or any other popular *sīra*) as we do about the life of the historical 'Antara ibn Shaddād. References to the narrative are few and scattered over intervals of centuries. Ibn Qutaiba (third/ninth century), Abu 'l-Faraj al-Iṣfahānī (fourth/tenth century), and all other known early sources do not refer to the existence of an extended fictional narrative based on 'Antara's life. Furthermore, Ibn an-Nadīm's bibliographical compendium *al-Fihrist,* written in the latter part of the fourth/tenth century and the major source of our knowledge of the popular literature of the time, makes no mention of such a work, which strongly suggests that popular epics were not yet prevalent, at least in Mesopotamia. If they were, it seems unlikely that they would have escaped the comprehensive view of the learned Baghdadian bookseller.[19]

Not until the sixth/twelfth century, in fact, does a reference to *Sīrat 'Antar* appear. In the biographical dictionary of eminent physicians, *'Uyūn al-anbā' fī ṭabaqāt al-aṭibbā'* (Founts of Information concerning the Classes of Physicians), Ibn Abī Uṣaibi'a mentions that Abu 'l-Mu'ayyad ibn aṣ-Ṣā'igh (fl. middle of sixth/twelfth century), a physician and minor poet, bore the nickname al-'Antarī because he supported himself in his youth by writing (*yaktub,* copying?) the stories (*aḥādīth*) of 'Antar al-'Absī.[20]

Corroboration of the existence of a narrative concerning 'Antar by the middle of the sixth/twelfth century appears in a work of a contemporary of Ibn aṣ-Ṣā'igh. The Baghdadian physician and mathematician as-Samau'al ibn Yaḥya 'l-Maghribī (d. circa 575–76/1180), a Jewish convert to Islam, mentions in his autobiographical account of his conversion that as a boy (between the ages of ten and thirteen) he was infatuated with reading all kinds of stories and tales; among his favorites were such long works (*ad-dawāwīn al-kibār*) as the stories of ʿAntar, Dhāt al-Himma, and Alexander the Great.[21]

Two centuries later, we have evidence for the existence of *Sīrat ʿAntar* in Egypt. The Cairene scholar Tāj ad-Dīn as-Subkī (d. 771/1370) admonishes copyists not to waste their time transcribing books "for which God has no use, like *Sīrat ʿAntar* [*al-kutub allatī lā yanfaʿ Allāh bi-hā ka-Sīrat ʿAntar*]."[22]

These three references are brief and made only in passing. But they suggest that by the early sixth/twelfth century the fragmentary *akhbār* concerning the life of ʿAntara had been drawn into the unified narrative framework of *Sīrat ʿAntar*, which had apparently attained some length and existed in written form in Mesopotamia-Syria and later in Egypt as well. Unfortunately, these references tell us nothing specific about its form or content, although their casualness and the fact that no contextual explanation was deemed necessary suggest that the *Sīra* was commonplace by this time.

The earliest extant major manuscript of *Sīrat ʿAntar* is dated 872/1466.[23] Its 910 folios contain less than half of the complete *Sīra*, but its text is mature and fully developed, differing no more from contemporary printed versions than they do from each other (in minor aspects of wording and narrative detail). This manuscript is important evidence that *Sīrat ʿAntar*'s written tradition was both widespread and stable by the middle of the fifteenth century, not only because of its text but also because of its origin. This is the manuscript Von Hammer-Purgstall bought in Egypt in 1801; originally, however, it belonged to the Imperial Ottoman Library of Sultan Mehmet II (r. 855–86/1451–81). This suggests that by his time the *Sīra* had gained fame and even a measure of respectability. That supposition is corroborated by the existence of an Ottoman-Turkish translation of the work undertaken for the same ruler. The unidentified translator states in his introduction that he embarked on his project because he was dissatisfied with earlier translation attempts. He also remarks that since the Arabic manuscript tradition had become unreliable, he based his translation on a collation of three separate Arabic versions.[24]

All this evidence suggests that by the middle of the ninth/fifteenth century *Sīrat ʿAntar*'s popularity and its written tradition had become stable. Nevertheless, for the next two centuries the extant manuscript tradition of the *Sīra* suffers a lacuna. No manuscripts have survived from the period between the late ninth/fifteenth and early eleventh/seventeenth centuries. Hereafter, however, manuscripts become plentiful, continuing to be copied until the end of the thirteenth/nineteenth century.

One might imagine that this gap of almost two centuries in the *Sīra*'s manuscript tradition would reflect diminished interest, but such is not necessarily the case. Few of the existing manuscripts of the *Sīra* are the work of one hand; the great majority are compilations of volumes of different date and size, copied by different scribes. This process of piecemeal compilation suggests that interest in the *Sīra* remained constant. Volumes were presumably kept until they became dilapidated and were then recopied. The older volumes were probably simply thrown away.[25]

Two redactions of *Sīrat ʿAntar* have been printed. One was first printed in Cairo in 1866–69, the other in Beirut in 1883–85. The *Sīra*'s great length makes detailed comparison difficult, but spot-checks indicate that the two versions are similar in style and event, although differences in wording and minor details exist. The greatest difference between them is that the Cairo version begins with a hundred-page version of the story of Abraham, while the Beirut version enters almost immediately into the story of ʿAntar. Both versions have been reprinted several times, which demonstrates that the *Sīra* has continued to attract modern readers.[26]

Such is the external evidence we currently possess for compiling a history for *Sīrat ʿAntar*. In addition to this, the narrative itself offers some internal evidence. The *Sīra* has rather extensive pseudo-historical pretensions; protestations of its historical veracity appear throughout.[27] In spite of this, one serious anachronism does intrude into the story's pre-Islamic setting: the appearance of Frankish Crusaders as the frequent and staunch allies of the Byzantine emperor. The presence of Crusaders indicates that the narrative was still absorbing material at least as late as the turn of the sixth/twelfth century. There is no mention of the Mongol invasions or Mamluk sultans of the seventh/thirteenth century, however, which suggests that the written version of the story had solidified by this time.

Although it seems probable that the general conception of the legendary ʿAntar became part of popular imagination fairly early, there is no evidence indicating the existence of an extended narrative of ʿAntar's life before the middle of the sixth/twelfth century, and even then we have no clear idea of the narrative's form or contents. It seems likely that written and perhaps oral versions of the epic were still evolving. A certain *terminus ante quem* for *Sīrat ʿAntar* in the form that we know it only arises in the middle of the ninth/fifteenth century, the date of the earliest extant major manuscript of the work.

Although we know little about the historical figure ʿAntara ibn Shaddād, therefore, it seems that his exploits caught public imagination and that he entered the realm of popular legend quite early. Care must be taken not to confuse or mix the specific manifestations that this legend assumed. To whatever degree ʿAntar figured in oral or written *akhbār* anecdotes in the early centuries of Islamic history, firm evidence of the existence of an extended narrative does not appear until the sixth/twelfth century. From the perspective of literary history what is new and revolutionary about the *Sīra* is not its content (much of which can be traced to preexisting *akhbār* materials), but rather its form: the new, extended, cyclic form of the *sīra* genre that transformed fragmentary *akhbār* material into a long, integrative story.

CHAPTER 3

The Narration of *Sīrat ʿAntar*

One of the immediate concerns of early students of *Sīrat ʿAntar* was to determine the identity of its author. Pioneers such as Baron von Hammer-Purgstall and Terrick Hamilton initially accepted the *Sīra*'s own assertion that it was composed by the famous medieval Arab philologist ʿAbd al-Malik ibn Quraib al-Aṣmaʿī (d. circa 208/823). Although they admitted that it had suffered "interpolations" and "augmentations" at the hands of storytellers and scribes, these early scholars felt that the greater part of the *Sīra* had indeed been composed—or at the very least collected and transcribed—by the third/ninth-century Arab scholar. Even when further investigation demonstrated the inaccuracy of this view, the search for a single author was not immediately abandoned. Von Hammer, for one, lost little time in proposing another candidate for the honor of authorship.[1]

Later scholars came to realize that *Sīrat ʿAntar* was not the work of any single individual but rather the product of a largely anonymous tradition of public storytelling. The style, tone, and structure of the epic—not to mention its very mass—along with the descriptions of *sīra* narration leave little doubt that this is the case. Nevertheless, although public narration of *sīra*s must have been a common feature of everyday life in the Arab world for centuries, it is only in the last three decades, when the tradition itself is dying, that researchers have begun to study the performance dimension of popular *sīra*s. Earlier Arab authors who mentioned storytellers usually did so only to warn against the mendacity of their narratives or to ridicule the folly and ignorance of those who attended their performances. Our few early descriptions of performances stem from incidental accounts by nineteenth-century Europeans, and even these are usually little more than generalized sketches rather than careful, reliable reportage. Fortunately, this situation has improved dramatically in recent years as folklorists and ethnomusicologists have undertaken the study of the one popular *sīra* still actively performed in Egypt, *Sīrat Banī Hilāl.*[2] Public performance is the crucible within which the *Sīra* was formed, and many aspects of these narratives are impossible to understand without an appreciation of the circumstances and necessities of their recitation. Hence, this chapter examines the early evidence on how *sīra*s were recited and integrates this with information provided by recent studies of *Banī Hilāl* performance.

The longest and most trustworthy early account of *sīra* narration occurs in Edward W. Lane's *Manners and Customs of the Modern Egyptians.* Lane lived in Cairo for various periods between 1825 and 1848 and found the local storytelling tradition still flourishing. He devotes three chapters of his book to discussing the "Public Recitations of Romances." The greater part of these chapters is concerned with plot-outlines of the more popular *sīra*s of the time, but Lane also describes how public narration proceeded:

> Reciters of romances frequent the principal ḳahwehs (or coffee-shops) of Cairo and other towns, particularly on the evenings of religious festivals, and afford attractive and rational entertainments. The reciter generally seats himself upon a small stool on the maṣṭabah, or raised seat, which is built against the front of the coffee-shop: some of his auditors occupy the rest of that seat, others arrange themselves upon the maṣṭabahs of the houses on the opposite side of the narrow street, and the rest sit upon stools or benches made of palm-sticks; most of them with pipe in hand; some sipping their coffee; and all highly amused, not only with the story, but also with the lively and dramatic manner of the narrator. The reciter receives a trifling sum of money from the keeper of the coffee-shop, for attracting customers; his hearers are not obliged to contribute anything for his remuneration: many of them give nothing; and few give more than five or ten faḍḍahs.[3]

In addition to offering this general description of how popular epics were typically performed, Lane also tells us which *sīra*s were narrated in his time, estimates the number of Cairene storytellers who recited specific works, and describes various methods of narration. According to him, public reciters of *sīra*s fell into three groups. The first were those termed *'shā'ir* (pl. *shu'arā',* poet). These narrators, who then numbered about fifty, specialized in reciting *Sīrat Banī Hilāl.* They did so "without book," to the musical accompaniment of a *rabāb* (a rebec or viol), and generally did not recite alone but had a companion with another instrument for additional accompaniment.[4]

The next group of narrators, second in number, were called *muḥaddith* (pl. *muḥaddithūn,* narrator). They specialized in reciting *Sīrat aẓ-Ẓāhir Baibars.*

Like the *shu'arā',* they composed their tales orally, without relying on written versions of the stories during performance. They depended on their own histrionic talents, however, rather than on musical accompaniment, to attract and hold their listeners' attention. Thus Lane remarks: "Much of the entertainment derived from recitations of this work [*Sīrat Baibars*] depends upon the talents of the *Mohaddit,* who often greatly improves the stories by his action, and the witty introduction of his own invention."[5]

The third group of narrators were those who specialized in *Sīrat 'Antar,* who, deriving their name from the story itself, were called *'Antari* (pl. *'Anātira*). This was the smallest class of narrators, in Lane's reckoning not more than six in all of Cairo. Unlike the other two types of narrators, *'Anātira* read their stories from books. They chanted the poetry and recited the prose "in the popular manner," without "the accompaniment of the rabab." Lane goes on to say that, "as the poetry in this work is imperfectly understood by the vulgar, those who listen to it are mostly persons of some education." Although best known for reciting *Sīrat 'Antar,* the *'Antarī* would also occasionally read from other works, such as *Sīrat Dhāt al-Himma, Sīrat Saif ibn Dhī Yazan,* and *The Thousand and One Nights.* Lane states, however, that recitation of the latter two works had become rare, since copies had become difficult to obtain and very expensive.[6]

If we may rely on Lane's testimony, therefore, three methods of *sīra* narration existed in early-nineteenth-century Cairo: oral composition to the musical accompaniment of a *rabāb,* oral composition without musical accompaniment, and storytellers who read from written copies of *sīra*s, reciting the prose "in the popular manner" and chanting the poetry. The question arises of how these three methods of narration interrelated. Were certain works intrinsically or historically linked to another means of narration, or could they (and did they) move from one form of recitation to another?

Lane's remarks suggest that the connection between a particular *sīra* and its manner of recitation was fairly well established in the Cairo of his time. His evidence agrees with other references to how these works were performed in nineteenth-century Egypt and Syria. The German consul J. G. Wetzstein wrote about hearing *Sīrat 'Antar* read aloud by "ein Rhapsode" in the marketplace of Damascus in 1857, mentioning as well that *Sīrat Banī Hilāl* was recited to the accompaniment of a *rabāb.* A year later F. Fresnel wrote that he had become acquainted with an *'Antarī,* a *reader* of the life of 'Antar.[7] Some of the evidence in this regard, however, is inconclusive. Here is Terrick Hamilton's testimony concerning *Sīrat 'Antar* (1820): "In Aleppo it is highly valued, particularly by the Armenians; and in coffee-houses, it is read aloud by some particular person, who keeps a sheet in his hand, to which he occasionally refers to refresh his memory."[8]

These remarks are typical of much early evidence regarding *sīra* narration. Hamilton tells us that *Sīrat 'Antar* was performed, but he is unclear regarding exactly how. Was the sheet in the storyteller's hand a prop or a necessity? It is difficult to say. Moreover, the fact that the *Sīra* was read in nineteenth-century Cairo does not mean that it was not composed orally in other areas or in other periods. Approximately one hundred years after Lane's description, R. Le Tourneau tells of a storyteller of Fez who recited the story of 'Antar without book to the accompaniment of a tambourine, a project that required one year to complete. This same storyteller also orally narrated *Sīrat Saif ibn Dhī Yazan* (this took four months), a work only rarely performed in the Cairo of Lane's time due to lack of manuscripts. It seems likely, therefore, that individual *sīra*s were simultaneously performed in various ways (sung or recited orally, read from a book, or recited orally with the book as an occasional reference or stage prop) in different parts of the Arab world. There also appears to be little doubt that over the course of time individual narratives could move from one performance medium to another. The style and structure of *Sīrat 'Antar*, as we shall see, indicate that the narrative was fashioned within the context of oral composition. Similarly, *Sīrat Banī Hilāl*, an epic that according to all evidence was only sung orally, also has a well-developed written tradition, which suggests that it too may have been read aloud by storytellers at certain times and places.[9]

Lane's remarks make it clear that in his time *sīra* narration was a craft. Reciters were paid professionals who not only specialized in narrating *sīra*s but even specialized in performing particular works. Like most artisans in late medieval Arab society, storytellers had their own guilds. Von Hammer remarked that he finally managed to purchase a copy of *Sīrat 'Antar* from the sheikh of the Cairene storytellers' guild. This guild is included both in the guild list compiled by Evliya Chelebi during his stay in Egypt in the 1670s and in the list compiled by the French in 1801. It is difficult, however, to obtain a precise idea of the size of this guild at different times. Evliya Chelebi claims that there were seven hundred members at the time of his visit. Two and a half centuries later Lane implies that somewhere between fifty and one hundred *sīra* reciters plied their trade in Cairo.[10] Furthermore, we know very little concerning the organization of this guild. U. J. Seetzen notes that at the time of his visit to Cairo in 1809 it was the practice of its members to meet at a certain coffee shop every Wednesday morning, but he does not say whether this was a long-established custom.[11]

At any rate, it seems certain that *sīra* narration, in one form or another, was a common part of daily life in many parts of the Arab world until relatively recently. Ṭāḥā Ḥusain, for example, recalls the daily narrations of the local *shā'ir* (reciter of *Sīrat Banī Hilāl*) as one of the ever-present background noises of his early childhood in the Upper Egyptian town of Maghaghah.[12] The advent of such modern entertainments as radio, cinema, and television has severely damaged the tradition, and public *sīra* recitation has all but disappeared. That a centuries-old, strong and well-developed narrative tradition should disappear so rapidly, apparently without the least trace of regret on the part of its once faithful audience, may seem remarkable; but in reality it is not difficult to understand. In his novel *Midaq Alley*, the Egyptian novelist Naguib Mahfouz offers a poignant portrayal of the passing away of *sīra* narration in a Cairene coffeehouse in the early 1940s, which provides valuable insight into the change of attitude of the *sīra* audiences:

> A senile old man is now approaching the cafe. He is so old that the passing of time has left him without a single sound limb. A boy leads him by his left hand and under his right arm he carries a two-stringed fiddle and a book. The old man greets all those present and makes his way to the couch in the middle of the room. He climbs up with the help of the boy, who sits beside him. He places the instrument and the book beside them and looks hard into the faces of the men present, as though searching for their reaction to his coming there. His full and inflamed eyes, filled with expectation and apprehension. . . .
>
> He picked up his instrument and began to pluck its strings. . . . He played a few introductory notes just as the coffee-house had heard him play every evening for twenty years or more. His frail body swayed in time with the music. Then he cleared his throat, spat, and said: "In the name of God." Crying out in his harsh-sounding voice, he continued:
>
> "We are going to begin today by saying a prayer for the Prophet. An Arab Prophet, the chosen son of the people of Adnan. Abu Saada, the Zanaty, says that . . ." He was interrupted by someone who entered at that point and said roughly:
>
> "Shut up! Don't say a single word more!"
>
> The old man lifted his failing eyes from his instrument and saw the sleepy, gloomy eyes of Kirsha, the tall, thin, dark-faced cafe owner looking down at him. He stared at him glumly and hesitated a moment as though unable to believe his ears. Trying to ignore Kirsha's unpleasantness, he began reciting again:
>
> "Abu Saada, the Zanaty, says that . . ."
>
> The cafe owner shouted in angry exasperation: "Are you going to force your recitations on us? That's the end—the end! Didn't I warn you last week?"
>
> A look of disappointment came into the poet's face and he commented critically: "I can see you have been living fast lately. Can't you take it out on someone else?"
>
> Even more exasperated, Kirsha shouted again: "I know what I said and

what I want, you imbecile. Do you think I am going to allow you to perform in my cafe if you are going to slander me with your vile tongue?"

The old poet sweetened his tone a little as he tried to soothe the angry man and said: "This is my cafe too. Haven't I been reciting here for the last twenty years?" The cafe owner took his usual seat behind the till and replied: "We know all the stories you tell by heart and we don't need to run through them again. People today don't want a poet. They keep asking me for a radio and there's one over there being installed now. So go away and leave us alone and may God provide for you . . ."

The old man's face clouded and he remembered sadly that Kirsha's cafe was the only one left to him, and indeed, his last source of livelihood and the only one which had done him well. Only the day before the "Castle" cafe had sent him away. Old as he was, and now with his living cut off, what was he going to do with his life? What was the point of teaching his poor son this profession when it had died like this? What could the future hold for him and how could he provide for his son? A feeling of despair seized him and increased in intensity when he saw the look of regretful determination on Kirsha's face. The old man pleaded: "Slowly, slowly, Mr. Kirsha. Public reciters still have an appeal which won't disappear. The radio will never replace us."

Firmly and decisively, however, the cafe owner replied: "That's what you say, but it is not what my customers say and you are not going to ruin my business. Everything has changed!"

In despair, the old man insisted: "Haven't people listened to these stories without being bored since the days of the Prophet, peace be upon him?"

Kirsha brought his hand down hard on the till and shouted: "I said everything has changed!"[13]

Sīra recitation had developed into a highly complex popular art, which could only be performed by specialized artists. Over the centuries specialization had doubtless improved the tradition. Stories had become extraordinarily long and complex, and reciters had developed different verbal and musical styles that could do much to enhance their delivery. But the same specialization that had ensured centuries of growth and stability for this narrative tradition also speeded its disintegration when it faced serious competition. The *sīra* performance tradition had become too large and complex to be able to survive a sudden shift in circumstances. One generation's break in the chain of narrators would be enough to ensure its destruction; once the chain is broken and no new performers are trained, all that remains is what has been transcribed on paper or recorded on tape.

At the same time that telling these stories had reached the point of demanding a lifetime's advocacy on the part of storytellers, listening to them had remained a casual affair for most of their audience. Individuals come to coffeehouses for many reasons: conversation, refreshment, to play backgammon or cards, to conduct business, to relieve boredom, to get out of a lonely house or a crowded apartment. Although one could momentarily become caught up in the story, listening to *sīra*s probably was an amusing diversion for most people, only one of the many daily attractions of the coffeehouse. As radio, cinema, and television developed in the Arab world, they provided audiences with more entertaining popular enjoyments, and the performance tradition of *sīra* recitation suffered accordingly.[14]

Although researchers such as Susan Slyomovics and Dwight Reynolds provide an excellent picture of present-day narration in Egypt, we still have few facts regarding the places and periods in which *sīra* performance flourished in earlier centuries and the identities and attitudes of the storytellers. Nevertheless, our information suffices to offer a general impression of the context in which these epics originated and developed. In terms of appreciating and understanding *Sīrat ʿAntar* itself, perhaps the most important point to remember is that it—like other *sīra*s—was created in the context of public recitation. Lane's description of *sīra* narration presents a picture of the quiet, pleasant atmosphere that must have prevailed during many such performances: a relaxed attendance to amusing tales heard more than once, an entertaining diversion after a long day's work, a source of extra attraction and excitement among the holiday crowds and bustle of one of the numerous feasts and festivals of the time. Nevertheless, the engaging sedateness of the scene Lane describes should not make us forget that, as with any live performance, public recitation of *sīra*s depended for its success on arousing certain levels of emotional and psychological engagement among members of the audience. Any narrator may offer a web of words, but a rhetorical demonstration only becomes a performance when it elicits emotional response from the audience. Evidence suggests that active audience engagement has always been an essential component of *sīra* recitation. Here, for example, is Von Hammer's description of *sīra* narration among the bedouin:

> You must have seen these children of the desert, how they are moved and agitated, and how they melt with sensibility, and burn with anger, how they torment themselves, and never again recover breath, how they laugh and lament, how they participate with the narrator and the hero of the narrative, in the charm of the description, and the madness of the passions. It is a real drama, in which the spectators are at the same time the actors. If the hero of the story is threatened with imminent danger they shudder and cry aloud, "No, no, no, God forbid! that cannot be!" If he is in the tumult of battle, mowing down ranks of the enemies with his sword, they lay their hands upon their own, and

> raise themselves up as if they would fly to his aid; if he falls into the snares of perfidy and treachery, their forehead contracts with angry indignation, and they exclaim, "The curse of God be upon the traitor!" If at last he sinks under the superior number of the enemy, a long and ardent sigh escapes their breast, accompanied with the farewell blessing: "God's mercy be with him; may he repose in peace!" If, on the other hand, he returns from battle victorious, crowned with glory, loud cries of "Praise to God the Lord of Hosts!" rend the air. Descriptions of the beauties of nature, particularly the Spring, are received with repeated *Taib!, taib!*, that is, Well! well!, and nothing equals the delight which sparkles in every eye, when the narrator draws at leisure and with ability a picture of female beauty; they listen with silent admiration; and when the narrator concludes his description with the exclamation "Praised be God, who created beautiful women!" they all exclaim in chorus, with the enthusiasm of admiration and gratitude: "Praised be God, who has created beautiful women!" Similar forms of expression, frequently intermingled with the course of the story, and lengthened by well-known sayings and circumlocutions serve the narrator as resting-places, as it were, to take a breath, or by them to continue the thread of the story without any new exertions of memory and imagination.[15]

This description, generalized and cast in the florid enthusiasm of early Romanticism as it may be, indicates that audience participation plays a significant role in successful *sīra* performance. The continual exclamation of the storytellers—praising God, describing the situation of the hero, exalting the beauties of women—elicited similar exclamatory responses from audience members and thus created a state of phatic rapport between performer and audience. The style of *Sīrat 'Antar* itself reveals the influence of the conditions that Von Hammer describes. During the excitement of battle scenes the tempo of the work's rhymed prose tends to quicken so that the tone and speed of language imitate the furied activity of battle. In external description—often, as Von Hammer says, of women or nature—the stylistic pace slows to allow the reader to be seduced at leisure into wondering admiration for the scene described. Reynolds's and Slyomovics's observations of *Banī Hilāl* performances confirm the importance of audiences' interactions with storytellers in creating successful performances.[16]

There are other ways to attract and hold audience attention besides purely stylistic modulation; adept use of narrative structure can also improve public performance. An example of this may be seen from this account of how *Sīrat 'Antar* came into being:

> A man by the name of Sheikh Yūsuf ibn Ismā'īl used to attend the outer court of al-'Azīz bi-'llāh [a Fatimid caliph of the fourth/tenth century]. Once there

> arose a scandalous rumor in the court of the Caliph which consumed the interest of the people in their homes and markets. This displeased al-'Azīz and he ordered the above-mentioned Sheikh Yūsuf to invent something for the people that would distract them from this story. This Sheikh Yūsuf was widely read in the history of the Arabs, knew many anecdotes and stories, and had gathered various reports from the works of Najd ibn Hishām, Juhainat al-Akhbār, al-Aṣma'ī, and other transmitters. So, he began to write the story of 'Antara and circulate it among the populace. They delighted in it and were diverted from everything else.
>
> Part of the subtlety of his artifice was to divide the book into seventy-two parts and arrange at the end of each part that the narrative was cut off at its point of climax. The reader or listener thus became so eager to learn what happened that he did not fail to seek out the part that followed. When he found it, however, it would end in the same manner as the first, and so on until the end of the story. He put into these books poems which had been recorded by the above-named Arabs, but continual recirculation among the scribes has corrupted the text.[17]

Despite the apocryphal nature of this story, it is interesting for a number of reasons. First, it suggests how popular *Sīrat 'Antar* must once have been. To claim that it was invented to replace popular gossip of the spiciest kind, related to the court, indicates that the *Sīra* was commonly known to have the power to attract and engage large portions of the populace. More important, however, are the remarks concerning Sheikh Yūsuf's trick of ending each section of the narrative at a climactic point. This does not refer to a physical division of the book—I have never seen a text of the *Sīra* divided according to this principle—but to the storytellers' ingenious habit of breaking off their narrative at exciting points in order to ensure the return of their audience the following day.

This technique of "cliff-hanging" is not an explicit organizational principle of *Sīrat 'Antar*'s frame, as it is in *The Thousand and One Nights*, but the narrative is eminently suited for the use of this structural device because it is filled with battles in which 'Antar or some other hero faces overwhelming odds or must rush to rescue a defenseless camp under attack. The frequent recurrence of such situations can make for monotonous reading, but this again suggests that *Sīrat 'Antar* was composed more for live recitation rather than for silent reading. In the slowed pace and histrionic immediacy of performance, the suspense and climax of battle would assume greater melodramatic potency than is possible during simple reading. And a narrator who stopped in the midst of a battle might leave the audience interested enough to return to hear the end of the narrative the next day. Indeed, we have several anecdotes that indicate that this technique could be overly effective:

A scoundrel sat in a coffee-house and began to read the lies that are called *The Story of ʿAntar*. A large number of the rabble and riffraff who loved to listen to such lies and fictions gathered around him, and when he saw that they were paying attention to him, he began to invent sayings which he ascribed to ʿAntar and other speeches which he attributed to ʿUmāra [ʿAntar's main rival in his love for ʿAbla]. The crowd became divided into two factions, each of which gave money to this scoundrel so that he would follow their inclination and praise the character they favored. This scoundrel, meanwhile, renewed his fictions and was engrossed in his lies until the approach of dawn when he said: "And while they were in the midst of battle and fighting, the dust cleared and revealed that ʿAntar had been taken prisoner . . . and we shall finish the story tomorrow night!"

One of the fools who had been listening to him said, "You have to finish it now! Here, take ten pounds!"

When the scoundrel refused and stopped his narration, the fool cursed him, so that their voices became raised with insults, and the matter ended in curses and blows. Finally, this madman went his way, for he remembered that he had *The Story of ʿAntar* at home. But he was illiterate and could not read it, so he headed for the house of his son. He woke him up, weeping all the while, and said, "My son, your father has been stricken with a great misfortune!"

His son said to him, "Has my brother died?" "No, it is worse than that!" his father replied. "Has the new house been destroyed?" "No, it is worse than that!" "Has my mother died?" "No, it is worse than that!" "Has the court decided against you in your case?" "No, it is worse!" "Has your cash been stolen?" "No, it is worse than that!"

"Then, what has happened to you, my father?" "O, my son, tonight they took ʿAntar prisoner! So get the book and finish the story, otherwise I shall kill myself!"

The son said, "But father, who is this ʿAntar? You are unhappy about a false story and a tale that is full of lies. What's ʿAntar to us? He was just a black slave who became famous for unjustly killing people in his lust for plunder and desire to have his own way."

The father replied, "Are you insulting ʿAntar, you son of a whore!" And he began to beat his son with his cane until he was covered with blood, all the while swearing that he was no longer part of the family and that he never wanted to see him again.

The poor son left the house cursing ignorance and his family, amazed that his father had descended to a state where his lack of education had made him act like an animal and had stripped from him the skin of humanity. One of his neighbors came up to him and asked about his condition. The son told him what had happened with his father. The neighbor replied, "I have always told your father to give up 'Antar. I tell him, come and become a Zughbī like me [i.e., listen to *Sīrat Banī Hilāl*], but he never listens to me."

The son could not help but laugh about the lack of intelligence of these two and said, "There is no doubt that *al-junūn funūn* [madness takes many forms]."[18]

In spite of its extravagant and humorous tone, this obviously satirical story contains grains of truth concerning the dynamics of the relationship between storyteller and audience. The overwrought father is a caricature, but as in all caricatures the elements of character that have been exaggerated must indeed have been present among *sīra* enthusiasts. 'Abd al-Ḥamīd Yūnis, for example, in his study of *Sīrat Banī Hilāl*, mentions that it was common for members of audiences to lend their allegiance to individual tribes or heroes of the narrative—a situation that could lead to arguments but could also obviously be quite lucrative for a storyteller who, like the one mentioned above, was willing to adjust the outcome of his battles according to which faction paid him best.[19]

The anecdote about the 'Antar fanatic reveals how potent the effects of talented narration could be; but we must also look at the reverse side of the coin. Audience response must have exerted substantial influence on how storytellers arranged and narrated their stories. The more warmly an audience responded, the more a storyteller would want (and feel relaxed enough) to improve his performance. Naturally, pecuniary considerations could also be important. Lane noted, for instance, that "the reciter is generally heard to greater advantage in public than when he is hired to entertain a private party; as, in the former case, his profits are usually proportioned to the talent which he displays."[20]

Audience response affected not only how competently a narrator would perform on any individual occasion, but also which parts of the narrative traditions flourished and which parts disappeared. Plots, characters, and events especially popular with audiences would be duplicated as long as they remained effective. This point must be remembered when one considers the repetitions that fill *Sīrat 'Antar*. Such repetition, viewed from within the context of public performance, should be understood less as a failure of aesthetic imagination than as an indication of public success. In any performance, the performer proposes while the audience disposes.[21]

It is important to remember, therefore, that *sīra* narration was more than the act of recitation on the part of the storyteller and passive attendance on the part of the audience. It was a dynamic situation in which the histrionic recitation of the narrator interacted with the active emotional involvement of the audience, a situation that could become, in Von Hammer's words, "a real drama, in which the spectators are at the same time the actors."

In summation, if it is difficult to give exact answers to the questions of when and where *Sīrat ʿAntar* originated and developed, the answer to the question of how it developed seems fairly clear. All evidence, both external and internal, indicates that the work is the product of a centuries-old tradition of public narration. This tradition, which had both oral and written currents, was the creation of specialized groups of narrators employing specialized methods of narration. While it once flourished in many parts of the Arab world, traditional *sīra* narration is presently on the verge of extinction, although the story of *ʿAntar* itself continues to be enjoyed in other media of popular entertainment—books, comic books, radio, television, and film.

CHAPTER 4

Literary Context and Literary History

MANUSCRIPT *HAZINE* 1145 in the Library of the Topkapı Palace Museum consists of the first three volumes of an Ottoman Turkish translation of *Sīrat ʿAntar*. The anonymous Ottoman translator remarks in his introduction that he undertook his project at the behest (*ishāra*) of Sultan Mehmet II (r. 848/1444–850/1446, 855/1451–886/1481). He then offers a brief account of the history of the epic, as well as a description of his approach to translating it.[1]

According to this account, fragmented stories of ʿAntar's achievements and verses of his poetry first circulated among the early Arabs; thereafter early philologists, such as Abu 'l-Hāshim ibn al-Kalbī, al-Haitham ibn ʿAdī, Abū ʿUbaida, and al-Aṣmaʿī (among many others that he names, who all flourished in the second/eighth and early third/ninth centuries), collected examples of these fragments to narrate and to recite in their literary assemblies (*majālis*). In this way, various parts of ʿAntar's story gained popularity among the tribes scattered throughout the provinces of the early Islamic empire. At a later stage, historians gathered the stories into organized accounts. Unfortunately, because of the diversity of early sources (increased by geographic dispersal) and the vagaries of transcription and ignorance of later scribes, versions of the *Sīra*'s text became marred by discrepancies and mistakes: some had many verses, some few; some mixed up the names of characters, changed events, or arranged the narrative in the wrong order; and some suffered in style and grammar because of the solecisms of their transcribers. As a result, earlier translations into Turkish were generally erroneous and were sometimes so garbled as to be incomprehensible. For this reason, the translator chose three Arabic manuscripts on which to base his text and spent two years editing, correcting, and translating, finally completing his project in 871/1466–67.[2]

This introduction is remarkable for the extent to which the attitude of its author corresponds to that of the nineteenth-century European scholars who later "discovered" *Sīrat 'Antar* for themselves. The Ottoman reveals a broader understanding of the genesis and development of the *Sīra*, realizing that it first existed as scattered anecdotes and verses transmitted orally and only later emerged as a unified composition. His apprehension of the literary processes involved, however, generally accords with that of von Hammer-Purgstall and Hamilton. Participants in the learned tradition, first philologists and later historians, were the ones who truly compiled and arranged the text of *Sīrat 'Antar*; thereafter it fell into decline and disarray in the hands of ignorant scribes and translators.

The Ottoman scholar's translation project is thus more than just a simple act of linguistic transmission based on the principle of semantic replication; it is part of an ongoing struggle of cultural salvation and historical regeneration. By translating the epic and presenting it to his monarch for safekeeping, he rescued it from the vicissitudes it suffered in its own linguistic and social milieu. He resuscitated it and saved it from the "folk."

Both this fifteenth-century Ottoman translator and the nineteenth-century European "discoverers" of Sīrat 'Antar, therefore, participated in heroic quests in which they sought to rescue the epic from the tragic depths of literary decline to which it had fallen, believing that their efforts would allow the *Sīra* once again to assume its rightful place in the elite literary canon. This striking parallelism of attitudes and efforts indicates the degree to which acts of literary scholarship involve issues of intercultural appropriation, class status, and social authority just as much as they do questions of textual accuracy, historical genealogy, or aesthetic appreciation. The Ottoman translator and his European successors are in fact unconscious adherents of the *Rezeptionstheorie* of folklore, which holds that most folklore is elite literature that has been "received" by the "ignorant folk" who thereafter garble and muddle it in the very process of making it their own.[3] In contrast, premodern Arab scholars, as we have seen, entertained little regard for *Sīrat 'Antar* and other popular epics precisely because they knew that these narratives were popular in origin rather than being elite works fallen on hard times.

These attitudes also illustrate the extent to which the gulf that separates elite from popular runs parallel through different linguistic, historical, and cultural environments. Suggestive as this example is, however, it provides only a partial picture of how the spheres of elite and popular culture or literature interact. Apprehending the true cultural and literary context of *Sīrat 'Antar* requires that we explore this issue on a more theoretical level. To do this, we must examine more closely the nature of the terms "elite" and "popular."

ELITE AND POPULAR

The distinction between popular and elite is an example of the "series of oppositions and antimonies that have plagued the social sciences since their inception . . . the individual versus society, action versus structure, freedom versus necessity, etc."[4] In this case, some dimension of culture—religion, literature, or art—is posited as falling into one of two categories: a high, elite, artistic "great tradition," civilized and learned, on the one hand; and a low, folk or popular, artless "little tradition," primitive and unlettered, on the other (the various designations depend on the researcher, discipline, and period).[5] There is nothing inherently wrong with such a dichotomy; often it is founded on a combination of firsthand observation, long-term research, and intellectual intuition. Nevertheless, one should maintain a critical attitude toward such terms; if applied unthinkingly, they can cloud as much as clarify the frame of reference.

The first thing to notice is that the conceptual antinomy of elite and popular (or folk—for the moment we consider folk and popular synonymous) is historically positioned and socially grounded. Hence, its use often presumes implicit prejudgments and unconsciously held values. Since the opposition was developed by "elite" thinkers, for example, there has traditionally been little question as to the relative merit or comparative stature of the two terms. "Elite" is positive, while "folk" or "popular" is negative (it may be pleasurable but it lacks redeeming social merit).[6] This valorization of cultural spheres is clearly exemplified by the institutional strength and cultural prestige of those who espouse it. Adherents of "elite" culture guard their authority and status jealously. All modern colleges and universities, for instance, offer programs that train selected youths into the mysteries of "learned culture"; relatively few of these same institutions offer programs—or sometimes even individual courses—focusing on the study of popular literature or folklore.[7] Indeed, one may argue that the primary purpose of modern "higher" education is to remove students from the realm of the popular by initiating them into the hidden mysteries of "advanced," "intellectual" culture.

In this situation some evenhandedness is called for. Elite and popular spheres of culture are historical presences that coexist and interact within and across most cultures. Even if we wish to valorize one sphere over the other, we must first understand the various ways that they interrelate and interact. This is the focus here.

Second, we must avoid treating the concepts of elite and popular as static monoliths. Each term encompasses complex internal pluralities that require elaboration and understanding. Commonly, the historical dynamism and internal diversity of elite culture are assumed, while the culture of the folk or the masses is considered to be innately static and monolithic. This is a misapprehension, since popular culture and literature are as innately vital and diverse as elite, in many instances more so. Hence, although general terms such as "elite" and "popular" have their uses, these should not blind us to the complexity of the phenomena they seek to describe.[8]

Third, too often the elite and the popular are studied as separate, independent spheres. This approach is fallacious, since the two spheres can only be understood in relation to each other. This is especially true of elite culture, since much of it consists of a process of conscious self-removal from popular or folk culture. Hence, rather than folk culture being a devolution of elite culture, as *Rezeptionstheorie* holds, the inverse is more correct. Elite culture draws itself out of popular culture and to a large extent identifies and defines itself against it. Although from a historical perspective each sphere develops and maintains its own genres, traditions, and values, the two nevertheless remain in constant interaction and tension. Each relies on the other as a resource and as a mirror, to draw from or react against as the situation requires.

THE INTERACTION AMONG ELITE, POPULAR, AND FOLK

Understanding the cultural, historical, and literary context of *Sīrat ʿAntar* requires a paradigm of the transmission and reception of literature in general. This can only be suggested in brief, attempting to offer a holistic picture of how spheres of literature interrelate. Rather than remaining bipolar, this paradigm distinguishes among elite, popular, and folk traditions. This is useful in that—broad as it may be—it is still more precise than a simple elite/popular opposition. Moreover, it facilitates detailed examination of some of the varied ways that literary spheres resemble or differ from one another. It also helps to prevent perpetuating a view of literary spheres as monolithic. There may be other significant types of literature that fall under the rubrics of elite, popular, and folk that require further specification, but at least this initial differentiation is a step in the right direction.

The following model of literary production and consumption distinguishes among those who produce texts, the venues in which texts are performed or consumed, the nature of their audiences, salient aspects of their internal characters as texts, their explicit aesthetic goals, and their general social and geographical contexts.[9]

	Elite	*Popular*	*Folk*
Producers	specialist	specialist	generalist/ specialist
	professional	professional	amateur
Venues	restricted hierarchical	public	public/private
Texts	restricted	accessible	locally accessible
	set	variable	variable
	unique	formulaic	formulaic
	equivocal	univocal	univocal
Audiences	educated	general	general
	specialist	diverse	communal
	adult	adult/child	adult/child
	hierarchical		
Aesthetic Goals	edification	entertainment	entertainment/ ritual
	singularity	repetition	repetition
Social/ Geographical	cosmopolitan	city/rural	city/rural
Contexts	(trans-city)	(transportable)	(local)

Producers

In elite literature, those who produce texts are called "authors"; but to use this term for all literary artists already skews our understanding of the broad cultural processes involved in literary production. Raymond Williams has pointed out that many other formations of literary and artistic production have also existed in history, such as traditions of oral-formulaic performance, theatrical companies, artisan guilds, and cultural movements that espouse a specific aesthetic stance (surrealism, futurism).[10] *Sīrat 'Antar* itself, as we have seen, was developed by a tradition of popular public oral and written performance whose participants in early-nineteenth-century Cairo even had their own storytellers' guild. For this reason, the more neutral term "producer" is adopted here.

In the above scheme, the essential distinction among producers is neither social status nor economic class, although these are important secondary considerations. The primary issue is that of professionalism—whether they regularly demand and receive compensation for their activities. In other words, the professional status of elite and popular authors separates them from their folk counterparts, who may be just as specialized (although some forms of folklore are communal) but who rarely receive explicit payment for their efforts. Payment can be introduced into a folk tradition, of course (such a process of professionalization is exemplified by the creation of government-sponsored folksinging groups or folkdancing troupes in many Middle Eastern or European countries), but this marks the first step in a movement from folk toward popular art.

Professionalism dramatically alters relations, putting producers at the mercy of consumers. To survive economically, producers must truly be "popular" with their audiences. From this perspective, the modern conception of the impoverished artist who pursues "art for art's sake" is a historical aberration from the normal relationship between elite producer and consumer, where the client/patron relationship has generally prevailed. (A society in which when a "starving" artist does not in fact literally starve is truly wealthy.)

Venue

Elite literature distinguishes itself from both popular and folk traditions primarily in terms of its exclusiveness. It intentionally limits its physical accessibility to general audiences by relying on communicative contexts of a private or restricted nature: private performance situations (contrast the performance context of the elite chamber music recital with that of the popular modern rock music concert), restricted storage environments (such as private personal and institutional libraries), or the expense that access (to manuscript copying or book purchasing, for example) entails. Correspondingly, entry into the restricted environment of elite culture costs more—in investments of time and money—than does the enjoyment of popular art. Elite literature is the domain of educated adults who can afford the luxury of "culture." Poor, or poorly educated, adults and partially educated children are excluded; they lack the requisite "cultural capital" (to use Pierre Bourdieu's term).[11]

Access to elite cultural and literary forms also tends to be hierarchical. Hence, hierarchies of status are marked by successive levels of restriction in producer/audience interaction. Exclusivity becomes an indication of elite status (the university lecture, for example, already a private elite activity, is transformed into the more restricted graduate seminar as students become more "advanced").[12]

Popular literature, in contrast, intentionally maintains its accessibility to a broad spectrum of people (including elite audiences, although they are frequently embarrassed about admitting their enjoyment of popular forms). Performance or access venues are more open, economically and socially. Aimed at a wide audience, popular literature prefers modes of presentation and language that are broad based, specifically designed to be understood by and accessible to most members of society.

Folklore, in this scheme, is more local. Although it aims at being generally accessible to all, it tends to be more restrictive than popular literature because of geographical remoteness, idiosyncrasies of local culture, particularities of performance style, and linguistic limitations imposed by the use of local dialects. Hence, texts move from folk to popular status through a process of being stripped of the dialectal or other locally specific features that hamper their general comprehensibility. In terms of venue, folk performance can be a public (even communal) endeavor or a private one, as when a storyteller entertains a small group of children.

Text

The elite tradition emphasizes the concept of a set, invariable text and hence valorizes the concept of textual integrity. This ideal is typified by the well-known story of the translation of the Septuagint, in which seventy monks, translating independently, all emerged from their cells with the same text. It is also typified by Walter Benjamin's logocentric concept of translation as returning a text to a state of "natural language."[13] In contrast, popular and folk literatures value versions over set texts. Hence, narratives move freely through different redactions, various genres, and even discrete media, such as oral performance, written texts, and in the modern age television, radio, and film versions (cf. the various versions and media presentations of "Robin Hood" or the *Arabian Nights*).

Elite literature also values complexity. Whether of a scholarly, scientific, or artistic nature, elite literature is a medium that creates specialized, often technical, terminology and promotes linguistic opacity so that only fellow initiates among the intelligentsia understand or appreciate it. Elite style and content purposely tend toward the difficult, polysemous, abstract, or allegorical. Popular texts and folklore desire immediate accessibility. Hence, they rely heavily on the use of structural and linguistic repetition and formula, while elite literature tries to minimize overt reliance on either.[14]

Aesthetic Goals

The aesthetic goals of elite literary production tend to be soteriological, founded on a belief in the morally redemptive powers of "great" literature. Elite literature is edifying, morally uplifting on both the individual and societal levels. This is why literary scholars must "rescue" works such as *Sīrat ʿAntar* that they consider to have fallen from their natural elite status. Access to such literature also entails certain formalities, rituals, and prerequisites. One "dresses up" for a symphony performance, which has its own ritual functions; one reads critical commentary on "masterpieces," the better to appreciate them.[15] The primary goal of popular literature and some kinds of folk literature is entertainment rather than moral edification. Folk literature at times differs from popular in being close to communal ritual, whether religious or social.

Social/Geographic Context

Finally, elite literature is a cosmopolitan (city-based) phenomenon. Popular literature exists wherever there is a sufficient economic base for its performers to prosper, whether in the city or in the countryside. Folklore is sometimes thought of as a predominantly rural phenomenon, but it is more accurately viewed as a regional one that exists within "local" groups in both metropolitan and rural settings.

This paradigm is not intended to suggest that these three spheres of literature are separate or isolated from one another. Clarifying their pertinent similarities and differences, however, allows a more precise investigation of their overlappings and interactions. Hence, the same topics, whether the life of the prophet Muḥammad, the Joseph story, Lailā and Majnūn, or beast fables like those in *Kalīla and Dimna*, can exist in each sphere of literature, although their performance contexts and literary treatments differ in each case. Furthermore, these categories are not uniformly present in all societies. Anthropologists have presented many examples of tribal cultures in which differences among these sectors have yet to be articulated. To a great extent, modern literary history is merely the record of the emergence of popular and elite literary spheres from folklore, as societies have grown more geographically broad based and homogeneous and more socially and economically rationalized, stratified, and complex.

This model also aims at clarifying the oral/written polarity that has been so popular, and at times so misleading, in recent years. The distinction between oral and written transmission is only of secondary importance in this paradigm, because each category of literature has various oral and written means of presentation. The task thus becomes one of discerning which forms of oral or written performance are typical of each category: the public lecture or formal theater in elite culture, for example; professional oral narration and musical performance and the sale of chapbooks and broadsheets in the popular tradition; and nonprofessional oral narration, song, and ritual text in folklore.

It also allows us to perceive more clearly the history of oral or written traditions and the nature of their interaction through time. Pre-Islamic Arabic poetry was predominantly oral, while 'Abbasid court poetry was a mixture of orality and writing; modern Arabic elite poetry is mainly written, while modern folk poetry remains predominantly—although not totally—oral. Yet although pre-Islamic poetry and modern Arab folk poetry both arose in contexts of pure orality, one has become "classical," the literature of the elite, while the other remains folk and popular. Writing, therefore, should be seen as a medium rather than an essential criterion for literary classification; although shifts from orality to writing and the consequent interplay between the two have social, formal, and performance implications, these must be studied on a case by case basis rather than being subject to generalizations based on *a priori* assumptions of how orality and writing relate in the Arabic or any other poetic tradition.[16]

Finally, this model tries to avoid the pitfalls of a class-based understanding of literary types. Issues of social class and economic context are of course crucial to the study of literary culture. But postulating crude correspondences between class and literary category can distort more than clarify our understanding of literary processes. Audiences who enjoy works of popular literature or folklore can be drawn from diverse classes. Aesthetic response may be tempered by social status, but it is not predetermined by it.

This model is theoretical, but it should also be clear from the preceding chapters that it helps to identify and to understand distinguishing characteristics that mark *Sīrat 'Antar* as a work of popular narrative. A brief survey of the history of Arabic popular literature will serve to situate the *Sīra* on a more concrete, empirical level as well.

SĪRAT 'ANTAR AND THE HISTORY OF ARABIC POPULAR LITERATURE

Any attempt to describe premodern Arabic popular literature is hampered by two factors. One is the large amount of basic philological, historical, and analytic work that still needs to be carried out in the study of premodern Arabic literature. The other is that, following their elite proclivities, few premodern Arabic littérateurs or scholars deemed popular literature worthy of notice; thus many of the details of its history and development remain unclear. For these reasons, the present survey must be considered introductory and provisional.[17]

The history of premodern Arabic popular literature, as described here, extends from the first/seventh to the twelfth/eighteenth centuries. For purposes of analysis, this time span may be divided into two, roughly equal, periods. The first period (first/seventh to seventh/thirteenth centuries) is characterized by a general adherence to an ideal of political, religious, linguistic, and cultural internationalism. During this time the ideal of a universal Islamic, Arabophone polity ruled supreme, even though by the period's end the gap between theory and reality had become considerable. A remarkable consequence of this ideal was the creation of the high, classical (*fuṣḥa*) literary tradition that, for most of this period, displayed an impressive combination of intellectual vigor and artistic quality. By the beginning of the seventh/thirteenth century, however, the vitality of this elite culture, along with adherence to the ideal that had fostered it, had somewhat declined.

Although the ideal of elite Islamic universalistic Arabic literature still received lip service during the second period (seventh/thirteenth to twelfth/eighteenth centuries) and was in fact still a reality in certain intellectual spheres—the religious and theoretical sciences, for instance—it was no longer a political, linguistic, or cultural reality. In the east, the Persian- and Turkish-speaking parts of the Islamic world embarked upon independent courses. In Spain Arabism was first attacked, then eradicated, while in much of North Africa it maintained an uneasy coexistence with local Berber dialects. Only in the Near East (the area corresponding to the present-day Arab world) did Arabic remain linguistically and culturally firmly entrenched; but even here political power passed to the control of non-Arab, and increasingly non- Arabic-speaking, ethnic groups: Kurds, Circassians, Turks. Much of the decline in the generally court-centered and court-sponsored high Arabic literary tradition may be attributed to the decreased presence of Arabic as the primary spoken language in royal courts.

For a literary tradition, the linguistic complexion of its audience has obvious consequences. This is an important consideration in understanding the history of premodern Arabic popular literature. During the first period, the elite was Arab or at least Arabized. But the general masses tended to absorb Arabic more slowly, and in many cases resisted giving up their preconquest languages and literary traditions for many centuries—if they did so at all. Hence, although popular literature flourished, it did so on the basis of formerly separate traditions coexisting and slowly converging. In the second period, the elite maintained only the most superficial presumption of Arabism; but by this time the masses had become, in general, Arabized. Hence, while elite Arabic literature went into decline, popular Arabic literature witnessed a great burst of creativity. For it, the Islamic synthesis had arrived.

A final criterion for this division into two periods is that, although there is ample evidence that popular literature thrived during the first period, hardly any actual texts from it survive. Here literary history must be written on the basis of secondary sources and reflections of popular traditions found in high literary texts. But a large number of works have survived from the second period; here literary history can be based on popular texts themselves.

Finally, a word concerning folklore. Society during this period was largely agrarian. Hence, we must assume the existence of lively literary and artistic folk traditions in the geographic area under discussion. Yet we have no ethnographic information concerning this tradition until the nineteenth century. Thus, it is impossible to discuss this tradition directly; nevertheless, its presence must be assumed as an important source of inspiration for the popular literature that coexisted with it.

FIRST PERIOD (FIRST/SEVENTH–SEVENTH/THIRTEENTH CENTURIES)

To give a complete picture of what is known about the popular literatures of each of the cultural traditions that contributed to the formation of premodern Arabic popular literature is beyond the scope of this discussion. A brief examination of those parts that became important ingredients of the resulting synthesis must suffice.

The Arab Contribution

Besides language, the Arabs' most important contribution was, obviously, Islam. For Muḥammad and his followers, Islam was both a continuation and a rectification of the Judeo-Christian religious tradition. The Qur'ān is full of references to earlier prophets. To elucidate these passages, early Muslims drew upon, refashioned, and made innovations in Judeo-Christian prophetic stories and traditions. In the high literary tradition, the result may be found in works of religious scholarship, such as the massive Qur'ānic commentary of Abū Jarīr Muḥammad aṭ-Ṭabarī (d. 310/923) and in historical literature: Islamic universal histories usually begin with the creation of the world.[18] Simultaneously, however, stories of prophets and, later, saints—disseminated by popular preachers and storytellers in the mosques and marketplaces—became an important ingredient of popular literature. Involved in the early stages of this process were a group of early transmitters, such as Wahb ibn Munabbih (d. 114/732) and Ka'b al-Aḥbār (d. 32/652–53), whose formulation of prophetic narratives became the major source for both high and popular literary traditions. We can obtain an impression of this genre at its early Islamic stage from a work attributed to Abū Muḥammad 'Abd al-Malik ibn Hishām (d. 218/833): *Kitāb al-tījān* (The Book of Crowns), which has been published with a similar work attributed to one 'Abīd ibn Sharya (fl. first/seventh century).[19] Later popular literature both expanded and embroidered these narratives, though such redactions often continued to be attributed to famous early transmitters such as Wahb. (The mature manifestation of this tradition of popular religious narrative is discussed later.)

Proverbs and fables, such as Aesop-like fables attributed to Luqmān the Wise, were prevalent in pre-Islamic Arabia and remained so in the premodern Islamic world.[20] More important from a literary point of view are the many pre- and early Islamic tribal traditions that the Arabs brought with them into Islamic culture. These formed the literary backbone of the Arabism that permeated Islamic cultural activity during this period. The continued strength of this Arabism may be illustrated by one of the major works composed by the prominent fifth/eleventh-century Andalusian writer Abū Muḥammad ʿAlī ibn Aḥmad ibn Ḥazm (d. 456/1064): a genealogical compilation that included a major section on pre-Islamic tribal genealogy.[21] Four centuries and a thousand miles away from pre-Islamic Arabia, a knowledge of its tribal structure was still deemed an essential ingredient of a cultivated person's education.

Arab tribal traditions and narratives covered a host of subjects. Like the religious narratives of the prophets, they became the bases for both high and popular literary traditions. The two pillars of premodern Arabic elite literature—*adab* (belles-lettres) and poetry—arose from and were permeated by pre-Islamic tribal sources and models. To understand the place of these traditions in popular literature, it is useful to classify them into three overlapping spheres: the heroic, the romantic, and the poetic.

Much pre-Islamic tribal narrative centered around important events and personalities of tribal and intertribal history. These narratives were basically anecdotal in form, usually consisting of prose interspersed with poetry. Little effort was made to develop continuous or synthesized narrative; a knowledge of context was assumed. An important group of heroic traditions fell under the heading *Ayyām al-ʿArab* (the Battle Days of the Arabs). These dealt with tribal skirmishes, battles, and feuds and the deeds of warriors and heroes. This body of narrative passed through a stage of critical scholarly scrutiny in the second/eighth and early third/ninth centuries and then entered elite historical and *adab* literature. But already at this stage a tendency toward enlargement and cyclic expansion is noticeable. We may assume that these narratives continued to find a popular audience and that this tendency grew. Half a millennium later, huge heroic cycles based to a significant extent on these narratives, the popular *sīra*s, appear.[22]

Other pre- and early Islamic traditional narratives important in later popular literature were stories of lovers. This genre especially developed in the first few centuries after Islam, when stories of such historical or semihistorical romantic couples as Jamīl and Buthaina, Qais and Lubnā, and Majnūn and Laylā flourished. Again, these accounts provided material for both high and popular literature. They mainly exist in anecdotal form, although the story of Majnūn and Laylā also became a longer, if somewhat loosely hinged, narrative.[23]

A third group of traditions relates to poets. One sure way to achieve renown in pre-Islamic Arabia was to be a talented poet. Poetry was highly prized, and both poems and details about their authors' lives were sought after, collected, and circulated. Few famous only for their poetry entered popular narrative tradition, but entry was easy for those who combined poetic renown with some other remarkable personality trait. Most of the warriors and lovers referred to above, for instance, were also famous poets. Another example of this phenomenon was the figure of Ḥātim aṭ-Ṭayyi'. Although neither a great warrior nor a famous lover, Ḥātim possessed virtues highly esteemed by the pre-Islamic Arabs: generosity and a highly developed sense of hospitality. According to tradition, he began life relatively wealthy but impoverished himself and at one point even sold himself into slavery in order to provide for his constant stream of guests. This trait, combined with his talents as a poet, excited popular imagination; he became the subject of many anecdotes and eventually full-length narratives. We later see the same process at work in regard to Abū Nuwās, historically a court-poet during the time of Hārūn ar-Rashīd. He caught the popular imagination as a combination of wit, humorist, and buffoon and became a subject of popular narrative.[24]

In regard to poetry itself, in the early centuries of Islam the difference between elite and popular poetry seems to have been based less on form than on quality. Popular poetry probably followed the tendency of the Arabic language by becoming lexically and grammatically simpler. To a certain extent, elite poetry followed the same path. Few contemporaries of any social class would have had difficulty in understanding the poetry of Bashshār ibn Burd (d. 168/784–85) or Abu 'l-Atāhiya (d. 210/825). But while popular poetry continued to follow the path of spoken Arabic toward linguistic simplification, resulting in the eventual abandonment of *i'rāb* (desinential inflection), elite poetry refused to do so. The split between the two literary traditions can to some extent be viewed as the result of this linguistic split in Arabic itself. From around the middle of the third/ninth century, elite poetry became characterized by its continued adherence to grammatical "correctness" and a general fascination with lexical opacity and rhetorical brilliance. Popular poetry, by contrast, became marked by linguistic and rhetorical simplicity. In certain forms it did not give up the full classical Arabic use of end vowels (*i'rāb*), but other forms began to develop in which it did and even had to do so. (The results of this process are discussed in the next section.)

One final body of Arab-inspired popular literature that later became important was not pre-Islamic in source, but arose with the coming of Islam. Islam and the astounding military successes that the Arabs achieved under its banner are remarkable world events. It is not surprising, therefore, that later generations were fascinated and formed an idealized picture of this period.

Hence, the life and deeds of the Prophet Muḥammad and those of his early followers in the conquests that ensued after his death were ripe material for popular literature. Again, although no such popular work on this topic has survived from this period, we can assume from the state of the material that appears in such early historical works as *Sīrat an-nabī* (Life of the Prophet) by Muḥammad ibn Isḥāq (d. 152/769) and the novelistic tone of the accounts of certain early Islamic transmitters such as Saif ibn ʿUmar (d. 200/815) that a process of popular fictionalization was under way.[25]

The Iranian Contribution

The other main source of premodern Arabic popular literature was Iran. Its lasting contributions were two: the pseudo-historical heroic cycle and the storybook. Iran had a thriving tradition of popular heroic narrative both before and after the coming of Islam. Some of these, such as *Sīrat Fīrūz Shāh* and *Qiṣṣat Bahrām,* came to exist in Arabic versions. More important is the possible contribution of the form itself. Although there is no direct evidence to support such a theory, it is tempting to view many of the popular *sīra*s that later appeared as the result of a combination of Arabic material and Iranian form.[26]

The most famous and influential Iranian storybook for premodern Arabs was *Kalīla wa-Dimna.* It was translated from Pahlavi into Arabic by ʿAbdullāh ibn al-Muqaffaʿ (d. 139/756) fairly early and enjoyed fame in this and many later redactions.[27] Its animal fables centered on the problem of how to survive and succeed in the intrigues of court life; they were of great interest to elite readers, for whom this problem was of no little import. Opposite in intent, in that it recommended renouncement of the world, was *Kitāb Bilauhar wa-Yūdāsaf,* based on a version of the Buddha story that became known in the West as *Barlaam and Ioasaph.* More important for popular literature, however, was the book that evolved into what is now known as *The Thousand and One Nights.* Many of the stories of the *Nights,* and of similar works such as the *Book of Sindbād* (*The Seven Viziers*), are of Iranian origin and are by no means the least interesting and entertaining part. But the supreme Iranian contribution was the concept of the frame story. Collections of anecdotes and stories abound in premodern Arabic literature; but they either center around a unifying theme, such as avarice *Kitāb al-bukhalāʾ* (The Book of Misers) by Abū ʿUthmān ʿAmr ibn Baḥr al-Jāḥiz (d. 255/868–69) or release from straitened circumstances in *al-Faraj baʿd ash-shidda* (Deliverance after Distress) by Abū ʿAlī al-Muḥsin ibn ʿAlī at-Tanūkhī (d. 384/994), or are miscellanies. The genius of the frame story is that it creates a context for telling stories and at the same time places no limits on the nature of the tale told. Both the *Nights* and the *Book of Sindbād* existed in Pahlavi versions. They existed in Arabic by at least the middle of the fourth/tenth century, and probably several centuries before.[28]

Other Contributions

Another potential source for popular literature, the Byzantine/Hellenistic Greek tradition, appears to have played little direct formative role in Arabic literature, although it made significant contributions to other realms of popular lore, such as magic, astrology, and wisdom literature. Greek was little spoken among the inhabitants of the lands conquered from Byzantium, while Syriac popular literature either was duplicated by the Iranian tradition or was concerned with subjects, such as Christian hagiography, that were of little interest to Muslims. Similarly, any Indian influence came secondhand through Iranian literature.[29]

As noted, much of our knowledge of the popular literature of this period comes from tracing back later developments through the reflection of similar material in elite literature. We thus surmise that the stories of lovers were popular at this time because they exist in later centuries and because they were popular, in different forms, in early elite literature. This deductive method must be followed because other evidence is generally absent. The few premodern Arab scholars who mentioned popular literature usually did so only to condemn it. But occasionally brief illuminations occur. One that deserves special mention is the account Ibn an-Nadīm (d. 385/995) gives in his bibliographical survey of books present in fourth/tenth-century Baghdad, *al-Fihrist* (The Catalogue). One chapter of this work is devoted to the books of "those who tell stories in the evening and tellers of fantastic tales [*al-musāmirīn wa'l-mukharrafīn*]." He begins by discussing the contemporary version of *The Thousand and One Nights*, which he calls by its Persian name: *Kitāb hazār afsān* (he also briefly mentions *Kalīla wa-Dimna* and the *Book of Sindbād*). Then he lists titles of books he has seen, categorized according to their national source or their type, with sections on the "Books of the Persians," "Books of the Indians," "Books of the Kings of Babylon," books concerning "Passionate Lovers during the Pre-Islamic period," and so forth. Relatively few of the books he mentions have survived, but the list of almost 200 titles—which includes only works that existed in writing as opposed to those that may have existed in oral form—shows the thriving state of popular narrative in his day. His categorization of books mainly according to their cultural sources also shows that a state of awareness concerning cultural diversity still existed.[30]

If little is known of the popular literature of this time, less is known concerning those who created and transmitted it. Ibn an-Nadīm refers to "those who tell stories in the evening and tellers of fantastic tales." He also tells of a littérateur who wanted to collect the best stories of all lands and so summoned storytellers (*al-musāmirīn*) to collect material from them.[31] Such scattered references suggest that popular performers of various types were ubiquitous but enjoyed very little social prestige. As far as the elite was concerned, storytellers contributed to the ignorance of the masses by injecting fiction in some of the very areas—religious tradition and historiography—where scholars were most trying to avoid it. Many storytellers, moreover, were professionals in competition with each other; to survive they not only needed to master a repertoire able to attract an audience but had to have the histrionic skills sufficient to enthrall it. Popular preachers preached "fire and brimstone" (*wa'd wa-taḥdhīr*); storytellers cultivated crowd-pleasing gestures and effects; mimics, jugglers, and buffoons were masters of their trade. The very exaggeration of such posturing put off the members of the elite; but at the same time the freedom of such a lifestyle apparently fascinated them. For it is just such sly and duplicitous, but rhetorically spellbinding, characters that became the protagonists of the elite genre of *maqāma* that Badī' az-Zaman al-Hamadānī (d. 398/1008) and Abū Muḥammad al-Qāsim ibn 'Alī al-Ḥarīrī (d. 516/1122) made famous.[32]

THE SECOND PERIOD (SEVENTH/THIRTEENTH–TWELFTH/EIGHTEENTH CENTURIES)

The beginning of this period saw Islamic society undergo a change. Many of the internal cultural and political tensions that made the earlier period so brilliant were either resolved or had run their course. The Mongol sacking of Baghdad in 656/1258 destroyed both the 'Abbasid Caliphate and any lingering illusions of the ideal of Islamic political unity. By this time, too, the concepts of Islam and of the Arabic language had also changed. Islam was now a mature world religion with well-developed and well-organized theological schools and doctrines, and although Arabic was now the first language of most of the inhabitants of the Near East, it was no longer the *'Arabiyya* of pre-Islam. Just as importantly, a unified view of the past had emerged. Although much time was henceforth devoted to studying and reconsidering the various intellectual currents and cultural achievements of the first period, few disputes concerning its intellectual framework arose. A measure of cultural synthesis had been achieved. In the sphere of popular literature, this synthesis produced a burst of creativity. Some new genres appeared; others came to maturity. Moreover, a suitable linguistic medium for popular literature emerged, one that stood midway between the Classical Arabic of elite literature and the dialects of the spoken language but was able to partake of either if necessary; we might call it Standard Written Middle Arabic.[33]

The continuing popularity of stories of the pre-Islamic prophets (*qiṣaṣ al-anbiyā'*) is attested by the existence of many manuscript copies of individual accounts, those of Abraham, Joseph, and Solomon being especially popular. Moreover, by the beginning of this period, whole books devoted to the subject had appeared. Prominent among these were the version of Abū Isḥaq Aḥmad ibn Muḥammad ath-Tha'labī (d. 427/1036), based primarily on accounts taken from Qur'ānic commentary, and the more fictionalized work of the apparently equally fictitious figure of al-Kisā'ī.[34] What distinguishes these works is their attempt to give a complete history of prophecy from an Islamic viewpoint. They organize pre-Islamic prophetic history so that it starts with the creation of the world and ends just before Muḥammad. Everything has now become a preface to Islam. Nor does popular religious history stop at this point. This period also witnesses the appearance of popular accounts of Muḥammad's life. Authorship of these works was attributed either to early historians, such as Abū 'Abdallāh Muḥammad ibn 'Umar al-Wāqidī (d. 207/823), or to such shadowy characters as Abu 'l-Ḥasan Aḥmad ibn 'Abd Allāh al-Bakrī (d. 694/1295).[35] Shorter, independent narratives were devoted to individual events in early Islamic history, such as the conversion of important early followers of Muḥammad—Abū Bakr or 'Umar ibn al-Khaṭṭāb, for example—or to the lives of early saints such as Tamīm ad-Dārī (d. 40/661) and later saints such as Abū Yazīd al-Bisṭāmī (d. 261/874).[36]

The early battles of Islam against the unbelievers of Arabia naturally came to be seen in a heroic light and became the subject of the popular *maghāzī* (campaigns) genre. These narratives never achieved the synthesized form that the "Stories of the Prophets" obtained. Instead they remained relatively short, independent narratives, each devoted to a single battle or adventure. Some were based on actual historical events, such as the battles of Badr, Uḥud, or Tabūk; others are fictional adventures. Although Muḥammad was their nominal protagonist, his cousin and son-in-law, 'Alī ibn Abī Ṭālib, became their real hero. Typically, a supplicant comes to complain of a misdeed to Muḥammad, who then sends 'Alī to right the wrong. With their emphasis on battle, the *maghāzī* are closely related to the genre of popular epic.[37]

Somewhat more substantial in narrative scope and organization are the *futūḥ* (conquest) works, which purport to describe the early Islamic conquests outside Arabia. Prominent among these are *Futūḥ ash-Sham* (Conquest of Syria), *Futūḥ al-'Irāq* (Conquest of Iraq), *Futūḥ al-Miṣr* (Conquest of Egypt), and *Futūḥ al-Bahnasā* (Conquest of Bahnasā [in Upper Egypt]). Like the popular biographies of Muḥammad, the narratives are commonly attributed to al-Bakrī or (pseudo–)al-Wāqidī.[38]

All of these works deal with actual historical figures and (to a certain degree) events. They may be described as pseudo-historiographical works into which a measure of fiction—more or less, as the case may be—has intruded. The popular *sīra* genre represents the reverse side of the coin; they are basically works of fiction adorned with a pseudo-historical and pseudo-historiographical overlay.[39]

The Thousand and One Nights is justly famous as one of the world's great storybooks. It is most associated with tales of magic and romance, but it may just as accurately be viewed as a panorama of premodern Arabic popular storytelling. Its frame story admitted diverse types of tales; in the course of its long development the collection absorbed a wide range of material, much of which also exists either in other sources or in independent redactions: animal fables; stories of early Arab lovers; religious tales of saints and prophets; stories of Harūn ar-Rashīd, his court-poet Abū Nuwās, and his favorite viziers from the Barmacide family; *sīra*-type works, such as the tales of "'Umar an-Nu'mān" and "'Ajīb and Gharīb"; and so on. The book is not just a collection, it is an encyclopedia; its comprehensive heterogeneity is one of its great points of attraction.

The *Nights'* history is complicated; to explore it adequately would require a full-length independent study. Scholars have delineated three main stages: pre-Islamic Persian; early Islamic, centered around Baghdad from the third/ninth to fifth/eleventh centuries; and late Islamic, centered in Egypt and Syria and coalescing in its mature form around the ninth/fifteenth and tenth/sixteenth centuries. We might add to this sequence a later European period, for the work's history in the West is a story in itself.[40]

The *Nights* is not the only premodern Arabic popular storybook. Other examples are *Kitāb al-ḥikāyāt al-'ajība wa-'l-akhbār al-gharība* (The Book of Wondrous Stories and Strange Tales), the story of *Azād-Bakht* (The Ten Viziers), the *Kitāb aṭ-ṭair al-nāṭiq* (The Book of the Talking Bird), apparently a version of the Persian *Tūtī-Nāma* (Story of the Parrot), and *Kitāb al-'anqā'* (The Book of the 'Anqā').[41] Popular literature abounded in anecdotes, usually involving originally historical figures and quite often humorous in tone. Some of these, such as those involving Abū Nuwās, the Barmacides, the wise-fool Juḥā, or the Mamluk vizier Qarāqūsh, became the subjects of special anthologies. Others remained part of various miscellanies devoted to amusing or entertaining stories (*nawādir*).[42]

Obviously, the popular narratives of this period covered a variety of subjects, were of different length, and were transmitted in different ways. Yet they share several characteristics. In their written form, their language was usually that of Standard Middle Arabic. Written in simple prose, they also admit large amounts of formulaic rhymed prose and poetry. They are commonly pseudo-historical: whether religious, romantic, humorous, or heroic, their protagonists are quite often based on historical figures. They also tend to have pseudo-historiographical frameworks: works are attributed to prominent early scholars and fictitious chains of transmitters (*isnāds*) are created. Moreover, they tend to have a pseudo-didactic purpose as justification: even the most outlandish or fantastic tale is justified as being useful as a "warning to those who would be warned [*ʿibra li-man yaʿtabir*]." Finally, there is a tendency toward cyclic expansion: anecdotes become woven into full-length narratives, narratives into huge cycles.

At the same time that popular narrative genres began to stabilize—around the seventh/thirteenth century—the first clear glimpses of the state of popular poetry appear. Classical Arabic poetry consisted of consecutive lines of two hemistichs each. Each line shared the same meter; while the hemistichs of the poem's first line rhymed, succeeding lines only shared the end-rhyme (*aa, ba, ca, da,* etc.). Genres of poetry (such as self-praise, panegyric, love, satire, wine, description, and elegy) had been set since the early days of Islam. Lapses in usage, *iʿrāb*, grammar, and prosody were not lightly countenanced by critics and scholars. Although popular poetry must have existed in the first period, it was largely ignored by the literary establishment and left unrecorded. This situation changed at the beginning of the second period when the *muwashshaḥ*, a strophic verse form that used some colloquial Arabic, and the *zajal*, a similar form composed completely in colloquial, rose into high literary favor. These forms were developed in Spain and were taken up by the Spanish elite by the sixth/twelfth century; soon afterward they became fashionable in the East. Their first major proponent there was the Egyptian poet Ibn Sanā' al-Mulk (d. 608/1211), who prefixed his anthology of Spanish and his own *muwashshaḥāt* with a valuable theoretical introduction to the genre.[43] A century later, another Eastern poet, Ṣafi 'l-Dīn al-Ḥillī (d. 749/1349), composed a similar work, which examines other popular verse forms as well. In this work, *al-ʿĀṭil al-ḥālī wa-'l-murakhkhaṣ al-ghālī* (The Current Weak Market and the Costly Bargain), he gives the classic summary of what became known as the "Seven Types" (*al-funūn as-sabʿa*) of popular poetry:

> All of the types of poetry among most investigators are seven. There is no disparity concerning their number among people of different lands. The disparity between Westerners and Easterners concerns two types of them. The seven mentioned by the people of the West, Egypt, and Syria are: regular poetry [*ash-shiʿr al-qarīḍ*] the *muwashshaḥ*, the *dūbait*, the *zajal*, the *mawāliya*, the *kān wa-kān*, and the *ḥamāq*. The people of Iraq, Diyār Bakr, and beyond confirm five of them, but they exchange *zajal* and the *ḥamāq* with the *ḥijāzī* and the *qūmā*.[44]

Of these seven types, al-Ḥillī says, three generally use correct language and classical meters: regular poetry (*al-qarīḍ*), the *muwashshaḥ*, and the *dūbait*.

The others use colloquial Arabic and do not necessarily employ any of the standard classical meters. The most important of these seven types, the *muwashshaḥ* and the *zajal*—whose subject is primarily love—are significant enough to deserve a separate excursus. Of the remaining forms, the *qarīḍ* is by far the most common. Most of the poetry appearing in the narratives described above, for instance, is of this type. The remaining forms are short and less common. The *dūbait* is a quatrain verse-form composed of four rhyming hemistichs, perhaps derived from the Persian quatrain. The *mawāliya*, most likely the ancestor of the modern popular *mawwāl*, usually consists of four hemistichs with the same end-rhyme as well, although expanded forms exist. Paronomasia, or punning, in the rhyme words is the outstanding characteristic of this form. The *kān wa-kān* is distinguished by a long first hemistich and a short second one; the *ḥamāq* by lines in the form of rhyming couplets (*aa*, *bb*, *cc*, etc.); and the *qūmā* by lines sharing the same end rhyme, but also having internal rhyme in the form *aaba*, *aaca*, *aada*, and so forth. The *ḥijāzī* has four hemistichs, three of which rhyme. Al-Ḥillī's typology was repeated by theorists and anthologists in the centuries that followed, but how accurate and how comprehensive it is for the popular poetry of the whole second period is open to question, especially since its formal criteria ignore the subject of thematic diversity. More research on this subject is needed.[45]

One final artform that deserves mention is the shadow-play (*khayāl aẓ-ẓill*). The only plays that have survived intact are three by the seventh-century Egyptian oculist Shams ad-Dīn Muḥammad ibn Dāniyāl (d. 710/1310). With their farcical intent and satiric tone, these are probably typical of the genre.[46]

In the first period there was a great deal of cross-fertilization between elite and popular literature in the sense that they shared the same source material, although they used it to different purposes; but by the second period the generic structures of both literary realms had become more settled; direct cross-influence declined, mainly, perhaps, because by this time high literature had become less vigorous and innovative. Nonetheless, other areas of cross-fertilization existed and are worthy of mention.

Popular Arabic literature exerted no less influence than high Arabic literature on the neighboring Islamic linguistic and cultural traditions. Indeed, linguistic transfer of works of popular literature was fairly common among premodern Islamic literatures. Versions of *Kalīla and Dimna*, the story of *Bilauhar and Yūdūsaf* (Baarlam and Ioasaph), the Alexander story, originally Arabic stories such as "Majnūn and Laylā" or "Ḥātim al-Ṭayyi'," and religious tales and hagiographies of prophets and saints existed concurrently in many languages.

Relatively few of the dozen major works of the *sīra* genre were widely translated in the Islamic world, despite the existence of equivalent narrative traditions in neighboring linguistic spheres. Of these, *Sīrat Amīr Ḥamza*, the story of the Prophet Muḥammad's uncle, became the most widespread; it was translated—or adopted—into Persian, Turkish, Urdu, Malay, and other Islamic languages. *Sīrat 'Antar* itself, however, despite being one of the best-known *sīra*s in the Arabic-speaking world, never achieved widespread diffusion in a popular (or elite, for that matter) translation.

What characteristics made *Sīrat 'Antar* so popular in Arabic but unpopular in other linguistic spheres, while *Amīr Ḥamza* crossed linguistic boundaries so easily? One answer to this question may be found by comparing the subject matter of the two narratives. The main difference is that the hero of the second is Islamic and transethnic, while the hero of the first is pre-Islamic, tribal, and Arabocentric. The translinguistic receptivity of Islamic stories among the various literary traditions of Islamic culture therefore appears to be an important consideration for their translatability. Another example is the figure of Baṭṭāl Ghāzī. He figures prominently in the Arabic *Sīrat Dhāt al-Himma*, but he is only one of its many heroes. Nevertheless, he becomes the main character of the Turkish *Destān-i Baṭṭāl Ghāzī*, presumably because his activities as a *ghāzī* (religious warrior) held obvious religious but also great cultural significance for Anatolian Turks during the eighth/fourteenth to ninth/fifteenth centuries. More Arabocentric tribal characters in *Dhāt al-Himma* did not make the transition into Turkish. Hence, for a hero to make a cultural transference, he or she must represent values attractive and acceptable to the receiving culture. Just as folklore must be shorn of local characteristics to enter the mainstream of popular literature within one culture, popular works must transcend limiting cultural features to achieve success in translation.

Sometimes in the course of its transference from one culture to another a popular work changed its social and literary venue. Hence, *Sīrat Amīr Ḥamza* became popular reading at the Mogul court, while, as we have seen, *Sīrat 'Antar* was translated for an Ottoman sultan. *The Thousand and One Nights* became a favorite of the European literary establishment in the eighteenth and nineteenth centuries. The issues of changes in cultural authority and audience reception are important here. The Ottoman translator undertook this task only a few years after Mehmet II had conquered Constantinople, during a period, in other words, in which the Ottoman Sultanate aimed at transcending the status of local *ghāzī* to assume a mantle of authority over the classical Islamic cultural tradition. From this perspective, presenting Mehmet II with a translation of the story of a prominent pre-Islamic poet is eminently politic. Similarly, Von Hammer-Purgstall and Terrick Hamilton lived in a period in which Western Orientalists, intent on mastering the literary and cultural traditions of the Muslim East, were fascinated by what they viewed as its seminal period, the pre-Islamic and early Islamic era. This explains their excitement about *Sīrat ʿAntar.* Such enthusiasm was not shared, however, by the European general public, perhaps because ʿAntar's warlike exploits evoked memories of Muslim military successes that, even in the early nineteenth century, were still too fresh for comfort. Greatly preferable were the exoticism, magic, and romance of the *Arabian Nights.*

PART II

Narrative Analysis

CHAPTER 5

The Heroic Cycle

THE WRITTEN VERSION of *Sīrat 'Antar* consists of a great mass of episodes, loosely or closely connected and interrelated to various degrees. Some are short and fairly straightforward others are long and intricate. In addition, multitudes of characters enter and leave the narrative, while the range of its geographical settings constantly modulates and expands. In its fifty-six hundred pages, the *Sīra* piles character upon character, episode upon episode, event upon event, and location upon location. The thematic world of the *Sīra* consists of many often-repeated events.

For example, during 'Abs's journey through Yemen several tribal kings see and fall in love with 'Abla, 'Antar's beloved.[1] These are not just chance incidents, however. 'Abla's beauty is so dazzling that almost all who see her fall madly in love, with the subsequent (for them) distressing consequence of having to face 'Antar's jealous wrath. 'Umāra ibn Ziyād falls in love with her early in the narrative (3:271ff.), as do Wāqid ibn Mas'ara (5:463–6:55), Mufarrij ibn Hammām (6:30–85), Rauḍa ibn Manī' (7:139–51), Bisṭām ibn Qais (8:248–9:281), Musaḥḥil ibn Ṭarrāq (9:339–60), Anas ibn Mudrika (9:397–10:420), and even the Persian Prince Azdashīr (33:266–82).

Similarly, at one point 'Antar undertakes the dangerous mission of winning one thousand 'Aṣāfīr camels as part of 'Abla's dowry. This achievement fails to satisfy her family; they soon arrange to send 'Antar to capture Queen Jaidā' as a bridal servant for 'Abla (7:152–8:233). Moreover, 'Antar is only one of the many lovers who fill the *Sīra* with quests for dowries. Naziḥ ibn Asīd falls in love and is set the task of capturing King Zuhair of 'Abs (14:315–80). Muqri 'l-Waḥsh must capture two thousand 'Aṣāfīr camels, then he is sent to fight 'Abs in order to earn the camels (19:347–20:400). In order to win their beloveds, Khufāf ibn Nadba must capture King al-Mutana'jiz (27:120–66); Ghaṣūb, camels and booty (35:387–411); and al-Ghaḍbān, 'Abla herself (40: 463–41:63)—to mention only a few examples.

It is clear that repetition is a common compositional technique here, but it involves more than the random reiteration of motifs. Contending with a rival and winning a dowry are less haphazardly chosen incidents than selected elements of larger narrative patterns that the *Sīra*'s oral storytellers relied on to create the epic's successive episodes. By means of this network of patterns, storytellers were able to create the episodes and stories that constituted individual oral performances of the epic. At the same time, mastery of these patterns allowed them to expand the narrative endlessly, transforming the fragmented anecdotal account of 'Antar's life into a full-scale, voluminous epic cycle. To understand how this was done, we cannot merely examine isolated examples of repeated events or attempt to index all the motifs that occur in the *Sīra*. Instead we must deduce the general configurations of the storytelling structures that govern the organization of these individual motifs. Beneath the seeming multiplicity of its episodes and events, the *Sīra* tells only one story—or more precisely one series of stories. This general sequence, which I term *Sīrat 'Antar*'s Heroic Cycle, is outlined below.[2]

THE HEROIC CYCLE

I. *The Rise of the Hero*
- A. Unusual Birth
  1. Unusual social status, either very low or high
  2. Peculiar, often illegitimate birth
  3. Unusual physical attributes as a child
- B. Preparatory Youth
  1. The youth practices the skills of war
  2. The youth acquires extraordinary accouterments
     - a. A wonderful horse
     - b. An unusual sword and/or suit of armor
     - c. An extraordinary helper
  3. The youth performs acts of unusual courage or strength
- C. The Hero Proves Himself or Herself
  1. The hero kills a lion
  2. The hero performs public deeds:
     - a. Defeats older or more prestigious opponents
     - b. Begins to go on raids
     - c. Defends the tribe
- D. The Hero Wins Public Acceptance

1. The hero performs some outstanding deed:
    a. Single-handedly defends the tribe
    b. Wins a tournament
2. The hero overcomes the resistance of a rival
3. The hero gains paternal acknowledgment

II. *The Love Story*
- A. The Hero Falls in Love and
    1. Flirts with the beloved
    2. Recites poetry
- B. The Hero Rescues the Beloved
- C. The Hero Overcomes the Opposition of the Beloved's Family by
    1. Obtaining a special dowry
    2. Capturing or killing an important person
    3. Defeating the beloved in single combat
- D. The Hero Defeats a Rival
    1. In the beloved's camp
    2. After seeking him or her out
    3. By stealing the beloved from the rival
- E. The Hero Marries the Beloved

III. *Heroic Service*
- A. The Hero Helps the Weak:
    1. Defenseless women
    2. Strangers in distress
    3. Supplicants and refugees
- B. The Hero Helps His Family and Peers by
    1. Rescuing captured family and fellow members of the tribe
    2. Rescuing friends and fellow heroes
    3. Rescuing captured rivals
    4. Helping lovers win their beloveds
- C. The Hero Helps Tribes and Rulers in Their Wars

IV. *The Death of the Hero*
- A. The Hero Dies by Being Killed
    1. Outright in battle
    2. Through accident or mishap
    3. Through duplicity, treachery, or magic
- B. Family and Friends Mourn and Bury the Hero
- C. Family and Friends Avenge the Hero's Death

These four clusters of story patterns cover the hero's entire life—from birth to death. More importantly, they determine the nature and order of the events. The Rise of the Hero focuses on the hero's birth, childhood, and attainment of adulthood; the Love Story charts the course of the hero's romances; Heroic Service organizes the great deeds of the hero's maturity; and the Death of the Hero relates the circumstances of the hero's lamented demise. These patterns combine to provide comprehensive narrative structures for each part of the hero's life story and in doing so allow a storyteller to continue his narration—potentially at least—forever.

Part of the genius of these story patterns is their flexibility and their inherent duality: they can both serve as a part within the whole and stand alone as independent narrative units. Each contains within itself the outline of a complete plot structure that, if necessary, can exist as an independent entity; yet each can also exist as a subsidiary part of the Heroic Cycle. To illustrate this point, the following sections describe basic thematic and structural features of these patterns and some of the ways in which *Sīrat 'Antar* transforms their abstract potentialities into concrete particularities.[3]

THE RISE OF THE HERO

The Rise of the Hero story pattern recounts the events of the hero's early years: the circumstances of his or her birth, the events of childhood, and his or her final ascent into adulthood. Yet *Sīrat 'Antar* is drawn to such biographical concerns only to the extent that they offer opportunities for conjuring exciting and dramatic situations. Growing up, therefore, is not the story of a person's smooth and effortless entry into a new phase of life but rather the result of a tumultuous struggle to prove one's worth and so win full status in the closed hierarchy of the adult world. In *Sīrat 'Antar* equality and social acceptance are not bestowed freely—they are won! It is the story of this prolonged struggle that provides the dramatic tension of the Rise of the Hero.

Unusual Birth

Heroes are destined to rise above the normal standards of society. To make their ascent more difficult—and thus their eventual successes more noteworthy—this story pattern frequently begins by placing them very low in society. It also conjoins in them contradictory qualities of intrinsic personal worth and external social disadvantage. While the virtues of heroes are uniform—great size and strength, martial prowess, innate nobility, and generosity—their social drawbacks are diverse. Since 'Antar possesses most of the social disadvantages found in the *Sīra*'s heroes, his story provides a good example of this pattern.

'Antar is set apart from his society from birth. The son of a freeborn Arab father and an enslaved Abyssinian mother, 'Antar combines the fiery pride and arrogance of his father with the physical attributes and low social status of his mother. Hence, his racial constitution symbolizes the combination of social advantages and disadvantages that makes his social status a matter of contestation throughout his life. On the one hand, 'Antar's extraordinary size, strength, and ferocity excite the early attention and admiration of others. He bullies older boys, teases the camp dogs, and becomes the camp nuisance.[4] Nevertheless, Shaddād's companions are quite aware that such high-spiritedness is a sign of future greatness and covetously try to claim a share in the child (2:125–28). On the other hand, 'Antar's black skin and African features appear to assure a life of ignominious slavery in his stratified and racially discriminatory tribal society. Thus the contradiction between the hero's inherent worth and his superficial social unworthiness is internally represented in the person of 'Antar himself. It becomes externally represented, however, as he strives to win paternal acknowledgment. 'Antar cannot alter his physical constitution—nor would he want to if he could. Nonetheless, he can change his society's perception of him. This struggle to win social acceptance, symbolized by winning his patrimony, provides the dramatic mainspring for the first part of his story.

Encumbering the hero with such social drawbacks is a favorite habit of the *Sīra*; 'Antar is just one of the many black slave heroes who fill its pages.[5] How the narrative sets its heroes at odds with society matters less than the essential fact that it does so. It may accomplish this in several alternative ways. 'Antar's story is typical of heroes who begin in the lower realms of society. Sometimes, however, heroes are not lowborn but highborn. The drama of their stories springs from another kind of individual-society confrontation. Unlike the lowborn hero, they do not confront social obstacles; instead their stories begin with their not fulfilling social expectations. In *Sīrat 'Antar*, such unwarriorlike behavior provokes just as great a scandal as warriorlike behavior on the part of the slaves. Bisṭām ibn Qais, for example, has the unacceptable quality of sitting among the women rather than pursuing such manly habits as hunting or fighting. The disgrace becomes so great that his father finally sends him away to another tribe, hoping that more masculine instincts will come to the fore there (8:254). 'Amr ibn Ma'dīkarib, alternatively, prefers eating to fighting. This idiosyncrasy costs his father, the great hero Ma'dīkarib ibn al-Ḥārith, great shame and considerable numbers of camels, since 'Amr reveals his heroic excess by consuming a whole camel at every meal (25:475–78).[6]

Sometimes the *Sīra* combines aspects of the lowborn and highborn hero by presenting heroes who fall from high to low social positions due to some early catastrophe. One example is Nāziḥ ibn Asīd, the son of a prince of 'Abs. While Nāziḥ is still a baby, he and his mother are captured on a raid so that he grows up an orphan. Heroes are innately indomitable, however, whatever their social position, and we first meet Nāziḥ as a young man fighting for equality and social acceptance in his adopted tribe. In the midst of this struggle he captures his real father, learns his true identity (for some reason mothers of captured children always seem to keep this a secret), and thus assumes his rightful station in life (14:31–81). The story of Mājid ibn Mālik is much the same (29:332–30:407).

One final type of social disadvantage that certain heroes must overcome in *Sīrat 'Antar* is that of gender. Some of the epic's greatest heroes—al-Jaidā' (7:152–233), Ghamra (27:126ff.), and 'Unaitira (56:53ff.)—are women. In general, being a woman is much less of a drawback for an aspiring hero than being a slave, and the motif of the female hero plays a more important role in the Love Story than it does in the Rise of the Hero.[7]

The circumstances of heroes' conceptions are often as exceptional as their later lives. 'Antar is conceived out of wedlock when Shaddād captures Zabība on a raid, but this is mild compared to other examples in the *Sīra*. 'Antar's children, for example, all have extraordinary conceptions. Maisara is conceived when 'Antar captures Mahriyya's wedding caravan, sleeps with her, kills her bridegroom, and then reunites her with her lover (25:413–29); al-Ghaḍbān, when 'Antar magically cures Sarwa of a mysterious illness, marries her for a day, and then loses her in the desert (35:449–51; 36:35–37); Ghaṣūb, when 'Antar first defeats Ghamra in single combat and then rapes her (27:149–51). The circumstances of the conceptions of 'Antar's other children and of the other heroes of the *Sīra* are equally unusual.[8]

This story pattern, which marks the hero as someone different from birth, serves two narrative purposes. First, the reader's attention is drawn to the heroes. Their peculiarities presage the great things to come: these are children who will have an unusual future; their stories deserve attention. If heroes' peculiarities serve to mark them for the external audience, however, within the story they serve the completely different function of creating a cleft between heroes and society. Society comes to view them as people of such low or liminal status that they fall beyond the pale of acceptability. Thus begins the struggle between hero and society. Heroes are destined to win this struggle, but they do not do so by giving up their peculiarities; rather they force society to accept them in spite of them. Heroes do not change to fit society; they alter society by forcing it to accommodate them.[9]

Preparatory Youth

Following the account of the hero's birth and early childhood comes the preparatory period of his or her youth. Here heroes practice and refine their martial skills and begin to accumulate the accouterments that help assure their future success. The story of ʿAntar himself provides the fullest account of this period. He secretly practices riding and the use of sword and lance while he tends his father's herds; he kills wild animals that threaten them; and he begins his extremely valuable partnership with his half-brother Shaibūb, who is to be his helper, counselor, and alter-ego throughout his career (2:131ff.). ʿAntar later obtains heroic accouterments: his wonderful black mare al-Abjar (the Stout) (2:220–21) and his deadly sword aẓ-Ẓāmī (the Thirsty) (2:265–66).[10] This period of preparatory youth also continues the secret alliance between the heroes-to-be and the readers. We alone are privy to the secret of their true worth and so are able to foresee the burst of heroic activity soon to come.

As heroes grow, so do their deeds, as they move from the periphery of societal awareness toward its center. ʿAntar quarrels with and kills two slaves, helps to protect his tribe against attack, and begins to go on raids (2:136ff). The feat that commonly symbolizes the hero's readiness to assume the full status of adulthood is the lion fight. Heroes encounter and single-handedly defeat this greatest and most dangerous of beasts and so display sufficient courage and strength to warn those who would dare to oppose them of the consequences that opposition will entail.[11]

With the hero's full emergence into the public arena, the stage is set for the climax of the Rise of the Hero plot pattern. This assumes two forms. In the case of highborn heroes, a situation arises that compels them to choose to act, and so fully assume the social positions that are naturally theirs, or not to act and irrevocably relinquish them. There is, of course, little doubt about which course they will pursue. Despite ʿAmr ibn Maʿdīkarib or Bisṭām ibn Qais's initial social deviances, at crucial moments, when their tribes are under attack and in deadly peril, they assume their true personas as tribal heroes and protectors. When five hundred raiders attack the otherwise undefended Tamīm camp, Bisṭām single-handedly drives them off. To dispel any further doubt about his courage, he proves himself again in the mock warfare of King an-Nuʿmān's tournament lists. His deeds multiply and his fame grows so that Bisṭām becomes the recognized hero or protector (*al-ḥāmī*) of the Banī Shaibān (8:253–59).[12] Similarly, when ʿAmr's tribe is attacked, he first roasts and consumes a whole camel and then takes a nap. Finally, he takes his father's horse and arms, saying that Maʿdīkarib has become too old and feeble to need them, and drives off the attackers.[13] From that time he becomes the recognized hero of the Banī Zubaid (25:475–79).

In the case of lowborn heroes such as ʿAntar, winning public acceptance is not a process of natural accession to an already existent social position but a matter of fierce struggle. Ironically, although lowborn heroes' deeds are all directed against their tribes' external foes, their real enemies are their rivals within their own tribes. Yet in this more important struggle heroes' strength and prowess avail them little. They cannot force their tribes to accept them by defeating each member in single combat (although they are sometimes tempted by this thought).[14] Instead they force their tribes to accept them by performing so many great deeds that their fellow tribe members either acquiesce, as do Prince Mālik, Prince Shāsh, and King Zuhair in 'Antar's case, or are forced by public sentiment to simulate acceptance, as do ar-Rabī' ibn Ziyād, Mālik ibn Qurād, and 'Antar's other implacable enemies within 'Abs. Failing this, heroes have little recourse but to leave their tribes, which 'Antar temporarily does on several occasions (2:208ff., 23:233ff., 26:33ff., etc.). Indeed, for 'Antar social struggle remains a lifelong issue. His enemies' sense of honor forbids them to accept a former slave as an equal, no matter how great his deeds. Led by ar-Rabī' ibn Ziyād, they continue to form shifting alliances against him throughout his life.[15]

With lowborn heroes, public acceptance is often symbolized by paternal acknowledgment. Except in the extraordinary case of 'Antar himself, who continues his struggle for social acceptance even after his father acknowledges him, paternal acknowledgment equals social acceptance. Indeed, conflicts between sons and fathers represent all the problems of the struggle between heroes and their societies. Shaddād is the only person whom 'Antar allows to strike him. Instead of raising his hand in return, he leaves the tribe (2:208ff.). At times the *Sīra* portrays this conflict differently, by staging instances of single combat between fathers and sons unaware of their familial relationship. The dramatic possibilities intrinsic in such encounters account for the *Sīra*'s fondness for this motif. It also serves as a dramatic final climax for the Rise of the Hero.[16]

The main theme of the Rise of the Hero, therefore, is not heroes' struggles against external enemies, although these conflicts provide the storyteller with wonderful opportunities to create drama and suspense. It is their struggles to win their birthrights, the place in society to which their innate talents and virtues entitle them. In the end, heroes do win social acceptance—sooner if they are highborn or later if they are lowborn. There is little question about their eventual success. If they did not succeed, they would not be heroes.

THE LOVE STORY

After or in the midst of their struggles for social acceptance, heroes enter the second major story pattern of the Heroic Cycle: the Love Story. Early Arab society customarily encouraged the marriage of first cousins as a way of preserving family unity and wealth. The *Sīra* reflects this custom: its heroes often fall in love with cousins. Nevertheless, the general rule in *Sīrat 'Antar* is that a male hero (female heroes rarely participate in this pattern) only falls in love with his cousin when there is some good reason for her family to reject his suit. This usually occurs with poor or lowborn heroes such as 'Antar. In such cases, the *Sīra* represents the right of first cousins to marry as a strongly supported principle and portrays the hero's being denied his cousin's hand as an injustice. The hero's struggle to win the beloved echoes his efforts to win social acceptance, the main theme of the Rise of the Hero. His cousin thus becomes one more patrimonial right that the hero must fight to win. Despite these implications, in *Sīrat 'Antar* ties of blood never overshadow the bonds of love. Heroes want to marry their cousins because of love, not social custom.[17]

The precedence of the ties of love is clearly emphasized by the alternative plot scheme of the Love Story. In this scenario, a hero falls in love with a girl who is not his cousin, while the beloved's family rejects him on the grounds that he is not part of the family. The *Sīra* portrays this as an injustice, since nothing should stand in the way of true love. In such situations, the beloved's first cousin, usually portrayed as arrogant and unattractive, often becomes the villain of the story because he insists on his right to marry his first cousin, even though she loves another. He thus becomes the second hurdle (after the parents) that blocks the lovers' happiness.[18] In either case, whether related to his beloved or not, the hero is faced with a situation where the delights of love can only be won through force of arms. To succeed in this struggle, he usually needs his considerable propensities for violent and determined action.

The Hero Falls in Love

Love in *Sīrat 'Antar* begins in one of three ways. If the beloved is the hero's first cousin, daily interaction provides ample opportunities for its spark to ignite. For example, 'Antar's youthful duties as a slave and thus servant to the women of his clan give him a chance to admire 'Abla every day—until others notice and object to their love (2:144ff.). Such daily exposure, however, is rarely needed to initiate the sweet pangs of love. When lovers meet as strangers, an exchange of glances or a glimpse of each other's faces suffices to cast one or both into the thralls of passion. Sometimes even this is unnecessary. A maiden's beauty provokes as much repute and discussion in *Sīrat 'Antar* as a hero's prowess and deeds. Often just hearing a description of a girl's beauty completely infatuates a hero or moves kings or emperors to go to war.[19]

The beauty of the beloved usually strikes the hero dumb—but not for long! Love inspires poetic outpourings. Because 'Antar cannot restrain himself from reciting love poetry publicly, he shames 'Abla's family and creates a scandal within the tribe (2:144ff.). The love poems that heroes recite in lonely solitude at the edge of their camps, during their far-off quests for dowries and glory, or, in happier circumstances, during the dalliance and flirtation of secretly arranged picnics or moonlight trysts provide some of the *Sīra*'s prettiest moments. If love is mutual and fortune smiles, the course of true love is smooth. Heroes such as ʿUrwa ibn al-Ward (43:39) and Prince Hiraql of Byzantium (53:260–64) meet and court their beloveds under ideal circumstances. In their cases, the interlude between first love and consummation is brief and pleasant. Such cases are exceptional, however; in *Sīrat ʿAntar* love usually creates nothing but trouble.

The Hero Rescues the Beloved

One major threat to the happiness of the lovers is the beloved's capture during a raid. Tribal society, as portrayed by the *Sīra*, is predatory and rapacious; heroes must stand ready to protect their tribes. One special concern during such attacks is the loss of their lovers or wives. ʿAntar is often distracted from his general defense of the camp by ʿAbla's cries for help (2:160–62; 2:185–88). In fact, ʿAbla falls captive regularly (5:463–6:85, 8:210ff., 9:299–10:420, 10:420–11:41, 12:122ff., etc.). Rescue of the beloved thus becomes a frequent motif. At other times, lovers suffer sudden separation from their beloveds. For example, Prince al-Ḥārith ibn Zuhair (13:280–93) and Mājid ibn Mālik (30:407–74) fall in love with young women from clans who have sought refuge with ʿAbs. Both princes meet with their beloveds and swear oaths of love. When they leave to visit their own tribes, however, each returns to find the beloved's campsite empty and her clan departed. So the heartbroken lover must set out to recover his beloved.[20]

Such sudden separations offer the storyteller numerous possibilities for creating suspense. Nevertheless, the true dramatic confrontation of the Love Story is not the lover's defense of his beloved from some outside danger, but rather his efforts to win over her family. In this struggle, two obstacles stand in the way of happiness: the father of the bride and the rival suitor.

The Hero Overcomes the Opposition of the Beloved's Family

The story of al-Ghaḍbān and Daʿda provides a good illustration of this part of the Love Story (41:8–63).[21] Al-Ghaḍbān is the son of ʿAntar and Sarwa (35:449–51). Since ʿAntar has lost contact with Sarwa (as tends to happen in his impromptu trysts), he remains unaware that she has borne him a son (36:65). Al-Ghaḍbān grows up as a slave among Sarwa's tribe, becomes a warrior, and eventually wins his freedom (40:463–41:8), thus ending the Rise of the Hero part of his story. Then he falls in love.

Al-Minhāl, a chief of the Banī Kināna, is dismayed when a former black slave requests his daughter's hand. Nevertheless, like most fathers of brides in

Sīrat 'Antar, he is aware that it is dangerous openly to refuse the suit of a powerful and impetuous hero. Instead he resorts to the path that almost all unwilling fathers pursue in the *Sīra*—procrastination and deceit. When Da'da falls captive, al-Minhāl encourages al-Ghaḍbān to rescue her, presuming that whether the youth succeeds or dies in the attempt he, at least, will be relieved of his problem. Al-Ghaḍbān rescues Da'da; but by this time al-Minhāl has conceived of another plan to rid himself of this unwelcome suitor. He declares that he wants to honor his daughter with the most glorious wedding ever seen in Arabia and therefore asks the youth to capture 'Abla, so that Da'da will have a fitting attendant for the wedding. Al-Ghaḍbān, being a hero, will undertake any mission to gain his beloved and immediately sets out for 'Abs.[22]

Here an event occurs that typifies the way *Sīrat 'Antar* interlaces its narrative. On his way to 'Abs, al-Ghaḍbān captures ar-Rabī' ibn Ziyād and his family in the desert. As if the *Sīra* considers the prospect of fighting 'Antar too dangerous to be justified for the sake of one beloved, it now gives al-Ghaḍbān another; he falls in love with ar-Rabī''s daughter. Ar-Rabī' adopts the same policy as al-Minhāl. He tells al-Ghaḍbān that he will only give his daughter in marriage to the person who delivers 'Antar's head as a dowry. Armed with another reason to fight the father he has never met, al-Ghaḍbān continues his journey toward 'Abs.

'Antar and al-Ghaḍbān meet, fight, and eventually discover that they are father and son. 'Antar decides to help his son in his quest, so, having achieved his mission in a way that will surprise al-Minhāl, al-Ghaḍbān sets out for home. (Apparently ar-Rabī''s daughter is no longer important, for no more is heard of her.) On his return, the young hero discovers a new obstacle. King Sa'b of the Bani 'r-Riyān has fallen in love with Da'da and has demanded her from al-Minhāl. The father, always forced to choose between the worst of two evils, decides that the danger at hand is more pressing than the one he has temporarily contrived to send away. He submits to King Sa'b's intimidation and agrees to the marriage. Fitting out a rich marriage caravan, he sets out to take his daughter to the Bani 'r-Riyān. Raiders attack the caravan, al-Ghaḍbān and 'Antar appear just in time to save the beloved, al-Minhāl flees (probably glad to be rid of his troublesome daughter), and al-Ghaḍbān marries Da'da.

Al-Ghaḍbān's Love Story contains the dramatic complications typical of this story pattern. The young hero rescues his beloved from outside attackers, contends with the demands of the girl's father, and faces the challenge of a rival suitor. Alternative plot twists are possible at the various stages of the story pattern. As we have seen, al-Minhāl sent al-Ghaḍbān to capture a person as part of his dowry demand. This demand is a frequent motif; but just as common is the demand that the hero obtain material goods.[23] The hero is never reluctant to undertake the dangerous task of winning a dowry—quite the opposite: he usually considers it a wonderful opportunity to win fame and glory. When 'Antar agrees to steal 'Aṣāfīr camels (4:345–5:462) or capture al-Jaidā' (7:152–8:233), he is initially unaware how dangerous and difficult these missions really are; but even when he learns of their true dangers, he remains steadfast in his desire to complete them.[24] Similarly, Rabī'a al-Mukaddam marries his beloved Hind without having to provide a dowry. After the wedding, however, this shortcoming so shames him that he secretly leaves his bride to go win a fine dowry (39:358–59).

Rabī'a's courtship of Hind reveals another recurrent motif: the bride herself, rather than her father, opposes the hero's suit. In this situation two scenarios are possible. If the bride is of normal strength, she resorts to trickery to rid herself of her husband or suitor. Kabsha sends Wizr ibn Jābir on difficult missions, hoping he will be killed (47:179ff.); 'Abla stabs Prince Azdashīr at the dinner table (33:282). If the beloved is a great warrior in her own right, however, she challenges her suitor to single combat. Hind agrees to marry Rabī'a only after he defeats her in battle (39:356–57), while al-Jaidā' temporarily falls out of love with Khālid ibn Muḥārib when he is unable to vanquish her (7:175–81).[25]

When all else fails, the reluctant father of the bride flees with his family from the unwanted suitor. 'Abla's father, for example, does this a number of times (8:242ff., 9:334ff.). Sometimes such flight initiates another love story. When Asmā''s father escapes an unwanted suitor by bringing his clan to the Banī 'Abs, she and Prince Mājid of 'Abs fall in love (30:447ff.)

The Hero Defeats a Rival

The confrontation between the lover and his rival assumes different forms. Typically, the rival appears while the hero is away winning the dowry. If the beloved's father favors the suitor, as Musaika's father favors Muqri 'l-Waḥsh (20:466), or at least values his promise to let a hero marry his daughter, as Ḥiṣn's uncle does (2:260–65), then he resists the rival's advances. In this case, the episode builds suspense as the bride's father delays the wedding ceremony long enough for the hero to return. If the father dislikes the hero, however, as often happens with 'Antar and his rivals, he often demands the latter's death as the price of accepting the rival and sets up a confrontation in this way (8:248ff., 9:34ff., etc.). Finally, if all else fails, the hero steals the beloved from his rival, as happens with al-Ghaḍbān, 'Urwa ibn al-Ward (26:14ff.), and Maisara (30: 454ff., 39:89ff.). However the lover finally wins the beloved—whether by returning in the nick of time to defeat his rival, defeating him in a desert encounter, or stealing the beloved from him—the suspense runs high, the fighting is fierce, and the outcome remains in doubt until the last possible moment.

The Hero Marries the Beloved

When their tribulations are over and the final obstacles that block their path have been removed, the lovers marry. Marriage ceremonies in *Sīrat 'Antar* are conventional, almost anticlimactic affairs. The greatest such celebration is, of course, the marriage of 'Antar and 'Abla (20:401–57). This wedding fills fifty pages, but it is just an expanded version of all of the weddings of the *Sīra.*[26] Guests are invited by the hundreds, animals are slaughtered by the thousands, wine is consumed by the caskful, feasts are held in continuous rounds, and poems praising the happy pair are constantly recited. Generally, however, the narrative is less interested in describing wedding celebrations and the marital bliss that follows them than it is in portraying the terrible yet sweet suffering that love provokes and the great deeds that it inspires in the earlier period of courtship. It is not the steady red glow of daily companionship that excites the imagination of the *Sīra*, but the white heat of passion.

The hero's early years are dominated by the themes and events of the Rise of the Hero and the Love Story. In due time these story patterns run their course. The hero overcomes the obstacles and challenges of these early struggles by winning social acceptance and marrying his beloved. The story, however, does not end here. *Sīrat 'Antar*, unlike the folk tale or romance, does not end with a formula such as "And they lived happily ever after" after the wedding banquet. One might even say that the story really begins at this point. Now the hero enters maturity, dominated by the themes and events of the third story pattern of the Heroic Cycle: Heroic Service.

HEROIC SERVICE

The keynote of Heroic Service is helping others. While the first two story patterns achieve such personal goals as gaining social acceptance and winning the beloved, in Heroic Service heroes turn their gaze outward to serve, rescue, and defend those in need. In general, these supererogatory activities fall into three categories. Heroes help those lesser, those equal, and those greater. A hero like 'Antar defends the weak—women, old people, slaves, and other nonwarriors; helps his peers—individuals from his family, friends, other heroes, and, of course, other lovers; and serves larger social groups—tribes or nations and those who represent them, such as kings or emperors. Since 'Antar is the hero to whom the *Sīra* allots by far the greatest number of heroic feats, his story exemplifies the events that typify this story pattern.[27]

The Hero Helps the Weak

ʿAntar defends the weak and helpless against the aggression of the strong. He protects two old women from the bullying harassment of an arrogant slave (2:136–42), rescues strangers from the rapacity of robbers (6:90–99, 9:319–30), and repeatedly saves women from his own and other tribes from captivity and enslavement (2:170–78, 2:181–90, 9:308–12, 18:27–77, 26: 34–38, etc.). ʿAntar, in fact, generally acts chivalrously toward all women, even those of enemy tribes (23:215, 36:59). Finally, he takes in supplicants or refugees from other tribes who seek protection (17:103, 26:43, 49:333).

The Hero Helps His Family and Peers

ʿAntar's relationships with his peers are based on noble sentiments and mutual esteem. He always rescues members of his clan or tribe (2:249–54, 16:13–16, 29:340–406), even those who hate and despise him (6:13–84, 7:130–39, 9:302). He also has many friends among the heroes of his own and other tribes (together they constitute a kind of intertribal league of heroes) and is always prepared to aid them should the need arise (22:188–23:217, 26:33–36, 26:88–27:110, 29:321–26). Having suffered the pangs of love himself, ʿAntar never refuses to help other lovers to win the hand of their beloveds (3:254, 14:38, 27:122).

The Hero Helps Tribes and Rulers in Their Wars

Apart from helping individuals, ʿAntar also supports larger groups. He stands ready to fight the enemies of his tribe, helping ʿAbs in its wars with the kings of al-Ḥīra and the shah of Persia (10:420–11:40, 11:41–12:175, 12:176–13:274, 49:333–51:62) and in its feuds with other tribes (14:381–17:102, 17:175–19:347, 25:430–70, 49:333–51:62). Even after quarreling and temporarily leaving his tribe, he forgets his anger and returns to help if it suffers attack (24:331, 55:458–59). ʿAntar also helps the great kings and emperors of his day: the king of al-Ḥīra (12:175–13:274, 33:205–34:306), the shah of Persia (28:227–72, 43:257–44:375, 51:62–82), the Ghassānid king in Damascus (32:157–66, 55:462–63), and the emperor of Byzantium (32:166–33:205, 53:197–266, 53:267–54:310, 54:311–55:389, 55:463–56:10). In fact, ʿAntar will help any tribe or ruler against outside threats or attacks, even one with whom he has just been at odds. For example, he aids Queen Ghamra in defeating the Sudanese kings who invade her lands (36:71–37:134). Then he assists one of these kings, Laun aẓ-Ẓalām, in his war with another of them, King Hammām (37:134–38:270). He helps King Hammām against his liege King

Damhār (38:262–68) and then helps all the Sudanese kings against the negus of Abyssinia (38:268–39:299).

NARRATIVE SITUATION VERSUS NARRATIVE PROGRESSION

The story pattern of Heroic Service differs radically from the previous two story patterns in its combination and use of such basic narrative tools as theme, structure, and context. The dramatic basis of the Rise of the Hero and the Love Story rests on a sense of long-term narrative progression. Both give the heroes long-range goals to fulfill and place a string of obstacles or trials in their way. As the hero struggles toward his or her goal, each success or failure assumes significance on two levels: its own and that of the story pattern's overall theme. When 'Antar rushes to help King Zuhair's ten sons who have fallen under sudden attack (2:170–75), for example, the resulting battle contains its own measure of suspense and excitement. Although the aura of immediate excitement ends with the battle, the event's overall significance does not, since 'Antar's victory is also important in regard to his struggle to achieve social equality. King Zuhair and several of his sons now favor 'Antar's case more strongly, and this shift in attitude will affect the shape of events throughout the remainder of the story pattern.

Hence, in the Rise of the Hero and the Love Story, the story pattern's larger theme is woven into the themes of its individual events. These larger themes serve two functions. They are smoldering sources of motivation for the hero that often generate narrative events. Of equal or even greater importance, however, is their role in unifying the events of the story pattern. Events otherwise random are no longer so; instead they are a part of the hero's tumultuous progress toward his or her final goal.

The thematic context of Heroic Service, however, is situational rather than progressive. Instead of pursuing their own personal goals, heroes adopt the more passive situation of helping others. They respond to rather than initiate action. Simultaneously, a multiplicity of individual deeds replaces the single overriding goal of the other story patterns. The narrative effectiveness of the descriptions of these individual deeds thus depends less on the cloak of contextual unity of one overriding theme than on the dramatic possibilities and qualities inherent in each situation. An example will illustrate this point.

On one of his many expeditions to rescue 'Abla, 'Antar, accompanied only by 'Urwa ibn al-Ward and his one hundred vagabond followers, attacks a whole campful of Kinda tribesmen. 'Antar would have been overwhelmed and the day lost except for the sudden appearance of Bisṭām ibn Qais and four of King Zuhair's sons, each leading a column of warriors. The Banī Kinda suffer defeat, while ʿAntar successfully rescues ʿAbla. The five armies celebrate their victory and then set out individually to return home, ʿAntar going with Bisṭām to live among the Banī Shaibān for a time (9:363–78). On his return journey to ʿAbs, Prince Mālik leaves his army to hunt alone in the desert and is captured by some passing raiders. At this point ʿAntar appears. When he sees the prince a captive, he immediately attacks, defeats and drives off the raiders, and rescues him. Both then return toward the army that Mālik was leading home (9:383–95).

Here are two rescues, each with its own intrinsic dramatic charge: suspense due to a dangerous situation, the excitement of battle, relief when the right side wins. ʿAntar's first rescue also has a second dimension of significance: it promotes the overall scheme of his Love Story—the guiding story pattern at this point. It is difficult to see a greater significance in the second rescue. ʿAntar's rescue of Prince Mālik forms an independent narrative entity, with no important connection with the events that precede or follow it. Indeed, if it were omitted, the overall continuity of events would not suffer. The incident seems only to provide ʿAntar with a gratuitous opportunity to display his heroic prowess. It is tempting to say that although this incident might have some minimal intrinsic value it carries no greater narrative significance.

One must be careful, however, about deciding whether such incidents in the *Sīra* are egregious or irrelevant, since a great part of the work falls in the same category. The whole purpose of ʿAbs's trip through Yemen (20:478–22:187), for example, is to provide ʿAntar with opportunities to perform great deeds and display heroic prowess. This, in fact, is the essence of the story pattern of Heroic Service. It presents the individual deed stripped of the enveloping cloak of thematic progression.

The only way the first three story patterns of the Heroic Cycle differ from one another is in their handling of theme. What heroes actually do in each is much the same: they fight, rescue, serve, save, attack, defend, and celebrate victories. But while the Rise of the Hero and the Love Story cloak their events with a context of thematic progression, Heroic Service creates a sense of thematic unity in a more static way. Here it is abstract ideals rather than long-term goals that motivate the hero. What unifies the diverse events of Heroic Service is the code of heroic honor.

THE CODE OF HEROIC HONOR

The best way to gain an appreciation of the ideals that constitute this code of honor is to compare the acts of the hero with those of ordinary warriors. In *Sīrat ʿAntar* tribal society is based upon a common pact of mutual self-defense among the freeborn members of a tribe. A warrior must help and protect other members of the tribe and vice versa. Hence, the tribe presents a united front against external threats. This system of social allegiance is hierarchic, however. A warrior's first loyalty is to the clan and then to the tribe, but larger (increasingly looser) bonds of hierarchic allegiance are also present. Traditional or temporary alliances may exist among tribes, or between a tribe and foreign rulers, such as the kings of al-Ḥīra and Ghassān, or, on a more international scale, with the Persian shah or the Byzantine emperor. When a hero like ʿAntar, therefore, exerts himself to protect his family, clan, or tribe against outside attack or participates in his tribe's feuds with other tribes or helps rulers who are his lieges, such as the king of al-Ḥīra, in their wars, he is only fulfilling the natural duties and functions of an ordinary warrior. In these situations what separates heroes from warriors is not what each does but rather the different scales on which they do it. While a warrior is content to fight one opponent, the hero dares to face hundreds alone. A warrior can conceive of situations in which surrender is the best policy; for the hero the choice lies only between victory and death. A warrior might try diplomacy or stealth; the hero faces every obstacle with a frontal attack. One major difference between a hero and a warrior in performing customary social duties, therefore, is that while warriors stop at a certain point, heroes—adhering to a different and higher code of action—transcend normal standards.[28]

Another important distinction is that the actions of warriors are circumscribed by the normal limits of social obligations and interests. Warriors do their duty, protect their families and tribes, or serve their lieges, but they never exceed or contravene socially accepted limits. Such is not the case with heroes, whose only limits are those that the code of honor dictates. Frequently these run parallel to those of everyday social responsibility, and thus no conflicts arise. But when they do arise, heroes do not hesitate to sacrifice social responsibility, or even personal interest, to the prescriptions of honor. When ʿAntar grants his protection to a slave with whom King Qais is angry (31:74ff.), he prefers to leave ʿAbs rather than break his promise. Indeed, ʿAntar breaks his ties of social allegiance to his tribe if his sense of honor so compels him. He aids strangers who are not members of his tribe, whom he has no real reason to help; he befriends enemies of his tribe; and he even fights against members or allies of his tribe if his honor demands it.[29]

If the core of Heroic Service is the willingness to help others, the essence of the code of heroic honor is that the hero cannot restrain himself or herself from helping others. This code is not some external social system—a list of rules for chivalric honor—but rather an integral part of the hero's nature. Even when it contravenes personal interests, the hero must help those in need. For example, one of ʿAntar's early foes within ʿAbs is the vagabond poet-hero ʿUrwa ibn al-Ward. Al-Rabīʿ ibn Ziyād turns him against ʿAntar; at one point

ʿUrwa challenges and fights the black hero (4:320–44). When he suffers defeat and capture, ʿUrwa becomes even more hostile toward ʿAntar; when ʿAntar asks for King Zuhair's help, ʿUrwa, out of spite, convinces the king to do nothing (9:305). Enraged at this, ʿAntar decides to ambush and kill ʿUrwa at the first opportunity. When ʿUrwa escorts his sister Salmā home from another tribe, ʿAntar sets out to ambush them. Before he can emerge from his hiding place to attack, raiders appear and attack ʿUrwa and his sister. As the raiders defeat and capture ʿUrwa, ʿAntar is tempted to stand by and let the raiders carry out his intentions. But when they try to rape Salmā, ʿAntar is unable to stand idly by:

> When ʿAntar heard Salmā's calls and cries and saw her and her brother surrounded by foes, God removed hatred and malice from his heart. Arab gallantry and *jāhiliyya* fervor moved him. With no rancor or grudge toward her remaining in his heart, he emerged from the side of the gully. He advanced toward the horsemen, and then rushing at them like a torrentous flood, he called out, "Here now, at your service, O Cousin! Rejoice in deliverance from enemies and the end of sorrow, grief, and misery! For God has answered your call and sent me to your protection so that I may save you from your enemies." (9:309–10)

After ʿAntar has driven off the raiders and freed Salmā and ʿUrwa, the latter's animosity is transformed to admiration and friendship. The two heroes reconcile and swear friendship, and throughout his life ʿUrwa remains ʿAntar's friend, companion, and ally.

Such actions indicate the compulsory nature of heroic honor in *Sīrat ʿAntar*. Although this code of honor has a superorganic sense, it is innately concrete for heroes. When justice is about to be transgressed, heroes are unable to stand by. Indeed, heroes do not merely follow this code of honor, they embody it. The function of the various deeds of Heroic Service is thus to provide an arena in which they can demonstrate this fact.

The code of heroic honor also serves to unite the great heroes of the *Sīra*. It provides the bond that secures their friendship. ʿUrwa becomes ʿAntar's friend and companion out of admiration, not gratitude, because he senses the other's innate nobility. The same holds true of other heroes. They befriend ʿAntar not because he is able to defeat them in battle. He often does this, but defeat by itself could not dispel their enmity—after all, they are heroes too! Rather, they relent because they sense mutual participation in the transcendent values of the heroic code and because they see in ʿAntar their own heroic virtues reflected on an enlarged scale.[30] Hence, participation in this code is what separates the warrior from the hero. Not all of the great warriors in the *Sīra* are heroes. Ar-Rabīʿ ibn Ziyād, al-Ḥārith ibn Ẓālim, and as-Sabīʿ ibn al-

Ḥārith are all fearsome fighters, but they are not heroes because they allow self-interest to overshadow noble impulse.

The existence of the theme of heroic honor opens the structure of the narrative. An event founded upon this self-sufficient theme need not lead anywhere or relate causally to other events. It creates a tableau, a heroic vista whose dramatic energy is complete in itself. It is Heroic Service's function to provide these heroic tableaus. *Sīrat 'Antar* tells us that some of its characters are heroes; Heroic Service demonstrates that this is true.

THE DEATH OF THE HERO

The final story pattern of the Heroic Cycle is the Death of the Hero. This is not a common story pattern for the obvious reason that heroes do not easily die; but it does have some interesting features. The Death of the Hero is composed of three parts: the death scene, burial and mourning, and revenge.

The Death Scene

With the *Sīra*'s incessant battles and numerous bouts of single combat, violent death is a common occurrence. (Death due to natural causes, however, is extremely rare; there are not more than three or four instances in the whole work.)[31] Because death is so frequent, death scenes, even those of heroes, do not usually receive much dramatic emphasis. Ordinary warriors are only narrative pawns, sword-fodder for the heroes, and the *Sīra* sacrifices them quite freely in its extended battle scenes. In their cases, the description of the heroes' coup de grace is reduced to a single line. One might expect, however, that the situation would be different when great heroes died, that their deaths would be accompanied by especially dramatic situations, long speeches, and all the other apparatus of melodrama. This, however, is not the case. With few exceptions, death comes just as swiftly and suddenly to heroes in *Sīrat 'Antar* as it does to all other warriors. The same formula is even used.[32]

There are several causes for the *Sīra*'s general lack of interest in death scenes. One is its conception of the hero. For *Sīrat 'Antar* the phrase "death of the hero" is a contradiction in terms. One reason warriors attain the status of hero is that they are impervious to death. Indeed, heroes in the *Sīra* come close to being archetypal manifestations of the life force. They are more energetic, more vital than ordinary people. Leading charmed lives, safe from death because they are do not fear it, they move enveloped in the glow of life's aura. Thus, they rarely die because of direct defeat on the battlefield; there are almost always extenuating circumstances: stealth, treachery, magic, or just pure accident. 'Antar, for example, is killed by an arrow shot in the dark (56:18–28),

Ghaṣūb and Shaibūb are killed in their sleep (49:336 and 55:423), the magic thrust of a jinni's sword kills al-Ghaḍbān (47:155), Rabīʿa ibn al-Mukaddam's horse stumbles in battle (40:424–28), Bisṭām ibn Qais is killed while drunk (51:83–84), and ʿUrwa ibn al-Ward is overcome by sheer numbers (52:114).[33]

Another reason for the *Sīra*'s lack of interest in long, drawn-out death scenes is its preference for portraying the deeds of the living rather than the throes of the dying. This can be seen in its use of narrative point of view. As soon as a warrior or hero is killed, the point of view immediately shifts away from the corpse to the reactions and action of the living. When a hero defeats an opponent, a new challenger appears immediately and battle continues or the loss is so great that the enemy army breaks and flees. The *Sīra* pays no further attention to the fallen. Even when a hero is slain, the narrative changes its focus to portray the reactions of his companions. Thus when al-Ghaḍbān (47:55) and Maisara (55:398) are killed, the epic immediately leaves them to describe first how ʿAntar is so overcome with emotion that he faints and then how he tries to obtain revenge (thus immediately proceeding to the revenge motif of the story pattern). Sometimes the *Sīra* weakens the shock of heroes' deaths by letting them occur offstage. Someone arrives to announce a friend or family member's death, then the narrative backtracks to relate how the person died (51:83–84, 52:114, 55:391–94).

That *Sīrat ʿAntar* is generally uninterested in dramatic death scenes, however, does not mean that it is unable to create them. ʿAntar, dying in his saddle as he protects his retreating family, is the greatest and most moving example of this (56:18–28). Muqri 'l-Waḥsh (30:468–71) and Rabīʿa ibn al-Mukaddam's (40:424–29) deaths are other examples of dramatically effective death scenes.[34]

Family and Friends Mourn and Bury the Hero

When death does succeed in carrying off the hero, general mourning prevails. Funerals (like weddings) are conventional affairs in the *Sīra*; one differs little from the other. Relatives and friends gather to weep and recite elegies, and mourning continues for a month or so.[35] ʿAntar, as usual, goes to extremes. He sets up a black tent that he calls the House of Sorrow and, refusing to leave it, sits and mourns fallen family members or friends for a year or more (47:163–64, 52:136–37, 55:431–32).

Family and Friends Avenge the Hero's Death

After the quiescent period of burial and mourning comes action. After the hero is mourned, he or she must be avenged. Revenge is, in fact, the most important part of the Death of the Hero. If the *Sīra* pays little attention to a hero's death scene, it is more than willing to describe at length the efforts the fallen hero's companions or family exert to gain revenge. (This anxiousness to get on with the more exciting motif of revenge is probably an important reason for placing so little emphasis on dramatic death scenes.)[36] In revenge, terrible and extreme action is the rule of the day. To avenge Shaddād, his wife and family slaughter 770 prisoners on his grave (36:56–59). 'Antar kills 600 enemy prisoners on Rabī'a ibn al-Mukaddam's grave (40:458–59). Maisara and 'Antar kill 1,300 Fazāra prisoners to avenge Ghaṣūb's death (49:346–47). And when a strange warrior kills al-Ghaḍbān, 'Antar's first inclination is to travel around and kill every stranger he meets. This, however, is too much for his friends, and they warn tribes of 'Antar's approach so that they can come out to meet him and assuage his anger. 'Antar finally relinquishes his plans to avenge al-Ghaḍbān when he learns that the murderer was a jinni and so beyond his reach (47:165–77). Even so, when an opportunity for revenge later appears, he immediately seizes it (54:305–10).

That revenge is an extremely common motivation throughout the *Sīra* is understandable, for it is a very flexible theme. First, it immediately justifies sudden hostile action. Warriors frequently appear and attack each other to avenge some previous killing (often one to which there has been no prior reference).[37] Revenge also offers unlimited possibilities for creating narrative chain reactions. Ḥassān ibn Thābit kills 'Urwa ibn al-Ward, for example, in order to avenge his brother's death. Then 'Antar kills Ḥassān in order to avenge 'Urwa's death (52:114ff.). On a grander scale, these chain reactions become part of the major feuds of the *Sīra*. Here the desire for revenge smolders under the surface for long periods, ready to be rekindled. Hence, the feud between 'Abs and Fazāra erupts periodically throughout the epic, motivated by the desire for revenge (17:175–19:347, 25:430–70, 27:178–95, 49:333–51:62, 56:44–49).

FROM STORY TO CYCLE

The importance that *Sīrat 'Antar* attaches to the theme of revenge in the Death of the Hero offers a significant insight into the cyclical impulse of its compositional method. Themes like revenge have the potential for creating short or lengthy cycles of chain reactions and thus give the work unlimited scope for narrative expansion. Revenge even enables the *Sīra* to transcend the limits of 'Antar's own life. It continues for three hundred pages after 'Antar himself dies because the Death of the Hero pattern demands the poetic justice and structural completion of vengeance. The *Sīra* thus introduces and establishes the identities of a whole new generation of heroes worthy of avenging 'Antar, which they eventually do, carrying his bones with them on a camel so that he himself witnesses it (58:235–86). Here one gains an insight into how important the Heroic Cycle is. The ready-made narrative schemes of the story patterns permit the *Sīra* to create new heroes at will. Moreover, they are flexible enough to provide endless opportunities for internal variation. In fact, there is no real reason why the *Sīra* could not have gone on and told the stories of 'Unaitira, al-Jufrān, and al-Ghaḍanfar for another five thousand pages. The Heroic Cycle does not tell the story of only one or two heroes in the *Sīra*: it tells the story of them all.

CHAPTER 6

Use of the Heroic Cycle: Compositional Principles

IT SEEMS CLEAR that the creators of *Sīrat 'Antar* began their task with a basic corpus of preexisting narrative materials and strategies. They had the themes and events of the 'Antar legend, the fictional reservoir of the other legends and *akhbār* of pre-Islamic Arabia, a willingness to absorb new events and materials (such as the Crusades), and, finally, a basic mastery over the forms, patterns, and dramatic strategies of the art of storytelling. The Heroic Cycle falls primarily into this last category, with its story patterns providing narrative models to which the storyteller returns time and again. Although these constitute a fund of themes and events, their most important contribution is the dimension of a ready-made and organized dramatic structure. Storytellers have a structural template on which to rely; the story patterns help them to unify and to integrate the diverse features of the *Sīra*'s preexisting narrative materials, to formulate the hazy life of a legendary character into a detailed individual life story, or to create completely new characters and to generate new events and episodes at will.

It is not, however, in its reliance upon story patterns that the *Sīra* reveals true greatness; rather it is in the masterfully fluent and economical way it uses them. The four story patterns have been presented here as individual units spread along the longitudinal scale of the hero's life because the material has lent itself to this approach and because it creates a clearer picture of each pattern's essential features. Nevertheless, we must realize that throughout this analysis we have been viewing these patterns in a radically different way than the manner in which a storyteller would view them or the manner in which they appear in the epic itself.

My approach has been deductive, comparing the details of stories of all of the epic's heroes to arrive at the composite picture of heroic action that I term the Heroic Cycle. Doing this has entailed a certain amount of representational distortion. While *Sīrat 'Antar* uses the story patterns in action, I have stripped them of their dimension of narrative momentum to examine them in quiescence. Although the elements of the story patterns exist in the *Sīra* as intertwined strands of a unified narrative cord, I have unraveled these strands to be able to identify their individual characteristics. Finally, while the *Sīra* naturally emphasizes the individual or particular aspects of the character or event that it portrays—no matter how many times similar events happen or similar characters appear, the narrative presents them as new and unique—I have stressed the shared aspects of such characters and events and taken special notice of how they resemble each other rather than how they differ. Now I must rectify this misrepresentation. Having viewed the story patterns of the Heroic Cycle on individual levels, we must broaden our analytic perspective and offer some idea of how the *Sīra* uses these story patterns, not statically but kinetically, not singly but conjoined, not universally but particularly.

There are, of course, limits to such an investigation. Works of literature are not mechanisms we can take apart, measure, weigh, describe, and then reassemble. There is such a thing as overanalysis. Therefore, this section briefly discusses five general compositional principles of which the narrative appears to make particular use while forming specific stories from the patterns of the Heroic Cycle. The principles are selection, repetition, variation of emphasis, displacement, and superimposition. The first three are basic to all fiction but deserve mention because they play such essential roles in the epic's variegated use of the Heroic Cycle. Displacement and superimposition (the terms are mine) are particular to the *Sīra.*[1]

SELECTION, REPETITION, AND VARIATION OF EMPHASIS

The discussion to this point should already provide some idea of the important roles that selection, repetition, and variation of emphasis play in the *Sīra*'s formulation of individual stories. If we assume that a storyteller begins with a general preconception of what kinds of activities and situations are "proper" for a hero to engage in (and this is essential to the whole idea of a Heroic Cycle), then selection has already begun. Indeed, selection is at work at every level of the epic's use of the Heroic Cycle.

No single hero's story contains all possible motifs and themes; a fair number do not even contain all four story patterns. Hence, although 'Antar, Muqri 'l-Waḥsh (23f.), al-Laqīṭ ibn Zurāra (21f.), Nāziḥ ibn Usayyid (19f.), Maisara

(38f.), and Ghaṣūb (43f.) are examples of heroes whose stories do, to a greater or lesser extent, run the Heroic Cycle's full gamut, such inclusiveness is not a necessity. The stories of some of the *Sīra*'s most prominent heroes encompass only one or two story patterns. Khufāf ibn Nadba's story (34), for example, contains only the Rise of the Hero and the Love Story, 'Abd Hayyāf's (52) only the Rise of the Hero and Heroic Service, and 'Āmir ibn aṭ-Ṭufail's (28f.) and Duraid ibn aṣ-Ṣimma's (17.2f.) only Heroic Service.

The process of selection continues within the story patterns themselves. Some heroes are highborn, some lowborn; some fall in love with their cousins, some with strangers; some encounter hostile beloveds' fathers, some benevolent fathers. In addition, numerous individual motifs and incidents may or may not be included in the stories of particular heroes. Among his many deeds, 'Antar kills a lion single-handedly (9.3) and fights in a tournament (61.5). Bisṭām ibn Qais fights in a tournament (13.1:8/258), but does not kill a lion. Al-Ghaḍbān kills a lion (50.3:41/8) but does not fight in a tournament; 'Amr ibn Ma'dīkarib and 'Āmir ibn aṭ-Ṭufail do neither. All of these characters are great heroes who play substantial narrative roles, but the Heroic Cycle contains innumerable options, and in the end it matters less which motifs a hero's story includes than how they combine to produce their cumulative effect.

Repetition is also an essential part of the *Sīra*'s use of the Heroic Cycle. That individual hero's stories fall into general patterns at all indicates the narrative's fondness for this technique. Indeed, repetition so pervades the epic—thematically, structurally, and stylistically—that it seems almost superfluous to cite examples.[2] If we think of all the opponents 'Antar defeats, the enviers he foils, the rivals for 'Abla's love he overcomes, the people in distress he helps, the armies he routs, and the rulers he serves, and then add to this all the similar events that occur in the stories of the *Sīra*'s other heroes, we gains an appreciation of the technique's prevalence. Ironically, the varied use of repetition is one of the *Sīra*'s main ways of individualizing its heroes' stories. We know what types of events are likely to occur but not exactly when or how often. 'Antar and 'Abs fight five hostile tribes in their trip through Yemen (26); structurally and thematically they could just as well have encountered one tribe or ten.

The *Sīra* does not try to avoid repetition. At times its fondness for it appears surprising, as with the double use of the Love Story in the case of al-Ghaḍbān (50.4–5). Such cases must, however, be seen in context. In oral performance, the storyteller would avoid such blatant repetition. Moreover, listeners would be less conscious of their overall exposure to repetition since each performance would focus on one or two episodes. With the written versions, readers could similarly be expected to confine their sessions to one or two episodes at a time. Viewed from a macro-perspective, however, the *Sīra*'s general attitude seems to be that if one has a good story, why not repeat it? 'Antar fights to hang his *mu'allaqa* poem twice (44, 55), he fights his way through Yemen twice (26, 51), he helps the Byzantine emperor against his Western vassals twice (62, 63, 64, 68), he defeats unrecognized sons in single combat three times (38.4, 44.6–7, 50.6), to mention only a few examples. The important thing to remember in the face of such innumerable repetitions is that the *Sīra*'s whole aesthetic and rhetorical stance is based upon the supposition that it can make its readers/audience believe that each event, no matter how similar to other events, is new and unique. The extent to which the work succeeds in accomplishing this is testament to its dramatic and suspenseful storytelling.[3]

The compositional principle of variation in emphasis is an obvious corollary to selection and repetition. While the *Sīra* uses the same story patterns or motifs in different stories (or even at different points in the same story), it varies their effects by stressing them differently. We see this principle at work when comparing the stories of all the heroes. 'Antar's deeds differ little from those of other heroes; but because he acts more often and because the story focuses on his point of view, he becomes the narrative's main hero.

The epic also emphasizes individual story patterns differently. In 'Antar's story, for example, it never ceases to mine the dramatic possibilities that the Rise of the Hero story pattern offers. Early in the *Sīra* (6.2), ar-Rabī' ibn Ziyād becomes 'Antar's chief opponent in his struggle to achieve social equality within 'Abs. Five thousand pages later, ar-Rabī' still refuses to accept 'Antar. Indeed, he continues to slander and scheme until the moment 'Antar kills him at the narrative's end (67). In the stories of other heroes, however, the *Sīra* tends to use the Rise of the Hero as a short, almost perfunctory means of introduction. Such heroes as Bisṭām ibn Qais (13.1), Muqri 'l-Waḥsh (23), 'Amr ibn Ma'dīkarib (32), Maisara (38.3), Ghaṣūb (43.7), and al-Ghaḍbān (50) first appear in the narrative as young lovers seeking dowries (that is, in the midst of the Love Story). After thus attracting attention to them, the epic pauses, backtracks, and fills in their characters by narrating the Rise of the Hero. Here the *Sīra* uses this story pattern less to generate events than to serve as an identifying marker. The extended version of the Rise of the Hero of 'Antar's own story has created certain expectations of what a young hero does. When similar sets of events appear (in much reduced forms) in the stories of subsequent characters, the reader/listener naturally suspects that they too will prove to be young heroes.

This connotative reduction can continue until single motifs convey, at least to a degree, the thematic and emotive messages of whole story patterns. Hence, when the *Sīra* introduces al-Ḥārith ibn Ẓālim (16.3), it does not try to indicate his heroic stature by pausing to recount his past deeds or the story of his youthful rise to fame; it merely states that he is a great warrior (11/61). Nevertheless, the epic takes a few pages (11/61–63) to describe his marvelous sword. Since wonderful weapons are a part of the Rise of the Hero pattern, and since only great heroes have great weapons, the *Sīra*'s claims for al-Ḥārith's heroic status become convincing by a kind of synecdochic logic.[4]

Describing the *Sīra*'s various uses of selection, repetition, and variation of emphasis at much greater length is unnecessary; observant readers will notice these principles at work throughout their perusal of the narrative. It is more important to appreciate the great measure of structural and thematic flexibility they allow. Within the limits of rhetorical credibility—and the *Sīra* is never afraid to stretch these limits—any motif or event associated with the Heroic Cycle can be employed or not, can appear once or repeatedly, or can receive greater or lesser emphasis throughout a particular hero's story. The epic keeps itself as open-ended as possible in its ranges of narrative choices—within the general thematic and structural limits that it itself imposes.

Up to this point, we have examined how *Sīrat 'Antar* uses the Heroic Cycle to create and organize the events of an individual hero's story. Now we must explore the narrative principles that allow it to integrate these individual stories into a complex and unified whole. Primary among these principles are displacement and superimposition.

DISPLACEMENT

Once *Sīrat 'Antar* has introduced the figure of 'Antar (5), it naturally concentrates on his story for a time. Quite soon, however, new heroes appear. These characters are surrounded by the events and concerns of their own versions of the Heroic Cycle, but their stories do not merely run parallel to those of 'Antar or other previously introduced heroes; instead they intertwine, and one important way they do this is displacement. An example will elucidate this narrative technique.

Shortly after the epic has delineated the main tensions and conflicts of 'Antar's Rise of the Hero and Love Story patterns, a new young hero briefly enters the picture. Ḥiṣn of the Banī Māzin, Prince Mālik's foster brother, comes to 'Abs seeking aid (7.7). In love with his cousin, he has returned from collecting her dowry to discover that in his absence a powerful rival is forcing the girl's father to marry her to him. 'Antar and Prince Mālik immediately agree to help. They return with Ḥiṣn to his tribe, 'Antar kills the rival, and Ḥiṣn marries his beloved.

It is clear that within the context of the patterns of the Heroic Cycle Ḥiṣn is in the midst of his Love Story. He has fallen in love, won the girl's father's permission, and collected the dowry by going out raiding. When he returns and encounters his rival, however, he feels unequal to the task and goes to 'Abs for help. 'Antar, meanwhile, is in the midst of both his Rise of the Hero and

Love Story patterns. Nevertheless, he is willing, because of Heroic Service, to help the supplicant. In the process of helping Ḥiṣn, however, 'Antar displaces him in his story pattern. Although 'Antar defeats the rival, Ḥiṣn marries the beloved.

This is displacement. The *Sīra*'s greater heroes intervene in the Heroic Cycles of its lesser heroes and, in the process, temporarily assume some of their dramatic functions. Two (or potentially more) heroes thus come to share the performance of a single heroic feat. When 'Antar helps Ḥiṣn defeat his rival, his deed of Heroic Service becomes congruent with Ḥiṣn's fulfillment of his Love Story. One of the great advantages of displacement is that it allows economical use of thematic materials. The epic introduces a new protagonist, Ḥiṣn, and so expands its cast of characters; it enlarges 'Antar's range of activities; and it does both without introducing any new themes or events, since Ḥiṣn's Love Story is in outline similar to 'Antar's or other versions of the Love Story.

Although displacement facilitates the introduction of new heroes, it leaves no doubt about their relative importance. Ḥiṣn's Heroic Cycle is clearly subordinate to 'Antar's, and he is only the first of numerous characters whom 'Antar helps to achieve the goals of various parts of the Heroic Cycle (usually some part of the Love Story). For example, he helps Prince al-Ḥārith (18), Muqri 'l-Waḥsh (25), Nāziḥ ibn Usayyid (20.7–8), Mājid ibn Mālik (38.2–3), and al-Ghaḍbān (50.9–10) defeat rivals and win their beloveds. He also helps Khufāf ibn Nadba win his marriage dowry (34.4f.), Prince Usayyid defeat his unknown son (19.4), and Bisṭām ibn Qais rescue his sister (13.3–4). In fact, most of the acts of Heroic Service that 'Antar renders for other heroes constitute displacement to a greater or lesser extent. By definition, a hero should be able to overcome difficulties without having to rely on the help of another hero. Therefore, when 'Antar aids other heroes, he displaces them not only in their roles in their Heroic Cycles, but also in heroic prestige and stature. Although there are times when friends appear to help 'Antar in the midst of difficult situations (7.5, 26.10, 21.6–7), the *Sīra* never suggests that they are rescuing him. 'Antar would continue to fight whether the reinforcements had come or not. Similarly, although 'Antar frequently rescues other heroes from captivity (11.2, 14.1, 27.1–3, 33.1, 36.5), when he is captured, he usually manages to free himself (9.2–4, 42.3, 48.17; but compare 46.5). The epic intertwines the events of its various heroes' stories, but it never leaves any doubt about the identity of its main protagonist.

Displacement enables *Sīrat 'Antar* to coordinate the multitudinous activities of the large number of heroes that it introduces and reintroduces into its narrative. Once so inserted, many heroes remain in the narrative to become members of 'Antar's band of companions. 'Urwa ibn al-Ward (14.1f.), Nāziḥ ibn Usayyid (19.4f.), al-Ḥiṭāl (21.5f.), Muqri 'l-Waḥsh (23.3f.), Māzin ibn

Shaddād (37.2f.), Mājid ibn Mālik (37.5f.), Maisara (39.4f.), Ghaṣūb (44.8f.), Sabī' al-Yemen (Muqri 'l-Waḥsh's son) (46.1f.), al-Ghaḍbān (50.8f.), and Zaid ibn 'Urwa (60.3f.) all number among 'Antar's heroic entourage. In addition, other great heroes—Bisṭām ibn Qais (13.3f.), 'Āmir ibn aṭ-Ṭufail (28.2f.), 'Amr ibn Ma'dīkarib (32.4f.), Duraid ibn aṣ-Ṣimma (29.8f.)—are also 'Antar's allies. Although as the major heroes of their own tribes they do not join 'Antar's entourage on a full-time basis, they respond to his requests for help, as he does to theirs.

SUPERIMPOSITION

Despite displacement's significance as a compositional and integrative principle, superimposition is even more important. In fact, it would be difficult to overemphasize its importance for understanding the dynamics of the epic's compositional techniques. While displacement allows the *Sīra* to coordinate and intertwine the activities of its protagonists, superimposition provides the integrative principle that enables it to interweave the activities (and the thematic structures that support them) of almost all of its characters, friends and foes. Indeed, until we appreciate how superimposition works, it is very difficult to grasp or sympathize with the *Sīra*'s aesthetic ideals or rationale. Once again, the easiest way to gain an idea of the nature of this narrative principle is to examine a few examples. Two will suffice.

One day Mālik ibn Qurād and his family (including 'Abla) come to the Banī Shaibān seeking refuge from 'Antar (13.1), After King Qais grants them refuge, his son Prince Bisṭām falls in love with 'Abla. Mālik will consent to his marrying her only on the condition that he bring 'Antar's head as his dowry present. Setting out to find 'Antar, Bisṭām encounters him in the desert seeking 'Abla. The two warriors fight, and 'Antar emerges the victor. He takes Bisṭām captive and proceeds with him to the Shaibān encampment (13.2). On their arrival, they learn the camp has been raided. Out of concern for his sister Su'dā's safety, Bisṭām forgets his love for 'Abla; he and 'Antar swear friendship and together manage to free Su'dā', 'Abla, and others who have fallen captive (13.3).

A second example: one day Khidāsh, the leader of a clan of the Banī Bishr, seeks refuge with his clan among the 'Abs. (38.1). King Qais welcomes them, but during their stay young Prince Mājid sees Khidāsh's daughter, Asmā', and becomes enamored. When Khidāsh learns of this affair, he fears scandal so he gathers his clan and secretly departs. Mājid discovers this and, heartbroken, resolves to follow. He informs 'Antar, his friend and mentor, of this plan, and 'Antar gathers his companions to accompany him (38.2).

We now learn that Khidāsh and his clan left their tribe because a young black warrior named Maisara proposed marriage to Asmā' (38.3). Both Asmā' and her father opposed this suit, but, knowing that they would be unable to withstand the demands of so powerful a warrior if they remained with their tribe, they fled to ʿAbs. Having now left ʿAbs again, Khidāsh and his clan meet Maisara, who has been searching for them, in the desert. He forces them to agree to return to the Banī Bishr. Just at this moment (38.4), however, Mājid and ʿAntar and his companions appear. They order Maisara to release Asmāʾ and her family; when he refuses, extended fighting begins. After Maisara defeats several of ʿAntar's entourage and fatally wounds Muqri ʾl-Waḥsh, ʿAntar enters the field and captures him. Mājid and Asmāʾ are reunited and eventually marry (39.4).

Comparing these two episodes from the perspective of the Heroic Cycle elucidates three interwoven dimensions of narrative action. First is the progress of the story patterns of individual characters, which in both episodes are those of the Love Story. In the first episode ʿAntar is engaged in the "defeating the rival phase" of the Love Story, while his opponent, Bisṭām—equally involved in his version of the Love Story—is on his dowry quest. Mājid and Maisara, in the second episode, also each pursue their individual versions of this story. They share not only the same beloved but the same dramatic function: both are searching for the fleeing family of the beloved. Nor is the Love Story the only story pattern represented in these two episodes. When ʿAntar and Bisṭām become friends and set off to rescue their loved ones, they enter into the roles of mutual Heroic Service. By accompanying Mājid and fighting on his behalf, ʿAntar and his companions are also engaging in Heroic Service. When Muqri ʾl-Waḥsh enters his fateful combat with Maisara, he begins the Death of the Hero pattern. Maisara and ʿAntar's bout of single combat, the climax of the second episode, is shaded with the themes and concerns of Maisara's Rise of the Hero story pattern (son struggling against father). We can see, therefore, that in terms of their individual actions all the themes and concerns of these episodes' major characters are generated from parts of the Heroic Cycle.[5]

The second dimension of narrative action involves coordinating the interaction and counteraction of characters in order to create the plots of individual episodes. The *Sīra*'s method of doing this in these two episodes is clear. It contrives dramatic complications by arranging for the courses of individual warrior's versions of the Heroic Cycle to intertwine and overlap so that they transit and collide. By arranging for ʿAntar and Bisṭām to be simultaneously in love with ʿAbla, and for Mājid and Maisara to be intent upon marrying the same girl, *Sīrat ʿAntar* sets both pairs upon collision courses. Once such courses are set, it is easy to involve other characters (such as ʿAntar and his companions in the case of Mājid's story) through Heroic Service and displacement. The epic thus constructs the plots of its episodes from the same thematic and structural material that it uses to pattern the courses of action of individual characters.

Once again, it is important to notice that both contestants in an episode—'Antar and Bisṭām, Mājid and Maisara—draw equally upon the Heroic Cycle for motives and patterns of action. By intersecting and overlapping individual characters' heroic courses the *Sīra* first creates plot complications and situations of conflict and then resolves them.

Finally, the third dimension of narrative action involves the task of coordinating the events that, although they stem from the action of individual episodes, continue to have repercussions or implications in later parts of the epic. Hence, although each of the illustrative episodes enjoys its own interior resolution—'Antar and Bisṭām become friends, Mājid wins and marries Asmā'—they also contain events that influence and transfigure the greater course of the narrative. Such events include the introduction or removal of important characters and the beginning or ending of long-term friendships or enmities. In Bisṭām, 'Antar gains a powerful friend and ally who often reappears, ever ready to come to 'Antar's aid. In the second episode, although Antar loses a close friend and ally in Muqri 'l-Waḥsh, he gains a son and new companion in Maisara, who remains a major character in the *Sīra* until his own death toward the epic's end (65.3). Moreover, once a conflict is formulated, the *Sīra* always has the option of reviving it. Maisara gives way to Mājid and allows him to marry Asmā', but he does not forget his love. Later he again tries to steal Asmā' from Mājid (40.2f.).

What is significant about these three interwoven dimensions of narrative action is that the *Sīra* generates the second two—the plots of its episodes and the general flow of its narrative action—from the same material that it uses to create the first: the stories of individual warriors. This is why an awareness of the contents and contexts of the Heroic Cycle is important. All the major characters of the two episodes discussed above are engaged in the unfolding of their own versions of the Heroic Cycle. Moreover, this is not only the case in these two episodes but in the epic as a whole. Once we analyze and compare the actions and motives of the *Sīra*'s contestants from within the context of the Heroic Cycle, we discover that almost all characters—friends and foes alike—perform the same types of actions for the same reasons. Love, honor, revenge, ambition: these are the forces that drive protagonists and antagonists alike in the epic.

This process of intermixing and dovetailing different characters' Heroic Cycles to produce the plots, themes, and events of the *Sīra*'s multilevel action is the narrative principle I call superimposition. The great advantage of this principle is the thematic and structural economy that it permits, for it frees the *Sīra* from having continually to create and devise new plot structures to produce the complications and conflicts of its episodes. Instead, the epic constructs complex narrative action from the same source that it uses to create the stories of individual heroes, generating new characters at will from its story patterns (or supplying preexisting characters with new stories) and using superimposition to arrange these characters' activities so that they become united in friendship or counterpoised in opposition.

In this situation, the difference between friend and foe becomes a matter of rhetoric rather than of ethics. The *Sīra* has no dastardly villains, but rather the intermixed and overlapping stories of characters who share ideals and deeds in ways that can generate conflict and opposition. Deciding which characters are protagonists and which antagonists thus becomes a matter of partisanship. Through its fashioning of narrative context and its use of such rhetorical devices as point of view, the *Sīra* convinces us that ʿAntar and Mājid are the protagonists of their respective episodes—that they are worthy of winning their beloveds' hands in marriage—while it is Bisṭām and Maisara who are the interlopers and unworthy rivals. If, however, we remove this partisan narrative context and judge Bisṭām and Maisara's stories on the merits of their themes and events, our attitude could easily be reversed, since their versions of the Love Story are just as orthodox and valid as those of ʿAntar and Mājid. A simple shift in narrative perspective could make them the true lovers and ʿAntar and Mājid the unworthy rivals.

Indeed, when the plots of these two episodes are compared free from the refraction of narrative partisanship, we can see that they present the same situations. Both begin with fathers fleeing with their daughters from powerful black slave/warriors and seeking refuge with another tribe. In both cases, the daughters gain new, highborn admirers in these tribes. Finally, both episodes end with the question of who is going to win the girl being decided through open combat between the rival lovers, the first time directly (ʿAntar vs. Bisṭām), the second time through displacement (ʿAntar defeating Maisara on Mājid's behalf). The only difference in these episodes is their outcome. In the first episode, the lowborn black warrior defeats his rival and wins the beloved, while in the second it is the highborn lover who (aided by ʿAntar) defeats his lowborn black rival and emerges as victor.

These two episodes are not exceptional in regard to the basic equivalence of their contestants' motives and patterns of action. Examination of the *Sīra* reveals that almost all of its opponents are engaged in the same types of activities—those of the Heroic Cycle. Hence, whether we sympathize with characters or not depends not on the merit of their activities but rather on the epic's manipulation of narrative context. We cheer ʿAntar on in his effort to kidnap al-Jaidāʾ for his wedding dowry (12), but three thousand pages later we object when al-Ghaḍbān embarks on his quest to kidnap ʿAbla for exactly the same reason (50.5). We are unsympathetic when such characters as King Muʿāwiya ibn an-Nazzāl (26.4) or King Masʿūd ibn Musād (26.7) attack ʿAbs and try to seize ʿAbla by force, but sometime later (32.4) we find ʿAntar helping ʿUrwa ibn al-Ward attack ʿAmr ibn Maʿdīkarib for exactly the same reason, so that ʿUrwa can seize ʿAmr's wife. Once ʿAmr is defeated, it is ʿAntar who urges ʿUrwa to kill him in order to claim Lamīs unopposed! When King an-Nuʿmān attacks ʿAbs because King Ẓuhair has refused to give up his daughter in marriage to him (16.2), we side with ʿAbs. Nonetheless, we often sympathize with ʿAntar when he embarks upon projects that involve helping lovers seize their beloveds from unwilling fathers (18.3, 20.8, 48.8). We are horrified when Hassān ibn Thābit kills ʿUrwa ibn al-Ward in order to avenge his brother's death at ʿUrwa's hand, but we cheer ʿAntar when he immediately sets out to avenge ʿUrwa's death (60.5–6). There is no real difference between the motives and acts of the rival pairs of Khufāf and ʿAntar and al-ʿAbbās and Sabīʿ ibn al-Ḥārith (34.4f.), but when both pairs set out to capture King al-Mutanaʿjiz, we side with ʿAntar and Khufāf. Finally, when the blinded Wizr ibn Jābir practices shooting arrows by sound for years in order to take revenge upon ʿAntar (69), is he not doing exactly what ʿAntar himself would do if the situation were reversed?

Of course, *Sīrat ʿAntar* justifies the actions of its chosen protagonists and denigrates those of its antagonists, but the nature and intent of the deeds of both groups are essentially the same. This is understandable, because they all come from the same source: the Heroic Cycle. Superimposition, therefore, is the most important of the five narrative principles necessary to understand the varied ways *Sīrat ʿAntar* uses the Heroic Cycle to generate the plots of its episodes, since it enables the epic to rely upon the same themes and patterns to produce all of its variegated narrative action.

CONCLUDING REMARKS

It is clear that the composers of *Sīrat Antar* relied upon different types of narrative material to form the basis of its stories. Modern researchers, from Baron von Hammer-Purgstall on, have tended to be interested in the elements that enjoyed some connection with preexisting or historical sources—the figure of ʿAntar, for example, or the fund of *akhbār* accounts of pre-Islamic Arabia that the *Sīra* drew upon or absorbed. We cannot deny the significance of these materials, but we must keep them in proper perspective. Anyone who would consider preexisting narrative elements to constitute the core of the epic while viewing purely "fictional" themes and patterns, such as those of the Heroic Cycle, as supererogatory additions or afterthoughts is viewing the matter in reverse. It is only because *Sīrat ʿAntar* has the Heroic Cycle to serve as its structural core and narrative ballast that it can so easily absorb and integrate this other body of originally foreign materials.

Moreover, an understanding of the Heroic Cycle and of the various ways that the epic puts it to use clarifies some of the structural and thematic aspects of the narrative that might otherwise appear odd. For example, Rauḍa ibn Manīʿ appears in the epic (7:13–51) in a brief embedded episode. Within the context of the Heroic Cycle, his appearance is neither digressive nor extraneous. Rauḍa is involved in the falling in love and fighting the rival parts of his Love Story, and his appearance gives ʿAntar, through superimposition, an opportunity to exercise the fighting the rival phase of his own Love Story. Whether Rauḍa's appearance is brief or extended thus becomes unimportant. The cause and nature of his appearance in the *Sīra* are completely orthodox: he is engaged in a part of the Heroic Cycle.

Similarly, there is nothing particularly unusual about the repetitiousness of ʿAbs's embattled journey through Yemen (26). Since the whole *Sīra* is, in a sense, an exercise in repetition, it is a subsidiary matter whether these repetitions occur frequently, as they do in this chain of episodes, or infrequently. All the events of these episodes conform to the Heroic Cycle and are thus perfectly in context.

Narrative unity in the epic, therefore, is not a matter of unfolding the events of one tightly woven and orchestrated chain of events. Rather it is based upon the extensive network of equally orthodox themes and patterns of the Heroic Cycle. Thematic polyphony, not structural unity, is the basis of the *Sīra*'s organization of its events. The unifying dimension of the work's innumerable episodes is their common foundation in the themes and actions of the story patterns. The wisdom of this organizational basis can be argued both negatively and positively. The *Sīra* cannot be said to be terribly interested in originality. It sticks to the themes and patterns that the Heroic Cycle provides. By relying upon these patterns, however, the epic maintains a unity of tone, intent, and dramatic charge throughout the whole of its fifty-six hundred pages. Its structural flexibility and open-endedness enable it to create an interesting narrative world by relying upon surprising recombinations of already familiar events. The individual elements of its stories and plots remain the same, but, as in a kaleidoscope, they constantly shift and rearrange themselves in new combinations; this type of narrative organization, like the kaleidoscope, has its own particular fascinations and charms.

CHAPTER 7

Compositional Models and Description

WE SAW in the previous chapter that *Sīrat ʿAntar* repeatedly draws on the story patterns of the Heroic Cycle for the plots of its episodes. In general, these patterns provide a broad framework for the creation and development of narrative action; they determine *what* events occur. However, they do not determine many aspects of *how* events are portrayed. To shape this dimension of the narrative, the *Sīra* relies on other structural matrices that I term "compositional models."

When ʿAntar engages in a struggle, for example, the story patterns provide his motives and set his goals, but it is the compositional models that dictate most aspects of how the chain of events in his struggle are depicted. Naturally, these models relate to and to some extent intermesh with the epic's story patterns, but they generally structure lower levels of narrative discourse: portrayal of event, description, narrative context, and style.

To list or describe the many compositional models at work in *Sīrat ʿAntar* would produce a large index. The task here is not to catalogue phenomena but to understand principles; hence, several typical examples demonstrate how these models work. The thrust of the discussion is analytic rather than descriptive.

The *Sīra*'s compositional models control many aspects of description, narrative technique, and style, but they do not encompass all of them. In order to provide a clearer, more well rounded picture of the epic's composition, therefore, I intersperse examination of its compositional structure with individual discussions of other aspects of narrative discourse. Although this approach may fragment discussion somewhat, in the long run it produces a more complete and coherent picture of the narrative's composition and style. It has the added advantage of utilizing quotations—some of which are lengthy—for more than one analytic purpose. The discussion progresses as follows. In this chapter, I describe theoretical and practical aspects of the *Sīra*'s compositional structure, followed by a brief discussion of its modes of description. In the next chapter, I investigate the epic's most important and most common compositional model—the battle scene—and certain aspects of how the *Sīra* handles point of view. The discussion closes by evaluating some of the strengths and weakness of the narrative's reliance on compositional models.

COMPOSITIONAL MODELS—THEORY AND PRACTICE: THE LION FIGHT

Early in the story, 'Antar begins his struggle for recognition and acceptance, in accordance with the Rise of the Hero story pattern. Initially, his father, Shaddād, opposes this struggle; at one point he even plots with his own brother Mālik and his nephew 'Amr ('Abla's father and brother) to murder 'Antar.

Lion Description 1

One day, when the youth takes the herds to graze, his enemies follow, intending to ambush and kill him. Once in the desert, however, 'Antar encounters another opponent: a lion suddenly emerges from a nearby gully.

1. wa-idhā huwa bi-asad kabīr[1]
2. qadr ath-thaur wa-akbar
3. mujallal bi-'sh-sha'r wa-'l-wabar
4. yaṭīr min 'ainai-hi 'sh-sharar
5. wa-yaqlib al-wādī idhā hamaz wa-hamar
6. shadūq shadqam
7. 'abūs ḍaigham
8. tusma' ar-ra'd min-hu idhā hamham wa-damdam
9. yalma' al-barq min 'ainai-hi idha 'l-lail aẓlam
10. hā'il al-manẓar
11. wa-qad kharaj min baṭn al-wādī
12. wa-huwa yamshī wa-yatamakhtar[2]
13. wa-huwa aghbar
14. afṭas al-mankhar
15. bi-anyāb aḥadd min an-nawā'ib
16. wa-makhālīb aḥadd min al-maṣā'ib
17. 'abūs al-wajh

18. tasma‘ ṣaut-hu ka-r-ra‘d
19. shadīd al-hail
20. ṣa‘b al-mirās
21. ‘arīḍ al-kaff wa-’l-asās (6.3:2/156: appendix IV, 1)

1. And suddenly a large lion appeared,
2. the size of a bull or larger,
3. covered with hair and fur,
4. sparks flying from its eyes,
5. overturning the gully when it hit and growled,
6. wide-mouthed, large-gaped,
7. stern, ferocious,
8. thunder would be heard from it when it roared and snarled,
9. lightning would flash from its eyes when night darkened,
10. fearsome of visage.
11. And it had emerged from the belly of the gully,
12. walking, pacing,
13. tawny,
14. flat of nostril,
15. with fangs sharper than disasters,
16. and claws sharper than calamities,
17. stern of face,
18. and you hear its roar like thunder,
19. violent of force,
20. intractable,
21. broad of paw and stance.[3]

Lion Description 2

Toward its end, *Sīrat ‘Antar* introduces its last great hero, ‘Antar’s son al-Ghaḍanfar. The young hero enters the narrative when he raids one of the shah’s treasure caravans; returning home, he and his companions encounter a lion.

1. wa-idhā qad i‘taraḍ-hum asad fī tilka ’ṭ-ṭarīq
2. wa-hājam ‘alai-him wa-mana‘-hum ‘an al-masīr wa-’t-ta‘wīq
3. wa-kān dhālika ’l-asad qad kharaj ‘alai-him min bain al-ghābāt wa-’sh-shajar
4. wa-huwa asad aghbar al-maḥjar
5. yaṭīr min ‘ainai-hi ’sh-sharar
6. wa-yaqlib al-wādī bi-ṣiyāḥ idhā za’ar wa-zamjar
7. la-hu anyāb aḥadd min an-nawā’ib

8. wa-makhālīb ashadd min al-maṣā'ib
9. wāsiʿ al-ashdāq
10. ʿabūs ḍaigham
11. afṭas al-anf adgham
12. yusmaʿ min ghargharat-hi 'r-raʿd idhā hamaz wa-hamham
13. wa-tanẓur al-barq min ʿainai-hi idhā aẓlam al-lail wa-aqtam
14. wa-huwa ka-anna-hu 'l-qaḍā' al-mubram (72.:57/137: appendix IV, 11)

1. Suddenly a lion blocked them on that road
2. and rushed upon them, preventing them from advancing or retreating.
3. The lion that had emerged upon them from the thickets and trees
4. was dusty of eye-socket,
5. sparks flying from its eyes,
6. overturning the gully with noise when it bellowed and raged,
7. with fangs sharper than disasters,
8. and claws keener than calamities,
9. wide of mouth,
10. stern, ferocious,
11. flat-nosed, black-nosed,
12. its growl sounding like thunder when it bit and roared,
13. and lightning flashed from its eyes when night darkened and blackened.
14. It was like inescapable fate.

More than five thousand pages and a multitude of characters and events separate these two lion descriptions. Nonetheless, they are almost exactly alike. Of the eleven lines of pure description in the second passage (lines 4–14), nine have exact or very similar equivalents in the first description.[4]

If such close correspondence of phrase and metaphor were unique, it would be a truly remarkable coincidence. In reality, such verbal correspondence is typical for the epic. There are, for example, eleven lion fights in the *Sīra*, and all but two contain some description. These descriptions vary in length, ranging from six lines to the twenty-one lines of the first example above; nonetheless, the wording used is strikingly similar. Phrases and metaphors are repeated time and again, exactly or with slight variations. Few lines of the epic's lion descriptions appear only once (cf. appendix IV).

The same holds true for the rest of *Sīrat ʿAntar*. The narrative repeats different sets of descriptive phrases to portray every aspect of its story: character types (such as mighty warriors, beautiful women, or powerful rulers); places (such as campsites, meadows, or palaces); static scenes (such as weddings, feasts, or funerals); and, most importantly, action scenes (such as battles, single combat, or travel). This is a mark of—and a result of—the compositional technique that produced the narrative. In order to appreciate aspects of the work's composition and style, we must briefly discuss a theory that elucidates the nature of this compositional technique before examining how it operates in the epic itself.

ORAL-FORMULAIC COMPOSITION

The theory of traditional oral composition, conceived and developed by Milman Parry and further developed and presented in its fullest form by Albert B. Lord, is founded on the observation that traditional epic narratives (Parry was essentially a student of Homer) contain many repetitions in wording, description, and event. Parry had the remarkable insight to perceive that—far from being signs of imaginative or artistic weakness—such repetitions stem from the oral narrator's constant reliance upon interiorized linguistic and structural models to compose tales. These models provide the building blocks that the oral narrator uses and reuses to structure and actualize the narrative; they comprise, in effect, the narrative vocabulary, syntax, and grammar of the particular tradition of heroic oral narration to which the storyteller belongs.[5]

A full exposition of this theory of traditional oral composition is available in the writings of Lord and Parry.[6] Its primary importance lies in the revolution in critical perspective it provides. Through it, we come to recognize repetition of phrase and event as a natural—indeed integral—part of certain narrative traditions. Acceptance, understanding, and enjoyment of fictional narratives depend significantly on our conception of their compositional and aesthetic principles. By identifying and clarifying previously unrecognized or misunderstood compositional principles inherent in certain traditions of oral narration, the Lord-Parry theory metamorphoses our critical attitude toward narratives stemming from such traditions. It marks a considerable advance in our knowledge of the multiple forms of literary creation.

The written version of *Sīrat ʿAntar* clearly reveals the imprint of compositional processes similar to those described by Parry and Lord. Hence, an awareness of the principles of their theory—classically formulated in Albert B. Lord's *The Singer of Tales*—significantly increases our understanding of the epic's compositional structure. We must employ this theory carefully, however. Important considerations of language, literary tradition, and culture separate the *Sīra* from the narrative traditions that Lord and Parry studied. Moreover, there is a significant difference in literary form between the metrical verse of the Serbo-Croatian storytellers that Parry and Lord observed and *Sīrat ʿAntar*'s rhymed prose.

This difference cannot be brushed aside. Recognizing resemblances between narrative traditions should not lead us to disregard differences. Moreover, this difference in narrative medium is particularly important in that it affects our employment of the two analytic terms that Lord and Parry developed: Parry defined the *formula* as "a group of words which is regularly employed under the same metrical conditions to express an essential idea," and Lord defined the *theme* as "groups of ideas regularly used in telling a tale in the formulaic style of traditional song."[7] In employing these terms, it is essential to remember that they were developed in the context of studying narratives composed in metrical verse. Indeed, the formula is expressly defined in terms of the presence of meter ("words employed under the same metrical conditions"). And to the extent that the theme is defined in terms of the formula ("used in telling a tale in the formulaic style"), it, too, seems to require that meter be present.

Automatically employing the concepts formula and theme, as Parry and Lord have defined them, to describe *Sīrat 'Antar*'s composition invites analytic distortion on two levels. First, it performs the Lord-Parry theory itself a disservice; by generalizing, we contribute to the confusion that has sometimes entered scholarly discussions of formula and theme.[8] Second, uncritically using concepts not originally intended to describe prose (albeit rhymed prose) narratives risks impairing the accuracy of our own analysis.

For these reasons, we must adjust our apprehension of these two concepts, ideally in such a way as to remain within the broad parameters of Parry and Lord's theory and simultaneously allow accurate description of the *Sīra.* This is easy to do with the idea of theme. Although its definition does link "groups of ideas" with "formulaic style," the theme, in general, is less dependent on aspects of literary form than formula. Lord, for instance, remarks that "the theme, even though it be verbal, is not any fixed set of words, but a group of ideas."[9] This (and Lord's general application of the term) suggests that although repeated verbal representation is intrinsic to the idea of theme, specific considerations of narrative form are not. For this reason, I retain the term "theme" in this discussion, since applying it to describe *Sīrat 'Antar*'s rhymed prose does not stretch definitional limits too far.

The same cannot be said for the term "formula," since it is expressly defined in terms of the presence of meter. Therefore, I instead employ the term "traditional phrase." The traditional phrase may be defined as *a group of words recurrently used in a narrative tradition to express a simple idea.* Although it obviously shares many of the features of the formula, this term is intended to identify instances of extensive verbal recurrence in a narrative without placing specific restrictions on literary form. In this regard, the traditional phrase, as conceived here, does not displace or abrogate the formula but rather subsumes it. The formula is one special form of the traditional phrase.[10]

In addition to adopting the terms "traditional phrase" and "theme," it is necessary to expand the analytic framework of the Lord-Parry theory in two directions: laterally and hierarchically. The task of precisely and accurately describing *Sīrat 'Antar*'s compositional structure requires more refined distinctions than the two terms by themselves allow. Before presenting this expanded analytic structure in full, it will be helpful briefly to describe its rationale.

This definition of the traditional phrase conjoins two elements: a recurrent group of words and a simple idea. Theoretically, this seems straightforward enough: a group of words recurrently used to express an idea in a traditional narrative is a traditional phrase. This suggests, conversely, that when the storyteller needed to express certain ideas—a lion description, for example—the narrative tradition provided certain groups of words with which to do so. Practical analysis reveals that this is a good general description of what we find in *Sīrat 'Antar*, but it also reveals that the situation is not always so straightforward. For example, in the two lion descriptions quoted above, we have the words *yaṭīr min 'ainai-hi 'sh-sharar* (sparks flying from its eyes). This is a recurrent group of words—they appear not only in the descriptions quoted above (1/4, 2/5), but in three other lion descriptions as well (appendix IV, 2/13, 3/4, 4/8)—used to express an idea (flashing lion eyes). We may assume, therefore, that this is a traditional phrase. Examination of the two lion descriptions, however, reveals that the *Sīra* also uses other phrases to express the idea of flashing lion eyes (cf. 1/9, 2/3); hence, there is not a one-to-one correlation of distinct phrases expressing a single idea. Nor is this example unique. *Sīrat 'Antar* constantly relies on different sets of recurrent word groups to express single ideas.

The problem with our definition of the traditional phrase, then, is that it offers one term to cover two elements of a dichotomy: groups of words (the signifier) and the essential underlying idea (the signified). Once expressed, of course, these two aspects are irremediably integrated, but for the purposes of analysis it is of immeasurable help to be able to consider them individually (just as modern linguists have profited from the conceptual division of language into *langue* and *parole*). Unless each aspect of the dichotomy inherent in the definition of the traditional phrase is given equal terminological status, confusion inevitably arises during any examination of the *Sīra*'s compositional technique.

The concept of theme suffers from the same deficiency. It too implies the same signifier/signified dichotomy (traditional verbal representation vs. groups of ideas) as the traditional phrase. Clear terms to express each aspect of this dichotomy are therefore necessary here as well. The concept of theme also needs refinement in another way. As it stands, it is too general; analysis of *Sīrat 'Antar* requires differentiating more clearly among various levels of thematic structure. Hence, it is necessary to expand the analytic structure hierarchically to create three levels of thematic analysis—the thematic unit, the theme, and the scene—along with their ideational correspondents—the dramatic idea, the dramatic element, and the complete dramatic structure. The relationships that govern these concepts are explained below.

Adjusted and expanded in these ways above, the analytic framework necessary to describe *Sīrat 'Antar*'s compositional models is as follows:

signified	*signifier*
simple idea	traditional phrase
dramatic idea	thematic unit
dramatic element	theme
complete dramatic structure	scene

This scheme clarifies the problems discussed above. First, it offers terms that distinguish between the ideational and verbal aspects of our original terms. This is important, since analysis of the *Sīra* becomes confusing unless the difference between signified and signifier is clearly maintained. Of course, these elements are integrally related. Only by experiencing their recurrent verbal manifestations can we induce the ideational structure of the epic's compositional models, and only by grasping the unity of these ideational structures can we understand the multiformity that often characterizes their verbal manifestation. Nevertheless, being able to separate the signified/signifier aspects of these concepts significantly facilitates discussion of *Sīrat 'Antar*'s composition and style.

Second, by elaborating this analytic structure beyond the two terms "traditional phrase" and "theme," we can distinguish more clearly the hierarchical relationships that prevail among different levels of compositional structure. A simple idea, such as "flashing lion eyes," is recurrently expressed by one or more different traditional phrases. The lion descriptions of our quotes and of appendix IV are, for example, thematic units representing the dramatic idea "lion description." One or more dramatic ideas form a dramatic element. This element finds verbal manifestation in the theme, which consists of one or more thematic units. We shall see, for instance, that lion descriptions, either alone or in combination with other thematic units, represent the dramatic element "the lion is described" in the *Sīra*'s lion fight accounts. Sets of dramatic elements combine to form complete dramatic structures. These structures are verbally expressed by groups of themes, which together compose the scene. Scenes, finally, form the raw material of the epic's larger narrative structure: the story patterns of the Heroic Cycle.[11]

Needless to say, the differentiation among levels of compositional structure that this analytic structure allows should not make us lose sight of their overall unity. Traditional phrases, thematic units, themes, scenes, and the ideational models they represent can only be understood in terms of their relations to one another.

Each analytical level also has great potential for compression and expansion. The phrase "one or more" appears repeatedly in the explanation above to emphasize this point. A thematic unit, such as a lion description, may consist of many traditional phrases or only one or two. The theme "the lion is described" may consist of the thematic unit "the lion description" alone or in combination with other such units. Compositional structures may be expanded indefinitely or telescoped to the point of nonexistence. Examples of this principle are offered below.

Moreover, it is important to note that as we ascend along our analytic hierarchy we move from levels of narrative stasis—that is, pure description—to levels of narrative dynamics—that is, sequential action. Traditional phrases and thematic units, being smaller elements, tend toward stasis, while themes and scenes, because they involve multiple dramatic relationships, are more kinetic.

Finally, there is the issue of how we identify and differentiate among compositional levels in the narrative. This process entails two steps. First, we use repetition; it is only because the storyteller repeats traditional phrases, thematic units, themes, and scenes that we can identify them. Piecemeal identification does not suffice, however. To understand the dynamics of the *Sīra*'s compositional modes, we must transcend the dimension of verbal manifestation and apprehend the nature and purpose of the structural models that lie behind it. In other words, to understand how *Sīrat 'Antar* creates its compositional structures we must understand the rationale of their use; we must perceive the dramatic and aesthetic effects the epic seeks to achieve in each of its different types of scenes. Once we understand the purpose of the whole, discerning the nature of the relationships among the parts presents little problem. The epic does not consist of traditional phrases, thematic units, themes, and scenes strung out randomly along the line of narrative sequence but rather of the dramatic relationships that these three elements express. The purpose of this compositional technique is to tell a story; to forget this for even a moment means that our analytic structure will collapse under the weight of its own abstraction.[12]

Appendix V presents outlines of all eleven lion fight scenes in *Sīrat 'Antar*. Comparison reveals that the *Sīra* relies on seven central dramatic elements to form their dramatic core. Let us examine these seven elements with a view toward obtaining an impression of their interrelation and interplay on an ideational level and their ratio of unity and variety on the level of verbal manifestation. The seven dramatic elements of the lion fight scene are:

1. The lion appears
2. The lion is described

3. Others react in fright
4. The hero reacts courageously
5. The hero fights and kills the lion
6. The hero reacts to his or her deed
7. Others react to the hero's deed

The lion fight scene begins with the appearance of the lion. Although there are occasions when word of the lion—or even the beast itself—is brought to the hero (see appendix V, 2e, f; 3a; 6b), the *Sīra* usually introduces the animal by having it startle the hero in the midst of some everyday activity, such as herding or traveling. The surprise provoked by the lion's appearance in this way injects an immediate sense of suspense and excitement into the confrontation.

After presenting the lion, the epic customarily describes it. This is a fluid theme in the lion fight; it usually occurs immediately upon the lion's introduction, but it may appear at later points (see appendix V, 2i) or even be omitted (see appendix V, 6, 7)—though when it does occur it naturally must precede the lion fight itself. The theme of lion description contains two types of thematic units: rhymed prose alone or rhymed prose supplemented by verse. Rhymed prose and verse each serve differing purposes. The prose descriptions purport to describe the particular lion of the moment; verse, however, generalizes the frame of descriptive context; poems (which rarely amount to more than three or four lines at a time) serve as an anonymous citation, preceded with a statement such as "it was like that of which the poet said . . ." In this way the epic insinuates that the lion presently being described is as fierce as those whose ferocity has become proverbial. Of these two forms, prose is the more frequent; it occurs without verse, while verse never occurs alone.[13]

Despite its descriptive pretensions, the function of the lion description is more dramatic than narrative, its purpose being less to describe an individual lion than to heighten narrative suspense. By magnifying our impression of the ferocity and menace of the beast, *Sīrat 'Antar* ensures our involvement in the narrative situation and increases our sympathy for the hero in his or her moment of peril. It is because the function of the lion description is primarily dramatic that the epic can rely on traditional phrases to depict all its lions. Moreover, just as description is a way of inducing narrative tension, length of description is a way of calibrating it. The longer the description, the greater our impression of the lion's ferocity and the higher our sense of narrative suspense.

Having introduced and described the lion, the *Sīra*'s next two dramatic elements portray the effect it produces on its surroundings. In general, the lion's appearance causes panic: animals bolt and shy away, servants scatter, even warriors suffer a moment's pause (see appendix V, 1c; 2b, e; 4b, d; 6a; 8c; 10d).

The hero's reaction, however, is the opposite: he or she welcomes the challenge the lion presents and rushes to engage it. While advancing on the beast, the hero may issue a challenge and/or recite a battle poem (again the theme has different representational possibilities) of self-praise, warning the lion of the hero's prowess (appendix V, 1f, g; 2h; 3e). The hero also makes sure that the heroic task is sufficiently difficult by removing armor and relinquishing some or all arms (if on horseback, by dismounting) and then faces the lion with only sword and shield, or only sword, or even with bare hands (appendix V, 1h; 2k; 3f; 4e; 5d; 6b; 7b; 8d; 9c; 10e, f; 11d).

Dramatic elements 3 and 4 are thus intertwined. Element 3 is optional but psychologically significant since the *Sīra* uses it to create dramatic contrast; by portraying the panic-stricken reaction of others to the lion, it highlights the courage of the hero and the magnitude of the deed. Moreover, these two elements together serve as a counterbalance for the lion description in the scene as a whole. The static moment of the hero's dismounting and preparing for the fight, removing armor, and perhaps reciting a poem echoes the static moment of lion description. Together they present a vivid tableau of heroic confrontation.

Most of the lion fight scene consists of dramatic buildup and aftermath; the fight itself is a straightforward affair. Typically it is presented counterpunctually, with the epic switching its focus back and forth between the lion and hero. The hero advances on the lion; the beast crouches. The lion issues a tremendous roar; the hero answers it with an even greater roar. The lion springs; the hero meets the spring with a mighty blow that usually cleaves the beast in two.[14]

Following the fight comes another psychologically important moment in the scene: the hero's consummation of victory. Again this finds thematic manifestation in different ways. The hero sometimes recites another poem of self-praise (appendix V, 21, 4h, 8g), at other times makes light of the deed and acts as if nothing significant has happened (appendix V, 7e, 11g). Almost always the hero shows disdain for the fallen opponent by wiping the sword clean on its fur and leaving its carcass to lie where it has fallen. Perhaps the reaction that most completely symbolizes the hero's attitude toward this foe occurs in 'Antar's first lion fight (appendix V, 1). After killing the lion with his bare hands, the young hero skins, roasts, and eats it. Having thus conquered and consumed danger, 'Antar falls asleep—resting his head on the lion skin.

The final dramatic element of the lion fight scene is the portrayal of others' reactions to the heroic deed. This element is crucial, being in one sense the point to which everything else has led. In *Sīrat 'Antar* it is not enough for the hero to perform a deed; for complete effect he must have witnesses who react positively to his actions. The witnesses may marvel in silence (appendix V, 11) or, more often, express their feelings by praising, congratulating, or even rewarding the hero (appendix V, 2m, 3g, 4g, 5g, 6e, 7c, 8h, 9e, 10i, 11f). Nonetheless, they must be present, for through them the *Sīra* voices the audience's favorable reaction. More significantly, they are a device to control this reaction, ensuring that the audience perceives the hero's deed from the correct point of view.

Having examined the seven dramatic elements of the lion fight scene and their most important forms of thematic representation, let us look at their interaction. The narrative effect of the lion fight issues from *Sīrat 'Antar*'s manipulation of three sets of contrastive pairs: the lion and the hero, the reaction to the lion of others and of the hero, and the reaction to the victory of others and of the hero.

The primary pair, of course, is the lion and the hero. Essentially this opposition contrasts danger facing the endangered, and its dramatic potency stems from the surprising reversal of states after the fight. A sense of inequality is essential to this confrontation; the lion must seem to present a real danger to the hero. This is why the lion description theme is important: it provides an effective technique for convincing the audience that the lion is indeed dangerous. The epic implies the hero's endangerment in other ways as well: the heroes dismount to face the lion on foot, remove their armor, and rely only on their sword and shield—or sometimes only on their bare hands—to kill the beast. Because the *Sīra* invests its heroes with such strength and power, convincing us that the lion truly presents a danger can be difficult. This in itself is a perilous situation. The epic cannot allow the audience to feel sorry for the poor lion; such an ironic undercutting of audience identification with the hero would be disastrous. Irony has no place in the *Sīra*; it would corrode its heroic world like acid.

To counter this threat, the *Sīra* introduces a third presence—the other—and thus introduces two more pairs of dramatic contrasts in the lion fight. First, the others who flee before the lion are contrasted to the hero, who thus not only becomes the endangered but the protector or defender as well. After the fight, the others' reactions are again contrasted with that of the hero. Whether the hero celebrates victory with a poem or—in a psychologically more subtle reaction—evinces indifference to the deed, the epic always describes the positive impression this act arouses in the others, who either react with mute astonishment or—more frequently—openly praise and congratulate the hero. The lion fight scene thus hinges upon three reversals of situation. The hero moves from apparent victim to victor, the lion moves from apparent victor to victim, and the other moves from panic and/or low opinion of the hero to security and/or high opinion of the hero.[15]

Arriving at the dramatic core of the lion fight scene allows us to appreciate the combination of unity and variety within and among its different versions.

The lion fight scene can be quite pliant, expanding or contracting themes according to the necessities of the moment. For example, it is not surprising that one of the fullest versions of the lion fight is its first occurrence. The *Sīra* cannot presume previous acquaintance with the scene's dramatic elements, so its thematic representation is correspondingly elaborate. The lion description is the longest one in the epic. ʿAntar challenges the lion in both prose and verse before fighting it, he kills the beast with his bare hands, and he skins and eats it afterward (appendix V, 1).

Subsequent versions of the lion fight scene, however, can be presented in reduced form since the audience already has attained a working knowledge of its nature. Poems may or may not appear, lion descriptions may be extended or reduced, lion fights may be short or drawn out, and the hero's celebration of his victory may be elaborate or momentary. In other words, dramatic elements may be thematically presented in full face or obliquely.

Examples of obliquely manifested elements are quite interesting because in them we more easily see the protruding bones of the *Sīra*'s compositional models. For instance, in the sixth lion fight Māzin fights the lion offstage (appendix V, 6). Servants bring news of the lion into camp; Māzin sets out to fight it and thus momentarily disappears from view; when he returns, he has already killed the lion and is portrayed returning to camp with his servants bearing the lion's carcass after him.

This is a disastrous weakening of the lion fight scene. A lion fight conducted offstage is not much of a heroic confrontation, and thus the scene loses a great deal of its dramatic impact. But there is a reason for this weakening. While Māzin is gone, his mother reveals that the youth's real father is Shaddād—a revelation that advances one aspect of Māzin's Rise of the Hero story pattern. It appears, therefore, that the *Sīra* sacrifices one element in its Heroic Cycle (the hero proves himself by killing a lion) for the sake of promoting another (the hero's unusual circumstances of birth).

Nevertheless, the epic does not entirely give up on its presentation of the lion fight theme. After Māzin's return, one of the camp's servants describes the fight to those who remained in camp (Māzin, being a hero, would never describe the fight himself). In this way, the *Sīra* manages to restore the effect of the lion fight theme in part and in so doing also sets the stage for and justifies Māzin's mother's congratulations on his victory (dramatic element 7). Even as it varies its portrayal of events, *Sīrat ʿAntar* tries to fulfill the demands of its compositional models.

This episode, by the way, is a good example of how *Sīrat ʿAntar* modulates narrative expectations by emphasizing thematic elaboration. Māzin is at this point a new character, but his lion fight confirms his heroic status. The lion fight scene's truncated nature, however, suggests that Māzin is not destined to become a character of the first magnitude. If he were, the *Sīra* would provide fuller versions of its themes. Such expectations are justified by Māzin's subsequent role: although he becomes one of 'Antar's band of heroic companions, he never becomes as prominent as other members, such as Ghaṣūb or al-Ghaḍbān.

Often we sense a principle of dramatic compensation at work in the epic's balancing of dramatic elements. When one is reduced, others gain in dramatic potency. For example, the seventh lion fight scene (appendix V, 7), with Hānī ibn Mas'ūd, completely lacks a lion description. As if to compensate, the *Sīra* magnifies Hānī's daring and might. Unarmed, he beards the lion in his thicket, dragging out the living lion by one hand to kill it with a single blow. The epic thus offsets the loss in narrative suspense that results from the omission of the lion description theme by emphasizing Hānī's endangered status and the heroic aplomb with which he carries out his deed.

Just as *Sīrat 'Antar* expands, reduces, and balances thematic units and themes within its scenes, it also intermixes and balances its scenes to weave the fabric of the larger concerns of the various parts of the Heroic Cycle. We have seen one example of this in the discussion of Māzin's fight; other examples are easily discerned. In the second lion fight (appendix V, 2), fleeing servants bring King al-Mundhir news of a nearby lion. At this point, the lion fight scene is interrupted by a description of Prince an-Nu'mān's arrival with a captured 'Antar. 'Antar informs al-Mundhir of his need for 'Asāfīr camels and, stirred by the thought of 'Abla, caps his account with a love poem. Having established 'Antar's credentials as a lover by introducing themes from the love scene (part of the Love Story narrative pattern), the epic resumes the lion fight theme where it left off—by again describing the panic of the king's attendants before the lion. Although there are times when the conflation of different scenes can weaken the dramatic effect of one of them (as in Māzin's lion fight), the *Sīra*'s compositional structure is flexible enough to accommodate conjunction and intermixture of scenes.

An advantage to grasping the dramatic essentials of scenes is that even when the *Sīra* intermixes them we can still put seemingly strange or anomalous incidents into their correct context. For instance, in the first lion fight (appendix V, 1), Shaddād, Mālik, and 'Amr stalk 'Antar in order to murder him. There is nothing strange about this; such intentions are a normal part of the Rise of the Hero story pattern.[16] Their subsequent actions do seem inexplicable, however; while creeping up on 'Antar, they observe his lion fight; thereafter, they watch him skin, roast, and eat the beast, and then go to sleep. This, we might suppose, is the perfect moment to ambush someone: while he is sleeping soundly after hard physical exertion and a large meal. Instead, Shaddād and his companions give up their plan and return to camp. This decision appears mysterious unless we realize that Shaddād and the others are filling the role of impressed and marveling witnesses to 'Antar's deed. In other words, by bringing Shaddād and the others out of camp after 'Antar, the *Sīra* provides a dramatic element integral to its lion fight scene (element 7).

So far only general aspects of compositional structure in the lion fight scene have been considered. Let us therefore close this discussion by examining the nature of its smaller components: traditional phrases and thematic units. In appreciating *Sīrat 'Antar*'s reliance upon such repeated elements, it is important to realize that the epic does not use them because of a paucity of artistic imagination or feebleness of linguistic capability. Rather, it is a question of aesthetic attitude. The *Sīra* aims to produce certain dramatic or aesthetic effects; since it can create and recreate these effects by modulating tested phrases, descriptions, and narrative sequences, it does so. It does not adopt traditional phrases and thematic units because it considers them to be the only way of telling its story, but because it considers them to be the best way.

We can see this principle at work in the lion descriptions assembled in appendix IV, but for variety's sake this point can be illustrated by examining another thematic unit of the lion fight theme, which portrays not a static lion description but a dynamic act. In nine of the lion fights, the hero kills the animal by striking a mighty blow with his sword. This act is portrayed in each of these scenes as follows:

1. wa nahad 'alai-hi . . . wa-'staqbal-hu bi-'l-ḥusām wa-ḍarab-hu ḍarbat baṭal humām ḥaqq-ha min yad 'Antar wa-qāl, "anā mā shaqait wa-anā ḥabīb 'Abla ma baqait!" wa-waqa' al-ḥusām fī jabhat-hi wa-mā zāl yaqṭa' ilā an waṣal ilā ṣurrat-hi wa-waqa' al-asad qiṭ'atain wa-ṣār 'ala 'l-arḍ shaṭrain. (appendix IV, 2:4/374–75)

[The lion] leapt upon him . . . and he ['Antar] met it with his blade and struck it the blow of a mighty hero, worthy of the hand of 'Antar. And he said, "I worry not; I am 'Abla's lover as long as I live!" The blade fell upon its forehead and continued cutting until it reached its middle. The lion fell in two pieces and became two parts on the ground.

2. wa-ma'a wathbat al-asad ḍarab-hu 'Antar bi-'ẓ-Ẓāmi 'l-abtar bain 'ainai-hi fa-ṭala' al-ḥusām min bain fakhdhai-hi wa-waqa' 'ala 'l-arḍ qiṭ'atain wa-saqaṭ fī wasṭ dhalika 'l-īwān juz'ain. (appendix IV, 3:5/457)

And with the lion's spring, 'Antar struck it with sharp Ẓāmī [Thirsty, the name of his sword] between its eyes. Then the blade emerged from between its thighs, and it fell upon the ground in two pieces and dropped down in the center of that Arch in two sections.

3. wa-sāwa 'l-asad fī wathbat-hi wa-ḍarab-hu bi-ṣārim-hi fa-ḥakam bain 'ainai-hi wa-lam [yazal] yaqṭa' ilā an kharaj min bain fakhdhai-hi. (appendix IV, 4:26/18)

And he [ʿAmr] faced the lion in its spring and struck it with his sharp-edged sword. And it fell exactly between its eyes and continued cutting until it came out from between its thighs.

4. wa-fi-l-ḥāl bādar-hu bi-ḍarba baʿd ʿan wathab ʿalai-hi wa-kanat al-ḍarba qad aṣābat-hu bain ʿainai-hi wa-ṭalaʿ as-saif yalmaʿ min bain fakhdhai'hi fa-waqaʿ al-asad shaṭrain wa-qad ṣār juz'ain wa-baqiya qiṭʿatain. (appendix IV, 5:27/101)

Immediately he [Daththār] fell upon it with a blow, after the lion had sprung toward him. The blow struck it between its eyes, and the sword emerged gleaming from between its thighs. Then the lion fell in two parts, for it had become two sections and was two pieces.

5. wa-hājam ʿalai-hi wa-ḍarab-hu bi-'l-ḥusām fī jabhat-hi wa-aṭlaʿ-hu yalmaʿ min ẓahr-hi. (appendix IV, 6:29/351)

And it [the lion] charged upon him [Māzin] and he struck it with his blade on its forehead, pushing it through so that it gleamed from its rear.

6. wa-hājam mithl al-barq ʿalai-hi fa-'staqbaluh al-Ghaḍbān bi-saif-hi al-yamān wa-ḍarab-hu bain ʿainai-hi kharaj as-saif yalmaʿ min fakhdhai-hi fa-waqaʿ shaṭrain wa-ṣār ʿala 'l-arḍ qiṭʿatain. (appendix IV, 8:41/5)

It charged upon him like lightning. Al-Ghaḍbān met it with his Yemeni sword and struck it between the eyes. The sword came out gleaming from its thighs. Then it fell in two parts and became two pieces on the ground.

7. wa-wathab ʿalai-hi fa-zāwagh-hu 'l-Ghaḍbān wa-ḍarab-hu bi-ḥadd al-ḥusām ʿala qimmat-hi akhraj-hu yalmaʿ min silsilat-hi. (appendix IV, 9:41/24)

And it sprang at him. Then al-Ghaḍbān sidestepped it and struck it with the sharp of his blade on its crown, thrusting it so that it gleamed from its backbone.

8. fa-wathab al-asad ilai-hā bi-surʿa fa-'staqbalat-hu ʿUnaitira bi-ḍarba jā'at bain ʿainai-hi thumma ṣār as-saif yahwī ilā bain fakhda-hi wa-dhālika min shiddat al-ḍarba wa-quwwat al-hamza fa-waqaʿ ʿala 'l-arḍ qiṭʿatain wa-'nqasam firqatain. (appendix IV, 10:56/55)

Then the lion sprang quickly toward her. Then ʿUnaitira met it with a blow between its eyes. Thereafter the sword sank to between its thighs from the force of the blow and the strength of the thrust. And it fell on the ground in two pieces, split into two portions.

9. wa-ḥamal ʿala 'l-Ghaḍanfar wa-ḥamal al-akhar ʿalai-hi wa-ḍarab-hu bi-'s-saif bain ʿainai-hi fa-min quwwat al-ḍarba wa-shiddat ḥail al-asad ṭalaʿ as-saif yalmaʿ min fakhdai-hi. (appendix IV, 11:57/138)

[The lion] rushed toward al-Ghaḍanfar and the other rushed toward it. And he struck it with his sword between its eyes. From the strength of the blow and the force of the lion's power, the sword emerged gleaming from between its thighs.

I quote all nine examples of this "killing the lion with a sword" thematic unit (as opposed to the hero killing it with bare hands) because this gives a sense of the semantic unity of its underlying dramatic idea and the combination of unity and variety of its linguistic representations. The simple ideas that combine to form the dramatic idea of lion killing here appear in the sequence the lion attacks, the hero responds to this attack, the hero strikes the lion a mighty blow, this blow not only kills the lion but severs it in two.

These examples of this dramatic idea confirm its essential unity. Hundreds, sometimes thousands, of pages separate lion fights, but the act of lion killing with the sword is depicted in similar fashion, using the same traditional phrases. The amount of verbal repetition that exists among these examples makes this fact seem indisputable. Of course, linguistic variety also exists. The *Sīra* often relies on different words to represent a single concept. For example, it uses the words *nahad* (leap, ex. 1), *wathab* (spring, ex. 2, 3, 4, 7, 8), *hājam* (attack, ex. 5, 6), and *ḥamal* (rush, ex. 9) to portray the lion's attack; while *istaqbal* (meet, ex. 1, 6, 8), *sāwā* (face, ex. 3), *bādar* (fall upon, ex. 4), *ḍarab* (strike, ex. 2, 5), *zāwagh* (sidestep, ex. 7), and *ḥamal* (rush, ex. 9) are used to depict the hero's response to this attack. Similarly, the hero may strike the lion *bain 'ainai-hi* (between its eyes, ex. 2, 3, 4, 6, 8, 9), on the *jabha* (forehead, ex. 1, 5) or on the *qimma* (crown, ex. 7); several words denominate the sword with which the hero strikes: *ḥusām* (ex. 1, 5), Ẓāmī (ex. 2) *ṣārim* (ex. 3), *saif* (ex. 6, 9), and *ḥadd al-ḥusām* (ex. 7). Similar examples of linguistic variation exist throughout the remainder of this thematic unit. Despite this variation, the words involved are either synonymous or, at the very least, freely interchangeable. If only two examples of the thematic unit were compared, the linguistic variation involved might appear great; but the amount of verbal duplication increases as further examples are compared, making the variation appear increasingly insignificant. After a comparison of all of the above-quoted examples, their inherent ideational and verbal congruence seem self-evident.

Again, the potential for expansion or compression that exists at every level of *Sīrat 'Antar*'s compositional structure must be recognized. The verbal rendition of a dramatic idea may be relatively long (ex. 1, 8) or short (ex. 5, 7).

We should also notice the aspect of localization that exists in some instances of the thematic unit. The first example belongs to the lion fight scene into which the *Sīra* has interwoven materials from the Love Story (appendix V, 2). Accordingly, before striking the lion, 'Antar swears by his love for 'Abla, thus maintaining the reverberations of the love scene throughout the lion fight. Similarly, in example 3 'Antar kills the lion at the request of and before the eyes of the Persian shah Anūshirwān. Hence, when describing how the dead lion, severed in twain, falls to the ground, the epic has the animal fall under the great Arch of Ctesiphon, concomitant in popular imagination (along with Shah Anūshirwān himself) with the idea of Sassanian splendor and might. By means of such localization, the *Sīra* grounds its repeated themes in the narrative circumstances of the moment.

Finally, I must reiterate that *Sīrat 'Antar* uses repeated verbal elements (phrases, themes, etc.) because it considers them the best way of depicting events. I have made frequent use of the word "dramatic" in this discussion, both in the determination of analytic concepts and in the analysis of the interrelated elements of the lion scene. This word is appropriate because it suggests the rationale for the *Sīra*'s repetition of phrase and description (disregarding, for the moment, the obvious rationale of compositional ease). Like all works of adventure, *Sīrat 'Antar* is interested in creating narrative suspense and dramatic effect. One major way it accomplishes this is to rely on pictorially vivid representations of actions. What better way to portray a mighty blow than to have the hero strike the lion, in mid-leap, on its head, have the sword cut until it appears gleaming at the animal's other end, and then have the lion fall, split in two? For *Sīrat 'Antar*, this is (we must assume) the most vivid, exciting, and dramatically effective way to depict a hero killing a lion with a sword. Since this is the best possible image, it is repeated—time and time again.

NARRATIVE TECHNIQUE: DESCRIPTIVE MODES

Before discussing *Sīrat 'Antar*'s compositional structure further, let us examine its descriptive technique. This subject cannot be examined exhaustively, but several examples of description can be analyzed to elucidate the basic principles that underlie the epic's descriptive modes. Let us begin by reexamining the first of the above-quoted examples of lion description.

As previously noted, one function of protracted description is to heighten narrative suspense. Having devised the confrontation between 'Antar and the lion, *Sīrat 'Antar* seeks to emphasize the lion's awesomeness. Concern, anxiety, and even a little fear are the feelings the epic evokes on 'Antar's behalf, so that the hero's success in the encounter provokes a sense of relief that he successfully survived the threat and impresses the audience (internal and external) with the ease and aplomb with which he did so.

In this lion description, the *Sīra* interweaves three types of portrayal. First, it enumerates physical attributes of the lion: the animal is large, perhaps larger even than a bull (lines 1, 2), it is also hairy (line 3), wide-mouthed (line 6), tawny (line 13), flat-nosed (line 14), and wide of paw and stance (line 21). Listing these attributes reinforces our awareness of the essential "lionness" of the animal (flat-nosedness, wide-mouthedness, tawniness, etc., being in combination features particular to lions). The epic also emphasizes the animal's large size; if meeting lions is worrisome, meeting large ones is especially unpleasant.

The second type of description lists affective impressions of the lion. It is not enough that 'Antar encounters a lion—and a particularly large one at that—the beast also appears threatening: its mien is stern, ferocious (lines 7, 17), violent (line 19), and intractable (line 20). Whether it really is any of these things is beside the point. This is how the animal impresses the onlooker—or so we are told.

Third, the epic uses metaphors to enhance the lion's physical attributes. Its eyes emit sparks and flash like lightning (lines 4, 9), its roar creates earthquakes and sounds like thunder (lines 5, 8, 18), and its fangs and claws are sharper and more frightening than the worst imaginable calamity (lines 15, 16).

In addition to these purely descriptive details, other aspects of the lion are unnerving. The animal appears suddenly (line 1); it emerges from the depths of a gully (line 11)—in the same way, perhaps, that primordial fears emerge from the depths of our unconsciousness; and it is advancing (line 12).

Thus, this thematic unit does not attempt realistic or naturalistic portrayal of detail but instead assembles disturbing associations: lionness and large size, a mien whose aspects evoke fear and dread, and attributes equated with such innately disturbing and dangerous natural events as shooting sparks, earthquakes, and thunderstorms. To convince us of the danger that the lion presents to 'Antar, therefore, the *Sīra* plays upon deep-seated attitudes. Sudden movements, large beasts, things emerging from the depths, and violent and uncontrollable natural forces are frightening or unnerving—no matter how well we control our emotions after the first startling moment. The lion, the epic implies, embodies and combines the dangers of all of these features or events. In fact, it is even possible to reduce the lines of our lion description to a kind of associative shorthand: 1. sudden movement–beast–large size, 2. large size, 3. beast, 4. fire, 5. earthquake, 6. beast, 7. ferocity, 8. thunder, 9. lightning, 10. ferocity, 11. emergence from the depths, 12. advancing movement, 13. beast, 14. beast, 15. disaster, 16. calamity, 17. ferocity, 18. thunder, 19. ferocity, 20. ferocity, 21. beast–large size.

This reliance upon associative equivalences is essential to *Sīrat 'Antar*'s descriptive techniques. The epic employs a standard repertoire of elemental polarities: largeness, darkness, hardness, downward movement, sternness or ferocity, startlingly swift movement, loud noises, bestiality, fire, and violent natural forces depict threatening or imposing phenomena and suspenseful situations; conversely, smallness, light, softness, upward movement, gentleness and good nature, stasis, sweet noises (song, laughter, poetry), and benevolent natural phenomena (still water, celestial objects, blooming flowers and trees, clement spring weather, dazzling jewels, etc.) portray pleasant phenomena and idyllic relaxation.

It is important to realize that these two associative polarities do not represent ethical opposites. Good and evil as moral absolutes play little role in the *Sīra*'s heroic world. 'Antar and the other inhabitants of this world are concerned with fulfilling the demands of heroic honor, which only incidentally coincide with those of morality. Rather, the *Sīra*'s descriptive polarities represent potentialities for violence and pacifism, danger and safety. Battle scenes, wild beasts, and great warriors are portrayed in terms of the first group of descriptive features; love scenes, feasts, and beautiful women are portrayed in terms of the second. 'Antar and other heroes, for example, are often described in ways similar to lions, being equated with hardness, ferocity, swift movement, fire (blazing eyes, flashes of steel), large size, and violence. Within this context, 'Antar's blackness and that of so many other great heroes of the *Sīra* is perfectly consistent and understandable: blackness or darkness belongs to the violent half of the epic's descriptive polarities.

Violence is not an ethically negative quality in *Sīrat 'Antar*. Indeed, warriors become heroes largely because of their unusually great capacity for violence. The hero does not overcome opposing violent forces through pacifism but rather through an ability to marshal even greater violence. Moreover, the hero is fierce not only in deed but in temperament. In the lion fight scene, for example, the lion roars just before it attacks the hero. Typically, the hero answers this roar with an even greater roar, symbolically outdoing the lion in ferocious expression before overcoming it in physical combat.

The three types of description delineated in the lion description (physical, affective, metaphoric) represent less hard and fast categories than descriptive tendencies—often intermixed. Listing physical attributes grounds the description of the subject portrayed (lion, woman, warrior, etc.). The affective and metaphoric types of description are of greater importance, however, for they place the object of description within the spheres of the *Sīra*'s associative polarities. Moreover, since the narrative consistently relies on these opposed spheres for its description, characters and events achieve significance only when they are portrayed in these terms. Look, for example, at this description of Mahriyya:

> fa-ra'au-hā ṣabīḥat al-wajh aḥsan min ash-shams wa-'l-qamar wa aḍwa' min al-fajr idha-'nfajar wa-ka-anna-hā min al-ḥūr al-'ain wa-qad kharajat min al-jinān au min banāt mulūk aṣḥāb at-tījān wa-'alai-hā qalā'id wa-'uqūd min az-zumurrud al-akhḍar wa-'l-yāqūt al-aḥmar wa-hiya fitna li-man la-hā yanẓur wa-'l-banāt allatī ma'a-hā yuqāribna-hā fī malā-ha wa-yushārikna-hā fī husn-hā wa-bahjat-hā. (30.2:25/419)
>
> Then they saw her, comely of face, fairer than the sun and moon, more luminous than the dawn when it breaks, as if she were one of the houris of Paradise who had come out of the Gardens, or one of the daughters of

> crowned kings. Upon her were necklaces and chaplets of green emerald and red ruby. She was a temptation to whoever looked at her, and the girls with her approached her in gracefulness and shared her beauty and splendor.[17]

This description presents no idea of what Mahriyya actually looks like. It indicates that she is beautiful only indirectly. The *Sīra* states that 'Antar and his companions *saw* her to be beautiful of face (affective description), favorably comparable to the sun and moon (celestial objects—light), as if (affective) she were an inhabitant of heaven (celestial), of the Gardens (celestial—benevolent natural phenomena), or as if she were a princess (up, in terms of social status and wealth). She is then metonymically equated with the emeralds and rubies she wears (pleasant natural phenomena) and with the attractiveness of her companions, who both reflect her beauty and, by their presence, increase it—beauty enhancing beauty. Mahriyya, we are told, renders distraught anyone who gazes at her (affective description).

There is not one item of individual, personal description here. On the contrary, the whole description exudes outward and upward. Through association Mahriyya is placed in the realm of beautiful, luminous, and precious phenomena; hence we conclude that she herself is beautiful and desirable. Similarly, the description of the warrior 'Assāf, brief though it is, firmly places him in the realm of dangerous and imposing phenomena.

> inna-hu kān min al-jabābira 'l-'utāh 'azīm al-khilqa shadīd az-za'qa ṭawīl al-qāma kabīr al-hāma idhā mashā sāwā bi-qāmat-hi 'l-ashjār wa-idhā takallam ash'al fī 'l-qulūb an-nār la-hu ṣaut al-asad al-haddār. (7.7:3/259)
>
> He was one of the arrogant oppressors, powerful of character, mighty of shout, tall of stature, large of crown. When he walked, he equaled the trees in his stature, and when he talked, he lit the fire [of fear] in hearts. He had the voice of a roaring lion.

Here we have outsized proportions of physique and temperament. 'Assāf is associated with large size, loud noise, violent character, and such dangerous phenomena as fire and roaring lions. It is interesting to see how the *Sīra* introduces trees—basically benevolent natural phenomena—into its threatening descriptive polarity by associating them here with 'Assāf's size. Just as violent natural phenomena are used to describe lions, now lions are used to describe this frightening and imposing warrior.

Description is accumulative in *Sīrat 'Antar*. There is little attempt at integrated portrayal or psychological insight; intensity of description is achieved through length, not through individualistic exactness or aptness. Important characters receive extended descriptions, minor characters little or no description. Description is always consistent. The different lines and the figurative members of the descriptive polarities serve to reinforce one another. Benevolent characters, such as Mahriyya, are described in terms drawn from one polarity, while violent characters, such as 'Assāf, are described in terms drawn from the other. Ambiguity and irony have no place in the narrative's descriptive modes.

This general technique of description, judged by the standards of modern realistic fiction, has obvious limitations; but it also has several advantages. First of all, it allows the *Sīra* to imbue its portrayal of character and scene with poetic emotiveness and tone. Metaphors, similes, and other figures of speech—traditional phrases grounded in the work's standard sets of associative polarities—stand ready at hand when extended description is called for. Just as importantly, the use of these descriptive sets enables the *Sīra* to establish an immediate sense of narrative context. From the first line of a description, the initiates among the audience know exactly what type of character has appeared (and can often guess what type of scene is about to be enacted). Thereafter, we wait to see which of the many plot possibilities the epic will choose to proceed with; anticipation plays just as important a role as curiosity in the mysterious dialectic of narrative suspense. Finally, as noted before, this technique of description gives *Sīrat 'Antar* exact control over the level of narrative suspense it wishes to create. Longer descriptions increase the importance of a scene or character and thus heighten narrative suspense; short descriptions indicate that the general movement of narrative event has not yet culminated.

CHAPTER 8

Compositional Models and Narrative Generation: The Battle Scene

I BEGAN DISCUSSION of *Sīrat ʿAntar*'s compositional models with the lion fight scene for two reasons. First, this scene is relatively short and self-contained and thus facilitates detailed examination. Second, it appears with sufficient frequency to illustrate the ratio of uniformity and diversity typical of the epic's compositional models but not so often that examining every example proves cumbersome. Although the lion fight scene is typical of the *Sīra*'s use of compositional models, however, it is not in itself a particularly important scene. Examination of it alone, therefore, provides little idea of how *Sīrat ʿAntar* uses a limited number of models to generate the great mass of its narrative. This purpose is better served through examination of what is without doubt the *Sīra*'s most important narrative scene—battle.

The *Sīra* begins by relating how Shaddād sets out on a raid with a small group of ʿAbs warriors. After traveling for some time, the raiders encounter a large and populous camp of the Banī Jadīla. Although the camp itself is too large for the ten raiders to attack, they steal a thousand camels and the black slave Zabība and her two young sons, Jarīr and Shaibūb, who have been herding the animals. The epic describes the Jadīla pursuit and the ensuing skirmish:

1. mā abʿadū ʿan ad-diyār illa ʾl-qalīl,
2. ḥattā ṭalaʿ min khalf-him ghubār,
3. qad thār,

4. wa-ʿalā ḥattā sadd al-aqṭār.
5. wa-ʾnkashaf al-ghubār,
6. wa-bān ʿan barīq zarad,
7. wa-lamīʿ khuwad,[1]
8. wa-khalāʾiq mā li-kathrat-hā ʿadad.
9. hādha wa-khalf al-ghubār ṣiyāḥ al-abṭāl
10. wa-hamhamat al-afyāl.
11. wa-lam yakun illā sāʿa ḥattā adrakū-hum
12. wa-hum la-hum ṭālibīn.
13. wa-nādau: "ilā ain tanjūn
14. "yā kilāb al-ʿArab
15. "wa-nahnu la-kum fī ʾṭ-ṭalab?
16. "fa-la-qad saʿaitum bi-arwāḥ-kum
17. "ilā ājāl-kum;
18. "wa-qad muttum ʿalā maut-kum
19. "wa-wabāl-kum!
20. "wa-ḍaʿū mā maʿa-kum min al-amwāl
21. "wa-ʾṭlubū li-arwāḥ-kum an-najāt
22. "qabl al-fawāt!
23. "wa-la-qad waṣal ʿalai-kum al-maut al-aḥmar,
24. "alladhī lā yubqī wa-lā yadhar."
25. thumma inna-hum ḥamalū ʿalā Banī ʿAbs ḥamla ṣādiqa.
26. qāl ar-rāwī:
27. fa-lammā naẓarat al-ʿashara min Banī ʿAbs ilā dhālika ʾl-hāl,
28. aʿannū khuyūl-hum,
29. wa-ʿtaddū bi-nuṣūl-hum
30. wa-waqafū yantaẓirūn al-qādimīn.
31. wa-lammā an waqaʿat al-ʿain ʿala ʾl-ʿain,
32. wa-taqābal kull min al-farīqain,
33. akabbat Banū ʿAbs ruʿūs-hā
34. fī qarābīs surūj-hā,
35. wa-ḥamalat mithl al-shawāhīn.
36. wa-athbatu ʾl-ajinna.[2]
37. wa-ʿamalat bain-hum al-asinna.
38. fa-sāl ad-damm wa-jarā.
39. wa-maddu ʾl-fursān ʿalā wajh ath-tharā.
40. wa-tarakū-hum li-waḥsh al-barr qirā.
41. wa-ʿind dhālika ʿamal al-battār.
42. wa-qadaḥat hawāt al-khail sharār.
43. wa-ʿamiyat al-abṣār.

44. wa-qallat al-anṣār.
45. wa-laḥiq al-jabān al-inbihār,
46. wa-ḥār.
47. wa-ṭalab al-harab wa-'l-firār.
48. wa-qaṣurat al-a'mar.
49. wa-kashafat al-astār.
50. wa-bāḥat al-abrār.
51. wa-ḍāqat al-aqṭār.
52. wa-lam yazalū 'alā hādhihi 'l-akhṭār
53. ilā niṣf an-nahār.
54. qāl ar-rāwī:
55. hādha wa-Banū Jadīla ma'a Banī 'Abs fī ḥarb wa-khiṣām wa-tajrī' al-maut ila 'ẓ-zawāl.
56. wa-lam yanalū min Banī 'Abs manāl,
57. wa-qad nafid min-hum al-māl,
58. wa-'adamu 'n-niyāq wa-'l-jimāl.
59. wa-'auwalū 'ala 'l-infilāl.
60. wa-qall 'azm-hum,
61. wa-'ajazū 'an liqā' khaṣm-him,
62. wa-talif jam'-hum.
63. fa-sāḥat Banū 'Abs 'alai-him,
64. fa-wallau min bain aidī-him ḥāribīn,
65. wa-ilā diyā-him ṭālibīn,
66. wa-hum yad'ūn bi-'l-wail wa-'th-thubūr,
67. wa-'azā'im al-umūr,
68. ba'd mā qutilat abṭāl-hum,
69. wa-ukhidhat amwāl-hum.
70. wa-sāq Banū 'Abs an-niyāq wa-'l-jimāl.
71. wa-ṭalabu 'd-diyār wa-'l-aṭlāl. (5.1:2/121–22)

1. They [the Banī 'Abs] had barely departed from the [Banī Jadīla] campsite
2. when there arose from behind them a cloud of dust,
3. that swirled up
4. and rose until it hid the countryside.
5. And the dust cloud lifted,
6. revealing the flash of chainmail,
7. and the gleam of helmets,
8. and creatures beyond number.
9. This, and behind the dust cloud—the shouts of heroes

10. and the roars of elephants.
11. They quickly overtook them,
12. for it was they whom they were seeking,
13. and they called out, "Where will you seek safety,
14. Oh Dogs of the Arabs,
15. while we seek you?
16. For you have brought yourselves[3]
17. to your appointed times of death;
18. you will have suffered death over and above your [final] death
19. and your [final] destruction!
20. Leave the animals you have taken
21. and seek safety for yourselves
22. before it is too late!
23. For to you has come Red Death
24. that spares not nor relents!"
25. Then they fiercely charged the Banī 'Abs.
26. The narrator said:
27. Then, when the ten Banī 'Abs saw this situation,
28. they reined in their horses,
29. prepared their lance-points,
30. and stood awaiting the advancers.
31. When eye fell upon eye,
32. and each of the two parties faced the other,
33. the Banī 'Abs lowered their heads
34. over the bows of their saddles,
35. and charged like falcons.
36. They steadied their shields.
37. And spear-points worked among them.
38. Then blood flowed and ran.
39. They laid low warriors over the face of the land
40. and they left them as feasts for the wild beasts of the field.
41. Then cutting blades worked.
42. And the hooves of horses struck sparks.
43. Sights were blinded.
44. And helpers were scarce.
45. Confusion overtook the coward,
46. and he wavered
47. and sought flight and escape.
48. Lives were shortened.
49. Veils were lifted.
50. The steadfast revealed themselves.

51. And quarters were close.
52. And they continued in these perils
53. until midday.
54. The narrator said:
55. Thus were the Banī Jadīla [engaged] with the Banī 'Abs in combat and contention and making Death gulp [lives] until noon.
56. They did not achieve their goal from the Banī 'Abs,
57. and their animals were lost to them,
58. and they were deprived of their camel mares and stallions,
59. and they became intent upon flight.
60. Their determination lessened,
61. and they were unable to withstand their opponents,
62. and their ranks broke.
63. Then the Banī 'Abs shouted at them,
64. and they turned before them, fleeing,
65. seeking their own lands,
66. bewailing [their] distress, destruction,
67. and the greatness of their misfortune,
68. after their heroes had been killed,
69. and their animals taken.
70. The Banī 'Abs drove the camel mares and stallions,
71. and sought out [their] lands and campsites.

This passage is cited in full because it provides—within a relatively short space—a complete rendering of the battle scene. The structure of this type of scene is fairly simple; it consists of four basic dramatic elements:

1. Attackers appear
2. Opponents respond
3. Fighting occurs
4. The fighting is resolved by one side fleeing

For the sake of brevity, I shall term these four elements Appearance, Response, Fighting, and Resolution. In this passage, Appearance consists of lines 1–25, which portray the appearance and approach of the Banī Jadīla. Response consists of lines 27–35, which describe the Banī 'Abs's reaction to the Jadīla pursuit. Fighting is composed of lines 36–53, and Resolution—in which the Jadīla flee—of lines 55–69. Lines 26 and 54 are frame elements, a dimension of the *Sīra* I shall not examine here, while lines 70–71 constitute the start of a new sequence of narrative events.

Since this is a short version of the battle scene, the number of its constituent thematic units is limited. Appearance consists of several such units. It begins with the "dust cloud" (lines 1–5), proceeds with the "description of the warriors" (lines 6–10), and ends with "challenge" (lines 11–24). The other themes contain only single units. Response consists of "the charge" (lines 25–35), Fighting of "battle description" (lines 36–53), and Resolution of "flight" (lines 55–69).

The dramatic relationships at play in the battle scene are obvious. In Appearance and Response, narrative tension arises through the antagonistic stance of the two parties. The epic often increases this tension by making the two groups very unevenly matched. In this scene, for example, the Banī Jadīla are portrayed as a great mass, while the Banī 'Abs number only ten warriors; as a rule, attackers outnumber defenders by at least ten to one. Alternatively, *Sīrat 'Antar* creates tension by having great armies clash—as when the Persians and Byzantines fight—or by having a *casus belli* of great dramatic import—as in the battles fought during the bitter internecine feud between 'Abs and Fazāra. Fighting generates its own intrinsic suspense: the audience follows the narrative while victory and defeat hang in the balance. Resolution, in turn, creates its own dramatic relief: the contest is decided when one side breaks and flees, and the matter is put to rest—temporarily or permanently.

As previously mentioned, the best way to become acquainted with the nature and range of *Sīrat 'Antar's* compositional models is to compare as many examples of single scenes as possible. In the case of the battle scene, there is certainly no lack of examples from which to choose. 'Abs and Jadīla engage in one short battle at the story's beginning and then part, never to meet again, but as the summary indicates, the battle scene appears innumerable times throughout the remainder of the epic. Unlike the lion fight scene, examining every example of the battle scene is not feasible. Rather than randomly choosing narratively unrelated examples, therefore, we shall compare the above-quoted scene with five sequential battle scenes drawn from the middle of the narrative. Examining a series of battle scenes clarifies how the *Sīra* uses scenes not only to portray narrative events but also (although on a lower level than the Heroic Cycle) to generate them as well. Here is a schematization of the first part of 'Antar's campaign of conquest in South Arabia and Africa (48.1–7:36/ 70–37/114):

I. DEPARTURE (36/70–75)

A. Cause (36/70–71)

Ghamra reminds 'Antar of his promise to help her regain her lands from the Sudanese, who have conquered them. 'Antar agrees to help her avenge her defeat immediately and recites a battle poem to hearten her.

B. Preparations for Departure (36/71–75)

'Antar orders Shaibūb to prepare for their departure the next day. Besides Ghamra and her few followers, they will take only Maisara, Ghaṣūb, Māzin, Sabī' al-Yemen, and 'Urwa ibn al-Ward and his hundred companions (approximately one hundred and fifty warriors in all). 'Antar and 'Abla say good-bye and exchange love poems. King Qais offers to bring all of 'Abs to help them, but 'Antar states that this is unnecessary. At this point, 'Antar recalls his grudge against ar-Rabī' ibn Ziyād and 'Umāra and recites a poem against them. King Qais placates 'Antar's anger.

II. TRAVEL (36/75–78)

They set out. After traveling for a time, Shaibūb suggests that they stop by Duraid ibn aṣ-Ṣimma's camp and enlist his aid, but 'Antar angrily replies that they need no one's help. Shaibūb skillfully guides them forward. Ghamra is amazed at his knowledge of the countryside, but he tells her that he remembers it from the time he was brought north as a slave while still a child. As they travel, 'Antar recalls 'Abla and recites a love poem. After traveling for some time, they come upon a pretty meadow and stop to rest for three days. Then they continue on their way.

III. ARRIVAL (36/78–80)

They approach Ghamra's former lands, which are now occupied by the Sudanese, ruled over by King Suwaidā ibn 'Uwaidā. King Suwaidā commands an army of 30,000, but is in reality just a vassal of the more powerful King Ghawwār of Sudan.

Shaibūb sets out alone to scout the camp. He returns and tells 'Antar that it is too large to attack and advises that they raid the camp's herds and thus draw pursuit out after them. 'Antar accepts this advice. He takes four men to raid the herds.

IV. BATTLE ONE (36/80)

1. 'Antar and his companions reach the herds.
2. They attack.
3. They kill two slaves and the rest surrender.
4. The 'Abs warriors drive the herds away.

V. REACTION (36/81–82)

A. Reaction One

1. Those herders who escape report ʻAntar's raid to King Suwaidā.
2. The king is furious.
3. He gathers his troops.
4. He sends his cousin Maimūn ibn Raḥmūn with 5,000 men to pursue ʻAntar.

VI. BATTLE TWO (36/81–84)

1. Maimūn overtakes ʻAntar and charges.
2. ʻAntar takes Maisara and Ghaṣūb and charges in turn.
3. Fighting (description).
4. ʻAntar recites a battle poem.
5. Ghaṣūb fights Maimūn and captures him.
6. The fighting continues until nightfall, when the Sudanese break ranks and flee.

VII. REACTION (36/85–89)

A. Reaction One

1. The Sudanese return and tell Suwaidā of their defeat; of 5,000 men, ʻAntar and his two sons have killed 1,500 and wounded 1,500.
2. The king is both incredulous and furious.
3. He gathers his troops.
4. He sends his cousin Ṣāʻiqa ibn ʻAlqam with 10,000 men to pursue the raiders.

B. Reaction Two

1. ʻAntar and his companions rejoin Ghamra and the others with their plunder.
2. ʻAntar wants to attack the camp itself, but Shaibūb again convinces him that drawing the enemy out of camp is still the better strategy.

VIII. BATTLE THREE (36/90–92)

1. Ṣāʻiqa and his men appear.

2. ʿAntar takes nine men to fight them.
3. Ṣāʿiqa is astonished that such a little group dares to face him. He sends 1,000 of his men to fight them.
4. ʿAntar and his men rout the 1,000 enemy soldiers (description of the fighting).
5. Ṣāʿiqa and all his men charge.
6. Fighting (description).
7. ʿAntar fights Ṣāʿiqa in battle and kills him.
8. Fighting continues until nightfall, when the Sudanese break ranks and flee.

IX. REACTION (36/92–37/103)

A. Reaction One

1. The Sudanese return and tell Suwaidā of their defeat; 1,500 of them have been killed.
2. The king is furious.
3. He gathers his troops.
4. His cousin Manīʿ ibn Munāʿ arrives for a visit. Manīʿ is a great warrior and offers to take 10,000 men after ʿAntar. Suwaidā accepts this offer.

B. Reaction Two

1. ʿAntar and his men rest.
2. ʿAntar asks Ghamra how Suwaidā managed to capture her lands with a mere 30,000 men. She replies that she was sick with worry over Ghaṣūb at the time, so she did not concentrate on resisting. Besides, King Ghawwār helped Suwaidā in the conquest.
3. Maimūn, still a captive, declares his willingness to join ʿAntar's side. Ghamra's father once gave him refuge. ʿAntar and Shaibūb trust his sincerity and free him, with the agreement that Maimūn will convince his followers to turn against Suwaidā in the midst of battle.

X. BATTLE FOUR (37/103–6)

1. Manīʿ ibn Munāʿ and his men appear.
2. ʿAntar takes 100 men to fight him.
3. It is close to nightfall, so both sides camp for the night. The next morning they draw battle lines.
4. Manīʿ enters the field for single combat and recites a battle poem.

5. ʿAntar comes out to fight him. He too recites a battle poem.
6. ʿAntar kills Manīʿ in single combat.
7. General battle ensues (description).
8. The Sudanese eventually break ranks and flee.

XI. REACTION (37/106–8)

A. Reaction One

1. The Sudanese return and tell Suwaidā of their defeat.
2. The king is furious.
3. He gathers his troops and decides to lead them.
4. He recites a battle poem.

B. Reaction Two

1. ʿAntar and his companions rest.

XII. BATTLE FIVE (37/108–14)

1. Suwaidā and his men appear.
2. It is close to nightfall, so both sides camp for the night. The next morning they draw battle lines.
3. Fighting begins (description).
4. ʿAntar fights Suwaidā in the midst of battle and captures him.
5. Both sides continue fighting until nightfall; the next day fighting continues until the Sudanese break ranks and flee.

XIII. DEPARTURE (37/114)

ʿAntar and Ghamra decide to attack King Ghawwār, but before doing so they attack the neighboring King Laun aẓ-Ẓalām so that their rear is secure when they enter Sudan.

The guiding impetus for ʿAntar's campaign into Yemen and Africa stems from the story pattern of Heroic Service. King Suwaidā, a vassal of the king of Sudan, has driven Queen Ghamra from her kingdom; ʿAntar promises to help her recover it (44.7). Initially, he is too busy to fulfill this promise (44.7–48), but when a moment's peace finally arrives, he eagerly embarks on a new series of battles on Ghamra's behalf, one of the longer conglomerations of episodes in the narrative (48).

Since 'Antar leaves 'Abs for several hundred pages, the *Sīra* begins by momentarily reviving thematic concerns central to the hero's relationship to the tribe. 'Antar and 'Abla bid one another farewell and pledge their love by reciting love poems. 'Antar then says good-bye to his liege, King Qais. The 'Abs king offers to assemble his warriors and accompany him. 'Antar, not wishing to trouble his overlord with his own affairs, declines this offer. In the midst of their interview, however, the hero recalls the ill deeds of the Ziyād clan against himself and recites a poem against them.

With these proceedings, the *Sīra* renews our awareness of important concerns of 'Antar's Heroic Cycle that it must leave untreated for the next few hundred pages. It touches upon 'Antar's Love Story (the scene with 'Abla and 'Antar's rivalry with 'Umāra ibn Ziyād), his Rise of the Hero story pattern (the enmity between 'Antar and ar-Rabīʿ ibn Ziyād), and his primary obligations of Heroic Service (to the ruler of his tribe, King Qais). As they travel, further aspects of 'Antar's Heroic Cycle are touched upon. The hero so burns with love for 'Abla that he bursts into poetry. Shaibūb's suggestion that they stop by Duraid ibn aṣ-Ṣimma's camp to engage his aid allows 'Antar an opportunity to reaffirm his heroic independence by angrily rejecting this idea—not out of ill will toward Duraid (both he and Duraid are great heroes, bound by mutual ties of heroic respect and admiration), but because seeking anyone's help is a breach of heroic honor. 'Antar naturally refuses to consider such an idea.

As is typical in travel scenes, 'Antar falls into the background and Shaibūb comes to the fore. It is Shaibūb who guides the group to Yemen; once there, it is he who scouts the enemy camp. Shaibūb also conceives of the group's battle strategy, and for once his practicality overcomes 'Antar's heroic impetuosity. Instead of attacking a camp of 30,000 warriors head on, as 'Antar urges, Shaibūb convinces his brother to raid the camp's herds and thus draw out a series of smaller bodies of pursuers.

We should notice here that just as the *Sīra* touches on ongoing narrative concerns that must lie fallow for a time, it also foreshadows future events. During the journey to Yemen, Queen Ghamra marvels over Shaibūb's knowledge of the countryside, and he explains to her that he remembers it from the time he was first brought north into slavery as a child. Shaibūb's ability to recollect the days of his early childhood becomes important at a future point when he meets long-lost relatives (48.17).

Turning to the battle scenes outlined above, we can see that all five are organized according to the four dramatic elements extrapolated from our first battle scene: Appearance, Response, Fighting, and Resolution. However, each battle also has individual traits. Battle one is short, encompassing only a few lines of text; 'Antar has a chance to kill only two slaves before the other herders surrender and cry for mercy. This battle functions less as a dramatic confrontation than as a precipitator of future confrontations.

Battle two is longer. It contains a battle poem by 'Antar and a short description of combat between Ghaṣūb and Maimūn. As noted, in *Sīrat 'Antar* attackers usually outnumber defenders at least ten to one. In this and the next battle, 'Antar and his companions are outnumbered a thousand to one.

Battle three has two parts. Suwaidā sends his cousin Ṣā'iqa against 'Antar. When Ṣā'iqa sees that only ten men oppose him, he sends a contingent of a thousand warriors to attack them. Only after their defeat does Ṣā'iqa attack with full force. This battle thus conflates elements of two battle scenes. There is only one Appearance and Response, but two-staged Fighting and Resolution.

In the fourth battle, fighting becomes more organized. Instead of impetuous pursuit and attack, warfare becomes structured. The two parties meet in the evening but wait until dawn to fight. They draw up organized lines of battle, and fighting begins with a bout of single combat between 'Antar and Manī' ibn Munā'. Single combat has its own ritualistic structure in *Sīrat 'Antar*. Typically, a warrior emerges from the battle line, recites a battle poem of self-praise, and issues a challenge to the enemy. An opponent emerges from the opposite line and responds with a poem of his own. Thereafter, the two fight. After one is captured or killed, the victor issues a new challenge and fights a new opponent or general battle ensues until one side is defeated or night falls and the two armies withdraw to rest. In the single combat of the fourth battle, 'Antar kills Manī' and routs his army in the ensuing battle.

In the final battle, between 'Antar and Suwaidā himself, aspects of the previous battle are repeated. Again the two groups first meet at nightfall and camp until morning before fighting. Again organized battle lines are drawn, but this time there is no structured single combat. Instead, 'Antar fights and captures Suwaidā in the midst of battle. Fighting continues, and by nightfall the Sudanese break and flee. With the war against Suwaidā completed, 'Antar kills the captured king in a fit of rage.

Interlinking the battle scenes are scenes of reaction. These customarily have two parts. On the one hand, news of his troop's defeat is brought to the enemy king, who first falls into a rage, then gathers his troops and prepares for a new battle. In the victor's camp, on the other hand, reaction consists of rest and consultation. Reaction is an optional but useful extension of the battle scene. It provides a moment of dramatic relief between the climaxes of battle and offers an arena for narrative transition. Details from the previous scene can be cleared up and put to rest, while the stage is set for the battles to come. This scene also gives the *Sīra* an opportunity to depict varied reactions to events within a single camp. Heroes are praised for their deeds in the day's battle, questions of strategy are argued, and new narrative lines—such as Maimūn's change of sides after the fourth battle—are introduced and developed.

THEMATIC UNITS AND TRADITIONAL PHRASES

Limitations of space prevent detailed examination of the thematic units and traditional phrases of the battle scene. This aspect of compositional structure should not be completely neglected, however. Let us look at the epic's varied use of two closely related thematic units within the compass of the battle scenes presented so far. The above-quoted 'Abs-Jadīla battle scene begins with the "dust cloud" description, immediately followed by "description of the warriors" (lines 1–10). These two thematic units also occur several times in the 'Antar-Suwaidā war, the first time being at the beginning of battle two when *Sīrat 'Antar* describes how Maimūn pursues and overtakes the 'Abs warriors:

> wa-idhā bi-'l-ghubār min khalf-hi wa-qad thār wa-sadd al-audiya wa-'l-qifār wa-aqbalat abṭāl as-Sūdān ka-anna-hum maradat al-jānn. . . . (36/80–81)
>
> And suddenly dust appeared behind him ['Antar] and swirled up and blocked the gullies and plains. And the heroes of Sudan advanced as if they were malevolent jinn. . . .

The second appearance of these thematic units also occurs in the context of pursuit, this time when Ṣā'iqa and his men overtake 'Antar and his companions at the beginning of battle three:

> wa-ṭala' 'alai-him min ṣadr al-barr ghubār wa-'alā ḥattā mala' al-aqṭār wa-fī dūn sā'a zālat al-ghibra wa-'nkashaf li-'l-fatra wa-bān min taḥt-hā barīq az-zarad wa-lamī' al-khuwad wa-rijāl ma li-kathrat-ha 'adad wa-Sudān. . . . (36/89)
>
> And there arose toward them from the heart of the land a dust cloud. And it rose up and filled the countryside. And in a short time the dust cloud dissipated and lifted for a while and revealed beneath it the flash of chainmail and the gleam of helmets and men—Sudanese—beyond number. . . .

These two examples share the same function as the corresponding thematic units at the beginning of the 'Abs-Jadīla battle scene: they represent withdrawing raiders' first sight of pursuit. This is a dramatically effective way of initiating a battle scene since narrative suspense builds as the *Sīra* introduces and describes the enemy's advance. Sometimes, however, thematic units appear even though there is no dramatic reason for them. Usually these are associative vestiges; we sense they are not needed, but that the storyteller felt that they belonged to the scene.[4] In battle four, for example, the *Sīra* does not use the "dust cloud" to introduce the pursuers. The epic describes how Manīʿ ibn Munāʿ and his men set out from camp after ʿAntar, then describes their progress until they overlook the ʿAbs tents. But the *Sīra* still manages to include the "dust cloud." Leaving Manīʿ overlooking the ʿAbs camp, it continues:

> wa-kān ʿAntar lammā abṣar ghubār as-Sūdān wa-qad ʿalā wa-ṭabaq al-arḍ wa-ʾl-falā rakab ilā liqāʾ-hum. . . . (37/104)
>
> When ʿAntar sighted the dust cloud of the Sudanese, which had risen and covered the ground and desert, he rode to meet them. . . .

It would have sufficed to state that ʿAntar rode to meet the enemy when they appeared; but a passing mention of the dust cloud was inserted, even though it fulfills no dramatic function. These thematic units, by the way, are not connected with the idea of pursuit as such; rather, they represent the idea of dramatic arrival. They are used for Manīʿ ibn Munāʿ's arrival at King Suwaidā's camp in the third reaction scene:

> wa-idhā bi-ghubār qad namā wa-ʿalā wa-thār ḥattā malaʾ ar-rawābī wa-ʾl-aqṭar sāʿa wa-ʾnkashaf ʿan abṭāl mithl al-usūd al-kawāsir. . . . (36/94)
>
> Suddenly a dust cloud appeared which grew and rose and swirled up until it filled the hills and countryside a while. And it lifted [to reveal] heroes like ferocious lions. . . .

Arrival, whether of friend or foe, is best portrayed as an exciting event. The "dust cloud" and other concomitant thematic units are one major way the *Sīra* creates this excitement.[5]

These examples suggest once again how thematic units may vary in length. None of the examples from the ʿAntar-Suwaidā war are more than half the length of those of the ʿAbs-Jadīla battle scene; indeed, the one portraying Manīʿ ibn Munāʿ's arrival at Suwaidā's camp is reduced to a single sentence. Diversity in lexical expression also occurs. The *Sīra* uses various words to express the rise of the dust cloud (*ṭalaʿ*, *thār*, *ʿalā*), to describe how it spreads across the countryside, and to denote the countryside itself (*al-aqṭār*, *al-audiya wa-ʾl-qifār*, *al-arḍ wa-ʾl-falā*, *ar-rawābī wa-ʾl-aqṭār*). In two examples, almost identical phrases are used to connote advancing warriors (*barīq az-zarad* [the flash of chainmail], etc.) of the ʿAbs-Jadīla battle and of Ṣāʿiqa's appearance in battle three. Other examples, however, differ. In one case the warriors are likened to malevolent jinn, in another to ferocious lions, and in a third (Manīʿ's arrival at ʿAntar's camp) the thematic unit is omitted. Moreover, although generally employed in battle scenes, these units are not essential to them, failing to occur, for instance, in the fifth and last battle scene of the ʿAntar-Suwaidā war. Despite their diversity in length, wording, dramatic function, and point of occurrence, the basic equivalence of these examples is clear; similarities of idea and expression among them are too great to be considered coincidence.[6]

Sīrat 'Antar uses five battle scenes in its portrayal of the 'Antar-Suwaidā war. As 'Antar and his companions continue their campaign south, the battles continue, once in 'Antar's war with King Laun aẓ-Ẓalām (48.8), four times in his first campaign against King Ghawwār (48.9–13), once in his war with al-Khātif (48.13), once in his second encounter with Ghawwār (48.14–16), and twice in his war with the Abyssinian negus (48.20–21)—and this is just 'Antar's Yemen-Africa campaign!

The extent to which *Sīrat 'Antar* repeatedly relies on a few compositional models to portray its narrative events becomes apparent here. Whenever a confrontation occurs, the epic has a well-developed repertoire of themes, thematic units, and traditional phrases to depict the resultant battle. Moreover, the *Sīra* can use the same set of dramatic elements that constitute the ideational structure of its battle scenes—Appearance, Response, Fighting, and Resolution—to structure the frequent instances of single combat that appear in its battles simply by endowing them with a different set of traditional phrases, thematic units, and themes.[7] On a much higher level, many of the major campaigns of the *Sīra*, including 'Antar's Yemen-Africa campaign, are just repetitions of this structure. 'Antar travels south and meets the enemy (Appearance), they respond to his incursion (Response), battles occur (Fighting), and the battles are decided (Resolution).

At this point, we perceive how the *Sīra* uses its compositional models not only to portray events but to generate them. It does this through repetition. Instead of having one battle decide a conflict, it uses half a dozen. Simultaneously, to prevent repeated scenes from becoming monotonous, the *Sīra* structures them hierarchically. Increasingly larger armies join in battle, and increasingly powerful and highly ranked rulers become involved as opponents and allies. When one king is defeated, his mightier liege stands waiting to take his place on the field of battle.[8] In this way *Sīrat 'Antar* uses its compositional models to transform a heroic story into a heroic cycle. Instead of one decisive battle between 'Antar and King Suwaidā, a series of five battles is offered. Instead of 'Antar's campaign in the south ending with his victory over Suwaidā, it becomes the first of a series of wars. New enemies appear, new battles must be fought, and the story continues.

NARRATIVE TECHNIQUE: POINT OF VIEW

Sīrat 'Antar, like all fiction, is a feat of rhetorical magic. Offering a fictional world as a replica of the world of empirical existence, the *Sīra*—with our compliance—draws us into and conducts us through its narrative cosmos. If the illusion is complete, we exist as free-moving witnesses, observers from Olympus. Nonetheless, this sense of divine omniscience is in reality a fata morgana; the *Sīra* constantly directs our attention, controls our reactions, and manipulates our sympathies—often in quite subtle ways. Primary among the narrative techniques that the epic employs to accomplish this task is direction of narrative point of view. To apprehend the extent, the nature, and the purpose of the *Sīra*'s use of this particular narrative technique, let us reexamine the previously quoted battle scene between the Banī ʿAbs and the Banī Jadīla.

The battle scene falls into four main parts. Lines 1–25 describe the appearance of the Banī Jadīla, lines 27–35 describe the Banī ʿAbs's reaction to this event, lines 36–53 describe the battle between the two groups, and lines 55–69 portray the Banī Jadīla's loss of courage and resolution and their flight. Each sequence entails a major shift of narrative perspective, although modulations of the *Sīra*'s direction of point of view occur throughout the text.

At the passage's beginning, we are objective observers. Having just seen how the Banī ʿAbs raided the Banī Jadīla herds, we now watch as they hurry homeward with their booty. In line 2, however, with the introduction of the dust cloud thematic unit, a change in point of view begins. The *Sīra* states that the dust cloud appears behind "them" (the Banī ʿAbs). Ostensibly our third-person objective point of view is maintained; but as the description of the dust cloud proceeds, objectivity begins to dissolve—increasingly our viewpoint merges with that of the Banī ʿAbs. By the time the dust cloud has risen, swirled, blocked the horizon, and begun to lift, our viewpoint has coalesced with theirs, and our curiosity and premonition about what the dust cloud is hiding are projected onto the ten ʿAbs raiders. Quite literally, we feel anxious *for* them.

Reason tells us that the dust cloud portends the approach of pursuing Banī Jadīla; but to create narrative suspense, *Sīrat ʿAntar* does not tell us who the approaching warriors are; not until the end of battle, when the attackers are put to flight, does it expressly name the Jadīla. So as not to dispel our curiosity too quickly, we are only told what the dust cloud hides by stages. At first, only partial glimpses are offered: the flash of chainmail, the glint of helmets, the gradually growing impression of an indistinct mass of creatures. Throughout this disclosure our viewpoint is that of the Banī ʿAbs.

Up to this point (line 8), narrative description has been purely visual. But now, as a further indication that the attackers are drawing increasingly near, sound is introduced (lines 9–10): first the indistinguishable cries of warriors, then (lines 13–14) the clear voice of challenge. If the mass of the approaching riders is threatening, their challenge is positively ominous; almost every line repeats the promise of death and destruction. At the end of their speech, the attackers identify themselves not as the Banī Jadīla, but as Red Death (lines 23–24).

Having aroused our anxiety and involvement by letting us identify with the Banī ʿAbs as they behold the approach of pursuers, the *Sīra* ends the sequence by switching back to third-person narrative (line 25). Once again we become objective observers standing outside the ʿAbs viewpoint. This shift serves two purposes. First, it relieves the tension built up by identifying with the ʿAbs as they watched the approaching attackers. More importantly, by separating us from the Banī ʿAbs again, the epic is able to impress us with their calm and brave reaction to the threat. They (unlike us?) do not consider flight. Instead they stop their horses, secure their arms, await the onrush of the attackers, then charge themselves (lines 27–35).

It is of significance here that although we witness the ʿAbs reaction from an objective viewpoint, it is not a neutral viewpoint. The *Sīra* maintains our identification with the Banī ʿAbs by keeping us in close visual contact with them. The Banī Jadīla are described from a distance: they are an indistinguishable mass, half-merged with the countryside, hurtling toward us in our consciousness, while the Banī ʿAbs are treated at close quarters: their actions (fixing their lance-points, bending down in their saddles as they charge) are clear and distinct. While the attackers are presented as massed together, vociferous, and threatening, the Banī ʿAbs are calm and self-assured. Confronted with the contrast of the distant, unidentified, and threatening attackers and the near, familiar, and steadfast Banī ʿAbs, there is no doubt about our sympathies. Are we not made to feel somewhere deep in our consciousness that the Banī ʿAbs are protecting us with their countercharge? Indeed, are we not viewing the action from behind the ʿAbs lines? By such subtle handling of point of view *Sīrat ʿAntar* ensures our allegiance to its preferred party during the battle scenes.

Here again the consistency of the epic's descriptive modes becomes apparent. The Banī Jadīla obviously harbor hostile intentions toward the Banī ʿAbs; their battle cry makes this abundantly clear; but even without this cry or any familiarity with previous events, their hostility is obvious. Portrayed as a dark, swiftly moving cloud on the horizon, approaching with flashes of light and indistinct roaring noises, what are the Banī Jadīla but the equivalent of an oncoming thundercloud? And thunderclouds bring storms.

Lines 36–40 portray the collision of the two groups and its effects. In terms of narrative viewpoint, we still view the action at close quarters and still favor the Banī ʿAbs. For example, the subjects of the verbs of lines 39–40 are unidentified, but are we not certain that it is the Banī ʿAbs who are laying their opponents on the field of battle and not the other way around? The whole psychology of the passage leads us to expect this to be the case.

As the battle proceeds (line 41 on), the narrative point of view loses its focus. There is no longer any "us" and "them"—there is only the tumult of battle. Simultaneously, description becomes less empirical and specific and more emotive and generalized. The details and images in the *Sīra* do not describe a sequence of action in the battle; rather, they play upon our anxieties concerning violent confrontations, connoting physical danger. Sharp blades and sparking hooves are deadly—especially when conjoined with loss of sight (41–44); room for movement is scarce (51); people die (48). In this situation true natures are revealed (49); will a warrior be steadfast (50) or succumb to fear (45–47)? The epic evokes these anxieties through generalized, psychologically directed description. It matters little whose cutting blades are at work, which horses' hooves are striking sparks, or whose sight is blinded. The cowards who fled are not identified, nor the steadfast who remained.

By placing its battle description on this abstract, generalized level, the *Sīra* induces our imagination to supply all of the details of the physical jostling and turmoil and the mental confusion and anxiety of battle. In this way, we mentally experience the fighting rather than merely visualizing it. The battle theme ends, however, by returning to third-person objectivity; by using the third-person plural of the verb in line 52, the narrative draws us out of the battle scene by emphasizing that it is "they" who are fighting, not us. The reference to time at this point reinforces this return to objectivity—as references to time do throughout the passage.

We emerge from the battle with the Banī Jadīla. It is they who are first mentioned when the contestants are once again individualized (line 55) and are the subjects of most of the sentences that follow (56–69). The Jadīla are destined to lose the battle, but it is interesting to see how *Sīrat 'Antar* portrays their flight. While their attack is presented in terms of action and force (swift movement, flashes and gleams of light, loud noises, ominous threats), their flight is the result of a diminishing and finally a loss of these characteristics. The *Sīra* does mention loss of life (line 66), but determination is the chief casualty the Banī Jadīla suffer. The latter lines of the passage consist of repeated negative phrases (56: "did not achieve their goal"; 57: "their animals were lost"; 58: "they were deprived"; 59: "they became intent on flight," etc.). Conversely, in the one line in this sequence in which they are the subjects, the Banī 'Abs act positively and aggressively. Their shout (line 63) causes the Banī Jadīla finally to turn and flee (notice the similarity of this exchange of shouts—Jadīla's challenge in lines 13–24 and the 'Abs shout of line 63—and the exchange of roars in the lion fight; see chapter 7). In one sense, this battle is less a conflict of agents than a reversal of energy. The Banī Jadīla appear moving swiftly, packed together, aggressive, and threatening; they depart vanquished, straggling, and full of cries of woe. After their departure, we remain alone again with the Banī 'Abs, who—after this brief interruption—continue their journey homeward (lines 70–71). They may have been in danger of losing their spoils, but they were never in danger of losing their central position in our narrative frame.

Manipulation of point of view is thus a crucial element in *Sīrat ʿAntar*'s narrative technique. Since such a large part of the epic consists of battle scenes, it is of some consequence that we sympathize with the correct side. But how can the *Sīra* ensure that we indeed do so? The narrative advocates no firm ethical structure: ideals of absolute right and wrong do not exist in it. As we saw in the discussion of superimposition in chapter 6, the same story patterns govern and motivate the actions of all of the epic's characters—friend and foe alike. Nor can the *Sīra* rely on narrative portrayal to differentiate between its protagonists and antagonists, since it uses the same traditional phrases and thematic units to describe all warriors and the same types of scenes to portray all their moments of conflict. When contestants are described in the same terms and do the same things in the same way for the same reasons, there is little reason why the audience should favor one side over the other in the *Sīra*'s continuous chain of battles.

This is clearly a delicate situation. Battles are the main way the epic creates and resolves narrative suspense; they are the moments of climax in its episodes. For the audience to become indifferent about the outcome of these battles would be a disastrous turn of events. To counter this, *Sīrat ʿAntar* relies on a number of ploys. One of these is narrative habit. All things being equal, we may be counted upon to sympathize with familiar characters against unfamiliar characters. But this ploy is not always applicable; the ʿAbs-Jadīla conflict, for example, occurs at the *Sīra*'s beginning; since both groups have just been introduced there is no real reason to favor one over the other.[9]

Another standard ploy is to make contesting sides numerically highly uneven, so that ʿAntar is sometimes outnumbered a thousand to one. This ploy can clarify cloudy or even adverse ethical situations. From a strictly ethical viewpoint, it is the ten ʿAbs warriors who are the aggressors in the ʿAbs-Jadīla conflict; it is the ʿAbs who attack Jadīla's camp, kill their slaves, and steal their animals. By rights we should sympathize with Jadīla rather than ʿAbs. Nevertheless, because the conflict is presented in terms of a large group attacking a small one, it is easy to sympathize with ʿAbs.

Even considering the numerical proportions involved, however, we would not sympathize with ʿAbs if the *Sīra* did not use its subtlest and most effective manipulative tool—point of view—in their favor. In literature we are prisoners of what we are allowed to see and how we are allowed to see it. If *Sīrat ʿAntar* had consistently presented events from the viewpoint of the Banī Jadīla, they would have won our sympathy; since we see events from the ʿAbs viewpoint, they become the episode's protagonists.

COMPOSITIONAL STRUCTURE AND NARRATIVE INVENTION: 'ANTAR'S HANGING OF HIS *MU'ALLAQA* POEM

We have seen that *Sīrat 'Antar* relies on compositional models to formulate and structure many aspects of its narrative. Moreover, the epic uses these models not only to portray events but often to generate them as well. Nevertheless, models have limits. Although they can provide a large measure of linguistic and structural infrastructure, they also imply parameters, in regard to both the types of events presented and how they are portrayed. The easiest way to illustrate this point is to look at an example.

One of the integral parts of the legend of 'Antar is the hero's hanging of his *mu'allaqa* ode (*qaṣīda*) on the walls of the Ka'ba in Mecca; any expression of the 'Antar legend must devote attention to this event.[10] *Sīrat 'Antar* is so filled with poetry that we might suppose that portraying this particular part of 'Antar's career would present little problem, but this is not the case. Recitation of poetry is not a dynamic narrative event in the *Sīra*; on the contrary, poetry serves mainly static functions. The *Sīra* uses verse for two narrative purposes: generalized description (objective poetry) and personal expression (subjective poetry). Examples of the first type are the short pieces of descriptive verse that are optional thematic units in the lion description. Such verse may be inserted into the description of any remarkable phenomenon, such as a beautiful woman, a fierce warrior, an exceptional horse or weapon, or a verdant meadow. An alternate use of descriptive poetry in the *Sīra* is to express generalized, gnomic sentiments, such as the pain of love, the dangers of familial duplicity or tribal dissension, or the usefulness of wealth. As a whole, the epic's descriptive poetry is diverse in topic but uniform in form, manner of presentation, and narrative function. The poems are short (rarely longer than ten lines, often only three or four lines); they are almost always presented as anonymous, typically being introduced by the phrase "it was as the poet said"; and they serve the function of generalizing and widening the frame of descriptive reference so that the object or event described moves from the realm of the individual to the realm of the proverbial.[11]

In contrast to descriptive poetry, which occurs relatively infrequently, subjective poetry is extremely common in *Sīrat Antar*. The narrative puts many poems into its characters' mouths to express personal sentiments. This type of poetry accords well with the concept of poetry as an expression of "a spontaneous overflow of powerful feeling."[12] Poetry ensues from the poet's suffering a state of heightened emotional tumult that demands immediate expression. 'Antar recites love poems when he is overwhelmed by passion, battle poems in the heat of battle, and elegies in the sorrow of funeral scenes. Although the *Sīra* has little interest in exploring the potential psychological complexities of its characters in the realm of narrative action, usually portraying internal states by means of objective description or comment, subjective poetry enables it to express characters' individual emotions and thoughts. These verses are thus the *Sīra*'s equivalent of monologues; they allow characters to assume greater individuality for the audience. The plight of an unhappy lover becomes more touching and he or she more real and sympathetic when a love poem is recited. In battle, a previously unknown warrior gains individuality by reciting a poem of heroic self-praise.

Despite this personalizing function, these poems remain conventional in language and idea. In general, they fall into four categories: love poems, battle poems (poems of heroic self-praise), panegyrics, and elegies (the first two types are much more prevalent than the second two).[13]

The *Sīra*'s poetry adds to narrative tone and atmosphere, but it is not essential to the story. Removing it would reduce the epic's charm but not unduly disturb its narrative continuity. This is because *Sīrat 'Antar* uses poetry for rhetorical or dramatic purposes. In essence, poems are thematic units.

Descriptive poems are an optional part of the *Sīra*'s descriptive themes, while the four categories of personal poems only appear in set situations: love poems in moments of union (love scenes or weddings) or—in the form of love laments—in moments of separation (travel scenes or feasts), battle poems in scenes of conflict (battle, single combat, lion fights), panegyrics during feast scenes, elegies during funerals. Poetry is extremely common, but largely ornamental, exerting little influence on the course of narrative events.[14]

This situation creates a problem when *Sīrat 'Antar* relates how 'Antar hung his *mu'allaqa* poem on the Ka'ba. The recitation of the poem is easy enough to portray. It would be possible to have 'Antar travel to Mecca, become inspired, recite his poem, and so impress his audience that they insist that he hang it upon the Ka'ba's walls. To portray the event in this way, however, would rob a central event of the 'Antar legend of much of its drama. One of the great feats of 'Antar's life would be reduced to an episode of a few pages. To magnify and dramatize this event, therefore, to transform it into a good story, the *Sīra* falls back on its preexistent web of narrative patterns and structures: the story patterns of the Heroic Cycle and the prestructured scenes of its compositional models.

'Antar's recitation of his *mu'allaqa* poem therefore becomes an event of heroic struggle, part of his Rise of the Hero story pattern. When he announces his intention to hang his poem, he meets violent opposition from the members of the South Arabian tribes present. Their opposition does not stem from poetic or aesthetic criteria; it is social and political. A black former slave cannot be awarded such an honor, and his North Arabian compatriots are not going to be allowed to foist him on the community as a whole. In order to portray this struggle, the *Sīra* turns to its basic structures of narrative portrayal: its compositional models. Let us examine the portrayal of this episode in more detail.

As may be seen from the summary (appendix I, 44ff.), 'Antar decides to compose his *mu'allaqa* poem in response to 'Umāra ibn Ziyād's taunts about his lack of poetic ability. While 'Antar's friends encourage him, his enemies within 'Abs gloat over what they presume will be an ignominious setback for the black hero, for they know that the other six *mu'allaqa* poets and the South Arabian tribes in general will bitterly oppose 'Antar in this matter. This premonition proves to be correct; when 'Antar announces his intention in Mecca, a riot ensues, even though he has obtained the support of the highly respected 'Abd al-Muṭṭalib, chief of Mecca's prestigious Hashimite clan and the unborn Prophet Muḥammad's grandfather. Warriors divide over the issue according to tribal affiliation, with the North Arabian ('Adnānī) tribes supporting 'Antar ('Abs being a North Arabian tribe) and the South Arabian (Qaḥṭānī) tribes opposing him.[15]

There is only one way to resolve such conflicts in *Sīrat 'Antar*. Battle lines are drawn, and 'Antar emerges onto the field of single combat to defend his poetic ability through force of arms. Subsequent events are as follows (44.4: 34/320–76).

1. 'Antar challenges the Qaḥṭānīs to single combat. He recites a battle poem. 'Amr ibn al-Akhyāl, whose father 'Antar has killed, emerges to face him. The two fight, and 'Antar kills 'Amr. (34/320–21)

2. Mālik ibn 'Amr ibn Darma al-Qainī, whose father 'Antar has killed, emerges. They fight, and 'Antar kills him. (34/322)

3. 'Antar recites a battle poem. 'Āyid ibn Ḥassān ibn Muṣād al-Kalbī emerges. They fight, and 'Antar kills him. (34/323–24)

4. Ṭāriqa ibn Sāriq of the Banī Bāriq emerges and recites a battle poem. 'Antar replies with a poem. They fight, and 'Antar kills him. (34/324–25)

5. 'Antar continues fighting and killing or capturing opponents until noon. Then he pauses to change his horse. His friends congratulate him and offer to fight for him, but he refuses their offer and returns to the battlefield. (34/325)

6. 'Antar challenges the Qaḥṭānīs and recites a battle poem. Ṭarafa ibn al-'Abd, one of the six poets already honored by having a poem chosen to be a *mu'allaqa*, emerges to face 'Antar and asks to hear another sample of his poetry. 'Antar bids him to recite something first, so Ṭarafa recites his *mu'allaqa* poem and challenges 'Antar to equal it. The black hero refuses to compete against a precomposed masterpiece and asks Ṭarafa to extemporize. He does so, and 'Antar answers. Ṭarafa admires 'Antar's poem and tells him that if his mother had been Arab he would willingly have supported his claim to hang a *mu'allaqa* poem. The two fight, and 'Antar captures Ṭarafa. (34/326–36)

7. Another *muʿallaqa* poet, Zuhair ibn Abī Sulmā, emerges to fight ʿAntar. He too recites his *muʿallaqa* poem and bids ʿAntar to match it. ʿAntar admires the poem but asserts that his *muʿallaqa* poem will surpass it. They fight, and ʿAntar captures Zuhair. (34/337–41)

8. A third *muʿallaqa* poet, Labīd ibn Rabīʿa, emerges and recites his *muʿallaqa* poem. They fight, and ʿAntar captures him. (34/341–46)

9. Amr ibn Kulthūm emerges and recites his *muʿallaqa* poem. ʿAntar asks him to improvise. Amr does so, and ʿAntar answers. Amr admires ʿAntar's poem but insists on combat, so ʿAntar fights and captures him. (34/346–54)

10. ʿAntar continues killing or capturing opponents until nightfall. ʿAbla and the ʿAbs women praise his deeds. In the morning, ʿAntar reemerges onto the battlefield. Hānī ibn Masʿūd offers to fight in his place, but ʿAntar declines his offer. (34/354–57)

11. ʿAntar challenges the Qaḥṭānīs and recites a battle poem. That day, he kills 150 opponents. Finally, the Qaḥṭānīs charge en masse. The ʿAdnānīs charge to help ʿAntar. As night falls, the battle is still unresolved, so the two sides fight all night. (34/357–60)

12. The next morning, ʿAbd al-Muṭṭalib manages to separate the two sides by placing idols between them. The two sides agree that twenty additional warriors will confront ʿAntar. If he defeats them, he will be allowed to hang his poem. (34/360–61)

13. ʿAntar emerges for single combat and recites a battle poem. A famed long-lived warrior, Hijām ibn Qitām (180 years old), faces him. The two fight, and ʿAntar captures him. (34/361–63)

14. Hijām's cousin ʿĀmir comes out, and ʿAntar fights and captures him too. (34/364)

15. ʿAntar recites a battle poem. Hijām's son Zaid emerges and also recites a battle poem. The two fight, and ʿAntar kills him. (34/364)

16. Qāhir ibn Hilāl emerges to fight ʿAntar. ʿAntar fights and captures him. (34/365)

17. An unnamed warrior emerges. ʿAntar captures him. (34/365)

18. Night falls, and ʿAntar withdraws to rest. ʿAbla decides to dress as a man the next day so she can see ʿAntar's deeds in person. The Qaḥṭānīs complain among themselves about their defeats. (34/366)

19. Morning comes, and ʿAntar takes the field. An old, never defeated warrior, al-Mirqāl, emerges to fight him. ʿAntar fights and captures him. (34/367)

20. ʿAntar continues to meet opponents in single combat until nightfall, killing or capturing forty more warriors. (34/367)

21. Night comes; ʿAntar withdraws for the night; ʿAbla praises him. (34/368)

22. The next morning, ʿAntar takes the field and recites a battle poem. A warrior named Jarīr ibn al-Ghūl emerges to face him. ʿAntar fights and captures him. (34/368–69)

23. ʿAntar recites a battle poem. Rabīʿa ibn as-Sakrān attempts to defeat him. ʿAntar captures him. (34/369–70)

24. Night falls, and ʿAntar rests. ʿAbla praises his deeds. The Qaḥṭānīs complain to Arabia's most famous poet, Imru' al-Qais, and ask him to do something. He promises them that he will face ʿAntar the following day. (34/370)

25. When morning comes, ʿAntar takes the field and challenges his opponents. Imru' al-Qais emerges from the Qaḥṭānī lines and recites his *muʿallaqa* poem. He and ʿAntar fight, but Imru' al-Qais soon feels himself outclassed and surrenders. ʿAntar waits for other opponents to appear, but no one else dares to fight him, so he withdraws to his tent. (34/271–76)

To portray ʿAntar's hanging of his *muʿallaqa* poem, *Sīrat ʿAntar* offers seventeen bouts of single combat (1–4, 6–9, 13–17, 21–24), refers to the hero fighting several hundred other opponents (5, 11, 20), and depicts a full-scale—if briefly portrayed—battle (11, 12). Nor are these conflicts the end of ʿAntar's struggles. In the pages that follow Imru' al-Qais's defeat, ʿAntar enters into an extended contest with his as yet unrecognized son Ghaṣūb, whom he finally manages to capture (44.5–8:34/37–35/411); engages his friend Hānī ibn Masʿūd, who challenges him in a sudden fit of jealousy, in a bout of single combat that after several days of fighting ends with Hānī admitting ʿAntar's superiority and the two heroes embracing in reconciliation (44.8:35/412–22); and, finally, submits to Imru' al-Qais's testing of his knowledge and mastery of the synonyms and metaphors of poetic diction (44.9:35/423–35). Only after all this is ʿAntar permitted to have his *muʿallaqa* poem recited and hung (44.9:35/436–41).

To portray ʿAntar's *muʿallaqa* hanging, therefore, *Sīrat ʿAntar* transforms a literary event into a war. This is how it dramatizes events: it creates and resolves conflicts. In turn, it structures these conflicts by using its compositional models to create scenes of battle and single combat. In ʿAntar's current struggle, single combat scenes run their familiar course of dramatic elements: Appearance, Response, Fighting, and Resolution. Warriors emerge from their lines of battle, issue challenges, and perhaps recite battle poems. Opponents emerge from the enemy lines and issue answering challenges and/or poems. The two contestants fight, and combat ends with one killing or capturing the other. With this, the stage is set for the next bout, since—as we can see above—single bouts readily evolve into series of bouts. Furthermore, just as bouts of single combat are modeled upon the same four dramatic elements, they are all portrayed by means of the same reusable traditional phrases, thematic units, and themes.[16] Like battle scenes, single combat scenes may be framed by scenes of reaction. ʿAntar fights until nightfall, when he withdraws to his camp to receive the praise of ʿAbla and the other ʿAbs women and the congratulations and offers of help of his fellow warriors (5, 10, 18, 21, 24). Simultaneously, his opponents complain among themselves and try to plan their next move (18, 24). When morning breaks, ʿAntar reemerges and issues his challenges, and the bouts of single combat resume.

Sīrat ʿAntar at times displays ingenuity and originality in its handling of this episode's single combat scenes. When the *muʿallaqa* poets reemerge to fight ʿAntar, for example, the epic has them recite their *muʿallaqa* poems instead of ordinary battle poems. This device has the effect of enhancing our final estimation of ʿAntar's own poem when it ultimately is presented, endowing it with a sense of culminating perfection. The poetic quiz that Imru' al-Qais gives ʿAntar is also marked with originality (as well as offering an insight into the *Sīra*'s creators' conception of the processes of poetic creation). Nevertheless, these incidents only adorn event; they do not affect its substance or ultimate course. Compared to the pervasive influence that the *Sīra*'s compositional models wield in regard to the general shaping and portrayal of events, these traces of individuality pale into insignificance. Even when the *muʿallaqa* poets recite their poems, their objections to ʿAntar's ambitions remain based on social, not literary, criteria (cf. 6, 9). Dazzling them with his poetic talent remains beside the point; to overcome their objections, ʿAntar must vanquish them on the field of battle. Although the Heroic Cycle and the compositional models are not the only sources that *Sīrat ʿAntar* draws upon to create and portray event, they are indisputably the most important ones.

The recitation of ʿAntar's *muʿallaqa* poem, when it finally occurs, remains static—*Sīrat ʿAntar*'s compositional models cannot make it otherwise. Nevertheless, the epic sets this event like a jewel at the pinnacle of a mountain of incident: numerous bouts of single combat, the adjusting presence of a prominent figure of Islamic religious tradition (ʿAbd al-Muṭṭalib), a major father-son struggle, an unexpected eruption between two great heroes (ʿAntar and Hānī), the inclusion of most of the other *muʿallaqa* poets in the narrative action, and the insertion of their poems into the story. *Sīrat ʿAntar* thus makes the hanging of ʿAntar's *muʿallaqa* poem the crowning event in a series of momentous struggles. In the process, it produces a successful and entertaining episode, but it also demonstrates the difficulty of transcending the limits of its compositional models.

Over half a century ago, Milman Parry offered the following remarks concerning the stylistic limitations inherent in the technique of oral verse making: "The oral poet expresses only ideas for which he has a fixed means of expression. He is by no means the servant of his diction: he can put his phrases together in endless numbers of ways; but still they set bounds and forbid him the search of a style which would be altogether his own." And some pages later: "The repeated use of phrase means not only that the poet is following a fixed pattern of words, it means equally that he is denying himself other ways of expressing the idea."

Parry directs his remarks to the question of style, and they do pertain to *Sīrat 'Antar*'s style. Their scope must also be expanded to include the *Sīra*'s models of composition (of which style is but one important reflection) as a whole. The *Sīra* can exhibit remarkable flexibility and even originality in its handling of details and general portrayal of event; but as a whole, its narrative invention is circumscribed by the borders erected by its compositional models. *Sīrat 'Antar* can stretch, squeeze, modulate, and interweave these models in innumerable ways. Rarely, however, does it escape them.

CHAPTER 9

The Uses of History

Sīrat ʿAntar is replete with historical self-consciousness. It contends that the events it relates actually occurred in the past and that its narrative was composed by scholars well versed in their sources, some even eyewitnesses to the events they describe. This historicist impulse is not unique to the *Sīra.* On the contrary, other popular *sīra*s and, indeed, many other genres of premodern Arabic popular literature make such claims, whether they be "Stories of the Prophets" (*qiṣaṣ al-anbiyāʾ*), popular hagiographies, accounts of the early battles of Muḥammad and his companions (*al-maghāzī*), or popular accounts of the later Islamic campaigns of conquest (*al-futūḥāt*). Even the stories of *The Thousand and One Nights* at times cloak their romances and fantasies in pseudo-historical garb.[1]

Scholars have remarked on this phenomenon, but they tend to evaluate the historicist dimension of popular *sīra*s according to the criteria of modern historiography. Too often they are so steeped in their academic training and elite intellectual background that they only apprehend popular texts through the filter of their own preunderstanding of what "true" historical study entails. In such cases, researchers usually reach the unsurprising conclusion that as works of history popular narratives are methodologically naive, aesthetically simplistic, and historically inaccurate—in short, inferior.[2]

Alternatively, scholars sometimes apply generalized intellectual classifications such as the image of "Islam," "Christianity," or "cultural identity" to popular works, on the assumption that the information they thus garner represents a direct reflection of the values or beliefs of popular audiences themselves. Unfortunately, such mechanical application of external analytic categories to popular literature invariably leads to a distorted understanding of popular texts, their audiences, and the dialectics of the relation between the two.[3]

More fruitful is an approach that seeks first to understand the nature of the historicist claims of popular works on their own terms. Once the popular representation of history is properly apprehended in one narrative or genre, it can then be compared to those found in other popular works or genres or to those of the neighboring elite or folklore traditions. Through such a process, we may eventually attain a composite picture of the vision of history that drives different types of narrative at specific times and places and thereafter suggest the nature of the "dominant social character(s)" (to use Raymond Williams's phrase) of their audiences.[4]

If we briefly define the discipline of history as an inquiry conducted by a qualified authority into the experiences of the past to produce an "organized account of real past events," then a narrative's self-identification as a historical work has rhetorical, empirical, and methodological implications.[5] The persona and voice of the historian, the selection of the events recounted, and the structure and style of the resulting account all play a role in drawing an audience into accepting the unified historical vision that a work seeks to promote. *Sīrat 'Antar* has clearly discernible dispositions in regard to each of these three aspects of historical narration and hence must certainly be judged a kind of history. What remains to be discovered is precisely which kind of history it is.

THE NARRATION OF HISTORY

Sīrat 'Antar begins its lengthy narrative by invoking its audience: "Hearken, O listener, to the accounts of the Arabs and to what transpired between Ya'rab and Qaḥṭān, and Fazāra and Dhubyān, and 'Abs and Ghaṭafān, and to the sons of Ma'dd ibn 'Adnān, and to what happened to them in times past" (1:4).

The *Sīra* thus introduces the names of some of the tribes and tribal groups that figure prominently in its story. Implicit in this process of identification, however, is the presumption of the audience's general acquaintance with the historical context for these tribal names. In other words, *Sīrat 'Antar* assumes that narrator and audience are united by shared background knowledge. Since the narrator can presume in the audience a familiarity with the contours of the past, his task is limited to organizing and supplementing this fund of common experience by elaborating the details that relate to one part of it. The *Sīra*'s invocation thus defines the horizon of expectations that henceforth link narrator and audience.[6] Centuries after the events have occurred, we are asked to return to a tribal, pre-Islamic Arabia of whose existence and historical landmarks we have some awareness.

This appeal to history is highly significant. In the first place, it demands that the audience reestablish, or more precisely re-create, its commitment to one part of its past. In this sense, *Sīrat 'Antar* precipitates an act of partial cultural reaffirmation (or, for the uninstructed, of partial cultural initiation). Through self-identification with this area of the past, the audience establishes for itself a shared communal bond that can provide one of the many abstract planes of mutual social interaction that every culture encompasses.

Beyond this, the *Sīra* offers instruction. It promises that the audience will now move beyond general knowledge to obtain a specific, detailed—and thus personally meaningful—account of what really occurred in the past.

Finally, by supplying particular details, the *Sīra* seeks to provide general truths. It organizes past events to make them intelligible for latter generations. By disclosing that the past involved patterned, meaningful configurations of events, the narrative promotes the hope (or illusion) that the present and future are similarly organized. In its goals and hermeneutic assumptions, *Sīrat ʿAntar* differs little from any other work of historiography.[7]

In general, printed versions of Arabic popular narratives emphasize their original oral provenance by beginning paragraphs with the stock formula *qāla 'r-rāwī*, "the narrator said." *Sīrat ʿAntar* uses this phrase constantly; but it also goes beyond the anonymous process of narration by attributing its text to a number of specific authors:

> Among the narrators of this wondrous, entertaining, and amazing *sīra* is the most eloquent person of his age who spoke of what transpired among the ancient Arabs, the highly learned ʿAbd al-Malik ibn Quraib al-Aṣmaʿī, may God Almighty rest his soul. He was one of the exceedingly long-lived [*al-muʿammarūn*] and lived for a long time in both pre-Islamic and Islamic times, reaching the reigns of both the first four and later Caliphs. . . . And he was among those who reported traditions [*hadīth*] directly from the Prophet of God. He used to say, "I heard from the Prophet of God such and such." (1:5)

Sīrat ʿAntar cites al-Aṣmaʿī (d. circa 208/823) as its main source but names as co-authors other early scholars of pre-Islamic literature, culture, and history:

> And among those who relate this wondrous *Sīra* are Abū ʿUbaida, Juhaina ibn al-Muthanna, al-Balkhī, Ḥammād, Sayyār ibn Qaḥṭaba al-Fazārī, al-Kāhin al-Ghasānī ath-Thaqafī, and Ibn Khidāsh an-Nabhānī. And each of these related what he witnessed and what he heard from those in whom he trusted from among those who attended the battles of the Arabs and who were accurate [in their reports]. (1:5–6)[8]

The *Sīra* thus frames its story with several levels of attribution. The first is the general tradition of anonymous storytelling of which it is a product. Whether the story is narrated publicly by a storyteller (through oral formulaic composition, reading, or some combination of orality and script) or read privately, it invokes the narrative context of public storytelling in which the *rāwī* openly attests to the veracity of the story.[9] Nevertheless, for *Sīrat 'Antar*, the *rāwī* is more than a mere storyteller or a phatic interlocutor of tale and audience: he represents a living link in a continuous chain of oral transmission that communicates knowledge of the past from one generation to the next. Of course, this chain of transmission is open to the charge of conveying falsehoods rather than historical facts. A work such as *The Thousand and One Nights* would not refute this charge. Rather it deflects it on the one hand by removing its narrator, Scheherazade, from specific time or identifiable place and on the other hand by universalizing her tale's import by placing it squarely on an ethical rather than historical plane.[10]

The *Sīra*, too, claims ethical significance for its text, but it bolsters this claim by asserting that the events it portrays are in fact true. Typical of this narrative stance is the following statement.

> This [narrative event] is a most wondrous affair that deserves to be recorded and written in golden ink, so that people of intelligence and knowledge can be warned by means of its statements, because I only collected and composed this *sīra* on the foundation of veracity, expert knowledge, and celebrated accounts [*akhbār*]. And I relate in it notable events that I took from composers of histories and from trustworthy transmitters. And I have collected a narrative [*ḥadīth*] as if it were pearls, precious jewels, and chains of gold, and only those who are possessors of insight, scholars, virtuous men, or great kings are fit to hear it, because it is a delight to beholders and a pleasure for the thoughtful. None among masters of *sīra* has collected its like in regard to traditions [*aḥdāth*], proverbs [*amthāl*], warnings [*'ibar*], unusual expressions, force of eloquence and courage, nobility of thought, varieties of marvels, and moral lessons. (54:311–12)

This passage reveals the three rhetorical strains upon which the *Sīra* relies to justify its existence. First, it is a source of marvels and wondrous events that will amaze its listeners. It also portrays deeds and sayings that are moral exempla, worthy of emulation by those who aspire to nobility and eloquence. And it only presents such events, deeds, or sayings as did in fact occur. Hence, by its own lights *Sīrat 'Antar*, regardless of how unbelievable parts of it may appear, depicts only the world of the possible, a fact well worth keeping in mind when we consider the potential political implications of the social message of the work.

By citing al-Aṣma'ī and other early scholars as its authors, the *Sīra* explicitly links itself to the group of philologists from the early Islamic period (second/eighth centuries) who collected and codified reports of pre-Islamic Arabia and thus became central sources for such information for later generations.[11]

The *Sīra* thus attests to being a work of early Islamic, rather than pre-Islamic, historiography, since al-Aṣma'ī and his colleagues collected accounts of events that had occurred decades earlier.[12] The *Sīra* does not confine its assertions of historical veracity to secondhand information collected by this generation of scholars, however. It also claims to contain primary accounts of the events it narrates, stating that its major narrator, al-Aṣma'ī, was one of *al-mu'ammarūn*, individuals famous for their long life spans, who actually witnessed many of the deeds that he describes. This assertion is emphasized by occasions in the text when al-'Aṣma'ī or other reporters shift from third- to first-person narration to provide specific descriptions of people or additional comments about the events they are witnessing.[13]

This, then, is the polyphonic narrative voice that *Sīrat 'Antar* modulates to emphasize its historical veracity. It claims that well-known scholars compiled the narrative in order to delight, mold, and instruct listeners and readers by providing an accurate account of the events of 'Antar's life, all of which in fact took place. From this perspective, its narrators can assert that the *Sīra* is a work of valid historiography. Before evaluating this assertion further, let us first inquire into the nature of the historical world that the epic depicts.

THE SUBJECT MATTER OF HISTORY

Historians create cohesive imaginary worlds that strive to organize, represent, and explain past events. The element of poetic fabrication that such worlds necessarily contain is forgiven (and at times forgotten) as a necessary evil, the cost of mimetic replication. Moreover, since historians strive to provide their audiences with as truthful a portrayal of events as possible, they attempt to maintain close control over the amount of fiction that enters their texts. If skillful narrative re-creation is central to historians' art, an unequivocal allegiance to the ideal of empirical veracity—no matter how impossible the complete attainment of such a goal may ultimately be—lies at the heart of their craft. Nevertheless, the fact remains that every historian relies on what Hayden White has called "the fictions of factual representation" to mold, fashion, and breathe life into the inert matter of assembled research data and thus create a coherent, vibrant narrative world.[14] *Sīrat 'Antar* does no less.

Biography

'Antar's life-line provides the most prominent cohesive thread in *Sīrat 'Antar*. The story begins with his birth, describes his youth, relates the many adventures of his adulthood, and concludes after his death. Throughout, the character of 'Antar rarely strays far from center stage. Although new characters enter and disappear from the scene, they exist mainly as foils or mirror-images of 'Antar's heroic attributes, ambitions, and enterprises. Warriors appear to be befriended or vanquished, kings to be served, and women to be rescued; when 'Antar moves on, secondary characters disappear, to be replaced by a cast new in name if not always in substance. To this extent, the central structuring line of *Sīrat 'Antar* lies closer to biography than to general narrative history.

Nevertheless, the *Sīra*'s focus on the figure of 'Antar does not mean that the arena in which he is moving remains completely formless. On the contrary, it possesses geographic boundaries and political and social processes that are highly structured—and necessarily so. It is only because such parameters are quickly established in the narration and remain stable throughout that the character of 'Antar can dominate its action so completely. This backdrop should not be ignored, for delineating the geographic contours and identifying the political and social operations of this narrative world enables us to understand how *Sīrat 'Antar* envisions the workings of history.

Geography and Politics

The topographical and emotive center of the *Sīra*'s narrative world is the Hijāz, the northwestern portion of the Arabian peninsula. Here lie the territories of the Banī 'Abs, where 'Antar is born, grows up, and achieves initial success. This area is the site of intense intra- and intertribal rivalries and hence provides the arena for much of the early action of the epic, as 'Antar overcomes numerous intratribal challenges to prove his worth to his own and then to other prominent clans in his tribe. On the emotional level, 'Antar's allegiance to 'Abs and its rulers becomes the first self/other demarcation in the story. Whatever his conflicts and rivalries with members or clans within his tribe, 'Antar never hesitates to protect them against outsiders. Through this process he finally wins their trust and affection. The tribe of 'Abs is also the point of departure and return for the many journeys that 'Antar undertakes. Despite the centrality of this area, however, it represents only the innermost of a series of concentric circles from which the hero continuously expands his range of activities.

The next circle envelops the tribes that neighbor the Banī 'Abs: the Banī 'Āmir and the Banī Fazāra, genealogically the sister-tribe of 'Abs. Both tribes alternate as major enemies or close allies throughout the *Sīra*. The Banī 'Āmir provide a hero who becomes one of 'Antar's closest friends and staunchest companions in battle, 'Āmir ibn aṭ-Ṭufail, while the Banī Fazāra are 'Abs's foes in the deadly feud that erupts during a horse race between the steeds Dāḥis and al-Ghabrā'. Farther afield lies the political cacophony of the rest of tribal Arabia. Numerous tribes appear in the *Sīra*, but they fall into two general genealogical categories, the North Arabian group of the Banī 'Adnān, to which

'Abs belongs, and the South Arabian federation of the Banī Qaḥṭān. This tribal division marks the second major self/other division in 'Antar's world. 'Abs usually considers northern Arabs friends and southern Arabs foes. In terms of the actual quarrels and wars, this allegiance has little practical value since 'Abs fights northern Arabs just as often, if not more often, than it does southern Arabs; nevertheless, to a certain degree it does follow the dictates of this ethnic division. Although 'Abs battles 'Adnānī tribes constantly, it does so only in defense, while it engages in offensive raids against Qaḥṭānī tribes and non-Arab armies. The distinction here appears to be that, although you might kill your brother with proper provocation, you never attempt to plunder his house.[15]

Lying geographically and emotionally between these two tribal groupings is the holy city of Mecca, a symbol for the potential of peaceful coexistence and political harmony between these two warring tribal federations. In the *Sīra* the most prominent personality in Mecca is 'Abd al-Muṭallib ibn Hishām, the Prophet Muḥammad's grandfather, a paragon of virtue, piety, and sagacity who often mediates and settles quarrels.

Beyond the fluid and ever-shifting alliances of tribal Arabia, the political topography of the *Sīra* becomes more stable. Within the next concentric circle lie the cities of al-Ḥīra, to the northeast, and Damascus, to the northwest. These are the seats of power of two Arab dynasties, the Lakhmids and the Ghassānids, respectively. The Lakhmid kings, Nu'mān ibn al-Mundhir and his brother and successor al-Mundhir ibn Nu'mān, hold nominal sway over the tribes of the Arabian peninsula; the Ghassānids control the tribes and regions of Syria. Each kingdom is a client state of one of the two great empires that lie beyond, the Lakhmids serving the Persian shah (*kisrā*) and the Ghassanids the Byzantine emperor (*qaiṣar*). Also within this circle are the various cities and kingdoms of Yemen, which 'Antar visits on his African campaign.[16]

These two empires, along with that of Abyssinia, fall in the third concentric circle. 'Antar frequently encounters the Persian shah, whose capital is al-Madā'in (Ctesiphon, near present-day Baghdad), throughout the *Sīra* and even visits the Byzantine emperor in Constantinople; but he only meets the Abyssinian negus during his excursion to Africa.

Finally, the outermost circle contains the remote lands and kingdoms of India to the east and the Franks to the west. The emperor of India enters the narrative when he invades Persia and Arabia and attempts to conquer Mecca. The Franks often appear as contingents in the armies of the Byzantine emperor in Syria. Late in the epic 'Antar also invades the lands of the west, North Africa, Spain, and Italy, to reconquer them for the Byzantine emperor. The concentric circles that fall outside the Arabian peninsula possess no emotive weight in the *Sīra*. 'Antar freely shifts alliances and helps one ruler or kingdom against another, depending upon the contingencies of the moment.

Although the geographic perimeters of this narrative world are well established, its actual details are of minor concern. Distance, for example, is of little import. During 'Antar's numerous journeys lip service is paid to well-known geographic distances only when it suits the purposes of the story. Typically, outward journeys take many days to complete, while the return trip is described in just a few lines. Similarly, although place names are frequent, the *Sīra* devotes little attention to arranging them in an organized geographic configuration. Instead, it relies again on the foreknowledge of its audience, who presumably are aware of the location of such major areas as Yemen or India or such cities as al-Madā'in or Constantinople. Less familiar place names, most fictional, gain ontological weight partly from the larger context created by known places and partly by the very act of being named. If the *Sīra* places a city in a particular area—Spain, for example—that is known to exist, why should that city not exist as well? *Sīrat 'Antar*'s stratum of actual fact induces belief in its less empirically established pronouncements.

The Political Regime

The political structure of the narrative world of *Sīrat 'Antar* may be characterized as familial, tribal, ethnic, hierarchical, and predatory. The basic unit of the tribe is the clan, which commands primary loyalty, followed thereafter by the tribe itself, intertribal self-identification (northern versus southern Arabs), and finally allegiance to the ethnic group. Ties to the last, however, are more a matter of general identification and sentiment than deeply felt affiliation. Arabs, Persians, Byzantines, Abyssinians, Indians, and Franks are all clearly defined ethnic entities, but this does not prevent them from fighting among themselves or from allying themselves with external groups against one or more factions of their own. At times, even tribal loyalties are more an ideal than a reality. 'Antar's clan, the Banī Qurād, is fiercely opposed within 'Abs by the rival clan of the Banī Ziyād, led by the strong-willed and powerful Rābi' ibn Ziyād, who often plots with outsiders against 'Antar. Similarly, the only close intertribal relationship mentioned in the *Sīra* is that between the sister tribes of 'Abs and Fazāra, who nonetheless are mortal enemies through much of the epic.

The political structure at each of these genealogical levels is uniform. Each clan has a chief, and the leader of the ruling clan in a tribe is its king (usually *malik*). Tribal kings are supported, aided, and at times opposed by members of their own clans (sons, brothers, cousins, etc.) and by leaders from other clans. Often they have a prominent advisor to whom they turn for counsel in moments of need, and invariably they have one or more heroes, such as 'Antar, who serve as leaders and champions in battle. This political system is replicated on the other levels of state organization, whether that of client-king or emperor. Each regime consists of a ruling family, extrafamilial counselors, and military heroes.

A series of hierarchical allegiances unites these theoretically independent ruling families. The Arab tribes generally consider the king of al-Ḥīra their ruler; he, in turn, serves the Persian shah. Counterparts to the Lakhmids are the Ghassānid kings of Damascus, who are clients of the Byzantines, as are, in general, the various rulers of the Franks. The kings of Yemen follow a similar progression of ascending steps of alternating power and subordination that ultimately concludes with the negus of Abyssinia, who is the overlord of southern Arabia and the Horn of Africa.

This uniformity of political regime serves the purposes of the story well. Each area that ʿAntar enters has a ruling family and leading heroes. When he fights and defeats these heroes in battle, he displays his martial prowess without destroying his opponent's political leadership. This allows defeated kings to acknowledge and admire ʿAntar's skill in battle without having to surrender their rule. Often the ʿAbs hero assumes the place of the hero(es) he has just vanquished.

As in the case of its representation of geography, the *Sīra* uses the ontological power of denomination to solidify its political paradigms. Every tribal or ethnic state has an explicitly identified king, heroes, ministers, or other subordinates. When possible, names of known historical figures fill these slots; otherwise, likely names are created to lend these figures some measure of individuality and substance.[17]

External relations among tribes and states are inherently inimical and predatory. Internally, however, the system of government is considered stable and just. It acknowledges the rights of the weak to aid and the needs of the poor for assistance, even if it does not always fulfill such obligations. Although the task of the minister or counselor is partly to provide stratagems for battle, these figures also represent sources of a political wisdom that sometimes ameliorates or even overcomes the passion for battle and revenge that characterizes the narrative world of *Sīrat ʿAntar*. At certain times, ministers serve their rulers by counseling peace rather than war.

Historical Context: Human and Divine

As noted above, the primary structuring device for *Sīrat ʿAntar* is the hero's biography. The narrative follows the events of ʿAntar's life in chronological sequence. Nevertheless the *Sīra* places this structure within the larger context of human and divine history. The story begins not with ʿAntar's birth but with the origins of the Arabs by telling how the four sons of Nizār divide his patrimony and migrate to different lands. Muḍar settles in the Hijāz, and his descendants become the Banī ʿAdnān; Iyād moves to the Yemen and begins the Banī Qaḥṭān; Rabīʿa founds the Banī Shaibān in Iraq; and Inmār's descendants in Syria become the Banī Ghassān. The *Sīra* briefly lists the four great wars of pre-Islamic Arabia:

1. The war of Nizār, which lasted 200 years
2. The war of Basūs between the tribes of Bakr and Taghlib, which continued for 40 years
3. The war of Dāḥis and al-Ghabrā', between ʿAbs and Fazāra
4. The war between Aus and Khazraj, which lasted 40 years and was finally settled by Muḥammad's emigration to Madina

After this concise survey of the origins of the Arabs and their most famous conflicts, the *Sīra* recounts the story of Abraham and his struggle with the cruel despot Nimrod. This narrative concludes with the account of how Abraham sent Hagar and Ishmael to the future site of Mecca, where they were blessed with the miracle of the well of Zamzam. The *Sīra* returns to tribal history, giving a brief summary of the war of Basūs, then narrows its sights to focus on the tribe of ʿAbs, introducing King Jadhīma and surveying important events in his reign, continuing with the story of the succession of Jadhīma's son, Zuhair, to the kingship of ʿAbs, and recounting how he won his wife, Tamāḍur, in marriage. Only after this preparation does the *Sīra* begin the story of ʿAntar himself.

In similar fashion, *Sīrat ʿAntar* does not conclude with ʿAntar's death. After describing the hero's burial, it relates how the power of ʿAbs thereafter disintegrates, as the tribe is attacked, defeated, and dispersed, and its leaders flee to live in exile. At this point, ʿAntar's custom of defending his tribe is assumed by his children. They reassemble the tribe and its leaders and exact revenge on their enemies. The *Sīra* ends with ʿAbs's entry into Islamic times, recounting the story of Muḥammad's struggles in Mecca, the conversion to Islam of ʿAntar's tribe and children, and the inauguration of the new world order, guided by the ethical and religious strictures of the new religion.

The *Sīra*'s prologue and epilogue thus place ʿAntar's biography in the larger contexts of Arab and Islamic history and award the hero a prominent position in each. Indeed, the contours of divine will and instances of God's direct intervention into history are evidenced throughout the narrative. It even assigns a cosmic role to ʿAntar himself:

> The transmitters and informants who relate the accounts of the ancient Arabs tell of the courageous Arabs of the Age of Ignorance [*al-jāhiliyya*], how they worshiped idols, and how they were attached to the worship of wooden im-

> ages and to the arts of divination. Satan had misled and deluded them. So God, may He be exalted, afflicted them with humiliation and deprivation. Their only interest at that time was to win supremacy over each other; each of them wanted to be supreme on the face of the earth and to vanquish heroes far and wide. They did not fear God, nor pay Him any heed or honor.
>
> So when God, may He be praised and exalted, desired to destroy the arrogance and pride of this people, He, may He be exalted, humiliated them and subdued them with the most insignificant and the humblest of his creatures. Nor was this difficult for Him. This was by means of the servant described as the "serpent of the depths of the ravine," fiery of heart, fine of birth, true in devotion, ʿAntar ibn Shaddād, who in his age was like a spark struck from a flint. Through him, God curbed the tyrants of the Age of Ignorance to pave the way for the appearance of our Lord Muḥammad, the best of men. (1:7)[18]

God intervenes to assist ʿAntar on several occasions (13:247, 36:41, 36:33) and even saves ʿAbla once (12:433). Although Muḥammad is yet to be born and Islam yet to be preached, the arrival of each is explicitly signaled throughout the narrative. ʿAbd al-Muṭallib and Mecca are anachronistically revered (6:89), a Christian monk foretells Muḥammad's birth (54:294), and future events from the prophetic period are referred to (23:251–52, 24:351, 25:389–90, 31:41, 31:48–49, 31:69, 47:170–74). Even ʿAntar, the *Sīra* observes, must submit to the will of God (29:360).

The tension between monotheism and polytheism is present in the narrative, although not emphasized. Persian armies who wish to turn the Kaʿba into a fire temple are repulsed (13:212). And when ʿAntar and many of his companions learn about Muḥammad and ʿAlī from an Arab soothsayer, they convert to the pre-Islamic version of the faith, Abrahamic Ḥanafī religion (47:169–79). ʿAntar invokes Muḥammad's name five times during his lifetime to win battles (54:339).

THE STRUCTURE OF HISTORY

The preceding survey suggests that *Sīrat ʿAntar* views history as encompassing the individual, the community, and the cosmos. It is a discipline in which identified authorities communicate their knowledge, based on first- or second-hand eyewitness reports, about past personalities and events placed in the broader context of communal and divine history. The historiographical ideals of *Sīrat ʿAntar*, therefore, generally correspond to those of the scholarly discipline of history, as pursued by practitioners of the premodern Islamic elite tradition of historiography or according to the Western models that dominate today. Nevertheless, if ideals are similar, practice differs.

The most notable disparity between the historiography of learned traditions and that of *Sīrat ʿAntar* revolves around the question of accuracy. In general, the learned tradition puts enormous emphasis on factual precision, while the *Sīra* is only theoretically interested in accuracy.[19] More interesting than simply noting this obvious distinction is inquiring into why this should be the case. Given the *Sīra*'s many affirmations of its desire to be accurate, why is it not so?

First, the narrative is accurate to a surprising degree, considering the nature of the already largely legendary materials with which it has to work. Much of our anecdotal knowledge of pre-Islamic Arabia comes from the corpus of narratives of wars and feuds among the pre-Islamic Arabs known as *Ayyām al-ʿArab* (Battle Days of the Arabs). The *Sīra* draws (rather accurately, in fact) from this corpus for its representations of the stories of such characters as Ḥāṭim at-Ṭayyi', Duraid ibn aṣ-Ṣimma, and Rabīʿa ibn Mukaddam, to name only a few examples.[20] Nor is the general political map that the narrative sketches so erroneous. Byzantium rules the north; the negus of Abyssinia the south. The shah of Persia and then Indian kings control the northeast and the far east, while various Frankish (i.e., barbarian) kings rule the northwest and west. Although elite Islamic historians such as Abū Jaʿfar Muḥammad ibn Jarīr aṭ-Ṭabarī or Abu 'l-Ḥasan ʿAlī ibn al-Ḥusain al-Masʿūdī provide extensive lists of dynasties, they often offer little more concrete detail than *Sīrat ʿAntar* in their presentations of the political configuration of the pre-Islamic world. Moreover, the two types of discourse in general share a similar historiographical perspective and serve an analogous social function in molding the consciousness of their audience. Michel Foucault has remarked:

> We tend to see, in an author's fertility, in the multiplicity of commentaries, and in the development of a discipline so many infinite resources available for the creation of discourse. Perhaps so, but they are nonetheless principles of constraint, and it is probably impossible to appreciate their positive, multiplicatory roles without first taking into consideration their restrictive, constraining role.[21]

The "restrictive, constraining role" that the *Sīrat ʿAntar* provides is not significantly different from that of elite historiography. One may even claim that popular narratives such as the *Sīra* exerted more influence in creating historical awareness in Arab-Islamic society. In Franz Rosenthal's words:

> Arabic historiography would have been no less remarkable as an expression of intellectual curiosity without the existence of its lowly sister, the historical novel, but it would have been much less of an instrument for making history a part of every Muslim's intellectual experience.[22]

Where the *Sīra*'s popular historiography diverges from elite history is in its choice of focus. First, it assumes that historical narration is predominantly a synthetic rather than an analytic activity. Next, it considers history to consist of the deeds of individuals rather than those of abstract formations, such as governments, classes, or peoples. Finally, it envisions history as representing a sequence of patterned rather than random events.

Sīrat 'Antar's preference for synthesis means that it is unwilling to leave gaps in the flow of its narrative. Since human history is a cohesive "emplotted" sequence of events, so too must be its representation.[23] Of course, the historian selects which incidents, or which categories of incidents, to emphasize in day-to-day life. In the case of *Sīrat 'Antar*, this means descriptions of battles, love trysts, travel, and feasts rather than, say, herding, farming, trading, or child-rearing. Nevertheless, within this chosen context, life proceeds day by day, and so must the account of it. Hence, when the *Sīra* shifts scenes from the activities of a major character, 'Antar for example, to simultaneous events occurring elsewhere, it always summarizes what has happened in the meantime. Similarly, this impulse compels the *Sīra*'s narrators, when faced with gaps in their historical knowledge, to fill them with suitable reproductions of what "probably" occurred (as did Thucydides, for example, when faced with similar circumstances).

Closely connected with this passion for synthetic, sequential narrative is the *Sīra*'s focus on individuals. The narrative concentrates on relating the events of 'Antar's life because that is the subject of its story. Yet this choice of subject is related to its overall vision of history, because in the *Sīra*'s view only the acts of individuals are meaningful. This is why each character is named, regardless of how fleeting his or her appearance in the narrative may be. Each character manifests an individual identity (although not necessarily a distinct personality) because it is only individuals who act, and it is only individual deeds, whether they lead to success or failure, that are the stuff of history. This focus on individuals is why the deaths of major characters in the *Sīra* provoke extended scenes of mourning; personages of major significance have disappeared from the stage of events, and their passing deserves commemoration.

Finally, the *Sīra* fills gaps of narrative event or concentrates on the successes and failures of individuals because it views the processes and issues of history as falling into clearly delineated patterns. History is the earthly enactment of divine, and hence universal, concerns and designs. Hence, it is the task of historians to structure their narratives accordingly. The epic's preselection of this hermeneutical grid has obvious consequences for the way in which it thereafter formulates its story. Although the events of early Arab history deserve report because they are of genealogical relevance, they pale in significance when compared to the stories of Abraham and Muḥammad. Similarly 'Antar's story is particularly significant because his life shares a theme of vital importance with that of these two prophets. Both prophets are virtuous individuals who struggle against immensely powerful enemies (Nimrod and the Meccans, respectively) and seemingly insurmountable obstacles to defeat hostile contemporaries and assure the spread of their beliefs. And this, on a more profane plane, is the central theme and main lesson of 'Antar's life as well. He too faces and overcomes the tremendous social impediments that his race and social status create in order to gain the social position and recognition that he truly merits. It is such stories that achieve historical noteworthiness. In the view of *Sīrat 'Antar*, they are what history is all about.[24]

The *Sīra*'s assumption that history is the expression of divine patterns universalizes its outlook. All individuals have similar motives and ideals, for example. And all governments, whatever their cultural origin, are portrayed as uniform in system. *Sīrat 'Antar*'s view of human society is cosmopolitan, because its conception of history is cosmic.[25]

MODULATIONS OF HISTORICAL PERSPECTIVE

Now that the historiographical and historical vision of *Sīrat 'Antar* is clear on its own terms, it is possible to compare it with the vision proffered by other narratives or other genres. One way to begin to do this is to examine the tension between the poles of the profane and the sacred in this corpus.

On the one hand, the popular Arabic histories of the *maghāzī* genre, which focus on the deeds of Muḥammad and 'Alī, for example, and the hagiographical biographies of saints or holy people both exhibit an understanding of history that closely resembles that of *Sīrat 'Antar*. These narratives also consider history to be the profane reflection of sacred patterns. Nevertheless, they differ in that they foreground the sacred much more pronouncedly. Such stories represent the earthly enactment of divine history. It is the tension between the necessities of profane history and the potentialities of the sacred that imbues them with narrative tension. Muḥammad, 'Alī, and saints such as 'Abd al-Qādir al-Jīlānī are known to be actual human beings, each defined by historical contingencies and individual characteristics. Nevertheless, these figures transcend normality in that they also represent direct doorways to the divine. Whether they successfully invoke God's help or whether God uses them as His instruments, these characters exist on the border between the profane and sacred. As such, their relationships to empirical reality and other characters approach myth. Although they do not dwell fully in the realm of myth, since they are not themselves divine and hence, to use Northrop Frye's definition, not "superior in *kind* to other men and to the environment of other men," they nonetheless hold within themselves the potential of temporarily achieving supernatural status. Much of the attractiveness and pleasure of their tales, in fact, rests on the audience's anticipation that when a crisis arises the mythic and supernatural potential inherent in such characters finds manifestation. Through such epiphanies, these stories render proof that at times, at least, the direct hand of God reaches out to influence temporal reality.[26]

On the other hand, narratives such as *Sīrat Banī Hilāl*, although preserving many of the same narrative assumptions and thematic structures found in *Sīrat 'Antar*, eschew the sacred realm to concentrate on the profane level of history. Life in *Sīrat Banī Hilāl* also revolves around individualism and the search for equity, but the narrative stresses the context of tribal society and the potential of extraordinary and heroic action on the earthly plane of history. Their heroes are "superior in degree to other men but not to [their] natural environment."[27]

A third narrative option is to move from the tension between the sacred and the profane altogether by embracing the realm of profane magic. These stories are full of supernatural events, but such events have nonsacred causes. The magical tales of *The Thousand and One Nights* or of such *sīra*s as *al-Malik Saif ibn Dhī Yazan* fall into this category.

Among these possibilities, *Sīrat 'Antar* lies somewhere between the first two. It ignores profane magic almost completely. Its frame, however, evokes the patterns of cosmic history, while its description of daily events focuses almost totally on the level of profane history. Ironically, in this sense it is elite models of traditional Islamic historiography, such as the works of aṭ-Ṭabarī or al-Mas'ūdī, that resemble the *Sīra* most closely, with their integration of human and divine history.[28] Nevertheless, they differ in their lack of emphasis on individuals as the most important agents in history, maintaining instead that meaning comes from understanding the broader patterns of events that emerge from the sweep of dynastic or world history. This enlarged focus means that such historians are less interested in the sequential events of an individual's life, except perhaps in the case of Muḥammad (into which, significantly, fictional or mythic elements thus enter), and are therefore less concerned with narrative synthesis. Instead they emphasize contiguity of event. Truth and meaning emerge, if at all, when separate events are studied, contemplated, and evaluated within the context of universal history. Synthesis occurs, again if at all, only at this highly abstract level. From this perspective, it is typical that individual personalities do not figure in 'Abd ar-Raḥmān ibn Muḥammad ibn Khaldūn's theory of history at all.[29] (Although it is telling that fictional material tends to creep in when such histories relate the lives of individuals, such as famous rulers like Hārūn ar-Rashīd.)

One of the consequences of this disparity of viewpoints is that the elite vision of history is generally realistic (i.e., pessimistic) about the ability of humans to perfect themselves. Elite historians often see history as a devolution from a Golden Age. Conversely, the popular view of history, at least as represented by *Sīrat 'Antar*, is generally optimistic in its outlook. In the *Sīra*, individuals are not crushed by history; as long as they possess sufficient energy and integrity they remain the masters of their fates. By molding their lives to accord with the divine plan, they achieve success. In this way they are figures who make history and, by reaching across time, come to personify their audiences' faith in its perfectibility.[30]

In this regard, *Sīrat 'Antar* does not function on the plane that Mikhail Bakhtin has called the "absolute past." In his view,

> The epic past is called the "absolute past" for good reason: it is both monochromatic and valorized (hierarchical); it lacks any relativity, that is, any gradual, purely temporal progressions that might connect it with the present. It is walled off absolutely from all subsequent times in which the singer and his listeners are located. This boundary, consequently, is immanent in the form of the epic itself and is felt and heard in its every word.[31]

In contrast to the novel, Bakhtin proceeds to argue, an epic world such as that in *Sīrat 'Antar* lacks "any openendedness, indecision, indeterminacy" (16). This argument holds a certain measure of truth, when viewed in relation to the modern novel. Nevertheless, it dramatically underestimates the appeal of the epic. It is the potential of an epic such as *Sīrat 'Antar* for not being "walled off absolutely from all subsequent times" that constitutes one of the genre's major sources of attraction and fascination.

If history and the modern novel focus on actuality, *Sīrat 'Antar* concentrates on potentiality. To the extent that pseudo-historical stories provide examples of human potential and capability (as manifested by individual examples) that under propitious conditions become extraordinary, they offer ideals of aspiration and action for ordinary individuals. As such, they are not narratives "walled off" in the absolute past; rather, they stretch out from the past to shape and stir the expectations and imaginations of their audiences about possibilities for action in the present and the future. In this way, they encourage comforts of courage and hope and the potential for positive initiative and action for individuals and groups much in need of this at times when elite histories have few such comforts to offer.

CHAPTER 10

Directions for Further Research

THIS STUDY has focused in some detail on aspects of the scholarly reception, hermeneutical context, historical background, generic framework, narrative structure, and compositional models of *Sīrat ʿAntar*. More could no doubt be said about each of these topics, but I conclude with some brief suggestions for possible directions for future research. Such lines of research may focus on *Sīrat ʿAntar* itself or may be comparative, investigating the *Sīra*'s relationship with other works —*sīra*s, other genres of Arabic popular literature, genres of Islamic popular narrative stemming from different linguistic traditions, or examples of non-Islamic world literature.

DETAILED STUDY OF THE *SĪRA*'S MANUSCRIPT AND TEXTUAL TRADITION

Appendix II offers an initial description of *Sīrat ʿAntar*'s manuscript tradition based on information collected from library catalogues. Much more information can be gleaned, however, by firsthand examination of the *Sīra*'s manuscripts. Such research will help elucidate the history of the epic's textual tradition, clarify issues of its stylistic and compositional stability and variance, and illuminate details of its social provenance and context. One can learn much by studying the material culture of the popular *Sīra* manuscript tradition—for example, by examining the quality of paper and script and by taking note of miscellaneous and extraneous comments recorded by owners and readers on title pages, pages, and margins. The textual traditions of Arabic and

Islamic popular literatures have their tales to tell about the literary and social contexts of the periods from which they stem. More effort should be expended on recording and evaluating this fascinating body of evidence.

INVESTIGATING THE INTERFACE BETWEEN ORAL AND WRITTEN

As part of a genre that has existed as both oral performance and written text, *Sīrat 'Antar* and the *sīra* genre as a whole represent excellent sources for exploring the varied relations between oral and written narrative. Care must be taken not to assume that one relationship holds for all members of the genre, since important distinctions no doubt exist among them. Nevertheless, with their vast corpus of manuscript and printed texts and a significant body of recorded oral performances for some works (such as *Sīra Banī Hilāl*), *Sīrat 'Antar* and other Arabic popular epics constitute a rich source for research in this area.

RELATION TO THE *AYYĀM AL-'ARAB* AND OTHER SOURCE MATERIAL

Quellenforschung should not be ignored in the study of the Arabic popular epic, but it must be put in proper perspective. Identifying probable historical sources is an important issue; *Sīrat 'Antar* appropriates, for example, many of the characters and stories that figure prominently in the *Ayyām al-'Arab* tradition. More significant is the question of how these popular epics thereafter adapt, modify, and utilize such historical sources. Hence, one must analyze *Ayyām* materials in *Sīrat 'Antar* not only to compare them with earlier versions, but also to see how the epic mobilizes them to serve its own narrative purposes.

CHARACTERS AND CHARACTERIZATION

Sīrat 'Antar relies on a relatively small number of stock character types. Space has not permitted any detailed examination of this dimension of the epic here, but it is a fruitful area for research. More study of the formulaic description of individual characters (heroes, kings, sages, beloveds, etc.) would be beneficial, as would examination of individual character types, such as Malcolm Lyons has initiated in the first volume of *The Arabian Epic*. One example of such treatment is further study of *ayyār*-type characters, such as Shaibūb, who serve as practical and wily helpers to heroes but who also become major figures in their own right in such independent narratives as *'Alī Zaibaq* and *The Thousand and One Nights* stories of "Aḥmad ad-Danaf and the Crafty Dalīla."[1]

Another character type deserving of more investigation is the warrior woman. Studies of the Arabic tradition by Remke Kruk and Nabīla Ibrāhīm and of Persian narratives by William Hanaway have broached this subject, but more work is still needed.[2]

The prominence of the black hero in *Sīrat ʿAntar* and also in such popular epics as *Sīra Banī Hilāl* and *Sīrat Dhāt al-Himma* also deserves further consideration.

Finally, character clusters that provide the impetus for much of the narrative action need study. One obvious example is the triad of the lover, the beloved, and the rival (and their respective families); this thematic unit should be examined in the context of narrative function but also in regard to its relation to the highly developed tradition of Arabic love poetry, in which stock characters such as the rival, the slanderer, and the malicious spy also appear. Another such cluster is the young hero, the older ruler, and the tension that arises between them, a theme that W. T. H. Jackson has studied, for example, in the context of the Western epic tradition.[3]

POETRY

Sīrat ʿAntar contains over 10,000 lines of poetry, some of it very good. Further investigation will illuminate the narrative purposes that this enormous corpus serves within the epic. These verses must also be critically analyzed in their own right from formal, aesthetic, and comparative perspectives.

AESTHETICS

Sīrat ʿAntar is a work of literature, the result of a highly developed popular tradition that sought to entertain and instruct its audiences. It deserves in-depth aesthetic evaluation. Some parts of the narrative are better than others; the epic as a whole is perhaps better than some examples of Arabic and world popular epics, perhaps worse than others. Criteria of aesthetic analysis and critical evaluation for these narratives should be developed, critiqued, and applied.

COMPARISON WITH OTHER WORKS

An enormous amount of groundwork remains in further study of *Sīrat ʿAntar*'s relation to other Arabic popular epics and to analogous works from other genres of Islamic and global popular literature. Each of the areas pursued or mentioned in this monograph can be explored in other *sīra*s or in larger comparative contexts, as can other topics that I may have omitted. The field is as wide open as it is exciting and rewarding. The length of Arabic popular epics makes this task daunting. Nevertheless, the subject is fascinating, edifying—and fun.

APPENDIX I

A Summary of *Sīrat ʿAntar*

This summary provides a coherent and easily consultable representation of *Sīrat ʿAntar*'s narrative action. The text on which it is based is *Qiṣṣat ʿAntara ibn Shaddād al-ʿAbsī*, published in Cairo in 1961 by Maktabat Muṣṭafa 'l-Bābi 'l-Ḥalabī. This edition comprises fifty-nine books, usually bound in eight volumes. Books 1–58 contain 96 pages each; book 59 contains 39 pages.

To allow readers to refer to the original version of an episode, or at least to gain a sense of the original episode's length, I provide corresponding book and page numbers separated by slashes (thus 6/85 refers to book 6, page 85) after each of the summary's episode headings. To facilitate reference to the summary itself in this study's chapters, I have numbered episodes and divided episode segments with decimals (thus 11.1 refers to episode 11, segment 1). References to equivalent parts of the summary and text are separated by colons (11.1:6/85 signifies episode 11, segment 1 of the summary, which corresponds to book 6, page 85 of the original).

Any summary is by necessity selective. Since this one is less than one-hundredth the size of the original, the large role that selection and omission have played should be obvious. It is appropriate, therefore, that I briefly describe some of the ways in which this summary does and does not reflect the original.

First, the differences. Although *Sīrat ʿAntar* contains at least ten thousand lines of poetry, apart from references to ʿAntar's *muʿallaqa* poem, little mention of this verse appears in the summary. Since poetry does not serve as a means of advancing narrative action, this omission does not affect the representation of this aspect of the *Sīra*. Still, the reader should be aware of it.

The summary is also shorn of most of the stylistic and rhetorical dimensions that make the *Sīra* exciting and suspenseful. It tells what happens, but does so in a way that, I fear, makes a poor story. In this respect, the summary is only a dim reflection of the original.

Finally, the reader must be warned that the summary makes difficult reading at times because it is so concise. *Sīrat 'Antar* constantly introduces a welter of new characters and events into its narrative. Hence, the summary often resembles less a skeleton than a labyrinth. This is unfortunate but unavoidable. To have made the summary more readable would have increased its length tenfold.

The summary has two strengths: completeness and organization. *Sīrat 'Antar* is a lengthy work, and previous students have offered only short, general descriptions or partial translations. Here the reader finds a portrayal of the whole epic's narrative action in a form more detailed and complete than any currently in existence. Moreover, unlike printed versions of the *Sīra*, which are divided into volumes, books, or chapters on a purely quantitative basis—so many pages to a chapter or book—the summary is organized according to the narrative's interior structure. Its main units correspond to the *Sīra*'s main episodic divisions, while its subunits attempt to recount the most important points of narrative action within episodes.

To introduce the characters and events of the *Sīra* would entail constructing a list of many pages. Therefore, I offer no cast of characters. Nevertheless, it is helpful to outline a hierarchy of five rivalries that come to play a role in the narrative:

1. The rivalry that develops between 'Antar and the Banī 'Abs clan of Ziyād, headed by the formidable warrior and political advisor ar-Rabī' ibn Ziyād. 'Umāra, ar-Rabī''s foppish and foolish brother, is also an important foil for 'Antar. He falls in love with 'Abla and is 'Antar's rival for her hand during much of the early portion of the narrative.

2. The bitter tribal feud that arises between the Banī 'Abs and the sister tribe of the Banī Fazāra (both belong to the Banī Ghaṭafān tribal group). This rivalry is also prominent in *Ayyām al-'Arab* sources, which center on the famous feud between 'Abs and Fazāra stemming from the horse race between the horses Dāḥis and al-Ghabrā' (see 22 below). In the *Sīra*, the feud centers on 'Antar and is portrayed as even wider and more bitter than in the *Ayyām*.

3. The long-standing enmity between the northern Arabian tribal bloc that traces its ancestry to the patriarchal figure of 'Adnān and the southern Arabian tribal bloc that traces its ancestry to Qaḥṭān.

4. The political rivalry between the Lakhmid kings, whose capital is the city of al-Ḥīra, situated just southeast of present-day Najaf, Iraq, and the Ghassānid kings of Damascus. Both of these ruling families were Arab, and their kingdoms served as buffer states against the tribes of the Arabian peninsula for the Persian and Byzantine empires, respectively.

5. The rivalry between the Persian shahs, whose capital was al-Madā'in, situated just southeast of present-day Baghdad, Iraq, and the Byzantine emperors of Constantinople.

Allegiances in *Sīrat 'Antar* are not always kept, nor enmities maintained. Nevertheless, a general awareness of this ascending series of rivalries should help readers weave their way through some of the geopolitical complexities of the *Sīra*'s world. The narrative begins with the story of Abraham, but the events of 'Antar's own life fall, supposedly, in the last half of the sixth century and the beginning part of the seventh century A.D.

SUMMARY

1. Introduction, 1/3–1/6

1.1. This is the story of 'Antar ibn Shaddād.

1.2. 'Abd al-Malik ibn Quraib al-Asma'ī is the story's primary compiler and composer, but he was aided by many other scholars, such as Abū 'Ubaida, Ḥammād ar-Rāwī, al-Kāhin al-Ghassānī, ath-Thaqafī, Ibn Khidāsh an-Nabhānī, Sayyār ibn Qaḥṭaba al-Fazārī, and Juhaina ibn al-Muthannā.

1.3. There were four great wars in pre-Islamic Arabia: 1. the wars of Nizār in Yemen, which lasted two hundred years; 2. the war of Basūs between the tribes of Bakr and Taghlib, which lasted forty years; 3. the war of Dāḥis and al-Ghabrā' between the tribes of 'Abs and Fazāra, which lasted sixty years; and 4. the war between al-Aus and al-Khazraj, which lasted forty years until it was settled by the Prophet Muḥammad. Of these wars, the best story is that of the war between 'Abs and Fazāra.

1.4. The Arabs before Muḥammad were hardhearted, arrogant, and impious people who ignored God and His commandments. In order to soften their hearts and pave the way for Muḥammad's message, God sent 'Antar down among them. Once they were defeated in battle by a mere black slave, the Arabs were no longer so self-confident and arrogant.

2. The Story of Abraham: Abraham and Nimrod (as told by Wahb ibn Munabbih), 1/8–1/76

2.1. After God destroyed Noah's people and punished the peoples of 'Ād and Thamūd, a son of Ham named Kūsh conquers a large kingdom in Kūtriyā.

2.2. Kūsh has two sons: Kan'ān and al-Hās. One day Kan'ān rapes a shepherd's wife named Sulkhā'. When the shepherd objects, Kan'ān kills him. Sulkhā' becomes his concubine and bears him a son named Nimrod.

2.3. Kan'ān has nightmares about the child and orders Sulkhā' to kill him.

She abandons him in the countryside, but a leopard suckles him. Nimrod grows up a cruel and wicked brigand.

2.4. Nimrod's power grows. Finally he defeats and kills his father, marries his mother, and takes over the kingdom. He learns astrology and magic and fashions idols in his image that he forces his people to worship.

2.5. Nimrod's minister, Āzar, has a son named Abraham. Nimrod has a nightmare about a male baby and orders all male infants in the kingdom to be killed. Nevertheless, God protects Abraham, who lives in a cave his first four years then returns to his parent's home.

2.6. Abraham grows up pious and upright. He refuses to worship Nimrod's idols and destroys them whenever he can. Nimrod tries to kill Abraham, but God always saves him, even from burning flames.

2.7. At the age of forty, Abraham begins to preach publicly. God produces nine miracles to save Abraham and warn Nimrod, but Nimrod is too blackhearted to take notice.

2.8. Nimrod constructs a box to which he ties vultures. He flies as high as he can and begins to shoot arrows in the sky to kill God. God has one of his angels cast Nimrod down again.

2.9. God sends a swarm of mosquitoes through the land. One enters Nimrod's nostril and then his brain, where it so torments him that he orders his servants to beat his head with mallets. He eventually dies from this beating. God destroys all of his people except Abraham and his followers.

3. The Story of Abraham: Abraham and Ishmael, 1/73–1/86

3.1. Abraham marries Sarah and travels with her to Egypt. He claims that she is only his sister, and the king there sees her and takes her to wife. When he draws near her, however, there is an earthquake. The king learns the truth; he returns Sarah and gives Abraham many gifts.

3.2. Among these gifts is a slave girl named Hagar. Hagar bears Abraham a son named Ishmael, but Sarah is jealous and forces Abraham to send them away. He takes them to Arabia and leaves them, trusting God to care for them.

3.3. When Hagar becomes thirsty, God reveals the spring of Zamzam. Passing tribes settle around the new spring, and Hagar and Ishmael grow rich by selling its waters.

3.4. Abraham wants to see his son. He visits him twice, but each time Ishmael is out hunting. The third time father and son finally are reunited.

3.5. God orders Abraham to sacrifice Ishmael. Satan tempts Ishmael to object, but Ishmael stones him and drives him away. Abraham almost carries out the sacrifice, but at the last moment God relents and orders Abraham to sacrifice a sheep instead.

3.6. Abraham builds the Ka'ba and, following God's orders, calls upon all to make a pilgrimage there. Then he returns home.

4. The Banī 'Abs, 1/86–2/119

4.1. Ishmael has many sons. Generations pass until the time of Nizār ibn Ma'dd ibn 'Adnan. Nizār has four sons: Muḍar, Rabī'a, Anmār, and Iyād. Upon Nizār's death, the four sons divide their inheritance and separate. Muḍar remains in the Hijāz, Rabi'a settles in Iraq, Anmār in Syria, and Iyād in Yemen. Each founds a major tribal group of the northern Arabs.

4.2. More generations pass, until the time of the end of the war of Basūs. The greatest king among the Arabs is Jadhīma ibn Rawāḥa of the Banī 'Abs.

4.3. Jadhīma is killed in battle by ar-Rabbāb, queen of the Banī Nabhān. Jadhīma's son, Zuhair, becomes king and avenges his father by killing ar-Rabbāb in battle.

4.4. King Zuhair goes to Mecca on pilgrimage. He likes the Ka'ba so much that he decides to build one for himself. Wiser heads dissuade him from this idea.

4.5. Zuhair falls in love with and marries a famous beauty named Tumāḍir. She bears him ten sons.

5. The Birth of 'Antar, 2/119–2/143

5.1. On a raid, Shaddād ibn Qurād and nine other raiders of the Banī 'Abs capture the black slave Zabība and her two small sons, Jarīr and Shaibūb. Shaddād fancies the girl and takes her as his share of the booty.

5.2. Zabība bears Shaddād a son, 'Antar. The baby shows great signs of strength. He beats up older boys and teases the camp dogs. Shaddād's fellow raiders try to claim a share in 'Antar, claiming that Zabība was pregnant with him at the time of her capture. Shaddād rejects their claims and the quarrel grows. King Zuhair hears of the argument. He orders the two parties to go to Bishāra ibn Quṭba, a judge respected among the Arabs. Bishāra rules in Shaddād's favor.

5.3. 'Antar grows up as Shaddād's slave. He tends the herds, killing wild animals that attack them with his bare hands. He and his brother Shaibūb also secretly practice the arts of war. 'Antar learns to ride and use the lance; Shaibūb is extremely swift of foot and becomes an expert archer.

5.4. 'Antar first attracts wider notice when he kills Dājī, the favorite slave of Prince Shāsh, son of King Zuhair. Dājī bullied two old women, and 'Antar comes to their defense. Prince Shāsh becomes 'Antar's enemy. Another son of Zuhair, Prince Mālik, admires 'Antar's courage and nobility and becomes his friend.

6. 'Antar in Love, 2/144–2/180

6.1. 'Antar falls in love with his cousin 'Abla. This love inspires him to begin to recite poetry. Mālik ibn Qurād, 'Abla's father and Shaddād's brother, and his son 'Amr are outraged at the scandal created by 'Antar's love poetry. They become 'Antar's enemies.

6.2. 'Antar creates another enemy in ar-Rabīʿ ibn Ziyād, whose slave he kills in a quarrel. Ar-Rabiʿ is the head of the powerful Ziyād clan in 'Abs and one of Zuhair's most influential counselors.

6.3. Shaddād is also scandalized by 'Antar's behavior. He plots 'Antar's death with Mālik and 'Amr, but they give up their scheme when they see him kill a lion with his bare hands.

6.4. 'Antar also wins some friends. He saves the women of the tribe from Qaḥṭānī raiders while all of the men are away on a raid. This act wins the favor of King Zuhair.

6.5. A few days later, 'Antar saves the ten sons of Zuhair from capture, which increases the king's fondness for him. 'Antar and Shaibūb begin to go raiding. They win great spoils, and Shaddād becomes rich from their efforts.

7. 'Antar's Fame Grows, 2/180–3/271

7.1. When the Qurād clan is invited to a wedding in another tribe, Prince Shāsh, ar-Rabīʿ, Mālik, and 'Amr send a party of slaves to ambush 'Antar, who is escorting the women of the clan. Before the ambushers can attack, another group of raiders attacks the caravan. 'Antar single-handedly drives them off.

7.2. The wedding over, the Qurād clan returns to 'Abs. They find the camp left defenseless and under attack. 'Antar drives the attackers away while Shaibūb kills the leader of the ambushing slaves, who was taking advantage of the battle to sneak up on 'Antar.

7.3. 'Antar learns that Shaddād is his true father. He demands paternal acknowledgment, but Shaddād angrily refuses and beats him. 'Antar decides to leave 'Abs.

7.4. In the desert, 'Antar meets and joins a raiding party of forty 'Abs warriors. They attack a camp and win great booty, but they refuse to give 'Antar more than a slave's share. Pursuit appears, and they leave 'Antar to guard the spoils while they fight a rear-guard action. 'Antar takes the opportunity to trade all of the spoils for a wonderful black horse named al-Abjar. His companions return to find their booty gone. They are angry, but their fear of 'Antar's might stills their complaints.

7.5. They travel on and capture a rich wedding caravan. With 'Antar's help, they manage to fight off the pursuit of the bridegroom, whom 'Antar kills. Shortly afterward the father of the bride appears with five thousand warriors. All the raiders wish to flee except 'Antar, who charges the attackers. The 'Abs warriors are only saved by the appearance of Prince Mālik and five hundred 'Abs.

7.6. When all return to 'Abs, 'Antar learns that his father has gone raiding. He follows and rescues Shaddād, who has fallen into captivity.

7.7. Prince Mālik's foster brother, Ḥiṣn of the Banī Māzin, comes to seek Zuhair's help in winning his beloved. Ḥiṣn has a powerful rival in 'Assaf, a hero of the Banī Qaḥṭān who is forcing Ḥiṣn's uncle to give his daughter to him. 'Antar and Prince Mālik agree to help. They arrive to find 'Assāf attacking Ḥiṣn's camp. 'Antar kills 'Assaf, and Ḥiṣn marries his beloved. During his journey with Ḥiṣn, 'Antar obtains a wonderful sword named aẓ-Ẓāmī.

8. 'Antar Wins His Freedom, 3/271–4/354

8.1. 'Umāra ibn Ziyād, ar-Rabī''s brother, falls in love with 'Abla. He is a foppish dandy but rich, so 'Abla's father favors his suit. 'Umāra and 'Antar come to blows, and Shaddād sends him back to tend the herds, forbidding him ever to carry arms again.

8.2. King Zuhair learns that an enemy army is approaching. He takes his warriors to intercept it, leaving only the Qurād clan behind to protect the camp.

8.3. The two armies bypass each other; suddenly the Qaḥṭānī army appears and attacks the camp. Shaddād and Mālik are hopelessly outnumbered; they beg 'Antar to come to their aid. 'Antar refuses to help unless he is promised his freedom and 'Abla's hand. Obtaining this promise, he attacks the enemy and drives them away.

8.4. Shaddād is glad he finally acknowledged 'Antar as his son, but Mālik seeks some way to keep 'Abla from 'Antar.

8.5. Ar-Rabī' convinces 'Urwa ibn al-Ward, a famous vagabond warrior-poet of 'Abs, to ambush 'Antar. 'Urwa does so, but 'Antar defeats and captures him. Then 'Antar rescues Shāsh, ar-Rabī', and his uncle Mālik, who have fallen captive to a raiding party.

9. The 'Aṣāfīr Camels, 4/355–5/462

9.1. Mālik decides to send 'Antar on an impossible mission. At ar-Rabī''s suggestion, he asks 'Antar for one thousand 'Aṣāfīr camels as a dowry for 'Abla. These camels are a special breed owned only by King al-Mundhir ibn Mā' as-Samā' of al-Ḥīra, the overlord of all of the Arabs.

9.2. 'Antar and Shaibūb find the camels and steal them. An-Nu'mān, King al-Mundhir's son, pursues them, and, overcome by sheer numbers, 'Antar falls captive. Shaibūb sees his brother disappear among the enemy and, thinking him killed, flees back to 'Abs.

9.3. 'Antar is brought before King al-Mundhir in chains. The king asks for his story and is impressed by his strength and eloquence. 'Antar proves his boldness by killing a rampaging lion.

9.4. The Ḥīran king is at war with his liege, Shah Anūshirwān of Persia. 'Antar wins al-Mundhir's friendship and gratitude when he helps defeat a Persian army against al-Ḥīra by killing the Persian general in single combat.

9.5. In spite of this short-term victory, al-Mundhir decides to make peace with the shah. Anūshirwān is agreeable to this because he now has more pressing problems. A Byzantine knight has appeared in the Persian court. In order to free Byzantium from the burden of yearly tribute to the shah, the knight challenges any Persian to defeat him in single combat. The shah cannot refuse this chivalric challenge and accepts the terms, but the Byzantine is invincible. For twenty-five days he defeats all who dare to fight him.

9.6. When he hears how 'Antar defeated his general, a desperate shah sends for him to come and face the Byzantine knight. 'Antar defeats him, thus winning Anūshirwān's favor and the jealousy of some of the Persian nobles.

9.7. 'Antar is royally entertained in al-Madā'in, the Persian capital, but he soon longs for 'Abla and home. He departs from first al-Madā'in and then al-Ḥīra laden with gifts, including the thousand 'Aṣāfīr camels he needs for his dowry, and heads for home.

10. The Struggle for 'Abla, 5/463–6/85

10.1. On his way home, 'Antar comes upon 'Abla weeping in the desert and calling his name. After Shaibūb returned with the news of 'Antar's presumed death, Mālik and 'Amr went raiding. They fell captive to Wāqid ibn Mas'ara of the Banī Kināna. Wāqid has heard of 'Abla's beauty and demands her as their ransom.

10.2. They all return to 'Abs, and Mālik and 'Amr bring 'Abla to Wāqid. 'Abla's father and brother are so ashamed of winning their freedom by giving her away that they decide to go live with Wāqid.

10.3. On the way back to Kināna, the party is attacked by a group of brigands led by the black warrior Ṭāriqat az-Zamān. Ṭāriqa kills Wāqid and takes 'Abla captive. Mālik and 'Amr flee. Ṭāriqa leaves a few men to guard 'Abla then sets off in pursuit.

10.4. In their flight, Mālik and 'Amr come across 'Urwa and 'Umāra, who are also out raiding. Ṭāriqa appears and captures them all. Then he and his prisoners return to the place where he has left 'Abla.

10.5. Meanwhile, ʿAntar has found ʿAbla. He quickly kills her guard and frees her. ʿAntar fights and kills Ṭāriqa and frees the other prisoners, who all hate ʿAntar but are forced to thank him for rescuing them.

10.6. On their way back to camp, ʿUmāra kidnaps ʿAbla. He soon falls captive to Mufarrij ibn Hammām of the Banī Ṭayyi'. Mufarrij falls in love with ʿAbla and tries to force her to agree to marry him by making her work as a slave in his tents.

10.7. Ar-Rabīʿ learns where his brother is. He and ʿUrwa go to rescue him, but they in turn are captured by Mufarrij.

10.8. ʿAntar sends Shaibūb to find ʿAbla, which he soon does. ʿAntar kills Mufarrij in battle, thus freeing all of the ʿAbs prisoners. Once again, ʿAntar's enemies are forced to thank him for their rescue.

11. ʿAntar and Prince Shāsh, 6/85–7/152

11.1. Mālik still wants to find some way to stop ʿAntar from marrying ʿAbla. He convinces Prince Shāsh to forbid ʿAntar to see ʿAbla. An angry ʿAntar decides to leave ʿAbs and emigrate to Mecca. On the way, he and Shaibūb rescue a family of the Banī Kinda from robbers.

11.2. Prince Shāsh goes hunting one day and falls captive to a group of the Bani 'l-Hārith. The family ʿAntar rescued live with this tribe, and, learning who he is, they help Shāsh escape.

11.3. On his way home, Prince Shāsh falls captive once again, this time to the Bani 'r-Riyān. ʿAntar has heard of his troubles. He and Shaibūb rescue Shāsh. Shāsh apologizes to ʿAntar for all he has done to him, and the two become friends.

11.4. On the way home, they meet Rauḍa ibn Manīʿ, a knight who has heard of ʿAbla's beauty and has come to marry her. He and ʿAntar fight; Rauḍa is impressed by ʿAntar's strength and nobility. He admits ʿAntar is the better man and presents him with the dowry he was bringing for ʿAbla as a gift. The two part as friends.

11.5. King Zuhair has been terribly worried about Shāsh. He is overjoyed to see him safe, and ʿAntar becomes dearer to him than ever. The king holds a large feast in his honor. The next morning, however, ʿAntar and Shaibūb have disappeared from camp.

12. ʿAntar and Khālid and al-Jaidā' of the Banī Zubaid, 7/152–8/233

12.1. Still anxious to instigate ʿAntar's death, ar-Rabīʿ and Mālik form the plan of having ʿAbla ask ʿAntar to capture al-Jaidā' bint Zāhir to lead the camel in their wedding procession. Al-Jaidā' and her husband Khālid ibn Muḥārib are king and queen of the Banī Zubaid. Both are famous warriors, and their wedding was the most sumptuous ever seen in Arabia to that time.

12.2. ʻAntar and Shaibūb come to the Banī Zubaid while Khālid has taken all of the men raiding. ʻAntar surprises al-Jaidāʼ while she is hunting alone and, after a hard struggle, captures her. Meanwhile, King Zuhair has discovered what ʻAntar is attempting. He gathers the ʻAbs warriors and sets out to help.

12.3. Left in camp in disgrace, ar-Rabīʻ and Mālik decide to emigrate from ʻAbs. With ʻUrwa, they take their families and leave camp. In the desert, they are captured by King Khālid of the Banī Zubaid.

12.4. When he learns what ʻAntar is doing, Khālid sends part of his force, led by the redoubtable warrior Maʻdīkarib ibn al-Ḥārith, to raid the defenseless ʻAbs camp. Then he takes his main force home to rescue his wife.

12.5. King Zuhair joins ʻAntar. Shortly afterward, Khālid and his men appear, along with their captives, among whom is ʻAbla. The two armies fight until nightfall.

12.6. The next morning Maʻdīkarib appears with more ʻAbs prisoners. ʻAntar has disappeared during the night, and the battle goes badly for ʻAbs.

12.7. ʻAntar appears with Khālid's head on his lance. He and Khālid went scouting the evening before. They met and fought the better part of the night until ʻAntar finally won. When they see that their king has been killed, the Zubaid break ranks and flee. The ʻAbs recover their prisoners and capture great booty. All head for home, but ʻAntar discovers that ʻAbla, Mālik, and ʻAmr are nowhere to be found.

13. ʻAntar and Bisṭām ibn Qais of the Banī Shaibān, 8/248–9/298

13.1. A messenger comes to the ʻAbs camp and announces that King al-Mundhir of al-Ḥīra has died and been succeeded by his son an-Nuʻmān. King Zuhair swears fealty to his new overlord. Meanwhile, ʻAntar has sent Shaibūb to discover where Mālik has taken ʻAbla. After forty days, Shaibūb returns with the news that Mālik has sought refuge with King Qais ibn Masʻūd of the Banī Shaibān and that Qais's son Bisṭām, a mighty warrior, has fallen in love with ʻAbla.

13.2. When Bisṭām requests ʻAbla in marriage, Mālik agrees but demands ʻAntar's head as dowry. Bisṭām sets out toward ʻAbs, but meets ʻAntar, who is on his way to Shaibān. The two fight, and ʻAntar captures Bisṭām after a difficult struggle.

13.3. Shaibūb goes to the Shaibān camp to scout out the best way to rescue ʻAbla. He returns to announce that the camp has been raided by the Banī Tamīm, whose leader Qanʻat ibn Ghiyāth wants to marry Bisṭām's sister Suʻdā. Upon hearing this, Bisṭām forgets about his love for ʻAbla. He is now more worried about his sister. He and 'Antar become friends. Together they gather the scattered Shaibān warriors and set off to rescue Su'dā and 'Abla.

13.4. They attack the Tamīm camp, and 'Antar kills Qan'at. The prisoners are rescued, and all return to the Shaibān camp to celebrate the victory. Mālik thanks 'Antar but is still hostile. He refuses to return to 'Abs unless one of King Zuhair's sons comes to assure him that he is no longer held in disgrace. So 'Antar asks Bisṭām to watch over 'Abla and leaves to bring one of the Zuhair's sons to escort Mālik and his family back to 'Abs.

14. Further Abductions of 'Abla, 9/299–10/420

14.1. When 'Antar returns to 'Abs, 'Urwa ibn al-Ward convinces King Zuhair to do nothing. 'Antar angrily decides to kill 'Urwa. One day 'Urwa visits his sister, who lives in another tribe. He finds her unhappily married and agrees to take her back to 'Abs. 'Antar waits in the desert in order to ambush him, but others beat him to it. Raiders attack and capture 'Urwa and his sister. 'Antar would happily stand by while 'Urwa was killed, but he feels sorry for his sister. So he attacks and drives off the raiders. 'Urwa is truly grateful, and he and 'Antar swear friendship.

14.2. Bisṭām sends 'Antar word that Mālik and his family have fled the Banī Shaibān and are living among the Banī Kinda. 'Antar and Shaibūb set out. 'Urwa tells 'Antar that he will gather his hundred vagabond followers and join him later.

14.3. On his way to Kinda, 'Antar saves the sister of a black warrior who is also named 'Antar from a brigand who has stolen her. 'Antar changes his double's name so he will not be attacked by mistake in the future.

14.4. Meanwhile, a mighty knight of the Banī Kinda named Musaḥḥil ibn Ṭarrāq sees and falls in love with 'Abla. Mālik agrees to a marriage but again requests 'Antar's death as the bride price.

14.5. 'Antar and Shaibūb arrive and learn that Musaḥḥil plans to take Mālik and his family to his own branch of the tribe. 'Antar waits and ambushes the caravan. He kills Musaḥḥil, but Mālik and the others flee back to the Kinda camp.

14.6. Reinforced by 'Urwa and his men, 'Antar decides to attack the Kinda camp. The enemy has seven thousand men, but 'Antar determines to rescue 'Abla or die in the attempt.

14.7. Battle is joined. 'Antar and his men are on the point of being overwhelmed when the Kinda warriors suddenly stop fighting and leave the battleground. Bisṭām and the Banī Shaibān have attacked their camp. Four of King Zuhair's sons also appear, each leading a column of the Banī 'Abs. All attack and win a great victory over the Kinda army.

14.8. Mālik still refuses to return to 'Abs as long as 'Antar is there. So 'Antar decides to go live with Bisṭām. The various armies head for home.

14.9. One column of 'Abs is lead by Prince Mālik. On the way home, he goes hunting alone and falls captive to a passing group of raiders. 'Antar happens to be among them and saves the prince. He is escorting him back to his men when they come upon another column of the army, which has been attacked.

14.10. A group of the Banī Khath'am, led by Anas ibn Mudrika, attacked the 'Abs army and took three hundred prisoners, including 'Urwa, 'Abla, and her brother 'Amr.

14.11. Anas falls in love with 'Abla. 'Amr agrees to let him marry her in return for 'Antar's death. At this point, 'Antar and Bisṭām and ten others attack. 'Antar wounds Anas, who flees. The captives are freed. 'Antar decides to return to 'Abs after all. He gives Bisṭām a large part of his share of the booty and bids him farewell. He and the rest of the 'Abs go home and celebrate their victories.

15. War among 'Abs, an-Nu'mān, and Anūshirwān: The Quarrel Begins, 10/420–11/411

15.1. 'Umāra complains constantly to his brother of his love for 'Abla, saying that he would rather see her dead than married to 'Antar. Ar-Rabī' approves of this idea and arranged for his friend Mufarrij ibn Hilāl of the Banī Shaibān to kidnap and later kill 'Abla.

15.2. Mufarrij, under the impression that 'Abla is just a disobedient slave, kidnaps her and awaits further instructions from ar-Rabī'.

15.3. 'Antar is mad with grief. He learns that it was ar-Rabī' who had 'Abla kidnapped, but he cannot prove it. Zuhair sends ar-Rabī' and his clan to live with the 'Abs sister tribe, the Banī Fazāra, in order to keep peace within his tribe.

15.4. Ar-Rabī' visits Fazāra, whose leaders share his hatred of 'Antar, then sets out to visit Mufarrij to finish off 'Abla, and then an-Nu'mān, the new king of al-Ḥīra.

15.5. Mufarrij orders one of his slaves to take 'Abla to the desert and kill her. The slave is about to complete his mission when Shaibūb appears and wounds him with an arrow. The slave, whose name is Bishāra, begs for mercy. In return for the hand of one of 'Abla's slave-women, with whom he has fallen in love, Bishāra promises to tell ar-Rabī' and Mufarrij that 'Abla is dead and to tell King Zuhair how ar-Rabī' instigated the kidnapping. Shaibūb agrees to this plan and returns to fetch 'Antar. Bishāra hides 'Abla and tells Mufarrij and ar-Rabī' that she is dead. These two then set out for al-Ḥīra.

15.6. At an-Nu'mān's court ar-Rabī' describes the beauty of King Zuhair's only daughter, al-Mutajarrida. An-Nu'mān becomes infatuated and decides to send ar-Rabī' to Zuhair to present gifts and ask for his daughter's hand. Mufarrij travels to Persia to help Anūshirwān quell a rebellion.

15.7. Ar-Rabī' heads for 'Abs with an-Nu'mān's caravan of gifts. He runs into 'Antar and his men, who are on their way to retrieve 'Abla from the Banī Shaibān. When 'Antar sees his rival leading a rich caravan, he disguises himself and steals all of ar-Rabī''s wealth, which he sends back to his clan to hide. Then 'Antar raids the Shaibān herds, picks up 'Abla and Bishāra, and sets out for home.

15.8. In 'Abs, 'Antar accuses ar-Rabī' before Zuhair of kidnapping 'Abla and demands the return of the many precious jewels she was wearing (which Mufarrij now has). Ar-Rabī' is amazed to see 'Abla still alive. But he accuses 'Antar of robbing him. Both ar-Rabī' and 'Antar are too powerful for King Zuhair to punish rashly, so he does nothing. He is, however, very displeased at an-Nu'mān's request for his daughter and determines to reject the suit.

15.9. Ar-Rabī' decides to get rid of 'Antar's evidence against him; he kidnaps the slave Bishāra. When 'Antar discovers Bishāra's absence, he gathers his men and sets out for the Fazāra camp, where ar-Rabī' is currently residing. King Zuhair, fearing the outbreak of open combat and a further split of 'Abs, sends his sons Shāsh and Mālik to keep the peace.

15.10. 'Antar finds Bishāra in the Fazāra camp. Ar-Rabi' has been sowing seeds of hatred against 'Antar among the Fazāra leadership, who come to his aid and attack 'Antar. 'Antar fights off the Fazāra and captures ar-Rabī' and 'Umāra. He sends them back to his tents to be kept prisoner.

15.11. King Zuhair has heard of the battle and comes to meet 'Antar to escort him back to 'Abs. As they enter the camp, they hear an uproar among 'Antar's tents. Prince Qais has seen ar-Rabī' and 'Umāra brought into camp as prisoners. He is outraged that 'Abs nobles should be held captive within their own tribe and releases them. Ar-Rabī' quickly gathers his supporters and ransacks the tents until he finds the wealth that 'Antar stole from him.

15.12. 'Antar is forced to admit that he attacked and robbed ar-Rabī', but he still demands the return of 'Abla's jewels. Failing to win assurance of their return, 'Antar gathers his clan and followers and emigrates from 'Abs.

16. War among 'Abs, an-Nu'mān, and Anūshirwān: The Quarrel Expands, 11/411–12/175

16.1. After leaving 'Abs, 'Antar hears that ar-Rabī' left with the Fazāra. He settles his clan in a camp near the lands of the Banī Shaibān. Once they are settled, he takes some men to raid the Shaibān herds.

16.2. Meanwhile, Mufarrij returns from the Persian wars. He learns that 'Antar raided his herds when he came to get 'Abla. Mufarrij goes to an-Nu'mān and asks for his help in recovering the animals. The king is angry at Zuhair for refusing his proposal of marriage, so he agrees to help. He sends an army of twenty thousand men against 'Abs under the leadership of his brother, Prince al-Aswad.

16.3. Nor is ar-Rabī' idle. With his friend Prince Ḥudhaifa of the Banī Fazāra, he enlists the services of al-Ḥārith ibn Ẓālim of the Banī Murra. They all set out to raid 'Antar's camp. They attack the camp while 'Antar is away, but he appears at the last moment, captures 'Umāra, Ḥudhaifa, and al-Ḥārith, and drives the rest of the attackers away.

16.4. Ar-Rabī' flees to the Banī Shaibān. A few days later, he and Mufarrij attack 'Antar's camp. 'Antar captures them and drives off their followers. From his prisoners 'Antar learns that al-Aswad and the Ḥīran army are on their way to attack 'Abs. 'Antar takes his men to help King Zuhair.

16.5. Shaibūb goes to scout the situation at the 'Abs camp. He returns to 'Antar with the news that al-Aswad has already attacked the 'Abs, defeated them in battle, pillaged the camp, and taken many prisoners, including King Zuhair and his sons.

16.6. Shaibūb has destroyed al-Aswad's water bags, and he advises 'Antar to attack the Ḥīran army at the next water hole. 'Antar agrees to this plan. He lies in wait for the enemy; after a few days, he sees al-Aswad and his thirsty, disorganized army rushing toward the water. 'Antar and his men attack and rout the Ḥīran troops. 'Antar releases the 'Abs prisoners, and all go to 'Antar's camp to celebrate the victory.

16.7. When they reach camp, 'Antar and his men discover that Mālik and 'Amr released ar-Rabī' and the other prisoners, who thereupon fled to an-Nu'mān.

16.8. An-Nu'mān receives word of his brother's defeat. He sends letters to all the tribes to help him against 'Abs. Among those who answer the call are al-Jaidā' and Ma'dīkarib and the Banī Zubaid. On the way toward an-Nu'mān, the Zubaid army captures Mālik and his family, including 'Abla. Mālik fled from 'Antar's camp after he released the prisoners 'Antar was keeping there. Ma'dīkarib sends his prisoners to al-Ḥīra; he attacks 'Antar's camp with the greater part of his army. 'Antar defeats the Zubaid army and captures Ma'dīkarib.

16.9. 'Antar and an-Nu'mān exchange prisoners: al-Aswad, Ma'dīkarib, and others for 'Abla and her much-contested jewels.

16.10. Warriors have flowed into al-Ḥīra from all the Arab tribes; prominent among them is Ḥujār ibn 'Āmir, the hero of the Banī Kinda. Anūshirwān has also helped by sending five thousand Persian troops. An-Nu'mān leaves al-Ḥīra leading thirty-five thousand men against the thirty-five hundred 'Abs warriors.

16.11. ʿAntar ambushes the Persian troops in a large gully. An-Nuʿmān suspected a trap and refuses to help the Persians, who have consistently rejected his advice. Few Persians escape ʿAntar's attack.

16.12. The ʿAbs return and fortify themselves in a mountain stronghold that an-Nuʿmān besieges. The two armies battle and hold rounds of single combat. Although outnumbered ten to one, ʿAntar and ʿAbs hold their own. An-Nuʿmān constantly receives reinforcements, but comes no closer to defeating his enemy. His anger turns to admiration for their courage and skill. Finally he decides that a victory, even if possible, would be much too costly, so he sends his minister ʿAmr ibn Nufaila to arrange peace with King Zuhair. Zuhair agrees to give the Ḥīran king his daughter in exchange for peace, so peace is made.

17. War among ʿAbs, an-Nuʿmān, and Anūshirwān: Anūshirwān Steps In, 12/175–13/274

17.1. When he hears how an-Nuʿmān let the Persian troops be cut apart without doing anything to help them, Anūshirwān becomes furious. He calls his son Khudāwand and orders him to collect an army of seventy thousand men, to remove an-Nuʿmān from his throne and replace him with Prince al-Aswad, and then to attack the Banī ʿAbs.

17.2. Khudāwand arrests an-Nuʿmān and declares al-Aswad king of al-Ḥīra. Al-Aswad immediately orders the Arab chiefs who are hostile to ʿAntar and ʿAbs to attack them. Two of those who respond to this order are Maʿdīkarib of the Banī Zubaid and Ḥujār ibn ʿĀmir of the Banī Kinda. These two invite the most prestigious chief of the Arabs, Duraid ibn aṣ-Ṣimma of the Banī Jusham, to join them, but Duraid refuses to help Persians defeat Arabs.

17.3. Ḥujār and an army of seven thousand Kinda come to the camp of the Banī Fazāra. The two tribes lay plans to attack ʿAbs. But ʿAntar has heard of the troops gathering against his tribe and launches a preemptive attack. He catches the Fazāra and Kinda unprepared, defeats them, and takes Ḥujār ibn ʿĀmir captive.

17.4. Ḥujār offers his friendship to ʿAntar and says that he and his men will help ʿAbs against the Persians. When Maʿdīkarib learns of Ḥujār's change of feelings, he too joins the ʿAbs. Feeling begins to turn from anti-ʿAbs to anti-Persian.

17.5. The ʿAbs and their allies fortify themselves within a mountain stronghold and await the Persian and Ḥīran armies. ʿAntar sends Ḥujār and ʿUrwa with some men to attack al-Ḥīra to try to free an-Nuʿmān.

17.6. Khudāwand and al-Aswad and their armies attack the ʿAbs. The two sides fight several days, with the Persian and Arab armies taking turn in attacking. The ʿAbs are severely outnumbered. They survive only because ʿAntar takes the field of single combat day after day and thus gives his men a chance to rest.

17.7. Ar-Rabīʿ ibn Ziyād, who has become al-Aswad's chief counselor, advises him to have the Arab and Persian forces attack ʿAbs together in one final effort. Before this can be arranged, however, an-Nuʿmān appears, having been freed by Ḥujār and ʿUrwa. All of the Arabs desert al-Aswad and go over to an-Nuʿmān.

17.8. Khudāwand is tired of fighting ʿAbs, whose courage he has grown to admire. When the Persian prince sees that he will now have to fight all the Arabs, he decides to make peace. An-Nuʿmān knows that there is no long-term gain in fighting the Persians and quickly accepts the Persian offer of peace.

17.9. Khudāwand has been greatly impressed with ʿAntar's skill in battle and asks to meet him. The two become friends, and ʿAntar accompanies an-Nuʿmān and Khudāwand to al-Ḥīra, where large feasts are held to celebrate the peace. An-Nuʿmān forgives his brother al-Aswad, and Khudāwand and the Persian vizier, al-Mūbadhān, convince Anūshirwān to forgive both an-Nuʿmān and ʿAbs.

18. ʿAntar Helps Prince al-Ḥārith ibn Zuhair, 13/273–14/315

18.1. On the way home from al-Ḥīra, ʿAntar and ʿUrwa encounter Shaibūb, who tells them that Prince al-Ḥārith ibn Zuhair has been taken captive. Al-Ḥārith fell in love with Lubnā bint Bakr of the Banī Zahlān. Lubnā loves al-Ḥārith, but she has two other suitors as well, her cousin Jarīr and the rich warrior al-Khaitaʿūsh ibn al-Ashʿath.

18.2. Al-Ḥārith and Shaibūb sneak into the Zahlān camp and flee with Lubnā. When Lubnā's absence is noticed, al-Khaitaʿūsh pursues them with five hundred warriors. He overtakes them and takes al-Ḥārith and Lubnā prisoner.

18.3. Shaibūb eludes capture and meets ʿAntar and ʿUrwa. He leads them back to the place where he left the Zahlān warriors. ʿAntar attacks them and rescues al-Ḥārith and Lubnā. They all continue on their way back to ʿAbs.

19. ʿAntar Helps King Zuhair's Brother, Prince Usayyid, 14/315–380

19.1. While ʿAntar is in al-Ḥīra, King Zuhair is visited by his brother Usayyid, who has been living in Mecca because his wife and infant son were stolen in a raid. Zuhair takes his brother on a picnic, during which Usayyid says that he plans to travel around Arabia and look for his family one last time.

19.2. The brothers fall asleep and awake to discover that they have been taken prisoner during the night. Their captor is a young warrior named Nāziḥ, who is a member of the Bani ʼl-Qiyān.

19.3. Nāziḥ came to capture King Zuhair as part of his dowry for his beloved, Ḍiya bint ʻAbbād. Nāziḥ is only a poor orphan, but his suit is favored by both Ḍiya and her father. He has, however, a powerful rival for Ḍiya's hand in Jāzim ibn Fātik of the Banī Naʻāma.

19.4. Nāziḥ takes his captives toward his tribe's camp. They meet ʻAntar and his companions, on their way home from al-Ḥīra. ʻAntar captures Nāziḥ and frees Zuhair and Usayyid. By an amulet that Nāziḥ is wearing, Usayyid recognizes him as his lost son. Father and son celebrate their reunion.

19.5. All decide to take advantage of the happy occasion to pause and celebrate the wedding of al-Ḥārith and Lubnā. After the wedding Usayyid decides to go with Nāziḥ to the Bani ʼl-Qiyān so that Nāziḥ can win Ḍiya and Usayyid can be reunited with Nāziḥ's mother, Salma. ʻAntar, Shaibūb, and ʻUrwa and his companions decide to help them. King Zuhair and al-Ḥārith and his new bride return to ʻAbs. There they learn that Prince Shāsh has been killed.

20. The War between ʻAbs and ʻĀmir, 14/381–17/102

20.1. Shāsh ibn Zuhair and Ḥudhaifa ibn Badr of Fazāra escorted their sisters to al-Ḥīra to marry an-Nuʻmān and al-Aswad, respectively. The weddings are celebrated and Shāsh and Ḥudhaifa depart for home together. On their way they quarrel, and Shāsh decides to proceed alone.

20.2. Shāsh encounters a warrior of the Banī ʻĀmir who is out hunting. They quarrel, and the hunter kills Shāsh and steals the fine presents that an-Nuʻman gave him. Shāsh's body is found by some of the Banī ʻAbs and brought home.

20.3. Zuhair mourns his son. Then he gathers his warriors to seek vengeance from the tribe in whose lands Shāsh's body was found, the Banī ʻĀmir.

20.4. Most of the leaders of ʻĀmir attended an-Nuʻmān's wedding and are still in al-Ḥīra. The ʻĀmir leaders who remain tell Zuhair that they know nothing of his son's death. Zuhair departs peaceably, but he sends his old nurse to the ʻĀmir camp to try to find out the identity of his son's murderer.

20.5. The hunter's wife tries to sell some of the possessions her husband stole from Shāsh's body. Zuhair's nurse recognizes them and reports to Zuhair. The ʻAbs king immediately gathers his men and returns to the ʻĀmir camp. The ʻĀmir leaders tell Zuhair that his son's killer has left their camp and that he should not hold a whole tribe responsible for the action of one man. Zuhair is about to agree, but ar-Rabīʻ ibn Ziyād calls out for revenge. The rest of the ʻAbs take up the cry and attack the Banī ʿĀmir. Battle rages for five days, until the holy month of Rajab begins and fighting stops. Zuhair goes to Mecca for the holy month.

20.6. Khālid ibn Jaʿfar, the king of the Banī ʿĀmir, also comes to Mecca on his way home from an-Nuʿmān's wedding and learns about the new war between his tribe and ʿAbs. He and Zuhair meet and exchange angry words. Khālid returns to ʿĀmir and sets up an ambush for King Zuhair. The ʿĀmir kill Zuhair on his way home from Mecca. Zuhair's oldest surviving son, Qais, becomes the new king of ʿAbs.

20.7. Meanwhile, ʿAntar is in South Arabia and knows nothing of the new war. He and his companions arrive at the camp of Nāziḥ's beloved and find the Bani 'l-Qiyān under attack. A powerful king of Yemen, Niqba of the Banī Ashtar, has heard of Ḍiya's beauty and has sent his son with seven thousand men to capture her. ʿAntar rushes into battle, kills Niqba's son, and forces the enemy to flee.

20.8. When Niqba learns of the defeat his troops have suffered, he gathers another army and attacks again. ʿAntar kills Niqba in battle. Niqba's good brother, Niʿma, is proclaimed king, Nāziḥ and Ḍiya marry, and Usayyid and Salmā have a happy reunion. ʿAntar and his companions head home.

20.9. King Khālid knows that his war with ʿAbs will be difficult to win if ʿAntar rejoins them, so he ambushes ʿAntar on his way home. ʿAntar and his men kill so many of the Banī ʿĀmir, however, that Khālid stops the fighting. He tells ʿAntar that he attacked him by mistake. ʿAntar is deceived by this explanation, and they make peace.

20.10. King Khālid returns to his camp to gather his warriors and allies, the most important of whom is al-Ḥārith ibn Ẓālim, and sets out to attack ʿAbs.

20.11. ʿAntar returns home and learns of Shāsh and Zuhair's deaths. King Qais has gathered an army and sets out to attack ʿĀmir. Ar-Rabīʿ has poisoned Qais's mind against ʿAntar, so the ʿAbs king leaves the black hero behind in camp.

20.12. The two armies meet, and things go badly for ʿAbs. No one can withstand the might of al-Ḥārith ibn Ẓālim, who defeats all who dare to face him in single combat.

20.13. Suddenly ʿAntar appears, and the tide of battle turns. ʿAntar fights and captures al-Ḥārith. Al-Ḥārith wants to be known as the greatest warrior of Arabia and is insanely jealous of ʿAntar, the only one who has ever defeated him. Once captured, however, al-Ḥārith makes a virtue of necessity. In exchange for his freedom, he promises to change sides and fight for ʿAbs.

20.14. Seeing that they will have to withstand both ʿAntar and al-Ḥārith, the Banī ʿĀmir retreat and fortify themselves in their camp. ʿAbs attacks them repeatedly. Among the heroes that ʿAntar captures in single combat is the young ‘Āmir warrior ‘Āmir ibn aṭ-Ṭufail. On the ‘Abs side, Prince Mālik and ‘Umāra fall captive. In order to recover these and other important prisoners, the Banī ‘Abs agree to a truce and stop their attacks.

20.15. Back at the camp, ‘Abs is once again torn by internal strife: ‘Antar and ‘Umāra argue. In order to maintain peace within the tribe, King Qais sends ar-Rabī‘ and ‘Umāra to live with the Banī Fazāra. Even at this distance, ‘Antar and ar-Rabī‘ and their feuding clans skirmish several times.

20.16. Meanwhile, King Khālid collects an army of forty thousand men and leads them against ‘Abs. King Qais learns of this army and sends for his allies. Ḥudhaifa ibn Badr, who is now king of the Banī Fazāra, is among those whose help Qais requests. Upon ar-Rabī‘ ibn Ziyad's advice, however, Ḥudhaifa refuses this request.

20.17. Ar-Rabī‘ lures ‘Antar out of camp and manages to capture him. He is attacked by a group of raiders from the Banī Khaulān. Ar-Rabī‘ flees, and the raiders take ‘Antar to their camp to decide what to do with him. They, in turn, suffer attack. ‘Antar manages to free himself and helps the Khaulān drive off their attackers.

20.18. King Khālid has attacked the ‘Abs and is on the point of defeating them when ‘Antar appears leading an army from the Banī Khaulān, who are now his friends. His presence demoralizes the Banī ‘Āmir, who flee.

20.19. King Khālid decides to go to al-Ḥīra and ask Prince al-Aswad, to whom he is related, for help against ‘Abs. Also at an-Nu‘mān's court is al-Ḥārith ibn Ẓālim, who is still trying to find a way to outdo ‘Antar. One night he gets very drunk and kills King Khālid in his sleep.

20.20. An-Nu‘mān is furious at this breach of court etiquette. He sends soldiers to arrest al-Ḥārith, who eludes pursuit. Al-Ḥārith gets hold of an-Nu‘mān's infant son, sneaks into court, and butchers the baby before his father's eyes. He flees al-Ḥīra and takes refuge with the Banī ‘Abs. King Qais welcomes him as the killer of his father's murderer and promises his protection.

21. ‘Antar and al-Laqīṭ ibn Zurāra, 17/103–17/174

21.1. King Qais suggests that it is time that ‘Antar and ‘Abla marry. ‘Antar happily concurs, but just then his half-sister Marwa arrives and begs his help. Her son al-Ḥiṭāl, a favorite of ‘Antar's, has been captured by al-Laqīṭ ibn Zurāra of the Banī Tamīm, and Marwa asks ‘Antar to rescue him.

21.2. Al-Laqīṭ is the most arrogant of the eighteen princes of the Banī Tamīm. When his brothers complain about him, al-Laqīṭ's father tells him that he cannot think so highly of himself unless he wins the famous beauty Badr ad-Dīn in marriage, captures one thousand ‘Aṣāfīr camels from an-Nu‘mān, and defeats ‘Antar in battle. Al-Laqīṭ sets out to accomplish these tasks.

21.3. He easily marries Badr ad-Dīn; her father has been warned in a dream to accept his proposal. Al-Laqīṭ then sets out for al-Ḥīra. On his way he captures al-Ḥārith ibn Ẓālim and delivers him to an-Nu'mān, who in gratitude gives him the thousand camels he desires.

21.4. On his return from al-Ḥīra, al-Laqīṭ captures al-Ḥiṭāl. When he learns that his captive is 'Antar's nephew, al-Laqīṭ takes him home and awaits 'Antar's arrival.

21.5. Shaibūb appears in the Tamīm camp and tells al-Laqīṭ that 'Antar is approaching. The Tamīm prince gathers three thousand men to meet him. 'Antar attacks the now defenseless camp, frees al-Ḥiṭāl, and raids al-Laqīṭ's herds. Then he and his companions return to 'Abs.

21.6. They arrive to find the camp being attacked by the Banī 'Āmir. The enemy has surprised and driven off Qais and his warriors, plundered the camp, and sent the 'Abs women to the 'Āmir camp as captives. 'Antar and his men join the battle. They fight the greatly superior number of 'Āmir all day. The next day al-Laqīṭ and his men arrive to reinforce the enemy. In spite of 'Antar's heroic efforts, the small group of 'Abs is about to be overwhelmed.

21.7. Help arrives from two directions. First King Qais and the reorganized 'Abs appear. Then al-Ḥārith ibn Ẓālim, who has escaped from an-Nu'mān and freed the 'Abs prisoners being held in the 'Āmir camp, joins the battle. The two sides fight all night, but finally the Banī 'Āmir break ranks and flee.

21.8. The 'Abs celebrate the victory, and once again Qais suggests that it is time for 'Antar to marry 'Abla. Still opposed to the marriage, Mālik and 'Āmir plot with ar-Rabī' and the Banī Fazāra to kill 'Antar. When the assassination attempt fails, Mālik and 'Āmir flee. They fall captive to the Banī Jabhān. 'Antar rescues them.

22. The War of Dāḥis and al-Ghabrā', 17/175–19/347

22.1. 'Antar returns to camp to learn that King Qais has become involved in a horse race with Ḥudhaifa of Fazāra. Cooler heads in both tribes try to stop the race, but Qais and Ḥudhaifa become increasingly angry with each other and refuse to heed advice. The time and place of the race are set.

22.2. Ḥudhaifa places a slave along the race course to hinder Qais's horse, Dāḥis, so that Ḥudhaifa's horse, al-Ghabrā', wins the race. Shaibūb, however, witnesses the cheating. King Qais refuses to pay the bet he had with Ḥudhaifa, and the two tribes part in bad temper.

22.3. Prince Mālik ibn Zuhair falls in love and gets married. To revenge himself against Qais, Ḥudhaifa kills Mālik and his new bride on their wedding morning. This act is too much for even ar-Rabī' ibn Ziyād, who takes his clan and moves back to ʿAbs. ʿAntar, a close friend of the murdered prince, goes to Fazāra and kills ʿAuf, one of Ḥudhaifa's brothers.

22.4. Meanwhile, an-Nuʿmān has learned that ʿAbs is harboring al-Ḥārith ibn Ẓālim. The king sends an army under command of Prince al-Aswad to attack ʿAbs and retake al-Ḥarith. Al-Mutajarrida warns her brother Qais about the army.

22.5. On ʿAntar's advice, King Qais makes a preemptive attack upon the Banī Fazāra before al-Aswad and his army arrive. The two tribes fight, but finally the old men of Fazāra come unarmed onto the battlefield and convince the sister tribes to stop their feuding. Ḥudhaifa and Qais declare a truce.

22.6. Leaving another sister tribe, the Banī Ghaṭafān, to protect their camp, the Banī ʿAbs set out to meet the Ḥīran army. After a few days of battle, ʿAbs surprises the enemy with a night attack. The Ḥīrans flee and their leader, al-Aswad, falls captive.

22.7. On their way home, the Banī ʿAbs are met by slaves who report that in their absence the Banī Fazāra have attacked and plundered their camp and slaughtered four hundred ʿAbs infants, including Qais's son.

22.8. The ʿAbs return to mourn and bury their dead. Leaving al-Ḥārith ibn Ẓālim to guard the Ḥīran prisoners, they set out to rescue their women from Fazāra. They storm the camp, recover their families, and take five hundred of the enemy captive. Qais gives every ʿAbs mother who lost a son one of the prisoners to slaughter in revenge. He himself kills the remaining hundred to avenge his own son.

22.9. ʿAbs prepares to finish off the regrouped Fazāra. Battle is joined, but ʿAbs sees al-Ḥārith ibn Ẓālim fighting on the enemy side. Because of his blind envy of ʿAntar, al-Ḥārith let himself be convinced by al-Aswad to change sides. Fierce but inconclusive fighting continues for several days.

22.10. ʿAbd al-Muṭṭalib, the grandfather of the future Prophet Muḥammad, appears. This highly respected Meccan leader has heard of the senseless feud. Through his mediation, ʿAbs and Fazāra make peace. He also arranges for al-Aswad to be released; since al-Ḥārith ibn Ẓālim has disappeared, peace is also made between an-Nuʿmān and ʿAbs.

22.11. Al-Ḥārith ibn Ẓālim flees to al-Ḥīra, where he hopes that al-Aswad's good offices will induce an-Nuʿmān's forgiveness. An-Nuʿmān initially agrees; but when al-Ḥārith begins to boast of his various evil deeds, the king has him killed.

23. Muqri 'l-Waḥsh, 19/347–20/400

23.1. An-Nuʿmān sees a way to punish ʿAbs when a young Syrian Christian knight, Muqri 'l-Waḥsh, appears at his court. Muqrī has come to win two thousand ʿAṣāfīr camels as a dowry for his beloved. An-Nuʿmān promises the camels to him in return for capturing or killing ʿAntar.

23.2. An-Nuʿmān tests Muqrī's skill in battle by holding a tournament. Muqrī defeats every opponent he meets. Satisfied, an-Nuʿmān gives him an army and sends him against ʿAbs.

23.3. When they hear about this new attack on ʿAbs, the Banī Fazāra join Muqrī and his army. Battle is joined, and the two sides fight for days. Finally, ʿAntar meets Muqrī in single combat. They fight for several days until Muqrī senses defeat and flees from ʿAntar, who sets out in pursuit.

23.4. ʿAbs and an-Nuʿmān's army continue to fight. Without ʿAntar, the ʿAbs are hard pressed. They are on the verge of defeat when ʿAntar and Muqrī return and, side by side, attack the Ḥīrans. They have become friends. When the Ḥīrans see this, they break ranks and flee.

23.5. The ʿAbs let the Ḥīrans go and follow the Banī Fazāra. The Fazāra scatter, but Ḥudhaifa and his clan refuse to flee. The ʿAbs surround the forty warriors of the ruling clan. They kill all except Ḥudhaifa's young son, Ḥiṣn, whom they spare because of his youth.

23.6. The Banī ʿAbs return home. They celebrate their victory, but they now regret the massacre of Ḥudhaifa and his clan.

24. The Marriage of ʿAntar and ʿAbla, 20/401–20/457

24.1. ʿAntar finally marries ʿAbla. ʿUmāra tries to stop the marriage by poisoning ʿAntar, but his scheme fails.

24.2. All of ʿAntar's friends from other tribes (al-Hiṭāl of the Banī Ghaṭafān, Hujār of Kinda, Maʿdīkarib of Zubaid, Bisṭām of Shaibān, and others) come with gifts and poems of praise for the couple.

24.3. The marriage is consummated.

25. ʿAntar Helps Muqri ʾl-Waḥsh Win His Beloved, 20/457–20/478

25.1. ʿAntar's wedding makes Muqrī long for his own love. ʿAntar promises to help him; he, Shaibūb, al-Hiṭāl, and ʿUrwa and his men set out with Muqrī for Syria.

25.2. Muqrī's beloved, Musaika, is a great beauty. Word of her beauty grows while Muqrī is away, and Badr, the son of King al-Ḥārith al-Wahhāb of Ghassān, requests her hand. Musaika's father has promised his daughter to Muqrī and rejects Badr's suit.

25.3. Badr decides to use force and attacks the camp with a great army. At this point Muqrī, ʿAntar, and the others appear. ʿAntar kills Badr, whose army then flees. But the power of the king of Ghassān is great. In order to avoid further trouble ʿAntar convinces Musaika's father and Muqrī to live with ʿAbs. They return together to ʿAbs but find the campsite deserted.

26. ʿAbs in Yemen, 20/478–22/187

26.1. The remnants of the Banī Fazāra have gone to al-Ḥīra and asked al-Aswad, Ḥudhaifa's brother-in-law, to avenge his death. Both al-Aswad and an-Nuʿmān become angry when they learn of Ḥudhaifa's death.

26.2. Al-Mutajarrida warns Qais of an-Nuʿmān's anger. King Qais decides to move ʿAbs to Yemen to find new lands out of an-Nuʿmān's reach.

26.3. The ʿAbs come to the territories of the Banī Harīqa, whose leader, King ar-Ramīm, welcomes them and gives them lands in which to settle. An important warrior of Harīqa, al-Akhyal ibn ʿAmr, becomes envious of ʿAbs's wealth. ʿAntar rejoins the tribe just as al-Akhyal stirs up the Harīqa against the ʿAbs and leads an attack on them. ʿAntar kills al-Akhyal in battle. The ʿAbs decide to seek new lands.

26.4. ʿAbs moves deeper into Yemen. On the way Muqri 'l-Waḥsh and Musaika marry. ʿAbs enters the lands of the Banī Saʿd. Their king, Muʿāwiya ibn an-Nazzāl, is at first friendly, but he falls in love with ʿAbla and attacks ʿAbs in order to take her. ʿAntar and the ʿAbs repulse the attack and move on.

26.5. They come to the lands of the Banī Tamīm. The Tamīm are allies of the Banī Saʿd, and the next day Muʿāwiya and King Jābir of Tamīm attack with a large army. ʿAntar kills Muʿāwiya, Muqrī kills Jābir, and the attacking army flees.

26.6. ʿAbs comes to the lands of the Banī Fahd, whose king is al-Jaun ibn Rauḍa. Al-Jaun and his warlord ʿAmr ibn Damra lead the tribe in an attack against ʿAbs. ʿAntar kills ʿAmr, and King al-Jaun sues for peace.

26.7. ʿAbs moves to the lands of the Banī Kalb, whose king is Masʿūd ibn Musād. King Masʿūd welcomes ʿAbs, but his tribe envies the visitors' wealth. Masʿūd sees ʿAbla and falls in love with her. In order to win her, he uses a witch, who tries to bewitch ʿAbla; ʿAntar and Muqrī happen upon her. She casts a spell on ʿAntar, but Muqrī is protected by an amulet he wears, and he kills her.

26.8. In spite of these provocations, the relations between ʿAbs and Kalb remain outwardly friendly. The Kalb disguise themselves as the Banī Kinda and raid ʿAbs, but they are beaten off. Masʿūd still burns with love for ʿAbla. He sends his chief adviser to Qais and formally asks for her hand. ʿAntar kills the adviser in a rage, and Masʿūd gathers his warriors for war.

26.9. Qais decides to leave the Kalb lands. King Masʿūd pursues and attacks them. ʿAbs drives off the attack, so Masʿūd gathers his allies. ʿAntar kills Masʿūd in battle, but the Kalb and their allies receive constant reinforcements and continue their attacks.

26.10. Finally ʿAbs receives help. King Niʿma of the Banī Ashtar, Nāziḥ of al-Qiyān, and Prince Amr ibn al-Hind, a brother of an-Nuʿmān, arrive leading armies. The enemies of ʿAbs flee.

26.11. Al-Mutajarrida has convinced an-Nuʿmān to forgive ʿAbs. To assure peace between ʿAbs and Fazāra, an-Nuʿmān decides to settle ʿAbs in lands further away from Fazāra. The ʿAbs are exhausted from the continual fighting in Yemen, so King Qais decides to accept an-Nuʿmān's offer. They change direction and head north.

27. The Way Home, 22/188–23/223

27.1. On the way home, ʿUrwa ibn al-Ward disappears while guarding the herds one day. ʿAntar, Muqrī, and Shaibūb go to look for their friend.

27.2. The next day Duraid ibn aṣ-Ṣimma of the Banī Jusham and his nephew Sabīʿ ibn al-Ḥārith raid ʿAbs's herds. When he learns whose herds he has raided, Duraid wishes to return the animals. Sabīʿ, however, rejects this idea. ʿAbs pursues the raiders. By chance, ʿUmāra happens to wound Duraid, and the ʿAbs retake their animals.

27.3. Meanwhile, Shaibūb leads ʿAntar and Muqrī to ʿUrwa, who has been taken captive by Ṣamīd ibn Mānīʿ, lord of the Banī Daurān. ʿAntar and Muqrī attack while Shaibūb sneaks into camp and frees ʿUrwa. ʿAntar kills Ṣamīd, and he and Muqrī alone put the Daurān warriors to flight. The heroes only refrain from plundering the camp because the women of the tribe ask for mercy.

27.4. ʿAntar and his friends return to ʿAbs. On their way back they defeat a Yemeni army on its way to attack ʿAbs.

28. ʿAntar and ʿĀmir ibn aṭ-Ṭufail, 23/223–23/288

28.1. ʿAbs settles on the lands an-Nuʿmān assigns, originally part of the lands of the Banī ʿĀmir. ʿUmāra is very proud of defeating so great a warrior as Duraid. He and ʿUrwa argue about ʿAntar. Angry about the constant dissension that surrounds ʿAntar, King Qais orders him and his followers, who by now number around five hundred, to leave ʿAbs.

28.2. ʿĀmir ibn aṭ-Ṭufail of the Banī ʿĀmir learns of ʿAntar's departure. Anxious to avenge his previous defeat, ʿĀmir attacks ʿAntar's camp. ʿAntar captures him and his men; when he generously lets his captives go free, ʿĀmir becomes his friend. He invites ʿAntar and his clan to come live with the Banī ʿĀmir.

28.3. There is constant feasting between ʿAntar and his new hosts. One day ʿAntar goes to get a new supply of wine. During his journey, he defeats and befriends the hero ʿAmr ibn Wadd, who was the Banī ʿĀmir's greatest warrior before he went to live in Mecca.

28.4. ʿAntar returns to the Banī ʿĀmir to learn that ʿĀmir ibn aṭ-Ṭufail has gone raiding and fallen captive to Zaid al-Khail of the Banī Nabhān. ʿAntar and his friends free ʿĀmir and steal all of Zaid's horses.

29. ʿAntar and Duraid ibn aṣ-Ṣimma, 23/288–24/376

29.1. On returning to the Banī ʿĀmir camp, ʿAntar learns that Duraid ibn aṣ-Ṣimma and his allies are attacking ʿAbs. Still angry at his tribe, ʿAntar decides not to help them.

29.2. At ʿAbs the two armies join battle. Ar-Rabīʿ ibn Ziyād manages to capture Duraid by trickery. Nevertheless, the ʿAbs get the worst of it in the fighting until they find a hero in al-Kalīm ibn Ṣārim of the Banī Ghurāb, who joins the fighting. Duraid's forces gain the support of al-Laqīṭ ibn Zurāra, who appears with five thousand men and joins the attack against ʿAbs.

29.3. The battle rages for days. In spite of al-Kalīm's efforts, the tide turns more against ʿAbs each day. Qais constantly sends messages to ʿAntar, who still refuses to help. Qais finally sends the women of the tribe to implore ʿAntar to help. The knight cannot refuse this request; he and his men go to help ʿAbs.

29.4. ʿAntar arrives just in time to rescue three hundred ʿAbs prisoners that Duraid, who has regained his freedom in an exchange of prisoners, planned to execute. The next day ʿAntar and Duraid meet in single combat. ʿAntar takes Duraid prisoner, and Muqri ʾl-Waḥsh takes al-Laqīṭ prisoner.

29.5. At this point, ʿAntar's brother Jarīr arrives with the news that Zaid al-Khail and the Banı Nabhan are attacking the Banī ʿĀmir. Concerned about ʿAbla's safety, ʿAntar takes ten men and goes to help. He fights and captures Zaid, whereupon peace is made between the two tribes.

29.6. ʿAntar returns to ʿAbs, where the battle is still in full course. Duraid's army has been strengthened by the arrival of Sabīʿ ibn al-Ḥārith, who has killed al-Kalīm and freed Duraid and al-Laqīṭ.

29.7. ʿAntar captures Sabīʿ; ʿĀmir ibn aṭ-Ṭufail captures Duraid; the enemy troops flee. The Banī ʿĀmir suggest that the ʿAbs come and live with them. Qais accepts the proposal, and the two tribes set about to celebrate their victories together.

29.8. They begin to discuss what they should do with the prisoners when al-Mutajarrida and Prince Amr ibn al-Hind arrive for a visit. Prince Amr arranges peace between Duraid and Qais. Sabīʿ still envies ʿAntar and challenges him to a duel, but suddenly falls ill. Duraid takes him home to his tribe.

30. Al-Abjar and Mahriyya, 24/376–25/429

30.1. 'Antar now considers the idea of hanging one of his poems on the Ka'ba, something only the greatest poets are allowed to do. He is distracted from this idea, however, when al-Laqīt ibn Zurāra sends a horse thief to steal al-Abjar, his horse.

30.2. 'Antar sends Shaibūb to locate al-Abjar. Shaibūb finds the horse and returns to 'Abs. Then he, 'Antar, 'Āmir, and the rest of 'Antar's company set out for al-Laqīṭ's camp. On the way, 'Antar meets and captures the wedding caravan of Mahriyya, the bride-to-be of al-Laqīṭ's brother, Mālik.

30.3. While Shaibūb sneaks into al-Laqīṭ's camp and resteals al-Abjar, 'Antar feels attracted to Mahriyya and takes her to bed. Thus al-Laqīṭ loses al-Abjar and his brother loses his bride.

30.4. Mahriyya tells 'Antar that she does not love Mālik; she loves her cousin. On the return journey, they happen upon this cousin. The lovers are reunited and return home. 'Antar and his friends return to 'Abs.

31. 'Abs and Fazāra at War Again, 25/430–25/470

31.1. The Banī Fazāra still thirst for revenge against 'Abs. Their king is now Ḥiṣn ibn Ḥudhaifa, whose chief counselor is Sinān ibn Abī Ḥarītha. The tribe wins an ally in al-Ḥārith al-Wahhāb of al-Ghassān, the Byzantine empire's vassal king in charge of defending the empire's Syrian marches.

31.2. Certain of their overwhelming strength, Fazāra warns King Qais of their coming attack. Qais asks King an-Nu'mān, an old enemy of al-Ḥārith, for help against the attackers. When al-Laqīṭ hears of the new war, he joins the Fazāra and Ghassān army, which thus numbers three hundred thousand men.

31.3. The two sides join battle, and fighting continues for several months. Ar-Rabī' ibn Ziyād kills al-Laqīṭ; finally 'Abs defeats its foes and forces Fazāra to sue for peace. The Banī 'Abs regain the rights of their original territories. After celebrating their victory, they bid the Banī 'Āmir farewell and return home.

32. 'Amr ibn Ma'dīkarib, 25/471–26/33

32.1. 'Urwa ibn al-Ward falls in love with Lamīs bint Hammām of the Banī Ghaṭafān. Unfortunately, Lamīs is already in love with and engaged to 'Amr ibn Ma'dīkarib of the Banī Zubaid. This 'Amr is the son of 'Antar's rival and friend Ma'dīkarib, who has grown old. 'Amr has proven himself to be an impressive warrior and has become the new hero of the tribe.

32.2. Unaware that he has a rival, 'Urwa takes his men and goes to woo Lamīs. He arrives just in time to witness 'Amr and Lamīs's wedding. Undaunted, ʿUrwa decides to kill the groom and steal the bride. He waits until they set out for the Banī Zubaid, then he attacks. The two heroes fight, and ʿAmr captures ʿUrwa.

32.3. The party travels on until they meet a black brigand, Sulaika ibn Sulaka, who has just raided the Zubaid camp. ʿAmr and Sulaika fight, and Sulaika captures his opponent. In desperation, Lamīs releases ʿUrwa. He fights Sulaika until nightfall, when the two groups withdraw to rest.

32.4. Battle is about to begin the next day when ʿAntar, Shaibūb, and Muqrī appear. They learned of ʿUrwa's plan and followed him. When Sulaika recognizes ʿAntar, he turns and flees. ʿAntar suggests that ʿUrwa kill ʿAmr and marry Lamīs, but ʿUrwa realizes that the two truly love each other. He sets ʿAmr free and all become friends.

33. ʿAntar Leaves ʿAbs Again, 26/33–26/88

33.1. That night ʿAntar dreams that ʿĀmir ibn aṭ-Ṭufail is in trouble. He and his friends say good-bye to ʿAmr ibn Maʿdīkarib and go to the camp of the Banī ʿĀmir, which they find under attack.

33.2. ʿAntar helps drive off the attackers. They manage to make off with fifty of the ʿĀmir women, including ʿĀmir's mother and sister. ʿAntar, ʿĀmir, and others set out in pursuit and recover the prisoners.

33.3. On their way back, they meet a small group of the Banī Kināna. The leader, Sarīʿ ibn Qādir, explains that he and his family left their tribe because of a quarrel between him and his brother. ʿAntar invites them to come and live with him, and they accept.

33.4. Sarīʿ's daughter Nuwār and her cousin Mālik ibn Qādim are in love. It happens, however, that Ḥiṣn of the Banī Fazāra sees Nuwār and falls in love with her. He asks for her hand, and her father accepts. ʿAntar and Ḥiṣn quarrel because ʿAntar forces a group of Fazāra raiders to return some animals they captured. ʿAntar, therefore, decides to help Mālik ibn Qādim win Nuwār.

33.5. When Nuwār is taken to Fazāra to marry Ḥiṣn, ʿAntar openly attacks the caravan and gives the young woman to Mālik. Both Ḥiṣn and King Qais become furious at ʿAntar for this act. ʿAntar decides to take his clan to live with Duraid ibn aṣ-Ṣimma. Sarīʿ takes his clan and returns to Kināna.

33.6. After traveling for two days, ʿAntar and his clan come to the lands of the Banī Juraish, who, upon hearing their story, invite them to visit for a time. Meanwhile, ar-Rabīʿ ibn Ziyād commissions the famed poet an-Nābigha 'dh-Dhubyānī to compose a poem ridiculing ʿAbla. This poem gains currency. An unlucky Juraish warrior shows a copy—without first reading it—to ʿAntar, who falls into a rage and kills him. This arouses the wrath of the Banī Juraish hero Muʿāwiya ibn Shakil. Full-scale fighting breaks out in which ʿAntar kills

Muʿāwiya and routs the Juraish warriors. Then he and his companions continue on their way.

34. ʿAntar Helps Khufāf ibn Nadba, 26/88–27/166

34.1. ʿAntar and his clan happen upon Duraid being attacked in the desert by the Bani ʾl-Ḥārith. Duraid was returning home after successfully helping his foster-son Daththār ibn Rizq marry his beloved, Suʿdā. Annoyed by his constant raids upon them, the Bani ʾl-Ḥārith decided to take this opportunity to ambush Duraid. ʿAntar rushes to help his friend, and together they drive off the attackers. Duraid thanks ʿAntar and, after hearing his story, insists that he and his clan come to live with the Banī Jusham.

34.2. At Duraid's camp, the two groups hold feasts and a tournament. One of the stars of this tournament is a young black warrior named Khufāf ibn Nadba. ʿAntar and Khufāf become friends.

34.3. Prince al-Ḥārith ibn Zuhair sends word to ʿAntar that Ḥiṣn has imprisoned Mālik ibn Qādim and is torturing him. ʿAntar disguises his men as Yemenis, raids Fazāra, and rescues Mālik.

34.4. ʿAntar returns to Duraid's camp to learn that Khufāf and his rival al-ʿAbbās have been fighting over their mutual beloved. The girl's father tells the two suitors that he who kills Prince al-Mutanaʿjiz, son of King Fāyiz of the Banī Quḍāʿa, will win his daughter's hand in marriage. ʿAntar undertakes to help Khufāf carry out this task. ʿAntar's enemy and rival, Sabīʿ ibn al-Ḥārith, promises to help al-ʿAbbās.

34.5. Al-ʿAbbās and Sabīʿ set out first. Luck is not with them. They lose their way in the desert and fall captive to al-Mutanaʿjiz and his Amazon-like sister, Ghamra, a formidable warrior in her own right. The siblings decide to hold their prisoners for ransom.

34.6. When word reaches Duraid of Sabīʿ and al-ʿAbbās's capture, he, ʿAntar, and Khufāf set out with two hundred followers to the camp of the Banī Quḍāʿa. King Fāyiz is expecting them, and battle is joined. ʿAntar captures Prince al-Mutanaʿjiz in battle and delivers him to Khufāf. At the same time, Sabīʿ ibn al-Ḥārith attempts to escape from the Quḍāʿa camp. Ghamra discovers him, and the two fight for two full days. By the end of this time they are so impressed with one another that they fall in love. Sabīʿ agrees to help King Fāyiz against his own tribe.

34.7. The fighting continues for several days. One night ʿAntar and Ghamra decide to go out scouting. They happen upon each other and, separated from their tribes, fight for several days. ʿAntar finally captures his opponent, only then discovering that he has been fighting a woman. Overcome by her beauty, he rapes her. He immediately regrets this act and, as compensation, gives Ghamra her freedom. Both return to their tribes, which are still fighting. The battle continues a few more days, but finally the Banī Quḍā'a are defeated.

34.8. Duraid forgives Sabī' for fighting for the enemy. But Sabī' still favors Ghamra's tribe and secretly releases all those who were taken prisoner, except al-Mutana'jiz, whom Khufāf personally guards day and night.

35. War between Byzantium and Persia (and Their Allies), 27/167–28/272

35.1. 'Antar and Duraid return to camp to discover that a force of 'Abs and Fazāra, led by King Qais, has raided in their absence and carried off 'Antar's family and relatives as prisoners. 'Antar and Duraid pursue the raiders. When they overtake Qais, however, the 'Abs king claims that he only raided the camp in order to induce 'Antar to return. 'Antar senses that his claim is deceitful, but he allows his former tribesmen to return home in peace.

35.2. 'Antar and Duraid set out toward their own camp. On the way they are attacked by an army of thirty thousand Ḥīrans led by Prince al-Aswad and Prince Amr ibn al-Hind. This attack has been prompted by ar-Rabī' ibn Ziyād and King Ḥiṣn of Fazāra, who have aroused an-Nu'mān's suspicion by telling him that Duraid wishes to replace him as king of the Arabs and is relying on 'Antar's help to do so.

35.3. The Ḥīrans attack, and the two armies fight all day. That night, however, the Ḥīrans suddenly depart because they receive word that a Syrian army led by King al-Ḥārith of Ghassān is attacking the Banī 'Abs. The treacherous Sinān ibn Abī Ḥarītha, the chief advisor of King Ḥiṣn, has persuaded Ḥiṣn that the time is ripe to take revenge on 'Abs and has convinced al-Ḥārith to help them.

35.4. King al-Ḥārith has promised to help Fazāra against 'Abs because he sees it as an excuse to launch a major invasion into Arabia and challenge the power of his rival, King an-Nu'mān, there. He and his army reach the 'Abs camp, but their attack is interrupted by a summons from Caesar to join him in an attack against Anūshirwān.

35.5. As King al-Ḥārith prepares his withdrawal, an-Nu'mān appears with an army and attacks him. The Syrians, however, outnumber their attackers, and an-Nu'mān and his army are put to flight.

35.6. 'Antar and Duraid receive news of these events. For the sake of Arab solidarity, they decide to help their nominal liege, an-Nu'mān. 'Antar decides that since King al-Ḥārith is away fighting the Persians, he will attack Syria, which al-Ḥārith has left unprotected in his rear.

35.7. Outside of al-Madā'in, the Persian capital, Anūshirwān has gathered his Persian and Arab troops, including an-Nu'mān and such prominent heroes as ʿAmr ibn Maʿdīkarib, Ḥujār ibn ʿĀmir, and Sabīʿ ibn al-Ḥārith, to face an attacking army composed of Byzantines, Franks, and Syrian Arabs. Fighting continues for several weeks, with the Persians generally getting the worst of it. Caesar suddenly asks for peace. He has received word that ʿAntar and Duraid are ravaging Syria in his rear.

35.8. ʿAntar, Duraid, and King Qais have attacked Syria and captured Damascus. Caesar brings his army west to meet them. When the two armies meet, it is the Franks who initiate battle. ʿAntar kills their leader, King al-Khailajān, in battle. Caesar decides not to risk an extended battle; after a few more skirmishes, he offers peace. The Arab forces accept his offer.

35.9. ʿAntar and his companions proceed to al-Madā'in, where they celebrate the withdrawal of the Christian armies with Anūshirwān and an-Nuʿmān.

36. The Story of Ḥātim aṭ-Ṭayyi', 28/273–29/331

36.1. During a feast hosted by Anūshirwān, conversation turns to a discussion of which man among the Arabs is the most generous. An-Nuʿmān alleges that it is Ḥātim aṭ-Ṭayyi' and relates anecdotes about his generosity.

36.2. Ḥātim's mother was exceedingly generous from youth. Her family became annoyed over this noble but costly habit and married her off to a well-known miser. She gives birth to Ḥātim, and it soon becomes clear that he outstrips even his mother in generosity, for he lavishes feasts on every passerby. Among his guests are itinerant poets who praise his generosity in their poems. Thus his fame spreads throughout Arabia.

36.3. Ḥātim's father cannot bear all this generosity and moves away to another tribe. Ḥātim and his mother continue to give away possessions until they finally have nothing left. A guest appears; in order to provide for him, Ḥātim has his mother sell him into slavery. Three months pass before Ḥātim's owner discovers his slave's true identity. He immediately frees Ḥātim and lavishes him with gifts so that he can continue his generous ways.

36.4. Another time, Ḥātim takes the place of a prisoner so that the man can return to his tribe and collect his ransom. Against everyone's expectations, the man returns and ransoms Ḥātim.

36.5. Anūshirwān's interest is aroused by these stories, and he sends for Ḥātim. On his way to the Persian capital Ḥātim meets and becomes engaged to Marya bint ad-Ḍaḥḥāk of the Banī Fahm. Continuing his journey, Ḥātim is attacked and taken prisoner. ʿAntar, on his way home from al-Madā'in, rescues him. In return, Ḥātim invites ʿAntar to his wedding, even though the southern Arab Banī Ṭayyi' are among ʿAntar's natural enemies. ʿAntar accepts this invitation and promises to come when the wedding is held.

37. New Relatives, 29/332–30/406

37.1. While ʿAntar is away in al-Madāʾin, King Qais learns that the wife and son of his murdered brother Prince Mālik are living in anonymous poverty among the Banī Kalb in southern Arabia. The ʿAbs king takes three thousand men to find them and bring them back.

37.2. A short time afterward, ʿAntar returns to ʿAbs. When he learns where Qais has gone and why, he takes Shaibūb and Muqri ʾl-Waḥsh and follows. While scouting in advance, Shaibūb meets an old couple and their son, Māzin. It turns out that Māzin is really the son of Shaddād and thus ʿAntar's half-brother. Shaibūb takes Māzin to meet ʿAntar, but finds ʿAntar and Muqrī being held prisoner by Sabīʿ ibn al-Ḥārith, who came upon them while they were sleeping and captured them. Shaibūb rescues them by trickery, and Sabīʿ flees.

37.3. While Qais is on his way, members of the Banī Kalb discover that young Mājid is the dead Prince Mālik's son. Because ʿAntar killed their king, Masʿūd ibn Musād, the Kalb are enemies of ʿAbs. They imprison Mājid and send word of him to their current king, Ḥassān ibn Masʿūd, who is living among another branch of the tribe.

37.4. Before Ḥassān has time to come, King Qais attacks. The battle initially goes well for ʿAbs, but Kalb reinforcements begin to arrive, and the tide turns. The situation improves, however, when ʿAntar appears bearing the head of the slain King Ḥassān on his lance. ʿAntar met the king, routed the army, and killed him. The grizzly spectacle of King Ḥassān's head disheartens the Banī Kalb. They sue for peace.

37.5. King Qais joyfully greets Mājid ibn Mālik and his mother. They all return to ʿAbs without further incident. Shaddād is delighted to learn of the existence of his son Māzin, who decides to remain with his newfound family. ʿAntar takes both him and Mājid under his special care and protection.

38. Mājid, Asmāʾ, and Maisara, 30/407–30/474

38.1. One day a clan from the Banī Bishr seeks refuge with the Banī ʿAbs. King Qais welcomes them and allows them to camp nearby. There young Prince Mājid meets Asmāʾ, the daughter of the clan's leader, and the two fall in love.

38.2. Qais is unhappy about this development, and the older generations on both sides forbid the lovers to meet. But ʿAntar favors the match and convinces King Qais to let the two marry. When the happy Mājid goes to tell Asmāʾ the good news, however, he finds that the Bishr clan, afraid of causing a scandal, has departed. Accompanied by ʿAntar and his companions, Mājid follows them.

38.3. The Bishr clan originally left their tribe because a powerful black warrior named Maisara fell in love with Asmā'. The girl's father, Khidāsh, opposed the match and to gain time sent Maisara away to win a dowry. He took his family and sought refuge with 'Abs. Upon leaving 'Abs, the clan encounters Maisara in the desert. The black warrior still loves Asmā' and forces the family to return toward their original home.

38.4. Mājid, 'Antar, and the others overtake them. Maisara challenges them to single combat. He manages to take Māzin and 'Urwa prisoner and badly wounds Muqri 'l-Waḥsh. At last, 'Antar enters the field. The two black warriors fight for several days, but 'Antar finally prevails and captures the younger man.

38.5. All head back toward 'Abs. On their way, however, they meet King an-Nu'mān, who is headed toward Mecca to consult a famous soothsayer concerning a recurrent dream. 'Antar decides to accompany the king but sends his companions home.

39. An-Nu'mān and Hānī ibn Mas'ūd, 30/475–31/73

39.1. An-Nu'mān dreamed that he was on a mountain being pursued by an elephant when suddenly a boy named Hānī ibn Mas'ūd appeared and saved him. The Meccan soothsayer advises the king to beware of the Persians and to seek out this Hānī ibn Mas'ūd. When an-Nu'mān returns to Iraq, he learns that Shah Anūshirwān has died and Prince Khudāwand has succeeded his father to the Persian throne.

39.2. One day Khudāwand is told of the beauty of Arab women. Intrigued, he asks an-Nu'mān to give him a sister or daughter to marry. When this request is refused, the enraged shah sends Iyās ibn Qabīṣa with an army and orders to replace an-Nu'mān as king of al-Ḥīra. An-Nu'mān learns of the approaching army and flees.

39.3. Iyās first secures possession of al-Ḥīra then pursues and overtakes an-Nu'mān. Battle is joined. An-Nu'mān is on the verge of losing when Hānī ibn Mas'ūd, a prince of the Banī Shaibān, appears and turns the tide. Hānī heard of an-Nu'mān's plight and decided to help him. The Persian army suffers defeat, and Iyās is forced to retreat to al-Ḥīra. An-Nu'mān goes to the Banī Shaibān and sends for reinforcements among the Arab tribes.

39.4. 'Antar has returned home from Mecca to discover that Muqri 'l-Waḥsh died from the wound he received from Maisara. More surprising, he learns that Maisara is his son. Maisara's mother is Mahriyya, with whom 'Antar had slept so many years before (see 30.3). When Mahriyya learned that 'Antar had taken Maisara prisoner, she came to 'Abs and revealed his true identity. 'Antar mourns his friend Muqrī, but is nonetheless delighted to find that he has a son. In the midst of these bittersweet events, Mājid and Asmā' marry.

39.5. Meanwhile, Arab troops flock to an-Nu'mān. Khudāwand counters by sending a large Persian army to reinforce Iyās. The two sides meet at Dhī Qār. The fighting is fierce, but eventually the Arabs win. The Persians break ranks and flee. ('Abs arrives too late to participate in the battle.)

40. 'Antar Leaves 'Abs, 31/74–32/100

40.1. When the 'Abs return to their camp, 'Antar and King Qais quarrel. 'Antar grants his protection to a slave with whom Qais is angry and refuses to let the king have him. He decides to gather his clan and leave the tribe.

40.2. 'Antar determines to settle in Syria. Before he travels very far, he learns that Maisara, aided by Māzin, has kidnapped Mājid's wife, Asmā'. Maisara still loves her and has convinced Māzin to take part in the abduction.

40.3. Having seized Asmā', Maisara and Māzin flee toward Syria. On the way, they meet a group of Syrian warriors, who overcome them and take them prisoner.

40.4. 'Antar takes the women and children of his clan to the Banī Ghaṭafān and leaves them in their care. With the men he pursues Maisara and Māzin. Ar-Rabī' ibn Ziyād has warned the Banī Fazāra, who now live in Syria as vassals to King al-Ḥārith al-Wahhāb, that 'Antar is coming their way. They and the Syrians set an ambush and manage to capture 'Antar and his men. They take them to King al-Ḥārith in Damascus, who throws them into prison.

41. The Death of an-Nu'mān, 32/100–32/137

41.1. Sabī' ibn al-Ḥārith meets Ḥānī ibn Mas'ūd in the desert. The two heroes fight. Sabī' captures Hānī and delivers him to Shah Khudāwand.

41.2. Khudāwand convinces Hānī that he has forgiven an-Nu'mān. When Hānī relays this news, an-Nu'mān returns to al-Ḥīra. Khudāwand lets him rule for a while to lull his suspicions, then lures him to al-Madā'in. When the Ḥīran king arrives, Khudāwand crucifies him. An-Nu'mān's closest allies—Hānī, Ḥujār ibn 'Āmir, and 'Āmir ibn aṭ-Ṭufail—flee to King Qais for protection. Iyās ibn Qabīṣa resumes rule of al-Ḥīra.

42. Another Persian-Byzantine War, 32/138–33/205

42.1. Caesar decides to wage war against Shah Khudāwand. He gathers his Byzantine and Frankish troops and orders King al-Ḥārith to help him. Leaving 'Antar and his companions in his dungeons, al-Ḥārith and his army join Caesar. When Khudāwand learns of this new attack, he takes his army to meet the invaders. The two armies join battle.

42.2. Among Khudāwand's knights is King al-Ḥārith's nephew, Abū Dūj. Abū Dūj is fighting against his uncle because the two have quarreled. Abū Dūj wanted to marry al-Ḥārith's daughter, but the Syrian king rejected his suit. After Abū Dūj proves his worth in battle by defeating all his opponents in single combat, Khudāwand gives him a thousand men to conduct a rear-guard attack on Damascus.

42.3. The governor of Damascus thinks that Abū Dūj has been sent by al-Ḥārith and opens the city's gates. Al-Ḥārith's daughter hates Abū Dūj; rather than fall prisoner to him she frees 'Antar and asks for his help against the attackers. 'Antar and his men defeat the Persian troops, and 'Antar kills Abū Dūj.

42.4. King al-Ḥārith learned of Abū Dūj's plan and followed him. He thanks 'Antar for saving his daughter and city, and the two become friends. When the king tells 'Antar how Khudāwand killed an-Nu'mān, 'Antar decides to help the Byzantines against the Persians.

42.5. King al-Ḥārith and 'Antar arrive at the battlefield just as the Byzantine army is getting the worst of things. With 'Antar's arrival the tide of battle quickly turns. Maisara kills the Persian general in single combat; disheartened, the Persian troops flee.

42.6. The Byzantine forces celebrate their victory. 'Antar and his companions are laden with gifts, and al-Ḥārith presents Maisara with a young noblewoman from his court so that he will forget his love for Asmā'. After several days of feasting, 'Antar decides to return to Arabia and rejoin his women and children.

42.7. On their way home, 'Antar and his men meet Duraid ibn aṣ-Ṣimma. Duraid heard that 'Antar had fallen prisoner and was coming to rescue him. On his way, Duraid met warriors from the Banī Fazāra who were lying in wait to ambush 'Antar on his return to Arabia. Duraid surprised and captured them. 'Antar and Duraid now take the prisoners and return to 'Abs. They pass the time by beating the Fazāra prisoners, but finally they feel sorry for them and release them.

43. War between Khudāwand and the Arabs, 33/205–34/306

43.1. 'Antar, King Qais, Ḥujār ibn 'Āmir, Hānī ibn Mas'ūd, Duraid, al-Aswad, and other Arab heroes and leaders meet to plan their revenge for Shah Khudāwand's murder of an-Nu'mān. They decide to go to Mecca and ask 'Abd al-Muṭṭalib to exert his considerable influence to unite all the Arab tribes against the Persians. Meanwhile, Shah Khudāwand gathers his troops and prepares to regain control over the Arabs.

43.2. After 'Abd al-Muṭṭalib sends letters to all the tribes of Arabia, men stream into Mecca. The Arab leaders choose Duraid as commander-in-chief, and he leads an army of seventy thousand Arabs against Khudāwand and Iyās's army of half a million.

43.3. Sabīʿ ibn al-Ḥārith, obstreperous as usual, fights on the Persian side. Khudāwand sends him with thirty thousand men to attack Mecca, while he himself engages the main Arab army. Sabīʿ attacks Mecca, but God sends a shower of meteors down upon his troops. With his army thus destroyed, Sabīʿ falls prisoner. Prior to this, however, he has managed to capture ʿAbla and other Arab noblewomen and send them to al-Madāʾin.

43.4. Khudāwand, meanwhile, meets the Arab army led by Duraid. The shah is astounded when he hears how his army was destroyed at Mecca, but he fights on with his main force. He captures ʿAntar and most of his clan in battle and sends them to al-Madāʾin in chains.

43.5. At al-Madāʾin, Khudāwand's eldest son, Azdashīr, sees and falls in love with ʿAbla. ʿAbla repulses his advances. When ʿAntar arrives in chains, Azdashīr threatens to kill him unless ʿAbla submits to his wishes. When ʿAbla still refuses, Azdashīr throws him before a mad elephant. ʿAntar kills the elephant by pulling off its trunk with his bare hands.

43.6. ʿAbla finally agrees to trade her virtue for ʿAntar's life. While dining with the Persian prince, however, she seizes a knife and kills him. Khudāwand's younger son approves of this deed, for he loves justice before all things—except perhaps the prospect of becoming shah. This son, Qubāz, frees ʿAntar and his companions on the condition that they return to the battlefield and kill his father, Khudāwand. ʿAntar arrives just in time to see Hānī ibn Masʿūd kill the shah in battle. With their leader's death and ʿAntar's arrival, the Persian army breaks and flees.

43.7. Qubāz proclaims himself shah. He releases ʿAbla and the other Arab women held captive in al-Madāʾin. On their way toward Arabia, these women fall captive to an anonymous black warrior who single-handedly defeats their escort. ʿAntar hears of this event. Overtaking the captive caravan, he retakes it, but the mysterious warrior escapes.

43.8. Back at al-Madāʾin, the remnants of the defeated Persian army, led by Iyās ibn Qabīṣa, refuse to recognize Qubāz as shah and lay siege to the city. The Arab army arrives, however, the Persian troops are forced to surrender, and Qubāz is recognized by all as the new shah. He immediately dismisses Iyās as king of al-Ḥīra and appoints al-Aswad in his place.

44. ʿAntar Hangs His Muʿallaqa (Suspended Poem), 34/306–35/443

44.1. The Arabs decide to return to Mecca and celebrate the Hajj. The leaders take turns giving feasts and parties for one another. At one of these feasts, ʿUmāra ibn Ziyād challenges ʿAntar's poetic ability, saying that he is not great enough to deserve the honor of having one of his poems suspended from the Ka'ba, a distinction awarded only to the greatest Arab poets.

44.2. 'Antar swears an oath not to drink wine or sleep with 'Abla before he too hangs a poem on the Ka'ba. His friends encourage him, while his enemies rejoice at the prospect of his failure. They know that the southern Arab tribes and the six poets who already have suspended poems (*mu'allaqāt*) will oppose 'Antar's desire.

44.3. 'Antar persuades 'Abd al-Muṭṭalib to recite the poem he wants hung. When the southern Arab tribes discover that the poem they are about to hear was composed by a black former slave, they riot. The northern Arabs ('Adnānīs) and the southern Arabs (Qaḥṭānīs), 'Antar's supporters and opponents, draw two battle lines.

44.4. 'Antar challenges all comers to single combat and defeats whoever dares to meet him. The poets challenge him. One by one, they appear, recite first their *mu'allaqa* poem then an extemporized piece, and defy 'Antar to do better. 'Antar answers their poems then captures them in battle: Ṭarafa ibn al-'Abd, Zuhair ibn Abī Sulmā, Labīd ibn Rabī'a, Amr ibn Kulthūm, and, last and most important, Imru' al-Qais. The southern Arabs refuse to give up and continue to send warriors to face 'Antar on the following days.

44.5. The day finally comes when no one dares to meet 'Antar in single combat. 'Antar returns to his tent to rest. At this point a new opponent, a black warrior, enters the field. Not wishing to disturb 'Antar's rest, Duraid aṣ-Ṣimma sends other knights to face the newcomer. But the stranger defeats everyone who faces him, and 'Antar is forced to return to the battlegrounds.

44.6. 'Antar and the stranger fight each other all day. The next day they fight again, this time without armor. When their weapons break, they wrestle. At last 'Antar defeats and captures the mysterious black warrior.

44.7. Queen Ghamra arrives. Driven from her lands in Yemen by the king of Sudan, she comes to Mecca to seek aid in regaining her kingdom. When she hears of the struggle between 'Antar and the mysterious knight, she rushes to 'Antar's camp to tell him that he has just captured his own son.

44.8. The young black stranger is Ghaṣūb, son of 'Antar and Ghamra (see 34.7). Ghamra raised Ghaṣūb, but always maintained that he was the son of one of their slaves. Noticing his prowess, she trained him as a warrior. When she sees that 'Antar is planning to kill him, Ghamra admits to 'Antar and her own tribe that the youth is indeed her son. Ghaṣūb left Ghamra's tribe because he fell in love and was out raiding in order to collect a dowry. It turns out that it was he who tried to make off with the 'Abs women on their way home from al-Madā'in (see 43.7). Father and son embrace joyfully.

44.9. Meanwhile, the southern Arabs see no alternative but to allow 'Antar to hang his poem. He declares that he will not do so until the other poets admit he is their equal. The poets choose Imru' al-Qais to test 'Antar's poetic skills by asking him for synonyms for sword, spear, armor, horse, camel, and snake. When 'Antar offers a few score synonyms and metaphors for each word, the poets decide that he deserves to pass the test. He is finally allowed to recite and hang his poem.

45. 'Antar and the Yemeni Maiden, 35/443–35/451

45.1. Sabī' ibn al-Ḥārith has been held prisoner in Mecca since he led the Persian attack against the city. He now escapes, severely wounding Hānī ibn Mas'ūd. 'Antar also prepares to leave the city. He must escort 'Abla home, but he promises to return and help Ghamra regain her lands. Maisara, 'Urwa, Shaddād, and other close companions of 'Antar remain in Mecca to await his return.

45.2. While leading the rest of 'Abs home, 'Antar has difficulties with 'Abla, who is jealous of Ghamra and Ghaṣūb. During a feast she demands that he show his love by kissing her foot. 'Antar angrily refuses and decides to take Shaibūb and return to Mecca.

45.3. On their way, 'Antar and Shaibūb meet a small caravan in the desert. In it is an unconscious maiden named Sarwa. Her parents are taking her to Mecca in the hope of finding someone able to cure her illness. 'Antar cures the girl with Muqri 'l-Waḥsh's amulet. Dazzled by her beauty, he asks her parents for her hand and marries her. Shaibūb also finds a lover among the women of the caravan. They camp for a few days, then 'Antar directs Shaibūb to take his new family to live with 'Āmir ibn aṭ-Ṭufail and the Banī 'Āmir until he returns.

46. 'Antar and the Jews of Khaibar, 35/452–36/34

46.1. 'Antar arrives in Mecca. He plans to help Ghamra regain her lands from the king of Sudan, but on his arrival he learns that his sons Maisara and Ghaṣūb and Muqri 'l-Waḥsh's son, Sabī' al-Yemen, have been captured by Sabī' ibn al-Ḥārith. Sabī' has found new allies among the Jews of Khaibar. Their hero, Jabbār ibn Sakhr, has befriended him. 'Antar and Ghamra take their men and set out to free the captives.

46.2. They arrive at the fortress of Khaibar when Sabī' and Jabbār are away. Confronted with this hostile force, Mīsha, the leader of the Jews, resorts to trickery. He releases 'Antar's sons, apologizes for imprisoning them, and invites 'Antar and his men to a feast held outside the castle walls. He drugs the wine; when 'Antar and his companions fall asleep, he takes them captive.

46.3. Ghaṣūb and Ghamra and her men do not attend the feast. When she notices how quiet the feast suddenly becomes, she investigates and sees the unconscious 'Abs warriors being bound. Gathering her men, she enters the fortress and shuts the main force of the Jews outside. The Jews have ʻAntar and his men as prisoners; Ghamra has Khaibar.

46.4. The Jews lay siege to their own fortress. The next day Ghamra and Ghaṣūb emerge and engage them in single combat. Seeing that things are not going according to plan, Mīsha sends a messenger to Jābir ibn Asad, the king of the Christian Arab tribes of the region, and asks for aid. Jābir gathers his men and comes to help.

46.5. Ghaṣūb decides to try to sneak into the enemy camp and release ʻAntar and his men. Meanwhile, the Jews receive more reinforcements: the local Byzantine garrison of fifteen hundred men. Mīsha instructs his allies to attack the front of the fortress. He takes his men and enters the fort through a secret passage in the rear. Ghamra has to fight on two fronts. Things look bad until ʻAntar and his men, freed by Ghaṣūb, enter the battle. Mīsha and his men are driven from the castle, which the ʻAbs resecure. That night, they set flame to Khaibar then attack the armies without. The enemy breaks and flees; the day is won.

47. The Death of Shaddād, 36/35–36/70

47.1. Shaibūb arrives with the news that he became separated from Sarwa and her family in the desert and does not know where they are and that Jabbār and Sabīʻ ibn al-Ḥārith raided ʻAbs and captured many prisoners, including King Qais and ʻAbla. Jabbār has fallen in love with ʻAbla, and he, his men, and his prisoners are now on their way toward Khaibar.

47.2. The two groups meet in the desert. When Sabīʻ sees ʻAntar, he flees, but Jabbār stays to fight. He kills Shaddād, but ʻAntar kills him in return. The prisoners are rescued, and ʻAntar and ʻAbla make up.

47.3. Shaibūb, Ghamra, and Ghaṣūb pursue and capture Sabīʻ ibn al-Ḥārith. All return to ʻAbs to mourn and bury Shaddād. To avenge his death, they kill all their male Jewish and Christian prisoners. The females, however, they set free to return home.

47.4. Meanwhile, a group of Yemenis meet Sarwa and her family lost in the desert and escort them home. Sarwa and her servant Saʻda bear ʻAntar and Shaibūb's sons, who are perfect likenesses of their fathers. They name them al-Ghaḍbān and al-Khudhrūf, but keep the identities of their fathers secret, claiming that both are the children of Saʻda and another slave.

48. ʻAntar and the King of Sudan, 36/71–39/305

48.1. After mourning Shaddād, ʻAntar, Ghamra, and their followers set out toward Sudan, guided by Shaibūb, who remembers the country from his childhood.

48.2. They come first to the lands of King Suwaidā ibn ʿUwaidā in Yemen. Suwaidā is a vassal of King Ghawwār of Sudan, who has appointed him overlord of the lands captured from Ghamra. When the ʿAbs forces arrive, Shaibūb first goes to scout the camp. Then ʿAntar takes five men and raids the herds.

48.3. King Suwaidā sends his cousin Maimūn ibn Raḥmūn with five thousand men to pursue the raiders. ʿAntar, Ghaṣūb, and Maisara defeat them all by themselves and capture Maimūn.

48.4. King Suwaidā sends another army, this time consisting of ten thousand men led by his cousin Ṣāʿiqa ibn ʿAlqam. ʿAntar faces them with ten men, kills Ṣāʿiqa, and routs the army.

48.5. Suwaidā sends another cousin, Manīʿ ibn Munāʿ, with ten thousand men. Meanwhile, ʿAntar's captive, Maimūn, turns against Suwaidā and says he will help ʿAbs against him. ʿAntar releases him and then goes to meet the army. He kills Manīʿ and defeats his army.

48.6. Gathering ten thousand more men, King Suwaidā now comes himself. With Maimūn's help, ʿAntar defeats his army and kills Suwaidā.

48.7. ʿAntar asks Ghamra if she has other enemies in the area. She says only King Laun aẓ-Ẓalām, another vassal of King Ghawwār. ʿAntar leads his men against Laun aẓ-Ẓalām.

48.8. Laun aẓ-Ẓalām has heard of Suwaidā's defeat and meets ʿAntar with an army of forty thousand men. ʿAntar captures him in single combat. During his captivity, he is seen weeping. He is sad because his son Ṣafwān is hopelessly in love with the daughter of King Hammām, ruler of Dhāt al-Aʿlām. Touched as ever by a love story, ʿAntar offers help. He and Laun aẓ-Ẓalām become friends and decide to join forces against King Ghawwār of Sudan, since Ghawwār and Hammām are allies.

48.9. King Ghawwār has heard of ʿAntar's victories. When he learns that ʿAntar is heading his way, he sends a large army commanded by his best general, Wajh al-Ghūl, against him. Aided by Laun aẓ-Ẓalām and his men, ʿAntar kills Wajh al-Ghūl and defeats his army.

48.10. Antar takes his forces into Sudan proper. Ghawwār sends another general, ʿAkkāsh, with fifty thousand men against the invaders. ʿAntar kills ʿAkkash and defeats his army.

48.11. Ghawwār sends another general, ʿAndam, this time with sixty thousand men. ʿAntar kills him and defeats his army. Shaibūb tells ʿAntar to kill as few of the enemy as possible because he recognizes the countryside as being where Zabība, Jarīr, and he originally came from.

48.12. King Ghawwār finally decides that he himself will lead his armies against ʿAntar. The two sides fight for a few days. Ṣafwān, King Laun aẓ-Ẓalām's infatuated son, disappears. He has been tricked and taken captive by Ghawwār. Shaibūb sneaks into the enemy camp and frees him.

48.13. The ʿAbs stage a night attack against the Sudanese and rout them. They decide that before pursuing they should take the fortress of al-Khāṭif ibn al-Khāṭifa, a mighty warrior noted for riding a giraffe in battle. ʿAntar kills him in single combat, while Shaibūb sneaks into the fortress and opens it for his forces, who capture it. Having thus secured its rear, the army continues into Sudan.

48.14. King Ghawwār is awaiting reinforcements from King Hammām. But when ʿAbs arrives, he gathers his troops and starts to fight them. The two armies fight a few days, when one night ʿAntar and Ṣafwān disappear. Shaibūb sets out to look for them while the rest of the ʿAbs continue the battle. They hold their own, but fifty thousand more troops, sent by King Hammām, arrive.

48.15. ʿAbs sorely misses ʿAntar's presence in battle. Many heroes fall captive to King Ghawwār in single combat before Ghaṣūb finally fights and captures him. ʿAntar and Ṣafwān have been tricked by Ṣafwān's beloved, Uʿjūba (King Hammām's daughter), and are now Hammām's prisoners.

48.16. The ʿAbs are hard pressed but notice that every day the size of Ghawwār's army shrinks. So one night they launch a surprise attack and rout what is left of the Sudanese. Messengers tell them that ʿAntar and King Hammām have become friends. Ghawwār's army was shrinking because Hammām was slowly recalling his troops.

48.17. Shaibūb arrived at King Hammām's castle to find that ʿAntar and Ṣafwān had escaped from their prison and taken King Hammām prisoner. King Hammām's wife recognizes Shaibūb. It turns out that Zabība is her sister and Shaibūb her nephew. All become friends.

48.18. Antar's army arrives. King Hammām agrees to let Ṣafwān marry his daughter. While they celebrate the wedding, a messenger arrives from King Damhār, King Hammām's overlord, ordering Hammām to pay his yearly tribute, so all set out to attack Damhār.

48.19. King Damhār meets them with ninety thousand men, but ʿAntar captures him in battle. That night they are preparing to kill him when Damhār recognizes an amulet that Ghaṣūb is wearing. It turns out that Damhār is Ghamra's uncle. Peace is made, and a celebration is held.

48.20. Now at peace with one another because of ʿAntar, all the Sudanese kings decide to throw off the overlordship of the negus, the emperor of Abyssinia.

48.21. The negus hears of this plan and sends his son-in-law al-ʿAbd Zanjīr with a large army to meet the attack. Al-ʿAbd Zanjīr and ʿAntar engage in single combat for seven days; on the eighth day ʿAntar kills him. ʿAntar attacks and captures the negus. They discover, however, that Zabība's grandfather was the present negus's great-grandfather, so Zabība is his aunt. Once again peace is made and feasts are held to celebrate.

48.22. 'Antar decides that it is time to return home. He and his companions make their way back to Ghamra's lands. She falls ill and dies. Ghaṣūb decides he wants to stay with 'Antar, so he lets another rule his tribe in his place. At long last, 'Antar and his men return to 'Abs.

49. The Story of Rabī'a ibn al-Mukkadam, 39/306–40/462

49.1. 'Amr ibn Ma'dīkarib comes to congratulate 'Antar on his safe return. On his way home 'Amr decides to raid the Banī Kināna. He attacks the almost empty camp and defeats several resisters when suddenly a young knight, Rabī'a ibn al-Mukaddam, appears, fights, and captures him.

49.2. Because he and his mother were stolen in a raid, Rabī'a grew up as a slave. He showed such strength and spirit, though, that his owner trained him as a warrior. Eventually, Rabī'a regained his freedom when al-Mukaddam won his family back in a raid.

49.3. Rabī'a releases 'Amr and offers to become his friend, but 'Amr is not used to being defeated and attacks Rabī'a. Rabī'a defeats and captures him again.

49.4. Some of Rabī'a's fellow tribesmen envy him. They try to rid themselves of him by convincing him to ask for the hand of Hind bint Qais ibn Mas'ūd of Shaibān. When Rabī'a hears descriptions of her beauty, he falls in love and swears to win her.

49.5. Rabī'a presses his suit at the Shaibān camp. Qais is willing to let him marry Hind, but Hind, a great warrior in her own right, refuses the suit.

49.6. In a tournament, Rabī'a defeats heroes of the tribe, such as Bisṭām ibn Qais, in single combat. Then Hind emerges onto the battlefield to fight him. When he defeats her, she falls in love with him and agrees to marry. They marry, but ten days later Rabī'a becomes ashamed of his lack of a suitable dowry. Without a word, he disappears to win one. His sudden absence causes a terrible scandal among the Banī Shaibān.

49.7. Accompanied only by his slave Miftāḥ, Rabī'a captures a rich caravan. He returns to his wife with this dowry, and all celebrate his victory.

49.8. One day while Rabī'a is away hunting, Fayyād ibn 'Alqama, a king of the Banī Kalb, appears to ask for Hind's hand. When he learns that she is married, he decides to steal her. He defeats everyone until Rabī'a returns and kills him.

49.9. Rabī'a takes Hind and his caravan of booty to Kināna. On the way, the caravan meets Duraid ibn aṣ-Ṣimma and his men. Hind once rejected Duraid's proposal of marriage, so he decides to attack the caravan. Rabī'a defeats him, but the two heroes end by becoming friends.

49.10. Rabī'a and his caravan next encounter 'Antar's sons and companions. They too attack the caravan, but Rabīʿa defeats them all. At this point, ʿAntar appears. He and Rabīʿa fight for several days. Finally Rabīʿa's sword breaks. When ʿAntar stops and offers to get him a new one, Rabīʿa is overcome by his nobility. They embrace and become friends.

49.11. Duraid, thinking ʿAntar might need his help, reappears. The friends now escort Rabīʿa home to hold a feast. Rabīʿa and ʿAntar become such good friends that ʿAntar marries Rabīʿa's sister. Worried about ʿAbla's jealousy, ʿAntar decides to let his new wife remain among her kin. After a few days' celebration, ʿAntar and his friends return home, where, at Duraid's request, he releases Sabīʿ ibn al-Ḥārith, whom he has been holding prisoner since the war with the Jews of Khaibar (see 47.3).

49.12. Rabīʿa brings his family to visit ʿAntar. On the way home, the party is attacked by Nubaisha ibn Ḥabīb of the Banī Diḥya. During the fighting, Rabīʿa's horse stumbles, and Nubaisha wounds him fatally. Rabīʿa fights long enough for his family to reach safety, then dies in his saddle while his foes look on, afraid to approach him.

49.13. At Rabīʿa's funeral, ʿAntar vows to avenge his death. He gathers his men and travels to the Banī Diḥya. He defeats them, but Nubaisha manages to escape and flees to the Banī Tamīm. ʿAntar pursues him. He defeats the Tamīm, but Nubaisha escapes once again and takes refuge among the Banī Wāʾil. ʿAntar follows and this time captures him. He takes Nubaisha and six hundred prisoners and slaughters them on Rabīʿa's grave. Among the poets who compose elegies for Rabīʿa is Ḥassān ibn Thābit.

50. Al-Ghaḍbān, 40/463–41/63

50.1. The shah has heard about ʿAntar's son Ghaṣūb and sends a message in which he asks ʿAntar to send the young hero to al-Madāʾin so that he can meet him personally. Ghaṣūb travels to the Persian capital, where the shah honors him with gifts and feasts. When a letter arrives one day from the Byzantine emperor informing the shah that a black warrior has stolen the tribute that Byzantium sent, the shah sends Ghaṣūb to recover it.

50.2. The black warrior is al-Ghaḍbān, the son of ʿAntar and Sarwa (see 45.3 and 47.4). He and his cousin al-Khudhrūf (Shaibūb's son) grew up as slaves among the Banī Kināna, but al-Ghadbān showed himself to be an outstanding fighter and began to go out on raids; on one of these he captures the Byzantine tribute.

50.3. Ghaṣūb overtakes al-Ghaḍbān, and the two fight. Al-Ghaḍbān defeats and captures Ghaṣūb, but lets him go. When al-Ghaḍbān returns home to discover that his master has been killed in a raid, he avenges his death and thus wins his freedom.

50.4. Al-Ghaḍbān falls in love with Da'da, the daughter of al-Minhāl, a chief of the Banī Kināna. Al-Minhāl is not happy about wedding his daughter to a black former slave, but one day Da'da falls captive to al-Munāzil of the Bani 'l-Māzin, and al-Minhāl promises to let al-Ghaḍbān marry her if he frees her. Al-Ghaḍbān eventually captures al-Munāzil and frees Da'da.

50.5. Da'da's father now asks al-Ghaḍbān to capture 'Abla as a servant for Da'da. So al-Ghaḍbān and al-Khudhrūf set out toward 'Abs. On the way they capture ar-Rabī' ibn Ziyād and his family. When al-Ghaḍbān falls in love with ar-Rabī''s daughter, ar-Rabī' also asks for 'Antar's head as dowry.

50.6. Al-Ghaḍbān meets 'Antar and his companions returning home from a raid. The young warrior challenges and defeats all of 'Antar's friends and family in single combat. Finally, 'Antar faces him. Father and son fight for three full days. While they fight, al-Khudhrūf and Shaibūb also fight each other. 'Antar defeats al-Ghaḍbān.

50.7. When al-Khudhrūf sees that al-Ghaḍbān has been defeated, he flees back to the Banī Kināna. Al-Minhāl is delighted to be rid of his unwelcome suitor; but when Sarwa learns that 'Antar has captured their son, she sets out with al-Khudhrūf for 'Abs.

50.8. Sarwa informs 'Antar and Shaibūb that al-Ghaḍbān and al-Khudhrūf are their sons. Fathers and sons embrace each other joyfully. 'Antar promises to help al-Ghaḍbān win Da'da, and they set out for Kināna.

50.9. Meanwhile, Da'da has acquired a new suitor, King Sa'b of the Bani 'r-Riyān. King Sa'b forces al-Minhāl to let him marry Da'da, but when al-Minhāl sets out in a caravan to take Da'da to King Sa'b, he is attacked by raiders.

50.10. 'Antar and al-Ghaḍbān appear and drive off the attackers. When al-Minhāl sees who his rescuers are, he flees as well. 'Antar takes Da'da back to 'Abs, where she and al-Ghaḍbān marry.

51. 'Antar in Yemen, 41/63–42/153

51.1. When his herders complain of drought, 'Antar decides to move his clan to greener territories to the south. Shaibūb suggests two good camping places in Yemen; 'Antar sends his sons with half the herds to one, while he takes the rest of the animals to the other.

51.2. As soon as they set up camp, 'Antar's sons are attacked by the local king, al-Hailaqān. They beat off his attack and kill him, but other tribes soon arrive to renew the fight. Once again, 'Antar's sons drive off their attackers.

51.3. Peace reigns for a time, but the defeated Yemeni tribes are not so ready to give up. They seek the help of the powerful warrior Prince Ja'far, who attacks 'Abs with an army of ten thousand men. Ja'far fights successfully against ʿAntar's sons in single combat. He is on the point of killing Maisara when ʿAntar and Shaibūb suddenly appear. ʿAntar kills Jaʿfar and his followers.

51.4. Having saved his sons, ʿAntar returns to his own camp. One day a passerby informs him that his sons have been captured by Ṣaʿṣaʿa ibn al-ʿAwwām of the Banī Muzaina. ʿAntar takes his companions and sets out to rescue them.

51.5. On their way, they encounter one of Ṣaʿṣaʿa's slaves, Muṭāwiʿ. Muṭāwiʿ helps Shaibūb sneak into the enemy camp to free the prisoners. ʿAntar creates a distraction by raiding the herds, and while Ṣaʿṣaʿa is thus engaged, Shaibūb and ʿAntar's newly freed sons attack from the rear.

51.6. The two sides fight for several days. The affairs of ʿAbs worsen when Ṣaʿṣaʿa is reinforced by King Manīʿ ibn Ḥajjāf and his men. The battle continues until King Qais appears with a thousand ʿAbs warriors and tips the balance. ʿAntar thanks Qais, who returns home. ʿAntar and his clan remain in Yemen a few more weeks, but must continually fight off attacks from the neighboring tribes. ʿAntar finally tires of this and leads his clan back to the Banī ʿAbs.

52. ʿAntar and the King of India, 42/153–44/375

52.1. One day a man appears and asks for ʿAntar's help. A group of foreign warriors has stolen his herds. ʿAntar agrees to help him and, gathering his companions, sets out in pursuit.

52.2. When he overtakes them, they tell him that they are the soldiers of ʿAbd Hayyāf, king of India, and warn him against invoking this powerful king's wrath. When ʿAntar insists they return the animals they have stolen, they all go to King Qais to ask him to mediate the quarrel between non-Arabs and an Arab with no connection to ʿAbs, so he sends them to Thābit ibn Ḥassān, a judge respected among the Arabs.

52.3. The judge decides against ʿAntar. He seizes the animals anyway and returns them to the Arabs. All fear the revenge of the king of India, but he is far away. ʿAntar stands before them, and no one dares oppose him.

52.4. ʿAbd Hayyāf is both a powerful king and a great warrior. When he learns how ʿAntar interfered in his men's affairs, he decides to teach the Arabs a lesson and sends his brother to collect tribute from them. The Indian prince is welcomed and honored by the Arab tribes. No one refuses him tribute until he comes to the Banī ʿAbs. There he and ʿAntar quarrel, and al-Ghaḍbān draws his sword and kills him.

52.5. When ʿAbd Hayyāf learns of his brother's death, he decides to invade Arabia and perhaps Persia as well. He sends for his ally King al-Akhḍar to join his attack. The two kings lead an army of half a million men into Arabia.

52.6. When 'Antar hears of the advancing enemy army, he gathers his friends and allies, such as Duraid ibn aṣ-Ṣimma, 'Āmir ibn aṭ-Ṭufail, and Bisṭām ibn Qais. The resultant Arab army numbers thirty thousand men. King al-Ḥārith of Ghassān sends forty thousand troops to help them.

52.7. The Indian and Arab armies meet and join battle. 'Abd Hayyāf deploys al-Akhḍar with thirty thousand men to attack the unprotected 'Abs camp and capture the women. Meanwhile, the fighting between the main armies alternates between single combat and full-scale attacks.

52.8. After a few days, King al-Akhḍar returns with the 'Abs women as prisoners. Then an even worse disaster befalls the Arabs. In an attack 'Antar's horse, al-Abjar, stumbles, and 'Antar falls and disappears under the enemy.

52.9. The Arabs are certain that 'Antar is dead. All except 'Abs flee. The Banī 'Abs continue to fight, but in spite of heroic resistance, they are hopelessly outnumbered and finally forced to flee.

52.10. King 'Abd Hayyāf now decides to attack al-Madā'in. 'Antar's sons and close companions refuse to admit defeat. They follow the Indian army to al-Madā'in, picking off stragglers on the way. The Indians besiege the Persian capital for nine months. 'Antar's sons and companions decide to return to Arabia and raise a new army; only al-Ghaḍbān refuses to leave and remains outside al-Madā'in.

52.11. Meanwhile, Duraid ibn aṣ-Ṣimma has been gathering a new army. All wish to avenge 'Antar; finally an army of one hundred thousand men collects and sets out for al-Madā'in.

52.12. The Arab army meets al-Ghaḍbān, and together they attack the flank of the Indian army led by King al-Akhḍar. Suddenly, in the midst of the fighting, 'Antar reappears. He was knocked unconscious and left among the dead in the previous battle. When he woke up, he wandered until he came across an old woman who took him in and tended his wounds. He finally regained his strength, found al-Abjar running wild in the desert, and, hearing about the new battle, set out to help.

52.13. On the way to the battle, 'Antar meets two youths. It turns out that they are his sons. The young men, Zaidān and Jār al-'Alam, are the sons of 'Antar and Bint Zaid al-Mukaddam, Rabī'a ibn al-Mukaddam's sister, whom 'Antar married shortly before Rabī'a's death. Their mother died, and the youths have been searching for 'Antar. All of the Arabs are delighted to see 'Antar again and to meet his newfound sons.

52.14. While the fighting continues, Shaibūb and al-Khudhrūf sneak into the enemy camp and release the Arab heroes who have been taken prisoner. King 'Abd Hayyāf formally divides his army into two parts: one to continue the siege of al-Madā'in and one to fight the Arabs. Fighting on both fronts continues for days.

52.15. 'Abd Hayyāf decides to challenge the Arab heroes to single combat. He enters the battlefield and defeats all who dare oppose him. While the enemy leader is thus occupied, 'Antar sends al-Ghaḍbān with ten thousand men to attack the Indian troops besieging the city. Under the force of al-Ghaḍbān's attack, the Indians break ranks and flee. The shah thanks 'Antar's son, who thereupon returns to rejoin the main Arab army.

52.16. The next day 'Antar emerges to meet 'Abd Hayyāf. The two heroes fight for several days, but they are evenly matched and neither prevails. The battle continues while they fight, but 'Antar and 'Abd Hayyāf come to admire each other's strength and nobility so much that they finally lay down their arms and embrace each other. They swear friendship and make peace. All celebrate the new peace for a full month, then, after the shah has honored 'Antar and his sons, the kings, heroes, and armies all return to their homes.

53. War between 'Abs and King Yaksūm, 44/376–45/450

53.1. On a raid several of King Qais's brothers kill the son of King Yaksūm, who rules over parts of the Yemeni coast and some of Abyssinia. Prince al-Ḥārith falls captive to one of Yaksūm's vassals, Ḥāṭil ibn Sāfiyya.

53.2. Enraged, Yaksūm sends an army of fifteen thousand men under the leadership of 'Amlāk, another of his vassals, to attack 'Abs. In the meantime, King Qais gathers his warriors to rescue his captive brother. 'Antar is unhappy about fighting fellow blacks, but Qais persuades him to help.

53.3. 'Amlāk and his army arrive at the 'Abs camp just as the Arabs are preparing to leave. The two armies fight. After a few days, 'Antar kills 'Amlāk, whose troops flee.

53.4. The 'Abs decide to go on the offensive. They arrange for the Banī Ghaṭafān and other allies to come and protect their camp while they are gone, then they set out for Yemen. When King Yaksūm learns of his army's defeat, he is furious. He gathers sixty thousand more troops, puts another of his vassal chiefs, Ghashīm ibn al-Miqdām, at their head, and sends them against 'Abs.

53.5. The two armies bypass each other in the desert. Ghashīm arrives at the 'Abs camp and attacks it. The Banī Ghaṭafān put up a spirited defense; but, although reinforced by Duraid ibn aṣ-Ṣimma and other friends of 'Antar, they lose ground. The Arabs are on the verge of defeat when 'Antar appears leading five hundred men. Shaibūb learned of Ghashīm's army, and 'Antar has returned to help defend the 'Abs camp. 'Antar kills Ghashīm and the Abyssinians flee.

53.6. In the meantime, King Qais and his army arrive at Hāṭil ibn Sāfiyya's fortress, where Prince al-Ḥārith is being held prisoner. The 'Abs take the fortress and free al-Ḥārith, but suddenly discover that they are no longer the besiegers but the besieged. Yaksūm has heard of their victory and sent an army to attack them.

53.7. Although greatly outnumbered, the Banī ʻAbs, inspired by al-Ghaḍbān's heroics, defend the fortress so valiantly that Shuraiṭ ibn Bahīm, the enemy general, is forced to send for reinforcements. Yaksūm sends another ten thousand men, and the Abyssinians manage to capture al-Ghaḍbān and Ghaṣūb. They are on the point of breaking through the walls when ʻAntar arrives and drives them back. At dawn the next day, ʻAbs wakes to discover that the enemy have struck camp and departed.

53.8. The Abyssinians retreated because they learned that Yaksūm was being attacked by the giant Ṭaud al-Aṭwād, king of the Isle of Qaimar. King Yaksūm recently refused to pay him tribute, so King Ṭaud sent an army to attack Oman, part of Yaksūm's dominion.

53.9. King Qais wants to pursue the enemy in order to rescue ʻAntar's captured sons, but ʻAntar is worried about leaving the ʻAbs women defenseless too long and persuades Qais to take the bulk of ʻAbs and return home. ʻAntar himself gathers his immediate companions (about 120 men) and follows the enemy army.

54. ʻAntar, Yaksūm, and Ṭaud al-Aṭwād, 45/450–46/52

54.1. Yaksūm takes his armies to Oman, where he is besieged by a large army led by Ṭaud's general, Khazāʻa the Mad. When the Abyssinians suffer heavy loses, Yaksūm decides to enlist the aid of al-Ghaḍbān and Ghaṣūb.

54.2. ʻAntar arrives. Unaware of this new war, he ends up skirmishing with Ṭaud's soldiers. When he rejoins his sons, now freed, they all decide to help their former enemy, King Yaksūm.

54.3. The fighting lasts for several days. Maisara, Ghaṣūb, and ʻUrwa fall captive, but al-Ghaḍbān finally kills Khazāʻa in single combat. The enemy flee back to their ships, taking their ʻAbs prisoners with them.

54.4. ʻAntar sets off in pursuit. Taking four thousand of Yaksūm's men, he heads for Qaimar. When King Ṭaud learns of his army's defeat, he gathers three hundred thousand men, puts half of them under the command of his mother, Sahm an-Nizāl, who is both a powerful warrior and a skilled witch, and sets out for Yaksūm's lands.

54.5. ʻAntar and Ṭaud's forces meet. The ʻAbs warrior kills Ṭaud in single combat, and the latter's army flees. ʻAntar pursues and leads his men toward the enemy capital, which Ṭaud left in the hands of ash-Shāmikh ibn Saʻīd. Ash-Shāmikh wants no part of the war. He releases the ʻAbs prisoners and, through their intercession, makes peace with ʻAntar.

54.6. While the former enemies celebrate their peace treaty, Yaksūm arrives with the news that Ṭaud's mother, Sahm an-Nizāl, has conquered Oman. ʻAntar finds time to arrange the marriage of ʻUrwa and Ṭaud's sister Wadʻa, who have fallen in love, then sets out for Oman with his men.

54.7. Sahm an-Nizāl wins the first battle with ʻAntar's enemy by using her witchcraft to create a hailstorm. ʻUrwa's new wife, Wadʻa, however, is able to counteract her mother's sorcery. Al-Ghaḍbān finally kills Sahm in battle, and ʻAbs captures the city. Yaksūm reascends his throne, and the next day ʻAntar and his companions set out for home.

55. ʻAntar Rehangs His Muʻallaqa Poem, 46/52–47/123

55.1. On the way home, Shaibūb informs ʻAntar that someone has torn his *muʻallaqa* poem down from the Kaʻba. Enraged, ʻAntar returns to ʻAbs and gathers an army to take to Mecca.

55.2. The man who dared tamper with ʻAntar's poem is al-Mustauʻir ibn Rabīʻa, a mighty southern Arab warrior. When he heard how ʻAntar had put up his poem by defeating the southern Arab tribes, al-Mustauʻir vowed to redeem their honor. He gathered fifty thousand men, came to Mecca, and tore down the poem.

55.3. ʻAntar and al-Mustauʻir arrange their troops. ʻAntar again defeats all of the southern Arab heroes in single combat. Finally, he and al-Mustauʻir face one another. After fighting for a few days, ʻAntar kills him.

55.4. The southern Arabs receive reinforcements, led by King az-Zibriqān. ʻAntar fights him and takes him prisoner. The next day ʻAntar is surprised when a new opponent takes the field. He is even more surprised to see that it is his son al-Ghaḍbān. Al-Ghaḍbān has decided that he is now more powerful than ʻAntar and is determined to prove it before the onlooking Arabs.

55.5. ʻAntar, laughing, meets his son on the field of battle. He soon discovers, however, that al-Ghaḍbān is in deadly earnest. The two heroes struggle for several days, but finally ʻAntar manages to defeat his son. The southern Arab tribes ask ʻAntar's pardon. He rehangs his poem and recites two others. Then he writes letters of protection to fifteen hundred tribes guaranteeing (and imposing) his protection. All return home.

56. The Death of al-Ghaḍbān, 47/123–47/179

56.1. Arriving home, ʻAntar holds many feasts to celebrate his new victory. He runs low on wine, however, so he and ʻUrwa set out for Syria to buy some more. On the way, ʻAntar meets and kills a jinni. He and ʻUrwa finally arrive at al-Madīna al-Baiḍā' (the White City). This marble city, originally built by

Alexander the Great, is now ruled by the Christian prince al-Lailmān ibn Marqūm.

56.2. ʿAntar raids the prince's herds. When al-Lailmān pursues, ʿAntar fights and captures him. It turns out, however, that the prince is Muqri ʾl-Waḥsh's cousin. For once, ʿAntar and his men are defeated; they flee back to ʿAbs.

56.3. Some years later ʿAntar and his sons, on a raid, meet a group of riders in the desert. When al-Ghaḍbān approaches to see who they are, the leader of the group kills him. Seeing his son lying dead, ʿAntar faints. He quickly regains consciousness and attacks the killers; but ʿAntar and his men are defeated and are forced to flee to ʿAbs.

56.4. All mourn al-Ghaḍbān. ʿAntar himself is inconsolable. He raises a black tent outside camp and refuses to leave it. All his friends come to cheer him up, but only the thought of revenge is able to bring him out of his tent. He decides to kill every stranger he meets until he finds his son's murderer.

56.5. This idea understandably worries ʿAntar's friends. They write ahead to all the tribes so that every time ʿAntar comes to a camp all come out and offer their condolences and thus turn away his anger. Finally, ʿAntar seeks the help of a soothsayer, Quss ibn Sāʿida. Quss tells him that it was not a man who killed al-Ghaḍbān, but a jinni—to avenge the jinni that ʿAntar killed.

56.6. Hearing this, ʿAntar gives up his plans for revenge. Quss goes on to tell him of the imminent appearance of a new prophet named Muḥammad and of the future greatness of the Arabs. After this peek into the future, ʿAntar and his friends return home.

57. The Story of Wizr ibn Jābir, 47/179–49/332

57.1. Wizr ibn Jābir is a great warrior of the Banī Nabhān. While hunting one day, he sees and falls in love with Kabsha, the daughter of the Arab chief Kabshān. Wizr proposes marriage, amasses a dowry, and marries Kabsha, but the girl considers him ugly and dislikes him.

57.2. Kabsha starts an affair with her cousin Mubādir, and together they plot Wizr's death: Kabsha urges him to win renown by fighting great heroes and capturing their wives or sisters to be her servants.

57.3. Taken in by this plan, Wizr sets out to capture Raiḥāna, the sister of ʿAmr ibn Maʿdīkarib. He manages to abduct her while ʿAmr is away visiting relatives; but when ʿAmr hears what has happened, he sets out after them.

57.4. Wizr returns home with his prisoner to discover that Kabsha and Mubādir have been cuckolding him. The leaders of Nabhān are worried about the consequences of Raiḥāna's abduction and advise Wizr to treat her honorably, which he does.

57.5. ʿAmr ibn Maʿdīkarib gathers men and raids the Banī Nabhān. Wizr fights and captures him, but asks that they be friends and that he be allowed to marry Raiḥāna. When he sees that his sister has fallen in love with Wizr, ʿAmr agrees, and the couple marry.

57.6. Wizr conducts many successful raids, and his fame grows. He becomes so conceited and arrogant that one day he dresses a ram in silk and jewels and begins to lead it around to all the neighboring tribes to make them pay protection money (*ghifāra*) to it.

57.7. Wizr still loves Kabsha, but one day he overhears her and Mubādir planning to poison him. He falls into a rage, kills them both, and burns their bodies.

57.8. ʿAntar is still mourning al-Ghaḍbān when Shaibūb informs him of Wizr's terrorization of the local tribes. Shaibūb tells ʿAntar that if he were a real hero he would not let tribes he promised to protect (see 55.5) be exploited like this. ʿAntar forgets his sadness and swears to kill and eat Wizr's ram. ʿAbla encourages ʿAntar to oppose Wizr as well, telling him that the Nabhān warrior is becoming more famous and feared than he.

57.9. ʿAntar takes Shaibūb and ʿAbla to the Nabhān camp. They arrive while Wizr is away raiding, but ʿAntar wastes no time. He seizes the ram, strips it of its finery, slaughters it, and forces Raiḥāna to cook and serve it to ʿAbla. Because Raiḥāna is the sister of his friend ʿAmr ibn Maʿdīkarib, ʿAntar does not abduct her or steal any of Wizr's animals. After killing the ram, he peacefully sets out for home.

57.10. When Wizr returns and learns what has happened, he swears vengeance. Taking Raiḥāna to witness his victory, he follows ʿAntar and overtakes him. While their wives watch, the two heroes fight. Finally, ʿAntar defeats and captures Wizr. He sends Raiḥāna home, but takes Wizr to ʿAbs as his prisoner.

57.11. Raiḥāna asks her brother ʿAmr to intercede with ʿAntar on Wizr's behalf. ʿAmr is reluctant, but he finally agrees. Arriving at ʿAbs, he finds that ʿAbla has already convinced ʿAntar to relent and release his prisoner. ʿAmr thanks him, and he and Wizr depart.

57.12. Wizr is determined to obtain revenge for his humiliation. He gathers his tribe, gains the help of his ally al-Minhāl ibn Nāqid of the Banī Wā'il, and sets out for ʿAbs. They attack while ʿAntar is away raiding. Ar-Rabīʿ sees an opportunity to humiliate ʿAntar and convinces King Ḥiṣn and the Banī Fazāra to join the attack. In the face of such overwhelming opposition, the ʿAbs are defeated. Their camp is plundered, and their women captured.

57.13. On the way back, King al-Minhāl sees and falls in love with ʿAbla. He and Wizr do not trust their recently gained allies, ar-Rabīʿ and King Ḥiṣn. They surprise and imprison them and then plunder the Fazāra camp. Al-

Minhāl reveals his love to 'Abla. She feigns agreement with the idea of marriage, but points out that he will have to kill 'Antar first.

57.14. Meanwhile, 'Antar and his companions are busy raiding the caravans and herds of King Wahb ibn Mauhūb of the Banī Ḥimyar and his allies. Ghaṣūb captures Wahb's nephew, Ṭāriq ibn Ghāsiq, the tribe's hero, and 'Antar exacts a rich ransom for him. After this success, the 'Abs raiders head for home.

57.15. On their return, they learn how Wizr and his allies have plundered 'Abs. 'Antar immediately sets out for the Banī Nabhān. Shaibūb scouts the camp and sees Wizr and al-Minhāl still celebrating their victories.

57.16. Antar sends 'Urwa and his men to raid the tribe's herds. When Wizr pursues, 'Antar ambushes them, and the two forces fight until nightfall. The next morning organized lines of battle are drawn, and fighting begins anew.

57.17. During the fighting, Wizr and al-Minhāl are reinforced by King Muljam ibn Ḥanẓala, his brother King Shārib ad-Dimā', and their men. 'Antar is reinforced, in turn, by the arrival of King Qais and the rest of 'Abs. Finally, 'Antar captures Wizr, Ghaṣūb captures al-Minhāl, and the enemy flees. 'Abs plunders the enemy camp and frees its women and prisoners, then they return home.

57.18. Al-Minhāl has treated 'Abla with great respect, so 'Antar releases him. But he has Wizr whipped daily and plans eventually to kill him. 'Amr ibn Ma'dīkarib asks for Wizr's freedom, however, and 'Antar agrees, out of friendship for him.

57.19. Wizr is perhaps more eager for revenge than ever. He goes raiding and by chance captures Khuṣaima, a foster son of 'Antar. When the boy's mother comes to 'Antar for help, he sends Shaibūb with a letter to Wizr demanding the youth's freedom. Wizr answers by imprisoning Shaibūb, whom he plans to crucify. The Banī Nabhān, however, are tired of Wizr's folly. They free Shaibūb and ask Wizr to take his clan and leave their camp.

57.20. Wizr moves to the Banī Jadīla, who welcome him. He sets about to assemble such allies as Muljam and Shārib ad-Dimā' and soon gathers a new army of twenty thousand men. Hearing of this, 'Antar and 'Abs decide to attack first. In the ensuing battle, 'Antar again captures Wizr and defeats the enemy army.

57.21. Once again Raiḥāna persuades 'Amr to plead for her husband's freedom. 'Antar agrees to free Wizr, but he blinds him first, promising to send him animals each year so that he does not starve. 'Amr takes Wizr home, still swearing that he will take revenge. 'Amr leaves him in disgust.

58. The Rekindling of War between 'Abs and Fazāra, 49/333–51/62

58.1. While 'Antar is in the midst of celebrating his victory, Shaibūb brings him a supplicant—a horse thief. He was bringing 'Antar a fine horse he had stolen when King Ḥiṣn came upon him and took the horse himself. ʿAntar, furious, sends Ghaṣūb to demand the return of the horse.

58.2. When Ghaṣūb arrives at Fazāra, he finds Ḥiṣn in the midst of a feast, drunk. Ghaṣūb decides to wait to talk to the king when he is sober. Meanwhile, talk turns to the day ʿAbs slaughtered the Fazāra nobles (see 23.5). Since this occurred before Ghaṣūb came to ʿAbs, he does not understand what they are talking about, so he goes to sleep. Ḥiṣn, full of drunken thoughts of revenge, kills the sleeping hero with a spear.

58.3. When Ḥiṣn's chief advisor, Sinān ibn Abī Ḥarītha, sees what has happened, he convinces the Banī Fazāra to flee. After Ghaṣūb fails to return the next day, ʿAntar sends Shaibūb to look for him. Shaibūb finds the young hero's body in the empty Fazāra camp.

58.4. ʿAntar grieves for his son then swears vengeance. He, King Qais, and ʿAbs pursue Fazāra. The Banī Fazāra, having failed to convince the Banī Shaibān to protect them, head for al-Ḥīra. ʿAbs overtakes them; when he sees Ḥiṣn, he is so overcome with emotion that he faints. The two tribes join battle and fight for two days, but Fazāra knows it has no chance of winning. Those not killed or captured flee during the night.

58.5. When he sees that the enemy has fled, ʿAntar, with Maisara, slaughters thirteen hundred prisoners captured in battle. Then ʿAbs returns home.

58.6. When King al-Aswad, Ḥiṣn's brother-in-law, hears Fazāra's story, he feels sorry for them and promises his protection. Later, learning of the slaughtered prisoners, al-Aswad writes to Qais and demands he hand over ʿAntar and Maisara.

58.7. King Qais, tired of the continual violence ʿAntar attracts, decides to obey al-Aswad's order. He plans to get ʿAntar and his son drunk and thus take them prisoner. ʿAntar foils the plan, however; angry at this attempted treachery, he gathers his clan and leaves ʿAbs.

58.8. On the advise of his minister, ʿAmr ibn Nufaila, King al-Aswad makes peace between ʿAbs and Fazāra, deciding to wait to deal with ʿAntar later. To equalize his relations with the two tribes, he marries his former sister-in-law and Qais's sister, al-Mutajarrida. Ar-Rabīʿ ibn Ziyād, for one, is very happy that everyone is uniting against ʿAntar.

58.9. ʿAntar and his clan go to ʿĀmir ibn aṭ-Ṭufail and the Banī ʿĀmir. When friends among ʿAbs send word that al-Aswad, Fazāra, and ʿAbs are plotting against him, he raids the ʿAbs herds.

58.10. ʿAntar is persuaded to return the ʿAbs animals he has stolen. He decides to take his clan to new lands in Iraq. Meanwhile, the Banī ʿAbs are unhappy that Qais drove ʿAntar away. Qais has no choice but to take his warriors and invite ʿAntar to return to the tribe. ʿAntar accepts; but before returning, they all decide to raid the herds of King al-Aswad.

58.11. When al-Aswad learns of Qais's new change of heart, he becomes so furious that he has al-Mutajarrida suffocated. He collects his allies, including 'Antar's old rival Sabī' ibn al-Ḥārith, and sends troops against 'Abs.

58.12. 'Antar and 'Abs defeat several armies al-Aswad sends against them. The Ḥīran king is ready to conclude peace; but when 'Antar demands Ḥiṣn's life as a precondition, al-Aswad refuses and sends several more armies to defeat. 'Antar has now captured such great chiefs and heroes as 'Āṭil ibn al-Muthannā of the Banī Sulaim and Khidāsh ibn 'Ilāqa of the Banī Shaibān. Al-Aswad is forced to ransom them and others at great cost.

58.13. Al-Aswad sends a new army against 'Abs, but 'Antar puts Ḥiṣn to flight, captures Sarī' ibn al-Ḥārith, and forces the rest of the army to flee. A new Ḥīran army, led by Hammām ibn 'Alqama of the Banī Hamdān, sets out. At first, things go well for them. 'Antar's saddle slips while he is fighting Hammām, who captures him. But 'Āmir ibn aṭ-Ṭufail rescues 'Antar as he is being taken to al-Ḥīra, and 'Antar returns to fight and kill Hammām. Once again, 'Abs is victorious.

58.14. Al-Aswad goes to al-Madā'in to ask the shah for help. Anūshirwān (apparently revived from the dead: see 39.1) gives him a Persian army and, with it and his own forces, al-Aswad himself sets out against 'Abs. 'Antar is warned of their approach and ambushes the enemy's vanguard. In the ensuing battle, he kills the Persian general Shahribān, defeats al-Aswad's army, and occupies al-Ḥīra.

58.15. Al-Aswad flees to the shah but finds that Anūshirwān now has more pressing problems. His governor in Isfahan has rebelled and has already defeated four imperial armies. The shah's minister, al-Mūbadhān, advises him to send 'Antar against the rebel. The shah is surprised at this suggestion, but accepts it. He sends a caravan of gifts to 'Antar in al-Ḥīra and asks him to come to al-Madā'in.

58.16. 'Antar and Qais come, and, under the good offices of the shah, are convinced to make peace with al-Aswad and Ḥiṣn. 'Antar also agrees to help Anūshirwān with his rebellious governor.

59. 'Antar in Iran, 51/62–51/82

59.1. Anūshirwān organizes an Arab-Persian army of twenty thousand men led by 'Antar, the other Arab heroes, and the Persian minister. With 'Antar and 'Abs in the vanguard, the army sets out for Isfahan. When the rebellious governor, Sharwīn ibn Jarwīn, is warned of their approach, he sends his general Shahrimān to meet them.

59.2. Shahrimān and his men meet 'Antar and the vanguard, pretend to join them, and that night attack them. Capturing 'Antar and most of 'Abs, Shahrimān takes them to Sharwīn.

59.3. When the Arab-Persian warriors learn that ʿAntar has been taken captive, they become very worried. Their leaders cheer them on, and they continue on their way. When they meet the enemy army, however, things go badly. They are on the point of defeat when suddenly ʿAntar and his men appear and attack Sharwīn's army from the rear.

59.4. ʿAntar has come because Sharwīn's minister, still loyal to the shah, has set them free. ʿAntar's appearance changes the tide of battle. He takes Sharwīn prisoner and defeats his army.

59.5. The Arabs and Persians collect their spoils and return to the capital. Sharwīn induces ʿAntar to intercede with Anūshirwān, and, to please ʿAntar, the shah forgives the rebel. He rewards all of the Arab leaders and holds feasts for several days. After this, all return home.

60. Friends and Family, 51/83–52/152

60.1. One day a messenger from the Banī Shaibān comes to ʿAntar to announce the death of his friend Bisṭām ibn Qais. Bisṭām courted and married a girl of the Banī Ramīs. During the wedding celebrations, however, the tribe was attacked by al-Hailaqān, a hero of the tribe who loved the same girl. Bisṭām was drunk, and al-Hailaqān killed him.

60.2. A grieving ʿAntar gathers his men to avenge Bisṭām. They raid the tribe's herds; thus enticing al-Hailaqān out of the camp, ʿAntar kills him in single combat. ʿAntar goes to Shaibān to mourn Bisṭām then returns home.

60.3. Meanwhile, ʿUrwa ibn al-Ward and his wife have had a son, named Zaid. As he grows up, the boy shows promising signs of becoming a good warrior. One day the young Zaid meets a friend of his father, Kaubab ibn Mujālī of the Banī Shaibān. Visiting this tribe, he sees and falls in love with a girl named Rabāba bint Mājid. ʿUrwa helps him arrange the marriage.

60.4. Rabāba is sent in a wedding caravan to be married among the ʿAbs. But the caravan is raided by a warrior named Zaid ibn Salmā. This Zaid is attracted to the bride and takes her as part of the booty. ʿAntar is away when this happens, but ʿUrwa, Zaid, and ʿAntar's sons pursue the raiders. They overtake them and attack, but are unable to overcome them until ʿAntar appears and kills Zaid. All return home, and Zaid ibn ʿUrwa and Rabāba finally celebrate their marriage.

60.5. One day Shaibūb tells ʿAntar that ʿUrwa has been killed. His killer is Ḥassān ibn Thābit of the Banī Dhubyān, who killed ʿUrwa to avenge his brother's death at ʿUrwa's hand.

60.6. ʿAntar buries ʿUrwa and swears revenge. He attacks and defeats the Banī Dhubyān, but Ḥassān escapes to take refuge with Dafāna ibn Ḥud of the Banī Quraiʿ. ʿAntar pursues him. In the ensuing battle, Dafāna kills ʿAntar's half-brother, Māzin ibn Shaddād. 'Antar kills both Ḥassān and Dafāna and plunders the enemy camp, then he and the 'Abs return home. 'Antar retires to his black tent outside of camp (which he calls his "House of Sorrow") and mourns 'Urwa and Māzin for a full year.

60.7. One day when 'Antar and King Qais go raiding they capture the wedding caravan of the bride of Murā'ir, the son of King Muljam ibn Ḥanẓala of the Banī Ṭayyi'. When he learns who the bride's husband-to-be is, King Qais wants to free her and return the booty. 'Antar, however, refuses to allow his king to demean himself in this way.

60.8. King Muljam collects seventy thousand men and attacks 'Abs. Qais wants to make peace, but 'Antar forces him to fight. The battle at first goes badly for the heavily outnumbered 'Abs, but Duraid ibn aṣ-Ṣimma comes to their aid, and the enemy is defeated.

61. 'Antar in Damascus and Constantinople, 52/152–53/197

61.1. There is now enmity between 'Antar and King Qais. Qais is tired of 'Antar's bellicose ways, and 'Antar thinks that Qais is getting weak and soft. So 'Antar decides to leave 'Abs for a time. He appoints Maisara to care for his wealth and clan in 'Abs then, taking Shaibūb, al-Khudhrūf, Muqri 'l-Waḥsh's wife and son, Musaika and Sabī' al-Yemen, and 'Abla, heads for Syria.

61.2. When they come to Damascus, they learn that King al-Ḥārith of Ghassān has just been killed. Since al-Ḥārith's heir 'Amr is only a boy, his older sister, Ḥalīma, becomes regent. Ḥalīma requests 'Antar's protection, so he assembles the people of the city and tells them that anyone who rebels against 'Amr must reckon with him. All swear obedience.

61.3. When they hear of al-Ḥārith's death, the shah and King al-Aswad decide to attack Damascus. On learning that 'Antar is protecting the regent, however, they give up their plans. Caesar is pleased that 'Antar's presence is keeping Syria quiet.

61.4. One of Caesar's nobles, Hābīl, plots a rebellion. Although Caesar arrests and imprisons him, Hābīl escapes, heads south, raises an army along the way, and decides to capture Damascus. 'Antar leads the Syrian army against the rebel and kills him. Then he heads for the rebel's homelands in northern Iraq and adds them to Prince 'Amr's territories.

61.5. When Caesar learns of 'Antar's victories, he sends for him to thank him personally. So 'Antar, Shaibūb, and al-Khudhrūf go to Constantinople. Caesar holds many feasts in 'Antar's honor and is very impressed with him. He holds tournaments in order to witness 'Antar's prowess, and 'Antar defeats all who face him.

61.6. Caesar would like a son of 'Antar at his court, so he sends a maiden to sleep with him. 'Antar, guessing this purpose, plans to kill the girl when he leaves. Meanwhile, all continue to feast and hold tournaments and wrestling matches. Caesar is amazed at the swiftness of foot of both Shaibūb and al-Khudhrūf.

61.7. 'Antar wishes to return to Syria, but one day he discovers that his mistress is missing. She and Kūbart, a Frankish prince living at the Byzantine court, have fallen in love and run away. Shaibūb follows them and stabs the girl, whose name is Maryam, but only wounds her. She and Kūbart get away safely.

62. 'Antar among the Franks, 53/197–53/266

62.1. One day envoys from King al-Lailamān, the Frankish Lord of the Sea and Isles, come to Constantinople. King al-Lailamān, who is Prince Kūbart's uncle, demands that Caesar deliver 'Antar to him because 'Antar killed Kūbart's brother and the Franks' former king, al-Khailajān (see 35.8), in a previous war between Persia and Byzantium. Caesar refuses and sends the envoys home.

62.2. 'Antar suggests that Caesar provide him with an army so that he can teach the Franks a lesson. The emperor gives him twenty thousand men and his son, Prince Hiraql. They embark on ships and head for al-Lailamān's lands.

62.3. They meet the Frankish king and his army at sea. The two sides begin to fight, but a storm arises and separates them. 'Antar and most of his army reach land and continue toward al-Lailamān's capital, Qal'at al-Ballūr (the Citadel of Crystal). Al-Lailamān has also landed and is on his way toward the Byzantines. When the two armies meet, 'Antar kills al-Lailamān, and the Franks flee.

62.4. Al-Lailamān's son Sarjwān mourns his father then gathers a new army. A battle takes place. 'Antar kills Sarjwān in single combat, and the Franks are forced to retreat into the city, which Prince Kūbart now rules.

62.5. 'Antar takes Kūbart prisoner in a battle outside the city walls. Both sides then settle down for a siege. Maryam, however, arranges a secret meeting with 'Antar one night. When he learns that she and Kūbart truly love each other, 'Antar's heart softens. There are several more secret meetings, and during one of them Prince Hiraql sees and falls in love with Marimān, al-Lailamān's daughter. 'Antar talks to Kūbart, who now repents his rebellion, and all become friends.

63. 'Antar and the Isle of al-Wāḥāt, 53/267–54/311

63.1. King Ṣāfāt rules the powerful rival Frankish kingdom of the Isle of al-Wāḥāt. When he hears of 'Antar's victories, he fears attack. Gathering one hundred and forty thousand men, he determines to attack first. ʿAntar, Hiraql, and Kūbart meet him with their armies. The fighting lasts several days, but ʿAntar finally kills Ṣāfāt and routs his army.

63.2. ʿAntar decides to invade Ṣāfāt's lands, but his way is blocked by the sudden appearance of a large river. He is advised to consult an old monk about how to get rid of the water. When the monk hears that ʿAntar is from Arabia, he asks if the battle of Dhī Qār has occurred. When ʿAntar tells him that it has (see 39.5), the monk is very happy because he knows that Muḥammad will appear soon thereafter. He tells ʿAntar how to get rid of the water, and ʿAntar successfully conquers the Isle of al-Wāḥāt.

63.3. In the city's palace, ʿAntar and his friends come upon a locked room. The lock is protected by magic; only ʿAntar is allowed to take the key and open the door. Inside they find a jinni who has been held captive since the day Alexander the Great imprisoned him there. In gratitude for being set free, the jinni brings ʿAntar al-Ghaḍbān's murderer. ʿAntar kills him with a magical sword and thus avenges his son (see 56.3–6).

64. ʿAntar in Andalusia, 54/311–55/389

64.1. A new enemy army appears from Spain. The king of Andalusia has a grudge against ʿAntar, who killed a cousin of his during the Persian-Byzantine war. Now the king, al-Janṭiyā'īl, has sent his son Prince ʿInān against ʿAntar. ʿAntar kills the prince in single combat and routs his army.

64.2. When al-Janṭiyā'īl learns of his son's death and defeat, he becomes furious. He gathers a new army of seven hundred thousand men, leaves his son ʿAbd al-Masiḥ in charge of his kingdom, and advances against ʿAntar.

64.3. ʿAntar has convinced Hiraql and Kūbart to try to conquer Andalusia, so the two armies meet each other halfway. King al-Janṭiyā'īl is a giant who rides an elephant in battle, but ʿAntar faces him unarmored and on foot and kills him. The Spaniards flee, and ʿAntar and his allies pursue.

64.4. When Prince ʿAbd al-Masīḥ hears how ʿAntar killed his father, he sues for peace. He and all the neighboring kings swear their fealty to the Byzantine emperor. In a triumphal procession, ʿAntar, Hiraql, and Kūbart visit the now compliant surrounding kingdoms of King Matrūs of Tunis, King al-Kardūs of Qairawan, King Mīkhā'īl of Cyrenaica, and King Hirmis of Alexandria and Egypt.

64.5. Two nephews of the dead al-Janṭiyā'īl, Kandrīyūs of al-Bahnasā and Sandarās of Ahnās, lead an army against the Byzantines. But with the help of his new vassals, ʿAntar defeats them.

64.6. ʿAntar longs for home. After they celebrate their latest victory, he and Hiraql bid Kūbart and Maryam farewell and depart for Byzantium. There they are honored by the emperor, who has 'Antar and Shaibūb's portraits painted. The two brothers return to Damascus.

65. The Deaths of al-Ḥārith, Maisara, and al-Hiṭāl, 55/390–55/404

65.1. 'Antar greets Prince 'Amr and is happy to be rejoined with 'Abla. A few days later messengers from King Qais arrive. Qais wants 'Antar to return to 'Abs. The hero decides to go home, and he and his company set out for 'Abs.

65.2. They arrive to find the tribe in an uproar. 'Antar's old friends Prince al-Ḥārith and his wife Lubnā (see 18) are dead. Al-Ḥārith was killed in battle by al-'Aiqafūr ibn 'Ar'ar of the Banī Zahrān, and Lubnā died from grief. 'Abs determines to avenge the murder.

65.3. The Banī Zahrān ally themselves with the Banī Nabhān and await the 'Abs attack. 'Antar and his tribe arrive, and battle is joined. Maisara kills al-'Aiqafūr in single combat, but the chief of the Nabhān, al-Muhalhil ibn Masrūq, kills both Maisara and 'Antar's nephew al-Hiṭāl (see 21.1–5). 'Antar kills al-Muhalhil, the enemy tribes flee, and 'Abs plunders their camps.

66. 'Antar, 'Amr Dhu 'l-Kalb, and the Death of Shaibūb, 55/404–55/433

66.1. On the way home, the 'Abs caravan of booty is attacked by raiders from the Banī Quḍā'a. 'Abs repels the attack, but in it 'Antar kills a cousin of the Quḍā'a hero 'Amr Dhu 'l-Kalb. When 'Amr learns of this, he swears revenge against 'Antar.

66.2. One day 'Antar meets 'Amr Dhu 'l-Kalb in the desert returning from a raid. When 'Antar orders him to turn over his plunder, 'Amr refuses. The two heroes fight for three days. By the fourth day 'Amr is so impressed with 'Antar that he dismounts from his horse and asks for peace. They become good friends.

66.3. Some days later Shaibūb is killed. His murderer is Ṣāliḥ, brother to the horse thief who stole al-Abjar, who was killed by 'Antar (see 30.1). 'Antar avenges his brother's death by killing Ṣāliḥ, but he is greatly saddened by his death. 'Amr Dhu 'l-Kalb and his sister al-Haifā' come to 'Abs to cheer up the hero. 'Abla and al-Haifā' become close friends.

67. 'Antar Kills ar-Rabī' ibn Ziyād and 'Umāra, 55/433–55/462

67.1. Ar-Rabī' ibn Ziyād and his brother 'Umāra rejoice at the deaths of 'Antar's relatives and friends. One day 'Abla overhears them saying that they hope this means that 'Antar himself will soon die. 'Abla angrily reports this conversation to 'Antar and demands that he take revenge.

67.2. A few days later King Qais holds a feast in honor of ʿAmr Dhu ʾl-Kalb. During the feast ʿAntar hears ar-Rabīʿ and ʿUmāra slandering him. Enraged, he draws his sword and kills them both on the spot.

67.3. The tribe falls into uproar over these internecine murders. When Qais suggests that ʿAntar leave ʿAbs for a time, he agrees. He gathers his clan and takes them to Iraq. ʿAmr Dhu ʾl-Kalb and his sister accompany him. On the way, al-Haifāʾ and ʿAntar fall in love and, with ʿAmr's blessing, marry. The marriage is kept secret from ʿAbla.

67.4. When the Arab tribes hear that ʿAntar has left ʿAbs, they see a chance to avenge their previous defeats and attack. ʿAbs is hard pressed. Among the many killed in battle is Qais's uncle Usayyid (see 19). When things are at their worst, however, ʿAntar appears and joins the fray. He learned of the battle and rushed to help. The attacking tribes are soon defeated, and ʿAntar returns to Iraq.

68. ʿAntar in Rome, 55/462–56/10

68.1. One day ʿAntar hears that Caesar has deposed King ʿAmr ibn al-Ḥārith in Damascus. When ʿAntar rushes to Syria and puts him back on his throne, the Byzantine emperor dares not oppose him. Instead, he sends his minister to renew their friendship and also to ask ʿAntar to help solve a new problem.

68.2. A letter has come from the king of Rome, Balqām ibn Marqus. King Kūbart has been deposed by his younger brother Buhinma ibn Nūrān. Buhinma is a great warrior who wants to avenge the Franks' defeats by ʿAntar. He has begun his campaign by attacking Caesar's vassal, the king of Rome.

68.3. ʿAntar agrees to help. He leads a Byzantine army to Rome, which is heavily besieged and on the point of surrender. ʿAntar and his men attack. ʿAntar kills Buhinma in single combat, and the Franks flee.

68.4. The Romans thank ʿAntar. Balqām's sister Maryam falls in love with him, and they marry. ʿAntar leaves. He takes Maryam as far as Constantinople; knowing she would not like desert life, he leaves her there. Caesar rewards him richly, and, laden with gifts, the ʿAbs warrior returns to Iraq.

69. The Death of ʿAntar, 56/11–56/52

69.1. Twenty years have passed since ʿAntar blinded Wizr ibn Jābir (see 57), who is still plotting revenge. Still blind, Wizr has learned to shoot arrows by sound; when he learns that ʿAntar has returned from the West, he sets out for his camp, guided by his servant Najm.

69.2. ʿAntar's clan has been celebrating his return with a week-long feast.

Wizr sneaks up to the camp, the dogs start barking, and 'Antar and Jarīr come outside to investigate. When 'Antar pauses to urinate, Wizr lets fly his arrow at the sound. The arrow hits its mark. 'Antar is severely wounded, but he makes not a sound. He overtakes and kills Wizr in silence. Jarīr does not notice that his brother is wounded until they return to the tent.

69.3. 'Antar knows he is dying and decides to take his clan back to 'Abs, where they will be safer. When they set out he is so weak that he has to ride in 'Abla's litter. The caravan is attacked, however, so 'Antar mounts al-Abjar. When the raiders see who it is, they back away, afraid to approach. Sitting on al-Abjar with his lance in his hand, protecting his clan while they hurry toward safety, 'Antar dies. It is hours before the raiders dare to approach him. When they see he is dead, they respectfully bury him.

69.4. All of 'Antar's friends mourn him deeply, while the world he held together begins to disintegrate. No one can mount al-Abjar, and the horse finally runs wild. Out of love for 'Antar, 'Āmir ibn aṭ-Ṭufail marries 'Abla so that she will have a protector. But she becomes extremely shrewish—continually comparing 'Āmir to 'Antar. 'Āmir grows so weary of her that he finally has her suffocated. When her father and brother complain of this, he kills them as well.

69.5. The Banī Fazāra see their chance for revenge and attack 'Abs. 'Abs manages to kill King Ḥiṣn and Sinān ibn Ḥarīitha, but Fazāra receives constant reinforcements and finally overwhelms them. The 'Abs camp is completely plundered, and the few survivors of the defeat scatter: one group goes to Mecca, one to the mountains, and one to Yemen. King Qais travels alone to Iraq and lives as a hermit. His son, Prince Zuhair, is among those who go to Mecca.

70. 'Unaitira and 'Abs, 56/53–57/103

70.1. After 'Antar's death, 'Amr Dhu 'l-Kalb and al-Haifā' return to the Banī Quḍā'a. Al-Haifā' gives birth to a black daughter who resembles 'Antar so much that she is named 'Unaitira (Little 'Antar). As the girl grows up, she displays remarkable signs of strength and skill in fighting, so 'Amr gives her a warrior's training.

70.2. One day 'Amr and 'Unaitira go raiding. They attack a tribe of the Banī Ḥimyar whose queen is Bint az-Zarqā, an aunt of Sabī' ibn al-Ḥārith. 'Unaitira fights and captures her. When Sabī' learns of this, he swears to rescue his aunt and sets off for the Banī Quḍā'a.

70.3. Meanwhile, Prince Zuhair ibn Qais is in Mecca, plotting his tribe's revenge. He sets out with those 'Abs in Mecca to reclaim the tribe's former camping grounds, but on the way they are attacked by a large raiding army.

'Abs is decimated. Only Zuhair and some thirty others survive the battle to flee to King al-Aswad in al-Ḥīra. The same army attacks and destroys the Banī Fazāra. The few survivors of that tribe are led by their current ruler, King 'Utaiba ibn Ḥiṣn, to al-Ḥīra to seek refuge with al-Aswad.

70.4. When Muḥammad begins to preach the new faith of Islam, both Zuhair and 'Utaiba lead their followers to Mecca and become Muslims. In the folds of the new religion, the old tribal enmities die, and 'Abs and Fazāra become friends. King al-Aswad dies in al-Ḥīra and is succeeded by his nephew al-Mundhir ibn an-Nu'mān. Zuhair and 'Utaiba return to al-Ḥīra to join his court.

70.5. 'Unaitira and her tribe are attacked by Sabī' ibn al-Ḥārith. When she engages Sabī' in single combat, she defeats and captures him. Seeing this, the Ḥimyar flee.

70.6. The defeated Banī Ḥimyar flee to al-Ḥīra to complain to King al-Mundhir. He leads an army of six thousand men against the Banī Quḍā'a, but 'Unaitira captures the Ḥīran king and defeats his army.

70.7. Remembering 'Amr Dhu 'l-Kalb's old friendship with 'Antar, Prince Zuhair goes to him to ask for al-Mundhir's release. 'Amr and Zuhair reminisce and weep over 'Antar; it is only now that 'Amr tells 'Unaitira that she is not his daughter but 'Antar's. 'Amr agrees to release al-Mundhir, 'Unaitira releases Sabī' and Bint az-Zarqā', and all become friends.

71. 'Unaitira Avenges 'Abla, 57/104–57/130

71.1. Now that she knows her true lineage, 'Unaitira plans her tribe's revenge. Together with Prince Zuhair she sends letters to all of 'Antar's old friends. Although many of 'Antar's fellow heroes, such as 'Amr ibn Ma'dīkarib, Hānī ibn Mas'ūd, and Duraid ibn aṣ-Ṣimma, do not come themselves, they all send men. The scattered remnants of 'Abs, among them Jarīr and al-Khudhrūf, also begin to appear, so 'Unaitira soon gathers a large army. She decides to begin her campaign by attacking 'Āmir ibn aṭ-Ṭufail to avenge 'Abla's death.

71.2. The 'Abs and 'Āmir armies meet and join battle. When 'Unaitira captures 'Āmir ibn aṭ-Ṭufail, however, his tribesmen flee. 'Abs celebrates its victory at its old campgrounds. 'Amr ibn Ma'dīkarib and Hānī ibn Mas'ūd come to offer their congratulations—and also to secure 'Āmir's safe release (he is destined to die opposing Muḥammad).

72. Al-Ghaḍanfar, 57/131–57/164

72.1. One day a message comes to 'Unaitira from King al-Mundhir of al-Ḥīra. Some Christian soldiers led by a brown warrior have attacked the caravan of tribute that al-Mundhir was sending to the shah. The king asks 'Unaitira to recover it.

72.2. The Christian leader is al-Ghaḍanfar, son of 'Antar and Princess Maryam of Rome (see 68.4). He has grown up in Constantinople as one of the emperor's favorites and is now a great warrior.

72.3. 'Unaitira pursues al-Ghaḍanfar. The two heroes fight, and 'Unaitira captures her half-brother in single combat. When Maryam learns of her son's capture, she comes to 'Unaitira and explains who he is. Brother and sister are happy to be united, and a long feast is held to celebrate. Al-Ghaḍanfar decides to remain with 'Abs.

72.4. More of 'Antar's scattered relations appear: Yāsir, the son of Maisara, and Laith al-Maidān, the son of Māzin—the sons of the girls that King al-Ḥārith of Ghassān had given their fathers (see 42.6); Usayyid, the son of Ghaṣūb; and ad-Dayyāl, the son of al-Ghaḍbān.

73. The Death of Qais and the Appearance of al-Jufrān, 57/165–58/234

73.1. One day King Qais, who has been living as a hermit along the banks of the Euphrates, is found by his brothers Naufal and Warqa. They remain together for a year then, hearing that 'Abs is reuniting under 'Unaitira, decide to go home.

73.2. On their way, they are attacked by the Banī Nabhān. Qais and Naufal perish, but Warqa escapes to tell the tale. 'Abs mourns the death of Qais, then they gather their allies and set out to avenge him.

73.3. On their way, however, they meet Princess Ḥalīma bint al-Ḥārith. A Frankish army has attacked Damascus and she has come to ask 'Abs's help against them. The Arabs decide to help her first and attack the Banī Nabhān afterward.

73.4. The attacking Frankish army is led by Prince al-Jufrān, the son of 'Antar's friend Kūbart (see 61.7; 62). The Arabs and Franks join battle, and the Arabs win until al-Jufrān challenges their heroes to single combat. Al-Jufrān defeats and captures all who face him: Khufāf ibn Nadba, Duraid ibn aṣ-Ṣimma, al-Ghaḍanfar, and even 'Unaitira. But even after the capture of these heroes, the Arab army continues to fight.

73.5. One day al-Jufrān's mother, who is with him, visits the Arab prisoners. Al-Jufrān is planning to kill them; but when Maryam sees that there are children of 'Antar among them, she stops him. She tells him that he would be killing his sister and brother, for he is really 'Antar's son, not Kūbart's as she raised him to believe. All are amazed at this news, but they are happy to be united. The fighting ends, and peace is made.

74. 'Abs Revenge, 58/235–58/286

74.1. When al-Jufrān learns that the Arabs are on their way to attack the Banī Nabhān, he offers to help. Their project is delayed once more, however, by the arrival of Prince Hiraql, who has come to invite them to pay their respects to Caesar. They go to Constantinople, but quickly return to Arabia. On their return, they meet a Sudanese army led by King Ṣafwān (see 48.8ff.), who has heard of their plan to avenge Qais and 'Antar and has come to help. The two armies pause to feast and reminisce about 'Antar's deeds.

74.2. Al-Jufrān swears that 'Antar must witness his revenge. They dig up 'Antar's bones, put them on a camel, and set out to attack the Nabhān. They defeat them in a pitched battle, but this does not satisfy their thirst for vengeance. They subdue all of the tribes who were hostile to 'Antar. After each victory, they ask 'Antar's bones if he is now satisfied. Receiving no reply, they proceed to the next tribe.

74.3. After the 'Abs and their allies defeat all they meet, they send letters to all the tribes and order them to attend 'Antar's new funeral. All come bearing gifts—out of fear or love. 'Antar's funeral lasts a month. There is general mourning, and many elegies are recited. Even Prince Hiraql and the shah's son come to do 'Antar honor. At the end of the month, all return to their homes.

75. 'Abs and Islam, 58/287–59/325

75.1. Pursuing a thief one day, al-Khudhrūf finds that it is his lost son 'Amr. Later 'Antar's brother Jarīr and 'Amr hear about Muḥammad. They become curious about the new religion and go to Mecca. (Some of the Prophet's early experiences and struggles are narrated.) When Jarīr and 'Amr witness Muḥammad's miracle of splitting the moon, they decide to remain in Mecca and enter Islam.

75.2. Al-Khudhrūf wonders what has become of his uncle and son, so he too goes to Mecca. Once there, he enters the new religion as well. All three become trusty messengers for the Prophet, who sends them to all the Arab tribes to invite them to join the new faith. Many older warriors, such as Duraid ibn aṣ-Ṣimma and 'Āmir ibn aṭ-Ṭufail, refuse to come and become opponents of the new religion. Prince Zuhair is already a Muslim and leads the 'Abs to Mecca to join the new faith en masse.

75.3. Al-Khudhrūf falls in love with 'Unaitira. She refuses to marry him, but Muḥammad reminds her that there is no celibacy in Islam. The two cousins marry and have many sons. The 'Abs remain with Muḥammad and help him in his struggles. They also play a prominent role in the worldwide conquests after his death. Of ʿAntar's children and family, al-Ghaḍanfar and al-Jufrān returned to their homes after ʿAntar's funeral. The rest take an active part in the new era of Islam and either win martyrdom in the wars of conquest or die of old age.

APPENDIX II

Sīrat ʿAntar in Manuscript and Print

This appendix has three parts: a list of extant Arabic manuscripts of *Sīrat ʿAntar*, a list of Ottoman-Turkish translations of the epic in manuscript, and some notes on the *Sīra*'s history of publication.

Manuscripts are listed by country and city, including:

1. The title of the library manuscript catalogue from which the listing was obtained.

2. Page and manuscript number references to the catalogues.

3. The number of volumes, parts, and folios the manuscript contains.

4. Its date, if known.

5. Its place of origin, if known.

6. Indication of whether the Abraham story is present or absent. Although we are still in the first stages of investigating the *Sīra*'s manuscript tradition, it appears that two major branches exist, those with the Abraham story and those without. It is still unclear how significant the differences that separate these branches are; further research is necessary.

7. The names of scribes, if known.

It should be noted that the compilers of the manuscript catalogues from which information has been gathered do not provide descriptions of equal fullness.

ARABIC MANUSCRIPTS OF *SĪRAT 'ANTAR*

Austria

Vienna

Die arabischen, persischen und türkischen Handschriftum der Kaiserlich-Königlichen Hofbibliothek zu Wien, Gustav Flügel, vol. 2.

A. 4–9, no. 783. 7 vols., 53 parts, 2,040 folios. Vols. 1–3, date 1466, belonged to the library of Sultan Mehmet II; vols. 4–7, late 18th century, bought in Cairo. Vols. 4–6 complement 1–3. Vol. 7 unconnected fragment. Abraham story present. Incomplete.

B. 9, no. 783 cont., 3 vols., 7 parts, 2,040 folios. Date? Abraham story? Incomplete.

C. 9–13, no. 784. 22 fragments, running between 33 and 144 folios. Mostly second half of 18th century. Scribes' names: 2. Ḥusain ash-Sharābī, 1780; 5. al-Ḥajj Ismā'īl, 1791 (Cairo); 6. 'Alī al-Mazārīqī, 1773; 8. 'Alī al-Mazārīqī ibn Ja'far ibn Yūsuf, 1783; 9, 10. Ḥusain ash-Sharābī, 1780; 11. al-Ḥajj Ismā'īl, 1790; 12. 'Alī al-Mazārīqī, 1766; 17. Muḥammad al-Qubā'ī (Qabānī?); 19. 'Alī al-Mazārīqī.

Denmark

Copenhagen

Codices orientales bibliothecae Regiae Hafniensis enumerati et descripti, August F. Mehren. 165, no. 303b. Fragment, 35 folios, numbered 9r.–47v., folios 16, 29, 30 missing. Late 18th century.

Egypt

Cairo

Fihrist al-makhṭūṭāt: Nashra bi-' l-makhṭūṭāt allatī iqtanat-hā 'd-Dār min sanat 1936–1953, Fu'ād Sayyid. 472. 35 vols., 35 parts, 3,492 folios. Date 1872. Abraham story present. Complete.

France

Paris

Catalogue des manuscrits arabes de la Bibliothèque Nationale, Baron William Mac-Guckin de Slane.

A. 629, nos. 3688–98. 11 vols., 3413 folios. Manuscript commissioned by Cardin de Cardonne in Istanbul. The copyist, P. Phillip, based this version on two different recensions of the work. Early 19th century. Abraham story? Complete.

B. 629, nos. 3699–3734. 36 vols., 2,788 folios. Composite version of diverse vols. 17th–18th century. Abraham story? Complete.

C. 629, nos. 3735–58. 24 vols., 2,079 folios. Composite of diverse vols. 17th–18th century. Abraham story? Complete.

D. 629, nos. 3759–82. 24 vols., 1,687 folios. Composite of diverse vols. 18th century. Abraham story? Incomplete.

E. 629, nos. 3783–89. 7 vols., 478 folios. Diverse vols. 17th–18th century. Abraham story? Incomplete.

F. 629, nos. 3790–91. 2 vols., 600 folios. Vols. 1–2. 15th century. Abraham story? Incomplete.

G. 624–31, nos. 3792–3808. 16 fragments, 37–72 folios each. 17th–18th century.

Germany

Berlin

Verzeichnis der arabischen Handschriften der Königlichen Bibliothek zu Berlin, vol. 8: *Die grossen Romane*, Wilhelm Ahlwardt.

A. 80–84, no. 9123 (We. 901–60). 60 vols., 4,161 folios. Composite of diverse vols. Mostly 1851 or 1844 (We. 930:1772; We. 959:1693). Abraham story present. Complete.

B. 84–87, no. 9124 (We. 961–1020). 60 vols., 4,161 folios. Composite of diverse vols. Beginning pages missing. Abraham story? Almost complete. Scribes' names: We. 961, Yūsuf ibn al-Ḥajj Muṣṭafā, 1773; We. 992, Muṣṭafā ibn Ḥusain ibn Harīsa (Huraisa?), 1783; We. 1020, as-Sayyid Najīb ibn Ḥasan al-Maghribī, 1830. Other vols., 1800 or later.

C. 87–89, no. 9125 (We. 1021–54). 34 vols., 2,513 folios. Composite of diverse vols. Mostly around 1800. Abraham story present. Complete? Scribes' names: Muḥammad Aṣlān ibn Sa'īd al-Ḥammāmī al-Ḥakwātī, 1836; as-Sayyid Muḥammad al-Bey al-Malqī, 1773.

D. 89–90, no. 9126 (We. 1055–69). 15 vols., 1,280 folios. Composite of diverse vols. Abraham story absent. Date? Incomplete.

E. 90–91, no. 9127 (We. 1070–85). 16 vols., 1,165 folios. Composite of diverse vols. Date? Abraham story absent. Incomplete.

F. 91–92, nos. 9128–29. 29 fragmentary vols., 719 folios. Date?

G. 92–95, no. 9130 (Spr. 1255–1311, 1313bis). 59 of 60 vols. (vol. 59 missing), 3,742 folios. Composite of diverse vols. 18th century. Abraham story absent. Almost complete.

H. 96–97, no 9131 (Spr. 1312–53). 42 vols., 2,649 folios. Abraham story present. Date 1853. Incomplete, approx. first two-thirds of story.

I. 97–98, nos. 9132–55. 4 fragments, 326 folios. 1750 and later.

J. 98–99, no. 9136. *ʿAntar-nāma.* Collection of the poetry from *Sīrat ʿAntar.* 329 folios, appr. 11,000 verses. Compiled for Sulaimān Bey, son of Muḥammad Amīn Pasha. Date 1798.

K. 99, no. 9137. 166 folios. *ʿAntar-nāma.* Selection of poetry from *Sīrat ʿAntar.* Date appr. 1800.

Gotha

Die arabischen Handschriften der herzoglichen Bibliothek zu Gotha, Wilhelm Pertsch. Vol. 4.

A. 363–67, nos. 2435–75. 41 vols., 3,576 folios. One hand. Abraham story? Date 1760. Complete. Scribe's name: Sulaimān ibn Jaʿfar al-Dimyāṭī.

B. 367–72, nos. 2476–96. 21 fragments, 932 folios. (No. 2496 from 1774.)

Munich

Die arabischen Handschriften der K. Hof- und Staatsbibliothek in München, Joseph Aumer. 271, no. 622. 19 fragments. Dates?

Great Britain

Cambridge

A Hand-list of the Muḥammadan Manuscripts . . . Preserved in the Library of the University of Cambridge, E. G. Browne.

A. 100, nos. 537–48. 12 vols., no. of folios? Date 1780. Abraham story? Complete? *A Supplementary Hand-List of the Muḥammadan Manuscripts . . . Preserved in the Library of the University of Cambridge,* E. G. Browne.

B. 315–16, nos. 1413–19. 7 fragments, no. of folios? Date? *A Second Supplementary Hand-List of the Muḥammadan Manuscripts in the University and Colleges of Cambridge,* A. J. Arberry.

C. 59, no. 340. A fragment of 58 folios. 18th century.

London

Catalogus codicum manuscriptorum orientalium qui in Museo Britannico asservantur. Part 2.

A. 319–21, nos. 670–73. 4 vols., 100 parts, 1,350 folios. Abraham story present. Date? Complete.

B. 321–22, nos. 674–79. 6 vols., 1,372 folios. Vol. 6 (no. 679) from before 1402. Composite of diverse vols. Abraham story? Incomplete.

C. 322, nos. 680–82. 3 vols., 463 folios. Fragment. Scribes' names: no. 680, Muṣṭafā ibn ash-Shaikh Aḥmad as-Sammām, 1761; no. 682, Aḥmad ibn ʿAbd al-Qādir al-ʿAṭṭār, 1761.

D. 322, nos. 683–84. 2 fragments, 298 folios.

E. 323, nos. 685–89. 5 vols., 621 folios. No. 689. Date 1654. Fragment.

F. 323, nos. 690–91. 2 vols., 386 folios. Fragment.

G. 323–24, nos. 682–85. 4 vols., 315 folios. Date 1751. Fragment.

H. 324, nos. 686. 43 folios. Date 1761. Fragment.

I. 663–65, nos. 1445–58. 14 vols., 2,806 folios. Date? Major part of work, beginning missing. Incomplete.

J. 665, no. 1459. 1 vol., 151 folios. Date 1437. Fragment.

K. 697–98, nos. 1836–40. 5 vols., parts 16–45, 1,999 folios. Date? Incomplete.

Manchester

Catalogue of the Arabic Manuscripts in the John Rylands Library, Manchester, A. Mingana.

A. 827–39, nos. 501–36. 36 vols., 3,394 folios. Abraham story present. Date 1720 and after. Various hands. Complete. Scribes' names: no. 501, al-Amīr Aiyūb ʿAbdallāh Khalwātī, 1813; no. 530, ʿAbdallāh ibn as-Sayyid ʿAlī at-Tūnisī, 1769; nos. 534–35, ʿAlī al-Mazārīqī Jaʿfar ibn Yūsuf, 1769. (Compare Vienna c. 6, 8, 12, 19.)

B. 840–44, nos. 537–55. 19 vols., 3,043 folios. Abraham story? Date 1800 and after. Various hands. Claimed author (no. 555): Amīn ibn Ismāʿīl al-Ḥumṣī. Complete. Scribe's name: no. 555, as-Sayyid Muḥammad Abu 'l-Yusr aṭ-Ṭarābulusī, 1812.

C. 846–52, nos. 556–71. 17 vols., 45 parts, (22, 42–44 missing), 3,118 folios. Abraham story present. Date mostly 1818. Various hands. Almost complete. Scribes' names: no. 556, Muḥammad ibn al-Ḥajj Sulaimān, 1818; no. 567, ʿAlī al-Mazārīqī ibn Jaʿfar ibn Yūsuf al-Jaʿfarī, 1819.

D. 852–62, nos. 572–607. 36 vols., 3,305 folios. Abraham story? Various hands. Date 1700 and after. Authorship ascribed to (nos. 582, 607): Yūsuf ibn Ismāʿīl ibn Ḥumṣ [*sic*] (compare B above). Complete.

E. 861–62, nos. 608–10. 3 vols., 963 folios. Abraham story present. Bought in Aleppo. Date ca. 1780. Incomplete.

F. 862–66, nos. 611–22. 12 vols., 58 parts (out of original 60, parts 1–2 missing), 3,078 folios. Various hands. Abraham story? Date mostly 1730–70. Almost complete. Scribe's name: no. 618, Jurjī Khūrī.

Oxford

Catalogi codicum manuscriptorum orientalium Bibliothecae Bodleianae, Alexander Nicoll. 152, no. 165. 27 vols., no. of folios? Date? Complete?

Holland

Leiden

Catalogus codicum orientalium Bibliothecae Academiae Lugduno Batavae, R. Dozy. Vol. 5.

A. 170–71, no. 2562. 2 fragments, no. of folios? Date? *Catalogus codicum arabicum Bibliothecae Academiae Lugduno Batavae*, 2nd ed., M. J. de Goeje and Th. Houtsma.

B. 348, no. 458. Fragment, no. of folios? Date?

India

Bankipore

Catalogue of the Arabic and Persian Manuscripts in the Oriental Public Library at Bankipore, Maulavi Muinuddin Nadwi. Vol. 15. 198–201, nos. 1103–10. 8 vols., 2,115 folios. Abraham story? Date 1851. One hand. Complete. Scribe's name: Aḥmad ibn Ibrāhīm.

Calcutta

Catalogue of the Arabic Manuscripts in the Buhar Library, Shams-ul-ʿUlamāʾ M. Hidayat. Vol. 2. 482–86, nos. 437–47. 11 vols., 2,166 folios. One hand. Abraham story? 19th century. Complete.

Turkey

Istanbul

Topkapı Sarayı Müzesi Kütüphanesi Arapça Yazmalar Kataloğu, Fehmi Edhem Karatay. Vol. 3. 353, no. 8644. 3rd part, 88 folios. Date 1444. Fragment. Scribe's name: Nāṣir ad-Dīn Muḥammad. Microfilm in Jāmiʿat ad-Duwal al-ʿArabiyya, Maʿhad al-makhṭūṭāt al-ʿArabiyya in Cairo. See Fuʾād Sayyid, *Fihris al-makhṭūṭāt al-muṣawwara*, vol. 1, 485, no. 497.

United States

Princeton

Descriptive Catalogue of the Garrett Collection of the Arabic Manuscripts in the Princeton University Library, Phillip K. Hitti et al.

A. 242, no. 731. 6 vols., 3,860 folios. Abraham story present. One hand. Date 1855. Complete. Scribe's name: Aḥmad ibn Muḥammad Murād al-ʿĀʾidī.

B. 242, no. 733. 4 vols., 571 folios. Abraham story absent. 18th century? Fragment.

OTTOMAN-TURKISH TRANSLATIONS

France

Paris

Catalogue des manuscrits Turcs (Bibliothèque Nationale), E. Blochet. Vol. 1. 149, no. 354. Part 4, 196 folios. Second half of 16th century. Fragment.

Germany

Berlin

Verzeichnis der orientalischen Handschriften in Deutschland: vol. 13, 1, *Türkische Handschriften*, Barbara Flemming. 273–74, no. 313 (no. 4079 Staatsbibliothek, Berlin). 130 folios. Date? Fragment.

Dresden

Catalogus codicum manuscriptorum orientalium Bibliothecae Regiae Dresdensis, Henricus Orthobious Fleischer. 2, no. 12. 175 folios. Date? Fragment.

Great Britain

London

Catalogue of the Turkish Manuscripts in the British Museum, Charles Rieu. 214, no. 7884. 117 folios. Ca. 18th century. Fragment.

Turkey

Istanbul

Topkapı Sarayı Müzesi Kütüphanesi Türkçe Yazmalar Kataloğu, Fehmi Edhem Karatay. Vol. 2.

A. 296, nos. 2805–7. First 3 vols., 1,501 folios. Date 1466–67. Originally copied for Sultan Mehmet II. Incomplete.

B. 297, nos. 2808–13. Various vols.: no. 2808, vol. 3, 588 folios, date?; no. 2809, vol. 6, 428 folios, date?; no. 2810, vol. 8, 696 folios, date?; no. 2811, vol. 8, 413 folios, date?; no. 2812, vol. ?, 317 folios, date?; no. 2813, vol. 1, 337 folios, date 1568–69.

NOTES ON THE PUBLICATION HISTORY OF *SĪRAT ʿANTAR*

Two different recensions of the *Sīra* have been printed. One was first printed in Cairo (hereafter C), the other in Beirut (hereafter B). C contains the story of Abraham, while B does not. Other differences are matters of wording and phrasing rather than overall style or sequence of events, in which the two recensions resemble each other closely, often exactly. I am not certain that the following list of publications is complete, but it will serve to offer an idea of how often the *Sīra* was printed.

Cairo (C)

1. 16 vols., 32 parts. Cairo: Maṭbaʿat Shāhīn, 1866–69.
2. 4 vols., 32 parts. Cairo: Maṭbaʿat al-amīra ʾsh-sharafiyya, 1888–93.
3. 32 vols. Cairo: Maṭbaʿat al-amīra ʾsh-sharafīyya, 1904.
4. 5 vols., ? parts. Cairo: al-Maṭbaʿa ʾl-ḥamīdiyya ʾl-miṣriyya, 1912.
5. 8 vols., 59 parts. Cairo: Maktabat Muṣṭafa ʾl-Bābi ʾl-Ḥalabī, 1961.

Beirut (B)

1. 6 vols. Beirut: al-Maṭbaʿa ʾl-adabiyya, 1883–85.
2. 10 vols. Beirut: n.p., 1893–1901.
3. 8 vols. Cairo: al-Maktaba ʾt-tijāriyya ʾl-kubrā, 1947.
4. 8 vols. Cairo: Maktabat al-Mashhad al-Ḥusainī, 1971.

APPENDIX III

Introduction to the Topkapı Manuscript (no. 1145)

Volume One of

The Story of 'Antar son of Shaddād, son of Qurād al-'Abs[1]

[1r.] In the Name of God, the Merciful, the Compassionate

Praise be to God who created Man in the best form, adorned him with eloquent speech and upright figure, and chose him from among the created things of the world, so that He said, "We have honored the sons of Adam,"[2] and "We made them peoples and tribes and nations."[3]

He favored the Arabs among them over the non-Arabs, and He selected from among the Arabs the people of Mecca and the Ka'ba[4] and exalted them with a noble prophet, Muḥammad, concerning whom it was revealed, "Indeed, you are sublime of character."[5]

Muḥammad uttered the primordial speech in the veracity of his summons in a proper, eloquent arrangement and in an upright, profound style; so that among his opponents the stentorian voices of the orators failed them, and the tongues of the fluent and the eloquent grew weak. Hence, they turned away from fighting with words to battling with swords, and from forbidding with speech to resisting with lances, and from conversing with talk to fighting with blades. Nonetheless, the lights of his guidance shone in the East and the West, and the secrets of his Message reached far and near. I bestow on him blessings equal in number to the grains of sand in the desert, through the ever-revolving nights and days. And I do the same for his virtuous family, and his pure Companions and Successors, who are the defenders on the battlefields of religion and the valiant on the battlefields of certainty.

Now then: this is a story [*sīra*] of ʿAntar of ʿAbs that I have translated from Arabic at the behest of he who has been adorned with [numerous] types of everlasting, divinely sanctified marks of favor and [diverse] kinds of eternal, intimate felicities. It is he who has filled the eastern and western parts of the earth with the upright decrees of his dominion, so that its near and distant environs have fallen into his lasso of obedience. He has raised the guideposts of religion, and he has drawn away the veil of doubt from the face of certainty with the true aim of his beliefs. *Verse*:

> It is he who has enriched all creatures,
> With gifts concerning which Desire dares not whisper.
> The light of Truth shines from his words;
> The lightning bolt of Might glistens on his cheeks.
> He is the rightly guided of the servants of God, the guide of His religion,
> The savior of the leaders on the path of truth, the succor of its protectors.

Indeed, he is the most magnificent Sultan, the magnified Khan of Khans, the Shadow of God [1v.] on earth, the Enlivener of state, world, and religion, the Master of necks of Caesars, the Bone-Crusher of Shahs, the Lord of the two domains,[6] the Ruler of the two seas, the Establisher of the foundations of the royal state, the Fulfiller of the fundaments of Ottoman rule, the Erector of the banners of Muslim holy law, the Raiser of the pinions of the Aḥmadī order, the Refuge for the weak of nations, the Vanquisher of the kings of Persians, Turks, and Kurds, the Lord of holy warriors and strugglers for religion, the Battler of infidels and recalcitrant profligates, the Preserver of the lands of God, the Protector of the servants of God, the Sovereign of the horizons, the rightful Vice-Regent of God, the Sultan, son of the Sultan, the Sultan Mehmet, son of Sultan Murād, son of Sultan Mehmet, son of Sultan Bayezid, son of Sultan Murād Khan Ghāzī, son of Sultan Orkhān, son of Sultan Othmān. O God, preserve the chain of their lineage in this order until the coming of the Hour and until the hour of the Coming! May the banners of religion remain aloft in the days of his harmonious rule! May the value of knowledge remain high in the time of his fortunate reign! May his supporters among the people of truth increase, and may his enemies among the folk diminish! O God, just as You have supported him as he promotes Your word, so perpetuate him! And just as You have illumined his spirit to organize the best interests of Your people, so immortalize him! *Verse*:

> Whoever has said, "Amen,"
> May God preserve his good name.

Indeed, this is a prayer that includes all of mankind: "Amen, O Lord of the Worlds!"[7]

INTRODUCTION

Masters of biography and experts of history have transmitted about this world champion, 'Antar ibn Shaddād, son of Qurād of 'Abs, wondrous and amazing stories and verses of poetry. Amongst the early Arabs, there were scattered stories. Arabs—such as Abu 'l-Hāshim ibn as-Sā'iba 'l-Kalbī, Ash'ath ibn Bakr ath-Thaqafī, Abu 'l-'Alā' Baṣrī, Abu 'l-Haitham ibn 'Adi 'ṭ-Ṭayyi', Ḥammād as-Sannānī, Abu 'Ubaida, Aṣmā'ī, Ibn al-A'rābī, Juhaina ibn Ghailān Yemenī, Abu 'l-'Aṭā' aṭ-Ṭayyi', and Abu 'l-Ḥasan ash-Shaibānī—wrote down these stories, poems, and proverbs. Each one of these esteemed men held sessions in which they composed some of the wondrous and strange tales [*ḥikayāt*] of the story of 'Antar. Each also recited appropriate verses for these sessions. Each of these compositions became popular and was read in its own province among the members of the tribe. All of these were compiled and organized, and this went on in this fashion for some time. Later, historians collected all of them and organized them, but since each compiler was a different person, the versions were different. Some stories were redundant, others deficient; [2r.] in some verses were many, in others they were few.

From among these different versions, certain individuals who were not grounded in the styles of Arabic and the rules of writing compiled disordered texts and translated them into Turkish. Parts of each of these versions of the story of 'Antar have come before this humble servant. Most of the verses mentioned in the Arabic were contracted, and much of the story was omitted. Even in the stories that formed the main part of the Turkish translation, the situation was such that the story's plot was impossible to understand. In most places I saw that the story did not hang together and remained totally incomplete. Some early parts appeared at the end, the story was disjointed, and contradictory phrases appeared. The end was different from the beginning, and there were mistakes in the proper names, titles, and patronyms of the warriors. Narrators attributed the heroic deeds of one warrior to another, and when warriors fought one another the narrators confused the killers with the slain. Further down, they would even relate the heroic deeds of the already dead warrior. In this way, contradictions filled the text. The examples of such mistakes are countless.

There are several reasons why these mistakes occurred in these initial translations. One is that they would rely on a single, defective Arabic text. Another is that those translating lacked knowledge of Arabic grammar and were ignorant of proper Arabic style and suitable ways of composition. Another is that they did not examine the story from its beginning to its end and hence did not understand its start from its finish. If they had done that, they would have paid attention to what came before and what came later so as not to create contradictions. They even sought to abridge the story, but with their selections they rendered it defective and incomplete. They just proceeded in a sloppy manner.

Seeing this situation, and also obeying the command of the Padishah of the World, this humble servant gathered together three copies of the histories of ʿAntar. I examined these three copies thoroughly, and, as is proper, I became fully conversant with the true version of the story. Whatever happened in the story and in the poetry that was superfluous, I collated. I corrected those places in the Turkish translations of the Arabic original that were possible [2v.] so that they agreed with the correct version that I had established. I provided suitable lines of poetry that had been omitted, and I completed the story where it was defective. Where success was possible, this is how I proceeded. In places where success was impossible, I made a new composition. I cited verses appropriate to the story in their entirety and inserted in their proper places the unusual stories that were missing in the above-mentioned translations, along with appropriate verses.

Thus, with the help of God and in the felicitous state of being in the shelter of the Padishah of the World, I brought forth this translation in a period of two years, freeing it from defects and mistakes and stripping from it the deficiencies of error. I named it "Glorious" [*fakhīr*], whose number of letters give the date in which it was completed [871/1466–67].

Now then, let us begin the story of ʿAntar . . .

APPENDIX IV

Lion Descriptions

THIS APPENDIX contains the eleven lion descriptions in *Sīrat 'Antar*. Perhaps the term "lion appearance" would be more accurate than "lion description," since lions six and seven have little or no description. I retain the word "description," however, to emphasize the point that the potential for description always exists, even if it is not always utilized. It would not be surprising, for example, to find that other recensions (performances) of the *Sīra* inserted lion descriptions at these points and removed them from other points. Whether the thematic slot "lion description" is filled or not, it always potentially exists when a lion is introduced. Remembering this general principle facilitates understanding of *Sīrat 'Antar*'s compositional technique.

In order to allow the reader to obtain an idea of the degree of lexical repetition that exists in *Sīrat 'Antar*, I adopt Lord and Parry's method of indicating formulas (Lord, *The Singer of Tales*, 45–50; Parry, "Studies in the Epic Technique of Oral Verse Making," 117–23 [*The Making of Homeric Verse*, 301–4]). My version of this basic technique rests on the following principles.

1. Words or phrases repeated one or more times in the *Sīra*'s lion descriptions are in italics. Different morphological forms of the same word (persons or tenses of a verb, singular-plural forms of nouns, comparative degrees of adjectives) are considered identical.

2. Identical words used in different connections are considered repetitions; but to indicate the slight differences of context, I underline such words or phrases (for example, the adjective *ṭawīl* "long" modifies the lion itself in 3, line 2, while it is used to modify its hair in 4, line 2). When individual words

are repeated but not the whole phrase, I italicize only the word (*ṭawīl* ash-sha'r); when the whole phrase is repeated, I italicize the entire phrase (*ṭawīl ash-sha'r*).

3. Synonyms or words of the same type (colors; words for lion noises: snarling, roaring, growling, etc.) are italicized in broken form when they recur.

LION DESCRIPTION 1 (2/156)

1. *wa-idhā huwa bi-asad kabīr*
2. *qadr ath-thaur wa-akbar*
3. *mujallal bi-'sh-sha'r wa-'l-wabar*
4. *yaṭīr min 'ainai-hi 'sh-sharar*
5. *wa-yaqlib al-wādī idhā hamaz* wa-h*am*a*r*
6. *shadūq shadqam*
7. *'abūs ḍaigham*
8. *tusma' ar-ra'd min-hu idhā hamham wa-damdam*
9. yalma' *al-barq min 'ainai-hi idha 'l-lail aẓlam*
10. hā'il al-manẓar
11. *wa-qad kharaj* min baṭn al-wādī
12. *wa-huwa yamshī wa-yatamakhtar*
13. *wa-huwa aghbar*
14. *afṭas al-mankhar*
15. bi-*anyāb aḥadd min an-nawā'ib*
16. *wa-makhālīb aḥadd min al-maṣā'ib*
17. *'abūs al-wajh*
18. *tasma' ṣaut-hu ka-'r-ra'd*
19. shadīd al-ḥail
20. ṣa'b al-mirās
21. *'arīḍ al-kaff wa-'l-asās*

LION DESCRIPTION 2 (4/374)

1. *wa-idhā hum bi-asad 'aẓīm jasīm* wasīm
2. *wa-huwa asad 'atīq fī qadr ath-thaur al-kabīr*
3. *wāsi' al-manākhīr*
4. *ṭawīl al-aẓāfir*
5. *wa-huwa shadūq shadqam*
6. *'abūs ḍaigham*
7. *afṭas adgham*
8. *tasma' ṣaut-hu ka-anna-hu ar-ra'd idhā za'ar wa-damdam*

9. wa-ʿawī-hu ka-anna-hu ṣakhr jabal tahaddam
10. *bi-shidq ka-anna-hu al-qalīb*
11. *wa-anyāb ka-annaha 'l-kalākīb*
12. *<u>wa-idhā</u> mashā wa-tamakhṭar*
13. *yaṭīr min ʿainai-hi 'sh-sharar*
14. wa-yuʿjab fī mishyat-hi
15. *wa-yahtazz* fī khaṭawāt-hi

LION DESCRIPTION 3 (5/456)

1. wa-hum [al-ʿabīd] yajurrūn *asadan ka-anna-hu 'th-thaur*
2. *ṭawīl qad jallal-hu 'l-wabar*
3. *wa-huwa yamshī wa yatamakhṭar*
4. *wa-yaṭīr min ʿainai-hi 'sh-sharar*
5. *wa-la-ju anyāb aḥadd min an-nawā'ib*
6. *wa-makhālīb ashadd min al-maṣā'ib*
7. *wa-huwa asad shadūq shadqam*
8. *ʿabūs ḍaigham*
9. *afṭas adgham*
10. *idhā hamaz hamham*
11. *wa-huwa aswad ka-'l-lail idhā aẓlam wa aʿtam*
12. *ka-anna-hu 'l-qaḍā' al-mubram*
13. *bi-shidq ka-anna-hu 'l-qalīb*
14. *wa-anyāb ka-anna-ha 'l-kalākīb*

LION DESCRIPTION 4 (26/18)

1. *wa-idhā bi-asad qad ẓahar*
2. *ṭawīl ash-shaʿar*
3. *aghbar*
4. *kabīr* ar-ra's
5. ghā'ir *al-maḥjar*
6. *wāsiʿ al-mankhar*
7. *ṭawīl al-aẓāfir*
8. *yaṭīr min ʿainai-hi 'sh-sharar*
9. *wa-tahtazz min-hu al-aqṭār*

LION DESCRIPTION 5 (27/100-1)

1. *idhā iʿtaraḍla-<u>hum</u> asad ʿaẓīm* al-khilqa . . .
2. wa-kān hādha l-*asad <u>aḥmar</u>*

3. *mujallal bi-'sh-sha'r wa-'l-wabar*
4. *'aẓīm al-mankhar*
5. man naẓar-hu yaqsha'irr badan-hi
6. wa-takād al-albāb 'ind ru'yat-hi an tazhaq

LION DESCRIPTION 6 (29/348)

1. *wa-qad ẓahar 'alai-*nā *asad 'aẓīm* fa-mā ra'ainā *a'ẓam* min juththat-hi wa-sharadat an-nūq wa-'l-jimāl min za'qat-hi

LION DESCRIPTION 7 (31/16)

1. *wa-idhā huwwa bi-sab' qad kharaj* min *ghābat-hi* wa-akhad aṭ-ṭarīda fī famm-hi wa-'ād bi-hā ilā *ghābat-hi*

LION DESCRIPTION 8 (41/5)

1. *wa-idhā bi-asad aghbar*
2. *'atīq aṣfar*
3. *ka-anna-hu* l-ba'īr
4. *au qiṭ'a min hajar kabīr*
5. *ḍaigham*
6. *la-hu anf* ajram
7. wa-ṣudgh *adgham*
8. *shadūq shadqam*
9. hamūsh ghashamsham
10. ẓahr-hu qaṣīr
11. wa-li-'ṣaulat-hi *hadīr*
12. *wa-lahu hamhama* wa-*zafīr*
13. *ka-anna-hu 'l-qaḍā'* idhā tamaṭṭā
14. au al-bāz idhā saṭā
15. *kufūf-hu 'arīḍa*
16. *wa-anyāb-hu* qātila
17. *wa-'ainā-hu* bāsila

LION DESCRIPTION 9 (41/24)

1. wa-'ind aṣ-ṣabāḥ *ẓahar 'alai-him asad 'aẓīm*
2. *qadr ath-thaur al-jasīm*
3. *bi-anyāb* maṣqūla
4. *wa-aẓāfīr* maghūla

5. *wa-huwa a'bas al-manẓar*
6. *ka-anna-hu qiṭ'a min al-ḥajar*

LION DESCRIPTION 10 (56/54)

1. *wa-idhā i'taraḍ-hum asad fī qadr ath-thaur al-kabīr*
2. *wa-la-hu zafīr* wa-shakhīr
3. *wa-huwa* yahdir *hadīr*
4. *ka-annahu* raḥa fī nīr
5. *wa-la-hu* shahīq wa-'iyāṭ
6. wa-'azm nahīḍ laisa fī-hi tafrīṭ
7. fa-'l-wail kull al-wail li-man bi-hi waqa'
8. *wa-la-hu anyāb wa-makhālib* ka-'l-khanājir

LION DESCRIPTION 11 (57/137)

1. *wa-idhā qad i'taraḍ-hum asad* fī tilka 'ṭ-ṭarīq
2. wa-hājam 'alai-him wa-mana'-hum 'an al-masīr wa-'t-ta'wīq
3. wa-kān dhālika *'l-asad qad kharaj 'alai-him* min bain *al-ghābāt* wa-'sh-shajar
4. *wa-huwa asad aghbar al-maḥjar*
5. *yaṭīr min 'ainai-hi 'sh-sharar*
6. *wa-yaqlib al-wādī bi-ṣiyāḥ idhā za'ar wa-zamjar*
7. *la-hu anyāb aḥadd min an-nawā'ib*
8. *wa-makhālib ashadd min al-maṣā'ib*
9. *wāsi' al-ashdāq*
10. *'abūs ḍaigham*
11. *afṭas al-anf adgham*
12. *yusma' min ghargharat-hi 'r-ra'd idhā hamaz wa-hamham*
13. *wa-tanẓur al-barq min 'ainai-hi idhā aẓlam al-lail wa-aqtam*
14. *wa-huwa ka-anna-hu al-qaḍā' al-mubram*

APPENDIX V

The Lion Fight Scene

THIS APPENDIX contains outlines of the eleven lion fights portrayed in *Sīrat ʿAntar.* Comparison of these outlines reveals that the lion fight scene consists of seven main dramatic elements:

1. The lion appears
2. The lion is described
3. Others react in fright
4. The hero reacts courageously
5. The hero fights and kills the lion
6. The hero reacts to his or her deed
7. Others react to the hero's deed

These elements occasionally assume diverse forms. Sometimes elements are expressed by only one thematic unit; sometimes several are used. Not infrequently, one or more elements are absent from a scene (cf. lion fights 3, 5, 6, 7, 9, 11). Even when fully present, elements need not appear in the order given above. Despite these variations, an examination of these scenes should convince the reader of the high degree of uniformity. To aid the reader in identifying elements, their numbers appear in parentheses after their respective lines in the outlines. Sometimes elements appear that are not integral to the lion fight scene (i.e., references to larger lines of narrative development). These are marked by a zero in parentheses (cf. lion fight 2, c–d).

LION FIGHT 1 (6.3:2/156–58)

a. ʿAntar is watching over his herds when suddenly a lion appears. (1)

b. The lion is described in prose. (2)
c. The herds smell the lion and scatter in fright. (3)
d. The lion is described in verse (3 lines). (2)
e. 'Antar rushes toward the lion. (4)
f. He threatens and challenges it. (4)
g. He recites a battle poem (7 lines). (4)
h. He decides to fight the beast bare-handed. (4)
i. Shaddād and his companions arrive while 'Antar is threatening the lion. They hide to watch the proceedings. (3 and 7)
j. 'Antar fights and kills the lion. (5)
k. He skins, roasts, and eats the animal, then goes to sleep. (6)
l. Shaddād and the others marvel at 'Antar's deed. They abandon their plans of ambush and leave him in peace. (7)

LION FIGHT 2 (9.3:4/370–76)

a. King al-Mundhir is out hunting when suddenly a lion appears. (1)
b. His attendants scatter in fright. (3)
c. Prince an-Nu'mān appears with 'Antar, whom he has just captured, in chains. (0)
d. Al-Mundhir asks 'Antar why he attempted to steal the 'Aṣāfīr camels. 'Antar tells the king of his love for 'Abla and, at the thought of his beloved, recites a love poem (22 lines). (0)
e. Back to the lion: al-Mundhir's attendants are still scattering. (3)
f. 'Antar fearlessly offers to kill the lion. (4)
g. Impressed by 'Antar's eloquence and boldness, al-Mundhir accepts this offer and orders his chains removed. (7)
h. 'Antar recites a battle poem to the lion (6 lines). (4)
i. The lion is described in prose. (2)
j. 'Antar fights and kills the lion with his sword. (5)
k. He wipes his blade on the lion's carcass. (6)
l. He recites a battle poem in victory (17 lines). (6)
m. Al-Mundhir marvels at 'Antar's courage, might, and eloquence. (7)

LION FIGHT 3 (9.6:5/456) [ELEMENT 6 IS ABSENT]

a. Shah Anūshirwān asks 'Antar to exhibit his might by fighting a lion. He has a lion brought to his tournament grounds. (1)
b. It takes ten slaves to control the lion's chains. (3)
c. The lion is described in prose. (2)
d. The lion is described in verse (4 lines, the same as in lion fight 11). (2)

e. ʿAntar recites a battle poem (6 lines). (4)
f. ʿAntar fights and kills the lion with his sword. (5)
g. The shah is very impressed by this deed. He praises ʿAntar and awards him fine gifts. (7)

LION FIGHT 4 (32.2–3:26/18–20)

a. ʿAmr ibn Maʿdīkarib is returning home with his bride and ʿUrwa ibn al-Ward, whom he has just fought and captured, when suddenly a lion appears. (1)
b. ʿAmr's horse shies. (3)
c. The lion is described in prose. (2)
d. ʿAmr flees from the lion, but then, more afraid that his new wife will think him a coward, returns to confront it. (3 and 4)
e. He fights and kills the lion with his sword. (5)
f. He wipes his sword clean on the carcass. (6)
g. ʿAmr's companions marvel at his deed. (7)
h. ʿAmr recites a battle poem in victory (19 lines). (6)

LION FIGHT 5 (34.2:27/100–101) [ELEMENT 3 IS ABSENT]

a. Duraid ibn aṣ-Ṣimma is helping Daththār ibn Rizq, his foster-son, win his beloved. On the way to her camp a lion suddenly appears. (1)
b. The lion is described in prose. (2)
c. Duraid's warriors ask him to allow them to attack the lion. Duraid wants to fight it himself, but Daththār begs for the honor of killing it, so Duraid gives him leave to do so. (4)
d. Daththār dismounts and approaches the lion, armed only with his sword. (4)
e. He fights and kills the lion with his sword. (5)
f. He wipes his blade clean on the carcass. (6)
g. All are impressed with Daththār's courage and might. (7)

LION FIGHT 6 (37.2:29/348–51) [ELEMENTS 2 AND 6 ARE ABSENT]

a. Shaibūb has just met Māzin and is staying at his camp. The camp's slaves come fleeing into camp; a fierce lion has appeared and is scattering the herds. (1 and 3)
b. Māzin smiles at the news, takes his sword, and goes to meet the lion. (4)

c. While Māzin is gone, Shaibūb learns that Shaddād is the youth's real father. (0)
d. Māzin returns, having fought and killed the lion. Slaves bear the carcass into camp, and one of them describes the fight. (5)
e. Māzin's mother congratulates him on his victory. (7)

LION FIGHT 7 (39.3:31/16–17) [ELEMENTS 2, 3, 7 ARE ABSENT]

a. Returning home from Mecca, 'Antar and his companions see a rider pursuing a wild ostrich in the desert. The rider kills the ostrich, but Māzin decides he wants to claim the prey and rides to fetch it. Suddenly a lion appears, seizes the ostrich, and retreats with it into his thicket. The rider, Hānī ibn Mas'ūd, asks Māzin for the ostrich. Māzin tells him how the lion took it. (1)
b. Hānī removes his armor, puts down his sword, and enters the thicket. (4)
c. Māzin is amazed at his courage and boldness. (7)
d. Hānī emerges from the thicket, dragging the ostrich with one hand and the living lion with his other. He strikes the lion a mighty blow and kills it. (5)
e. Hānī invites Māzin to share his prey. (6)

LION FIGHT 8 (50.2:41/5–6)

a. Al-Ghaḍbān is returning home after raiding the shah's caravan when a lion suddenly appears in his path. (1)
b. The lion is described in prose. (2)
c. Al-Ghaḍbān's companions are frightened of the beast. (3)
d. Al-Ghaḍbān dismounts, removes his armor, and attacks the lion with his sword. (4)
e. He fights and kills the lion. (5)
f. He wipes his sword clean on its carcass. (6)
g. He recites a battle poem in victory (13 lines). (6)
h. His companions are impressed with his deed and congratulate him. (7)

LION FIGHT 9 (50.5:41/24) [ELEMENTS 3 AND 6 ARE ABSENT]

a. Al-Ghaḍbān has captured ar-Rabī' ibn Ziyād and is on his way to find 'Antar. Suddenly a lion appears. (1)

b. The lion is described in prose. (2)
c. Al-Ghaḍbān dismounts, removes his armor, and attacks the lion with his sword. (4)
d. He fights and kills the lion. (5)
e. Ar-Rabīʿ is amazed at this deed. (7)

LION FIGHT 10 (70.1:56/54–55)

a. ʿAmr Dhu ʾl-Kalb and ʿUnaitira set out on a raid. Suddenly a lion appears in their path. (1)
b. The lion is described in prose. (2)
c. The lion is described in verse (5 lines). (2)
d. ʿAmr is frightened of the lion, but he decides to kill it. (3)
e. ʿUnaitira precedes him, saying that she wants the honor of this deed. (4)
f. She fights and kills the lion, using a sword that was once ʿAntar's. (5)
g. All marvel at her deed. (7)
h. She wipes her sword clean on the dead lion. (6)
i. ʿAmr is pleased with her and congratulates her. (7)

LION FIGHT 11 (72.2:57/137–38) [ELEMENT 3 IS ABSENT]

a. Al-Ghaḍanfar and his companions are returning from a successful raid when a lion suddenly appears and blocks their path. (1)
b. The lion is described in prose. (2)
c. The lion is described in verse (the same 4 lines as in lion fight 3). (2)
d. Al-Ghaḍanfar tells his companions that he will handle the lion. He dismounts, removes his armor, and, bearing only his sword, approaches the lion. (4)
e. He fights the lion and kills it with a mighty sword blow. (5)
f. His companions marvel at this blow. (7)
g. Al-Ghaḍanfar wipes his blade clean on the carcass, remounts, and rides on, acting as if nothing has happened. (6)

Notes

INTRODUCTION

1. The ethnographer Vasili V. Radlov's study of Turkic epics, *Proben der Volkslitteratur der nördlichen türkischen Stämme*, vol. 5: *Der dialect der Kara-Kirgisen*, was enormously influential on the studies of H. M. and K. M. Chadwick, whose *The Growth of Literature*, with its wide purview of epic, has in turn greatly influenced later scholars.

2. Scholars' understanding of the international scope of epic and their increasing awareness of the diversity of its social origins and contexts are already evident in such surveys of epic and heroic literture as C. M. Bowra, *Heroic Literature*; and Jan de Vries, *Heroic Song and Heroic Legend.* This awareness has increased with the passage of time, as the overviews of Felix J. Oinas, ed., *Heroic Epic and Saga: An Introduction to the World's Great Folk Epics*; and A. T. Hatto, ed., *Traditions of Heroic and Epic Poetry*, demonstrate. For discussion of the enormously influential research of Milman Parry and Albert Lord on oral-formulaic folk epics, see chapter 7 below.

3. The text of *Sīrat 'Antar* used for this study is *Qiṣṣat 'Antara ibn Shaddād al-'Absī.* This version is divided into 59 books of 96 pages each, except book 59, which has 39 pages; for other printed versions of the *Sīra*, see appendix II. For an overview of premodern Arabic and Islamic popular literature, see chapter 4 below. See also Peter Heath, "Arabische Volksliteratur im Mitteralter," in *Neues Handbuch der Literaturwissenschaft*, vol. 5: *Orientalisches Mittelalter*, ed. Wolfhart P. Heinrichs, 423–39; and Boaz Shoshan, "On Popular Literature in Medieval Cairo," *Poetics Today* 14, no. 2 (1993): 349–69.

4. This is the modern generic designation. The literal meaning of *sīra* is "a going" or "a mode or manner of going," coming from the verbal root *s-y-r*, which means "to betake oneself" or "to travel." From the primary meaning of "going" arose a series of secondary meanings—"mode of behavior or conduct" and then the story of such conduct: "biography" or "stories of the ancients" (*aḥādīth al-awā'il*). In addition, in the plural, *siyar*, the word acquired the associated meaning of "military expeditions or the actions or affairs thereof." (See Muḥammad ibn Mukarram ibn Manẓūr, *Lisān al-'Arab*, under "*sīra*," 4:389–90; and Edward W. Lane, *Arabic-English Lexicon*, 1:1483.)

Sīra is the singular form of the word; *sīrat* is the form of the genitive construct (*Sīrat ʿAntar* is the story *of* ʿAntar); the usual plural form is *siyar*, but I use the plural *sīra*s in order to simplify matters for nonreaders of Arabic. Another common Arabic term for works that fall under the category of popular *sīra*s is the more general determination *qiṣṣa* (story). For a discussion of the words used to indicate different types of fictional narratives in Arabic, see C. Pellat et al., "Ḥikāya," in the *Encyclopedia of Islam*, 2nd ed., 3:367–77 (hereafter, EI^1 for the first edition and EI^2 for the second edition). The term *sīra* is used consistently in this study in order to avoid confusion; but readers should not be surprised to find works we call *sīra*s titled *qiṣṣa* in the bibliography.

In regard to literary classification, one must take care to distinguish between the use of the word *sīra* to denominate historiographical, empirical biographies (the most famous being Ibn Isḥāq's biography of the Prophet Muḥammad, *Sīrat an-nabī*) and pseudo-historical, fictional narratives such as *Sīrat ʿAntar*. For a discussion of the term *sīra shaʿbiyya* in the context of Arabic literature, see Fārūq Khūrshīd and Maḥmūd Dhihnī, *Fann kitābat as-sīra ʾsh-shaʿbiyya*, 2nd ed., 33–50. For discussion of a premodern popular biography of the Prophet Muḥammad attributed to Abu ʾl-Ḥasan al-Bakrī, see Boaz Shoshan, *Popular Culture in Medieval Cairo*, 23–39.

5. On the pseudo-historiographical nature of these works, see Rudi Paret, *Die Geschichte des Islams im Spiegel der arabischen Volksliteratur*; Franz Rosenthal, *A History of Muslim Historiography*, 186–93; David Pinault, *Story-telling Techniques in the* Arabian Nights, esp. 21–24; and chapter 9 below.

6. ʿAntara is the Classical Arabic form of the name; in colloquial usage the final *a* (*tāʾ marbūṭa*) is dropped to leave ʿAntar. This study uses the Classical Arabic form of the name (ʿAntara) to refer to the historical figure of the pre-Islamic poet ʿAntara ibn Shaddād and the colloquial form (ʿAntar) for the legendary hero of the *Sīra*.

7. On the modern study of popular *sīra*s, see Giovanni Canova, "Gli studi sull'epica popolare araba," *Oriente Moderno* 57 (1977): 211–26; Peter Heath, "A Critical Review of Scholarship on *Sīrat ʿAntar ibn Shaddād* and the Popular *Sīra*," *Journal of Arabic Literature* 15 (1984): 19–44; and chapter 1 below. For brief discussions and summaries of prominent popular *sīra*s, see Fārūq Khūrshīd, *Aḍwāʾ ʿala ʾs-siyar ash-shaʿbiyya*; and Malcolm C. Lyons, *The Arabian Epic: Heroic and Oral Story-telling*, esp. vol. 3.

For bibliograpical background on the *sīra*s themselves, see Victor Chauvin, *Bibliographie des ouvrages arabes ou relatifs aux Arabes, publiés dans l'Europe chrétienne de 1810 à 1885*, 3:112–43; and Wilhelm Ahlwardt, *Verzeichnis der arabischen Handschriften der Königlichen Bibliothek zu Berlin*, esp. vol. 8: *Die Grossen Romane*, which includes summaries of many of these narratives.

Of the works mentioned, *Fīrūz Shāh, Bahrām, Saif, az-Zīr, ʿAntar, Dhāt al-Himma, Amīr Ḥamza, Baibars, ʿAlī Zaibaq*, and the *Banī Hilāl* have been published, often numerous times, in Beirut and Cairo (see bibliography). *Iskandar, Ghazwat al-Arqaṭ, al-Badr-Nār*, and *Ḥākim* remain unpublished. *Aḥmad ad-Danaf* is present in part in *The Thousand and One Nights*, but a full-length unpublished version exists in manuscript in the John Rylands Library in Manchester, England.

8. *Fīrūz Shāh* and *Bahrām Gūr* are Arabic versions of works that originally stem from the Persian tradition of popular epic. On the first, see William L. Hanaway, Jr., "Persian Popular Romances before the Safavid Period"; and, for a partial translation, his *Love and War: Adventures from the "Fīrūz Shāh Nāma" of Sheikh Bīghamī*. On Persian and Arabic versions of *Bahrām*, see Mechthild Pantke, *Der arabische Bahrām-Roman: Untersuchungen zur*

Quellen- und Stoffgeschichte. For the premodern Persian tradition of popular literature, see Jan Rypka, *History of Iranian Literature*, 617–43, 670–73. On the Alexander (*Iskandar*) legend in Islamic literatures, see *EI*[2], 4:127.

9. On *Saif*, see Rudi Paret, *Sīrat Saif ibn Dhī Jazan: Ein arabischer Volksroman*; and *EI*[1], 4:71–73; for *az-Zīr Sālim*, Jaroslav Oliverius, "Aufzeichnungen über den Basūs-krieg in der Kunstliteratur und deren Weiterentwicklung im arabischen Volksbuch über Zīr Sālim," *Archiv Orientalni* 33 (1965): 44–64; and his "Themen und Motiv im arabischen Volksbuch Zīr Sālim," *Archiv Orientalni* 39 (1971): 129–45; on *'Antar*, *EI*[2], 1:518–21, Bernhard Heller, *Die Bedeutung des arabischen 'Antarroman für die vergleichende Literaturkunde*; H. T. Norris, *The Adventures of Antar*; and Khūrshīd and Dhihnī, *Fann kitābat as-sīra 'sh-sha'biyya*; for *Amīr Ḥamza*, *EI*[2], 3:152–54; for *Dhāt al-Himma*, *EI*[2], 2:233–39; and Udo Steinbach, *Ḍāt al-Himma: Kulturgeschichtliche Untersuchungen zu einem arabischen Volksroman*; for *Baibars*, *EI*[2], 1:1126–27; Helmut Wangelin, *Das arabische Volksbuch von König eẓẒāhir Baibars*; and Georges Bohas and Jean-Patrick Guillame, trans., *Roman de Baibars*.

10. On the *'ayyār* figure, see *EI*[2], 1:794; and Lyons, *The Arabian Epic*, 1:118–27; for the Arabic tradition, see Muḥammad Rajab an-Najjār, *Ḥikāyāt ash-shuṭṭār wa 'l-'ayyārīn fī 't-turāth al-'arabī*; for this figure in premodern Persian epic, see Hanaway, "Persian Popular Romances," 129–77.

11. For the *Banī Hilāl*, see *EI*[2], 3:387; Svetozár Pantøůček, *Das Epos über den Westzug der Banū Hilāl*; Bridget Ann Connelly, *Arab Folk Epic and Identity*; Susan Slyomovics, *The Merchant of Art: An Egyptian Hilali Oral Epic Poet in Performance*; and Dwight Fletcher Reynolds, "Heroic Poets, Poetic Heroes: Composition and Performance in an Arabic Oral Epic Tradition in Northern Egypt"; and his *Heroic Poets, Poetic Heroes: Composition and Performance in an Arabic Oral Epic Tradition in Northern Egypt*.

12. Chapter 4 contains an overview of the various genres of premodern Arabic popular literature; see also Shoshan, "On Popular Literature in Medieval Cairo," 349–69. On the broader concept of "popular culture" as seen from the perspective of a historian, see his "High Culture and Popular Culture in Medieval Islam," *Studia Islamica* 83 (1991): 67–107; and his *Popular Culture in Medieval Cairo*, esp. 67–78.

13. On the manuscript tradition of the *Nights*, see Muhsin Mahdi's edition and study of the earliest extant manuscript, *The Thousand and One Nights (Alf Layla wa-Layla), From the Earliest Known Sources*. For a recent study of the *Arabian Nights* that takes into consideration the influence public performance had on the style and structure of its tales, see Pinault, *Story-telling Techniques in the* Arabian Nights. On the performance of *Sīrat Banī Hilāl*, see especially the studies of Connelly, Slyomovics, and Reynolds cited in note 11 above.

14. Two recent exceptions are Jan Knappert's *Islamic Legends: Histories of the Heroes, Saints, and Prophets of Islam*, which collects stories from throughout the Islamic world, and John Renard's *Islam and the Heroic Image: Themes in Literature and the Visual Arts*.

15. One example of this is scholars' use of the Lord-Parry theory of oral-formulaic epic composition, which has been applied promiscuously to all manner of literary genres; see chapter 7 below.

1. THE MODERN "DISCOVERY" OF *SĪRAT 'ANTAR*

1. For a description of Europe's reception of *The Thousand and One Nights* as well as a full bibliography of previous research on the subject, see Mia I. Gerhardt, *The Art of Story-*

telling: A Literary Study of the Thousand and One Nights; and Muhsin Jassim Ali, *Scheherazade in England: A Study of Nineteenth-Century English Criticism of the Arabian Nights.*

2. William Jones, *Poeseos Asiaticae Commentariorum* (London, 1774), 323. Quote translated by Terrick Hamilton, in *Antar: A Bedoueen Romance*, 1:xx–xxi.

3. For Von Hammer's account of his discovery of *Sīrat ʿAntar*, see Joseph von Hammer-Purgstall, "On Arabian Poetry, Especially the Romance of Antar," *New Monthly Magazine* (London, 1820): 12–14. This is a translation of his German article that appeared in *Jahrbücher der Literatur* (Vienna, 1802), which I have been unable to obtain. For a description of the manuscript that Von Hammer bought in Cairo, see G. Flügel, *Die arabischen, persischen und türkischen Handschriften der Kaiserlich-Königlichen Hofbibliothek zu Wien*, 2:4–9.

4. Joseph von Hammer-Purgstall, *Fundgruben der Orients* (Vienna, 1802): 2:304–6. Translated by Hamilton in *Antar*, 1:xix-xxii. I have changed Hamilton's ʿIbla back to Von Hammer's original ʿAbla, the correct form of the name.

5. On al-ʿAṣmaʿī, see *EI*[2], 1:717–19.

6. A. J. Arberry, *The Seven Odes: The First Chapter in Arabic Literature*, 154.

7. Terrick Hamilton, *Antar: A Bedoueen Romance*, 4 vols. (London: John Murray, 1819).

8. Von Hammer, "On Arabian Poetry."

9. Ibid., 153–54. Al-Maʾmūn's mother was, by the way, of Persian ancestry, not African; see "al-Maʾmūn," in *EI*[2], 6:331–39.

10. Von Hammer, "On Arabian Poetry," 160–61.

11. Hamilton, *Antar* (1820 ed.).

12. Ibid., 1:xii, xxviii.

13. Ibid., 1:xxix, xxiv.

14. Ibid., 1:xvii.

15. For a description of the public's reaction—such as it was—to Hamilton's translation, see Cedric Dover, "The Black Knight," *Phylon: Atlanta University Review of Race and Culture* (1954): 52–55.

16. An excellent bibliography of the studies, translations, and texts related to *Sīrat ʿAntar* that appeared during the nineteenth century is Victor Chauvin, *Bibliographie des ouvrages arabes ou relatifs aux Arabes*, 3:113–26.

17. A. Caussin de Perceval, "Notice et extrait du Roman d'Antar," *Journal Asiatique* (August 1833): 99. The translation is from "The Romance of Antar," *Asiatic Journal* n.s. 27 (September 1838): 57*n*2.

18. Ibid., 98. For the text of Muḥammad's remarks, see Abu 'l-Faraj al-Iṣfahānī, *Kitāb al-aghānī*, 8:243 (Būlāq, 7:101). Flattering as they are, one should perhaps not give too much credence to the authenticity of Muḥammad's remarks. Such comments by the prominent religious figures of early Islam regarding pre-Islamic or early Islamic poets are a common topos in the biographies of poets.

19. Caussin de Perceval, "Notice," 99–106.

20. "The Romance of Antar," 57.

21. Fulgence Fresnel, *Lettres sur l'histoire des Arabes avant l'islamisme*, 41–43.

22. Joseph von Hammer-Purgstall, "Sur l'auteur de roman de chevalerie arabe Antar," *Journal Asiatique* (April 1838): 384; translation from "The Romance of Antar," 57.

23. Von Hammer, "Sur l'auteur," 386–88. See Ibn Abī Uṣaibiʿa, *ʿUyūn al-anbāʾ fī ṭabaqāt al-aṭibbāʾ*, 2:290-97. The Ibn ʿArabshāh Von Hammer refers to is the fifteenth-century Aḥmad ibn Muḥammad ibn ʿArabshāh, secretary, historian, and littérateur; see *EI*[2], 3:711–12.

24. Heinrich Thorbecke, *Antarah: Des vorislamischen Dichters Leben.*

25. A. Perron, "Lettre sur Antar," *Journal Asiatique* (December 1840): 481–526.

26. Thorbecke, *Antarah*, 32.

27. Ibid., 33.

28. Edward W. Lane, *Manners and Customs of the Modern Egyptians*, chapters 21–23, pp. 397–430.

29. Ignaz Goldziher, *Muhammedanische Studien* (English translation *Muslim Studies*), especially vol. 2 (see Goldziher's index for references). See also his "Ein orientalischer Ritterroman," in *Jubilee Volume in Honor of Bernhard Heller on the Occasion of His Seventieth Birthday*, ed. Alexander Scheiber, 7–13.

30. Alphonse de Lamartine, *Vie des grands hommes*, 1:267–345; also *Voyage en Orient*, 2:473–507.

31. Hippolyte Taine, *Philosophie de l'art*, 2:344–45.

32. Ibn an-Nadīm (fourth/tenth century) calls *The Thousand and One Nights* (as it existed in his time) "truly a coarse book, without warmth in the telling [hackneyed]" (Muḥammad ibn Isḥāq ibn an-Nadīm, *Kitāb al-fihrist*, ed. Gustav Flügel, 304; translated by B. Dodge, *The Fihrist of al-Nadīm: A Tenth-Century Survey of Muslim Culture*, 2:714). For examples of Muslim religious scholars' reactions to popular stories and storytellers, see Johannes Pedersen, "The Islamic Preacher: *Wāʿiẓ, mudhakkir, qāṣṣ*," in *Ignaz Goldziher Memorial Volume*, ed. S. Löwenger and J. Somogyi, 1:226–51; and also his "The Criticism of the Islamic Preacher," *Die Welt des Islams* 2 (1953): 215–31; see also Goldziher, *Muhammedanische Studien*, 2:161–66; and Ch. Pellat et al., "Ḥikāya," in *EI*[2], 3:371.

The famous Egyptian scholar Jalāl ad-Dīn as-Suyūṭī (d. 911/1505) describes how he at one point became so incensed at the fabrications of a popular religious storyteller (*qāṣṣ*) that he issued a *fatwā* against him. Popular outcry against his judgment was so great, however, that he rescinded it and never dared to approach the issue again; see his "Maqāmāt al-intiṣār bi 'l-wāḥid al-qahhār," in *Sharḥ maqāmāt Jalāl ad-Dīn as-Suyūṭī*, ed. Samīr Maḥmūd ad-Durūbī, 225–33. A fifteenth-century Morrocan *qāḍī* (judge) similarly tried to forbid the narration or hearing of such works as *Sīrat ʿAntar* and *Sīrat Dhāt al-Himma*: see H. Pérès, "Le roman dans la littérature arabe des origines à la fin du Moyen Age," *Annales de l'Institut d'Etudes Orientales* (Algiers) 16 (1958): 33. (One must remember, of course, that educated Westerners had much the same attitude toward their own popular literature: see Victor E. Neuberg, *Popular Literature: A History and Guide*, especially 161–62, for nineteenth-century attitudes.)

There were exceptions to the general disdain for popular literature among Muslim scholars; the most prominent of these was the great historian/sociologist Ibn Khaldūn, who devoted several chapters of his famous introduction to history to the popular poetry of his time: see ʿAbd ar-Raḥmān Ibn Khaldūn, *Kitāb al-ʿibar*, the author's introduction (*al-Muqaddima*), 1:1124–69; translated by F. Rosenthal, *The Muqaddimah: An Introduction to History*, 3:412–80.

33. Cf. Chekri Ghanem, *Antar, pièce en cinq actes*; Aḥmad Shauqī, *ʿAntara*; and Maḥmūd Taimūr, *Ḥawwāʾ al-khālida.* For a partial list of attempts at modernizing the *Sīra*, see Fārūq Khūrshīd, *Aḍwāʾ ʿala 's-siyar ash-shaʿbiyya*, 53.

34. See Gerhardt, *The Art of Story-telling*; and Ali, *Scheherazade in England.* John Barth is an example of a modern author who has been inspired by the *Nights*; see his *Chimera* and *The Last Voyage of Somebody the Sailor.* N. A. Rimsky-Korsakov composed both a *Scheherazade* and an *Antar* suite. And the 1992 Walt Disney film *Aladdin* is only the latest in a long series of film and storybook versions of *Thousand and One Nights* stories for children and adults.

35. Both Von Hammer and Caussin de Perceval, for example, published continuations of the *Nights* (Chauvin, *Bibliographie,* 4:89, 162, and 4:97, 150, respectively), while Von Hammer also engaged in heated debate with Silvestre de Sacy over the origins of the *Nights* at the time when he was so vigorously defending ʿAntar's literary greatness (Chauvin, *Bibliographie,* 4:1–3).

36. C. Dover, "Terrick Hamilton: A Forgotten Orientalist," *Calcutta Review* (1954), quoted in Arberry, *The Seven Odes,* 156.

37. Scholarly interest in the ways folk and popular literature are composed and performed stems only from the end of the 1960s, with the publication of the studies of Milman Parry and Alfred Lord and the development of modern cultural studies.

38. On this process, see Raymond Schwab, *The Oriental Renaissance: Europe's Rediscovery of India and the East 1680–1880,* trans. Gene Patterson-Black and Victor Reinking; Edward Said, *Orientalism*; Maxime Rodinson, *Europe and the Mystique of Islam,* trans. Roger Veinus; Hichem Djaït, *Europe and Islam: Cultures and Modernity,* trans. Peter Heinegg; and Albert Hourani, *Islam in European Thought.*

39. Two reference works that deserve special notice are Chauvin's *Bibliographie* and Wilhelm Ahlwardt's impressive résumé of *sīra* literature in the eighth volume of his catalogue of the Arabic manuscripts in the Royal Library in Berlin: *Verzeichnis der arabischen Handschriften der Königlichen Bibliothek zu Berlin.*

40. Bernhard Heller, "Der arabische ʿAntarroman," *Ungarische Rundschau* 5 (1916): 83–107; *Der arabische ʿAntarroman: Ein Beitrag zur vergleichenden Literaturgeschichte*; *Die Bedeutung des arabischen ʿAntarroman für die vergleichenden Literaturkunde*; and "Sīrat ʿAntar," *EI*[2], 1:518–21. I have been unable to obtain the second of Heller's works, but the similarities in content and approach of his other studies on *Sīrat ʿAntar* suggest that it was largely subsumed into his third study and that all of his works on the *Sīra* are essentially continuations and enlargements of his first study.

41. Heller, "ʿAntarroman," 84–86. See especially *EI*[2], 1:519.

42. Only about half of the manuscripts of *Sīrat ʿAntar* have the Abraham story. For a list and brief descriptions of these manuscripts, see appendix II.

43. Heller, *Die Bedeutung,* 99–100.

44. Ibid., 183–84. This is not to say that motif classification is not itself useful; see, for example, Hasan El-Shamy, *Folk Traditions of the Arab: A Guide to Motif Classification*; and Malcolm C. Lyons, *The Arabian Epic,* vol. 2.

45. Heller, "Sīrat ʿAntar," *EI*[2], 1:519.

46. Quoted by Heller in *Die Bedeutung,* 187.

47. Ibid.

48. Rudi Paret, *Sīrat Saif*; Henri Grégoire, "Comment Seyyid Baṭṭāl, martyr musulman du VIII siècle, est-il devenu dans la légende le contemporain d'Amer (+836)?" *Byzantion* 11 (1936): 571–75; Marius Canard, "Delhemma, épopée arabe des guerres arabo-byzantines," *Byzantion* 10 (1935): 283–300; and his "Delhemma, Sayyid Baṭṭāl et

Omar al-No'mān," *Byzantion* 12 (1937): 183–88; Helmut Wangelin, *Das arabische Volksbuch von König eẓẒāhir Baibars*; and Udo Steinbach, *Ḍāt al-Himma: Kulturgeschichtliche Untersuchungen zu einem arabischen Volksroman.*

49. Rudi Paret, *Die Geschichte des Islams im Spiegel der arabischen Volksliteratur.*

50. Rudi Paret, *Die legendäre Maghāzī-Literatur*; Steinbach *Dāt al-Himma*; and Lyons, *The Arabian Epic*, 1:8–54.

51. The calls for further analysis of these works are common enough (e.g., Paret, *Sīrat Saif*, 93; Franz Rosenthal, *A History of Muslim Historiography*, 189), but not always fulfilled; see, for example, Marius Canard, "Les principaux personages du roman du chevalerie arabe Ḍāt al-Himma wa-l-Baṭṭāl," *Arabica* 8 (1961): 160; Mechthild Pantke, *Der arabische Bahrām-Roman*; and Nabīla Ibrāhīm, *Sīrat al-Amīra Dhāt al-Himma*, 253–54. Comparison to historical events and other works of literature also forms part of Wangelin's *Baibars* and Steinbach's *Dāt al-Himma.*

52. J. Oliverius, "Aufzeichnungen über den Basūs-Krieg in der Kunstliteratur und deren Weiterentwicklung im arabischen Volksbuch über Zīr Sālim," *Archiv Orientalni* 33 (1965) 44–64; and "Themen und Motiv im arabischen Volksbuch von Zīr Salīm," *Archiv Orientalni* 39 (1971): 129–45. Also, 'Abd al-Ḥamīd Yūnis, *al-Hilāliyya fi 't-tā'rīkh wa 'l-adab ash-sha'bī* (Cairo: Maṭba'at Jāmi'at al-Qāhira, 1956).

53. Mūsā Sulaimān, *al-Adab al-qaṣaṣī 'ind al-'Arab.* In spite of this work's virtues, it is also a good illustration of the spread of certain unfortunate Western prejudices among Arab scholars. Sulaimān relies on nineteenth-century European scholarship concerning *Sīrat 'Antar* and accordingly wants to find in the *Sīra* an "Arabian *Iliad*"; see 100–138.

54. See Khūrshīd and Dhihnī, *Fann kitābat as-sīra 'sh-sha'biyya*; and Khūrshīd, *Aḍwā' 'ala 's-siyar ash-sha'biyya.*

55. Armand Abel, "Formation et constitution du roman d'Antar," in *La poesia epica e la sua formazione*, 717–30.

56. Gustav E. von Grunebaum, "The Hero in Medieval Arabic Prose," in *Concepts of the Hero in the Middle Ages and the Renaissance*, ed. Norman T. Burns and Christopher J. Reagan, 84.

57. See Giovanni Canova, "Gli studi sull'epica popolare araba," *Oriente Moderno* 57 (1977): 211–26; Bridget Ann Connelly, *Arab Folk Epic and Identity*; Susan Slyomovics, *The Merchant of Art*; and Dwight Fletcher Reynolds, "Heroic Poets, Poetic Heroes." Reynolds's dissertation has a full and up-to-date bibliography of recent articles on *Sīrat Banī Hilāl*, 34–42. Pertinent collections of articles may also be found in Micheline Galley, ed., *Association internationale d'étude des civilizations méditerranéennes: Actes du IIième congrès*; *Edebiyāt: A Journal of Middle Eastern and Comparative Literature* n.s. 2, nos. 1–2 (1988), devoted to Middle Eastern oral literatures; and *Oral Tradition* 4, nos. 1–2 (1989), devoted to Arabic oral traditions. Finally, Lyons's three-volume *The Arabian Epic* contains useful essays on common themes in the genre, offers a comparative motif index, and provides brief plot summaries for ten major works of the *sīra* genre, including *Sīrat 'Antar.*

2. The History of 'Antara, 'Antar, and *Sīrat 'Antar*

1. Abū Muḥammad 'Abdullāh ibn Muslim ibn Qutaiba, *Kitāb ash-shi'r wa-'sh-shu'arā'*, ed. Muḥammad Shākir, 1:250–54; Abu 'l-Faraj al-Iṣfahānī, *Kitāb al-Aghānī*, 8:237–46 (Būlāq, 7:148–53). Later sources only repeat the information these works contain.

2. Cf. R. Blachère, "'Antara," *EI*², 1:521–22.

3. The geographical territories of the Banī 'Abs lay in the Hijāz region of central Arabia; genealogically they were 'Adnānī (northern Arabs).

4. Ibn Qutaiba, *ash-Shi'r*, 1:250; al-Iṣfahānī, *al-Aghānī*, 8:239.

5. al-Iṣfahānī, *al-Aghānī*, 8:239–40.

6. Ibid., 8:244. In *Sīrat 'Antar* the principal foe of the Banī 'Abs in the war of Dāḥis and al-Ghabrā' is the Banī Fazāra, a subunit of the Banī Dhubyān. This war, which reputedly lasted forty years, became one of the most famous feuds of pre-Islamic times.

7. al-Iṣfahānī, *al-Aghānī*, 8:240; Ibn Qutaiba, *ash-Shi'r*, 1:251.

8. al-Iṣfahānī, *al-Aghānī*, 8:243.

9. For Ibn al-Kalbī and Abū 'Amr ash-Shaibānī's accounts, see al-Iṣfahānī, *al-Aghānī*, 8:245. For Abū 'Ubaida's account, see Ibn Qutaiba, *ash-Shi'r*, 1:252.

10. al-Iṣfahānī, *al-Aghānī*, 8:244.

11. Cf. Wilhelm Ahlwardt, *The Divans of Six Ancient Arabic Poets*, 33–52. For other editions of 'Antara's *diwān*, see Blachère, "'Antara," 1:521–22; and Fuat Sezgin, *Geschichte des arabischen Schrifttums*, 2:113–15.

12. Blachère, "'Antara," 1:521.

13. Cf. Abū Muḥammad al-Ḥasan al-Hamdānī, *al-Iklīl min akhbār al-Yaman wa-ansāb Ḥimyar: al-Kitāb al-'āshir fī ma'ārif Hamdān wa-'uyūn akhbār-hā*, ed. Muḥibb ad-Dīn al-Khatīb, 168–70. For an English translation of this anecdote, see H. T. Norris, *Antar*, 51–52.

14. Cf. P. O'Flinn, "Production and Reproduction: The Case of *Frankenstein*," *Literature and History* 9, no. 2 (1983): 194–213, partially repr. in Bob Ashley, *The Study of Popular Fiction: A Source Book*, 23–39.

15. Some English-language equivalents to the many popular culture manifestations of 'Antar are the legend of Robin Hood, the tales of King Arthur and the Knights of the Round Table, and even (in modern times) the tales of *The Thousand and One Nights*.

16. In modern Arabic the plural of *khabar* (*akhbār*) is used for the daily news; indeed, the general range of the subject matter of the early Arabic *akhbār* tradition is reminiscent of the types of material covered by the departments of a modern newspaper or magazine.

17. For more on the early North Arabian *akhbār* tradition, see Werner Caskel, "Die einheimischen Quellen zur Geschichte Nord-Arabiens vor dem Islam," *Islamica* 4, no. 3 (1927): 331–41; and his "Aijām al-'Arab: Studien zur altarabischen Epik," *Islamica* 3, supplement (1931): 1–99.

18. *Sīrat Dhāt al-Himma* is slightly longer than *Sīrat 'Antar*. The longest of the other *sīras* (*Saif ibn Dhī Yazan*, *al-Malik aẓ-Ẓāhir Baibars*, *Fīrūz Shāh*, and the combined cycles of the *Banī Hilāl*) are about half the length of these two works, that is, about the length of the Būlāq edition of *The Thousand and One Nights*.

19. Cf. Abu 'l-Faraj Muḥammad ibn Abī Ya'qūb ibn an-Nadīm, *al-Fihrist*, 304–8 (English trans., 2:712–24). In spite of the lack of mention of a definite story of 'Antar, we do have evidence that the name 'Antar at an early period became a byword for bravery. In a debate between a Muslim and a Christian monk from around 800 A.D., the monk sarcastically remarks that his cowardly opponent is "no 'Antar": see K. Vollers, "Das Religionsgespräch von Jerusalem (um 800 A.D.) aus dem Arabischen übersetzt," *Zeitschrift für Kirchengeschichte* 29 (1908): 49–50.

20. Ibn Abī Uṣaibi'a, *'Uyūn al-anbā' fī ṭabaqāt al-aṭibbā'*, 2:290–97.

21. Martin Schreiner, "Samaw'al b. Jaḥyā al-Magribī und seine Schrift *Ifḥām al-Jahūd*," *Monatsschrift für Geschichte und Wissenschaft des Judenthums* n.s. (1898): 417–18 (German trans., 127).

22. Tāj ad-Dīn as-Subkī, *Mu'īd an-ni'am wa-mubīd an-niqam*, ed. D. W. Myhrman, 186. This particular remark is also quoted in Muḥammad Zaghlūl Sallām, *al-Adab fī 'l-'aṣr al-Mamlūkī*, 1:121.

23. See appendix II. There is also a small segment of *Sīrat 'Antar* dated before 806/1402 in the British Library. The ninth/fifteenth-century Arab biographer as-Sakhāwī mentions a miller named Khalīl who owned quires (*kurrasa*) of *Sīrat 'Antar*, *Sīrat Dhāt al-Himma*, and stories of the Companions of the Prophet. The miller gave them to a sheikh to perform, although without apparent success. This event is cited by Boaz Shoshan, "On Popular Literature in Medieval Cairo"; see also Muḥammad ibn 'Abd ar-Raḥmān as-Sakhāwī, *Tuḥfat al-aḥbāb wa-bughyat aṭ-ṭullāb*, 181.

24. See chapter 4 below and appendix III.

25. Cf. Franz Rosenthal, *A History of Muslim Historiography*, 188; and my own research with *sīra* manuscripts.

26. The *Sīra* itself claims that it exists in several redactions, a complete Hijāzī version and abridged Syrian or Iraqi versions. I agree with Bernhard Heller's opinion ("Sīrat 'Antar," in *EI*^{2}, 1:520) that as determinations for places of origin these terms are purely fictional. To accept the *Sīra*'s designations for itself would lead to confusion if further examination of the manuscript tradition reveals diverse redactions (what if one finds different versions both claiming to be Hijāzī?). I have therefore used the place of first publication to designate the two versions in print (see appendix II). This allows room for further creation of clear distinctions, should future research reveal this necessity.

All of the printed versions of *Sīrat 'Antar* have been cheap popular editions (with bad paper and miserable bindings). It would be interesting to investigate the current and past size of the *sīra*-buying audience, if the various publishers of *sīra*s keep records on numbers of volumes printed and sold. It would also be worthwhile to interview publishers and editors in order to ascertain their attitudes toward *sīra*s, why they use different editorial formats even when the same texts are used, how profitable *sīra* sales are, and so forth.

27. See chapter 9 below.

3. THE NARRATION OF *SĪRAT 'ANTAR*

1. See chapter 1 above.

2. See note 11 in the introduction for bibliographical references to these studies. As noted in the introduction, although the Arabic, Persian, and Turkish traditions of public narration are not identical, they are neighbors, and critical examination of the evidence from one tradition can inform our understanding about aspects of the other. For the Persian tradition, see Mary Ellen Page's "Naqqālī and Ferdowsi: Creativity in the Iranian National Tradition"; and William L. Hanaway, Jr., "Persian Popular Romances before the Safavid Period." For the Turkish tradition, see the studies of Pertev N. Boratav and Irène Mélikoff cited in the bibliography.

3. Edward W. Lane, *Manners and Customs of the Modern Egyptians*, 397–98. In the three chapters that Lane devotes to describing "Public Recitations of Romances" (chapters 21–23), he offers partial summaries of three *sīras*: *Banī Hilāl* (400–406); *Baibars* (407–19);

and *Dhāt al-Himma* (421–31); see also his *Arabian Society in the Middle Ages: Studies from a Thousand and One Nights*, 126–27.

4. Lane, *Modern Egyptians*, 398–400. As remarked above, *shā'irs* are the only type of *sīra* reciters still present in Egypt, and they are very few in number. The viol that Lane refers to is called a *rabāb* (or *rabāba*). In Lane's time storytellers used a square-box viol-type instrument that usually had one, sometimes two, horsehair strings. For a picture, see Lane, *Modern Egyptians*, 399. Modern *rabābas* use a coconut shell with the top cut off for a sound box, have two horsehair strings, and are played with a horsehair stringed bow. In Lane's day this variety of viol was called a *kemangah*, now the common term for violin. For a description and picture of this instrument, see Lane, *Modern Egyptians*, 362–63.

5. Lane, *Modern Egyptians*, 406 (the quotation is from 419).

6. Ibid., 419–20.

7. Fulgence Fresnel, "Quatrième lettre sur l'histoire des Arabes avant l'islamisme," *Journal Asiatique* (1838) 503; J. G. Wetzstein, "Der Markt in Damaskus," *Zeitschrift der Deutschen Morgenländischen Gesellschaft* 11 (1857) 493–94.

8. Terrick Hamilton, trans., *Antar: A Bedoueen Romance*, 1:xviii.

9. A good impression of the size and nature of *Sīrat Banī Hilāl*'s manuscript tradition may be obtained from Wilhelm Ahlwardt's descriptions in *Verzeichnis der arabischen Handschriften der Königlichen Bibliothek zu Berlin*, vol. 8: *Die Grossen Romane*. For a brief survey of recent investigation of this tradition, see Dwight Reynolds, *Heroic Poets, Poetic Heroes*, 34–35. Much work still needs to be done in this area; but for initial forays, see A. Ayoub and Bridget Connelly, "A propos des manuscrits de la geste des Banū Hilāl conservés à Berlin," *Association internationale d'étude de civilizations méditerranéennes: Actes du IIième congrès*, ed. M. Galley, 347–63; and Micheline Galley, "Manuscrits et documents relatifs à la geste hilalienne dans les bibliothèques anglaises," *Littérature orale arabo-berbère* 12 (1981): 183–92. Evidence suggests that the same epic can be performed in different ways. For example, Cathryn Anita Baker studied a literate Tunisian reciter of the Banī Hilāl who was well acquainted with written versions of the epic, but who nonetheless reworked the material in his oral renditions of the story: see "The Hilālī Saga in the Tunisian South." Similarly, audience reception of performed works can differ; see Bridget Connelly's chapter on "Punning as Understanding," in *Arabic Folk Epic and Identity*, 119–46, for more on this point. Finally, for an extensive discussion of the different venues and social contexts in which the *Banī Hilāl* epic is currently recited, see Reynolds, *Heroic Poets, Poetic Heroes*, 102–36.

10. For Lane's estimates, see note 3 above; for Evliya Chelebi's, see his *Seyahatnamesi*, vol. 10: *Misir, Sudan, Habeş*, 361. For the French list, see André Raymond, "Une liste des corporations de métiers au Caire en 1801," *Arabica* 4 (1957): 150–63. See also Gabriel Baer, *Egyptian Guilds in Modern Times*, 26.

11. U. J. Seetzen, *Reisen durch Syrien, Palästina, Phönicien, die Transjordan-länden, Arabia Petraea und Unter-Aegypten*, 3:397-98, quoted in Baer, *Egyptian Guilds*, 116.

12. Ṭāḥā Ḥusain, *al-Aiyām*, vol. 1, chapters 1–2.

13. Naguib Mahfouz, *Zuqāq al-midaq*, 5–6; *Midaq Alley*, trans. Trevor Le Gassick, 3–6.

14. For descriptions of the modern context for the recitation of *Sīrat Banī Hilāl*, see Susan Slyomovics, *The Merchant of Art*, 71–76; Reynolds, *Heroic Poets, Poetic Heroes*, 102–36; and Connelly, *Arab Folk Epic and Identity*, 55–68. Mary Ellen Page notes how lim-

ited an importance storytelling had for the regular customers of the Iranian coffeehouses she visited, even for those who were regular listeners when a storyteller was present:

> Another aspect of the storytelling phenomenon is the question of why the audience continues to go to the coffee house day after day to hear a story-teller. Part of this has already been touched upon in regard to the other [social] functions which the coffee house fills. It is worth repeating that the attachment is at least as much to the coffee house as to the storyteller. The proof of this seems to be in the fact that regulars do not follow their storyteller to another coffee house nor do most of them cease frequenting a coffee house when their storyteller leaves. When Ḥabīb Allāh left Shiraz only a handful of men ceased going there daily. One or two of Ḥabīb Allāh's regulars began appearing at the Chahār Faṣl [where another storyteller performed], but things went on pretty much as they always had. ("Naqqālī," 50–51)

On visits to Cairo I made it a habit to ask if and where *sīra*s are still performed. I was often told that they are and was directed to coffeehouses in the older parts of the city. At these coffeehouses, however, I was told that *sīra*s had not been recited there for a number of years. This suggests that former audiences are not even aware that common *sīra* recitation has disappeared. That it has in the traditional part of central Cairo itself is beyond doubt. Wandering around the quarters surrounding Sayyidna 'l-Ḥusain during Ramadan, one sees crowds gathered in many a coffeehouse, but they congregate to watch late-night movies on television. The only live entertainment consists of occasional performances by *mawwāl* singers. These, however, tend to be government-sponsored events occurring in tents especially erected for the occasion. Such performances occur in the new squatters' settlements that have grown up around Cairo in the last decades, filled with village emigrants to the city who (in Susan Slyomovics's words) "bring their storytellers with them" (personal communication). (For the analogous case of the rapid decline in Arabian Nabaṭī poetry, see Saad Abdullah Sowayan, *Nabaṭi Poetry: The Oral Poetry of Arabia*, 2–3.)

New media can also give a boost to certain genres, as did the arrival of the tape cassette to popular *mawwāl* singing in Egypt in the 1970s and 1980s. The 30- to 60-minute length of these ballads made them perfect for dissemination by cassette. For this genre, see Pierre Cachia, *Popular Narrative Ballads of Modern Egypt.*

15. Joseph von Hammer-Purgstall, "On Arabian Poetry," 17.

16. See the references to Slyomovics and Reynolds in note 14 above. For further analysis of *Sīrat 'Antar*'s style and composition, see part II of this book.

17. This anecdote was first published in the anonymous article "'Antara al-'Absī," *al-Hilāl* 5 (Cairo, 1896–97): 730. Its original source is unknown, but several volumes of a manuscript of *Sīrat 'Antar* in the John Rylands Library in Manchester, England, ascribe the *Sīra* to one Yūsuf ibn Ismā'īl ibn Ḥumṣ (see appendix II). Perhaps one of these volumes is its source. It is also quoted by Mūsā Sulaimān in *al-Adab al-qaṣaṣī 'ind al-'Arab*, 102–3. Al-'Azīz bi-'llāh was a Fatimid caliph who ruled from 365/976 to 386/996. H. T. Norris has noted in *The Adventures of Antar* (55) that one objection against accepting this anecdote is linguistic: it is doubtful that Arabic was at that time prevalent enough among ordinary Egyptians for them to become enthusiasts of a story related in it. Stylistic, textual, and historical evidence also testifies against accepting the veracity of this story.

18. This story appears in the Egyptian magazine *at-Tankīt wa-'t-tabkīt* 1 (1881):

10–11, ed. ʿAbdullāh Nadīm. Only one volume of this magazine appeared. (I thank David Ruedig for bringing this magazine to my attention.) This is not the only anecdote that satirizes audience reaction to *sīra* narration. Iskandar Bey Abkāriūs, in *Minyat an-nafs fī ashʿār ʿAntar al-ʿAbs*, 4–5, writes:

> We have heard of a certain man of Ḥumṣ who used to attend the circle of storytellers every night and listen to the story of ʿAntar. One night he tarried in his shop until after sunset and so arrived without having had supper. That night the narrative concerned the battle of ʿAntar with Kisrā [the Persian shah]. The storyteller read until the point when ʿAntar fell captive to the Persians so that they threw him in chains and imprisoned him. Here he broke off the narrative, and the audience dispersed.
>
> The man became very agitated, and the world darkened before his eyes. He went home sad and downcast. When his wife brought him food, he kicked the table so that the plates broke, and the food was scattered on the floor. He cursed his wife violently, and when she answered him back, he struck her severely. Then he went out and wandered restlessly through the markets. Finally, overcome by his mood, he went to the house of the storyteller. He found him asleep, but he awakened him and said, "You put the man, chained, into prison, and then you come home without a care!? I beg you! Finish the story for me until the point when you remove him from prison! I can't sleep or find peace as long as he is in this condition. See how much you collect from the audience in your night's work, and I will give you the same now." So the storyteller took the book and read the rest of the narrative until ʿAntar left prison. The man said to him, "May God grant you happiness and peace of mind! Take this money, thank you!"
>
> Then he returned happily home, asked for food, and explained to his wife how the story-teller had put chains on the foot of ʿAntar, and then she brought him food to eat. How could he even have tasted food while ʿAntar was imprisoned and in chains?
>
> He said, "But now I have gone to the house of the storyteller, and he read me the story until he removed him from prison. Praise be to God! My soul is happy, so bring me whatever food you have and forgive my excesses!"

This story is also quoted in Sulaimān, *al-Adab al-qaṣaṣī*, 100. Norris gives another translation of it in *Antar*, 68–69. In spite of the exaggeration of these stories, there is probably some truth to them. Hamilton (*Antar*, xviii) mentions, for example, that the famous explorer of the Arabian peninsula J. L. Burkhardt wrote to him about *Sīrat ʿAntar* and related that "when he was reading a portion of it to the Arabs, they were in ecstasies of delight, but at the same time so enraged at his erroneous pronunciation, that they actually tore the sheets out of his hands."

19. ʿAbd al-Ḥamīd Yūnis, *al-Hilāliyya fī 't-taʾrīkh wa-'l-adab ash-shaʿbī*, 199.

20. Lane, *Modern Egyptians*, 398.

21. It is important not to underestimate the role audience reaction plays in a storytelling tradition. Yūnis notes, for example, that audience members were always ready to correct the storyteller if he made a mistake or omission (*al-Hilāliyya*, 154); see also Connelly, *Arab Folk Epic and Identity*, 62–63; Slyomovics, *The Merchant of Art*, 75–76; and especially Reynolds, *Heroic Poets, Poetic Heroes*, 177–206. Page ("Naqqālī," 49) noticed in her work

with Persian storytellers that they shied away from narrating unknown material: "A storyteller will not recite material which is unknown to the audience. The audience, he feels, will not come back every day, and pay, to hear a story they have never heard before."

Audience reaction, of course, influences not only the contents of a narrative tradition, but its very life. In Egypt I met a young *mawwāl* singer named Hishām Mitqāl, a son of the well-known *mawwālī* Mitqāl al-Qinawī. Hishām's uncle, Shammandī Mitqāl, knows portions of the *Sīrat Banī Hilāl*, and I asked Hishām why he had not learned it as well. He replied that there was no point to it since the audiences did not want to listen to long works anymore. This is the moment of breakage in the narrative tradition that spells its doom. See also Connelly, *Arab Folk Epic and Identity*, 62.

It would be interesting to determine what factors made long epic cycles suddenly popular: the spread of Arabic as a vernacular, the influence of other (Persian or Turkish?) narrative traditions, a change in social conditions and self-perceptions as Arabic-speaking groups began to lose political power and prestige, the onslaught of the Crusades, or just literary spontaneous combustion? It is difficult at this point to estimate with any degree of certainty the relative importance of these and other literary or social factors.

4. LITERARY CONTEXT AND LITERARY HISTORY

1. Fehmi Edhem Karatay, *Topkapı Sarayı Müzesi Kütüphanesi Türkçe Yazmalar Kataloğu*, 2:296, nos. 2805–7.

2. *Hazine* 1145, folios 1a–2b. The translator dates his project by using the *abjad* alphabet chronograph, *fakhīr*. For a translation of this Ottoman introduction, see appendix III.

3. On this theory and its present standing among folklorists, see Michael Zwettler, "Classical Arabic Poetry between Folk and Oral Tradition," *Journal of the American Oriental Society* 96, no. 2 (1976): 198–212. For a recent discussion of the interrelationship between "high" and "popular" culture, see Boaz Shoshan, "High Culture and Popular Culture in Medieval Islam."

4. John B. Thompson, "Editor's Introduction," in Pierre Bourdieu, *Language and Symbolic Power*, trans. G. Raymond and M. Adamson, 11.

5. Robert Redfield, *Peasant Society and Culture*, offers what has become one classic formulation of this dichotomy, the distinction between great tradition and little tradition:

> Let us begin with a recognition, long present in the discussions of civilizations, of the difference between a great tradition and a little tradition. (This pair of phrases is here chosen from among others, including "high culture" and "low culture," "folk and classic cultures," or "popular and learned traditions." I shall also use "hierarchic" and lay culture.") In a civilization there is a great tradition of the reflective few, and there is a little tradition of the largely unreflective many. The great tradition is cultivated in schools or temples; the little tradition works itself out and keeps itself going in the lives of the unlettered in their village communities. The tradition of the philosopher, theologian, and literary man is a tradition consciously cultivated and handed down; that of the little people is for the most part taken for granted and not submitted to much scrutiny or considered refinement or improvement. . . .
>
> The two traditions are interdependent. Great tradition and little tradition have long affected each other and continue to do so. . . . Great epics have arisen

> out of elements of traditional tale-telling by many people, and epics have returned again to the peasantry for modification and incorporation into local cultures. . . . Great and little tradition can be thought of as two currents of thought and action, distinguishable, yet ever flowing into and out of each other. (41–42)

6. Differences of tone, political outlook, and aesthetic premises separate Redfield's concept of great and little traditions from F. R. Leavis's high culture conservatism and critique of mass culture in *Mass Civilization and Minority Culture*, on the one hand, and Walter Benjamin's classic essay against the fascist consequences of modern mass society, "The Work of Art in the Age of Mechanical Reproduction," in *Illuminations: Essays and Reflections*, trans. Harry Zohn, ed. and intro. Hannah Arendt, on the other. Nevertheless, there is a similar tendency to fall back on dichotomies of concept, expression, and attitude.

7. On the status and history of the modern study of popular culture and culture studies, see the introductions of Bob Ashley, *The Study of Popular Fiction: A Source Book*; Chandra Mukerji and Michael Schudson, eds., *Rethinking Popular Culture: Contemporary Perspectives in Cultural Studies*; and Simon During, ed., *The Cultural Studies Reader*. For a case study of the uneasy interaction between intellectuals and modern American popular culture, see Andrew Ross, *No Respect: Intellectuals and Popular Culture*.

8. Boaz Shoshan's breakdown of major cultural groups in Mamluk Egyptian society is useful here: see "High Culture and Popular Culture in Medieval Islam," esp. 69–88. And as Peter Burke has pointed out, the relationship among different cultural groups is always interactive and porous, marked just as much by processes of "negotiation" as by anything else: see "From Pioneers to Settlers: Recent Studies of the History of Popular Culture: A Review Article," *Comparative Studies in Society and History* 25, no. 1 (1983): 181–87, esp. 187.

9. Although I use the word "texts," this model equally applies to other art forms. My conception of this paradigm has been influenced by the models for verbal communication developed by Roman Jakobson in "Closing Statement: Linguistics and Poetics," in *Style in Language*, ed. Thomas A. Sebeok, 350–77; by the dynamics of cultural production outlined by Raymond Williams in *The Long Revolution*, esp. 57–86, and *The Sociology of Culture*; and by Stuart Hall's classic essay "Encoding, Decoding," in During, *The Cultural Studies Reader*, 90–103.

10. Williams, *The Long Revolution*, 57–86.

11. For Pierre Bourdieu's use of this term, see *Language and Symbolic Power* and *Distinction: A Social Critique of the Judgement of Taste*, trans. R. Nice.

12. Cf. David Johnson's remark: "Therefore the appropriate figure for thinking about the literature realm is not a network [his figure for the oral realm] but a hierarchy" ("Communication, Class, and Consciousness in Late Imperial China," 37, in *Popular Culture in Late Imperial China*, ed. David Johnson, Andrew J. Nathan, and Evelyn S. Rawski, 34–72). Although Johnson's article is stimulating, I cannot agree with overreliance on the dichotomy of literate/illiterate to determine audiences and their "consciousness." For a more discriminating analysis, see in same volume Robert E. Hegel's article, "Distinguishing Levels of Audiences for Min-Ch'ing Vernacular Literature," 11–42.

13. Walter Benjamin, "The Task of the Translator," in *Illuminations: Essays and Reflections*, 69–82.

14. This is intended as a general statement, whose exceptions must be recognized. Some genres of folk or popular literature rely to an extreme extent on aspects of equivocal verbal play. An example of this is the Arabic *mawwāl* or some performance aspects of the

popular *sīra.* For the first, see Pierre Cachia, "The Egyptian Mawwāl," *Journal of Arabic Literature* 8 (1977): 77–103; for the second, Bridget Ann Connelly, *Arab Folk Epic and Identity,* 119–46.

15. Cf. Matthew Arnold, "The Function of Criticism at the Present Time," in *The Portable Matthew Arnold,* ed. and intro. Lionel Trilling, 234–67; also Leavis's *Mass Civilization and Minority Culture.* Compare also Niccolò Machiavelli's letter of December 10, 1513, to Francesco Vettori, in *The Letters of Machiavelli,* ed. and trans. Allan H. Gilbert, 142, in which he describes how he spends his days in exile. After passing the day in the company of peasants, he writes:

> On the coming of evening I return to my house and enter my study; and at the door I take off the day's clothing, covered with mud and dust, and put on garments regal and courtly; and reclothed appropriately clothed, I enter the ancient courts of ancient men, where, received by them with affection, I feed on that food which only is mine and which I was born for, where I am not ashamed to speak with them and to ask them the reason for their actions; and they in their kindness answer me; and for four hours of time I do not feel boredom, I forget every trouble, I do not dread poverty, I am not frightened by death; entirely I give myself over to them.

16. On the controversial and still evolving issue of the relationship between orality and writing, see Walter J. Ong, *Orality and Literacy: The Technologizing of the Word*; Jack Goody, *The Interface between the Written and the Oral*; Albert B. Lord, *The Singer of Tales*; Ruth Finnegan, *Oral Poetry: Its Nature, Significance and Social Context*; and Paul Zumthor, *Oral Poetry: An Introduction,* trans. K. Murphy-Judy.

17. There is no single extensive modern study devoted to the history of premodern Arabic popular literature; for recent work in the area from a historian's perspective, see Boaz Shoshan, *Popular Culture in Medieval Cairo,* as well as his articles cited in the bibliography. Single authors and works can be approached through Carl Brockelmann, *Geschichte der arabischen Litteratur* (hereafter *GAL*); and, more recently, Fuat Sezgin, *Geschichte des arabischen Schrifttum* (hereafter *GAS*), which only goes to the 430 A.H.; as well as through individual articles in the *Encyclopedia of Islam,* both old and new editions. Dated, but still useful, is Victor Chauvin, *Bibliographie des ouvrages arabes relatifs aux Arabes.* Also useful for descriptions and summaries of individual works and for gaining an impression of the whole range of popular literature is volume 8 of Wilhelm Ahlwardt's manuscript catalogue, *Verzeichnis der arabischen Handschriften der Königlichen Bibliothek zu Berlin.* For narrative, see also Henri Pérès, "Le roman dans la littérature arabe des origines à la fin du Moyen Age," *Annales de l'Institut d'Etudes Orientales* (Algiers) 16 (1958): 5–40. For the development of Arabic in the premodern period, see the article "'Arabiyya" by Ch. Rabin et al., in EI^2, 1:561–83; Johann Fück, *'Arabiya: Recherches sur l'histoire de la langue et du style arabe,* trans. Claude Denizeau; and Wolfdietrich Fischer and Helmut Gätje, *Grundriss der Arabischen Philologie,* Part 1: *Sprachwissenschaft.*

18. Aṭ-Ṭabarī's commentary is entitled *Kitāb jāmi' al-bayān fī tafsīr al-qur'ān.* For historiographical methodology in premodern Islam, see "Tā'rīkh" by H. A. R. Gibb, in EI^1, suppl., 233–45, republished in Hamilton A. R. Gibb, *Studies on the Civilization of Islam,* ed. Stanford J. Shaw and William Polk, 108–37; Franz Rosenthal's *A History of Muslim Historiography*; and B. Lewis and P. M. Holt, eds., *Historians of the Middle East.*

19. Abū Muḥammad ʻAbd al-Malik ibn Hishām, *Kitāb at-tījān fī mulūk Ḥimyar*; see also F. Krenkow, "The Two Oldest Books on Arabic Folklore," *Islamic Culture* 2 (1928): 55–89, 204–36. For Kaʻb al-Aḥbār, see *EI*[2], 4:316–17; for Wahb ibn Munabbih, *EI*[1], 4:1084–85; for ʻAbīd ibn Sharya, Brockelmann, *GAL*, 1:100; and Sezgin, *GAS*, 1:260; and for Ibn Hishām, *EI*[2], 3:800–801.

20. For Luqmān, see *EI*[1], 3:35–37, Brockelmann, *GAL*, 2:63, 65–66; and Chauvin, *Bibliographie*, 3:1–82. For proverbs, see "al-Mathal," by R. Sellheim et al., in *EI*[2], 6:815–28; and Chauvin, *Bibliographie*, vol. 1.

21. Ibn Ḥazm, *Jamharat ansāb al-ʻArab*; for Ibn Ḥazm himself, see *EI*[2], 3:790–99. This pan-Arabism did not go uncontested; it was resisted by what became known as the *shuʻūbyya* movement: see Ignaz Goldziher, *Muhammedanische Studien*, 1:147–216.

22. For the *Ayyām al-ʻArab*, see Werner Caskel, "Aijām al-ʻArab: Studien zur altarabischen Epik." *Ayyām* material is prominent in several later *sīras*, especially *az-Zīr Sālim* and *Sīrat ʻAntar*.

23. For these early lovers, see Brockelmann, *GAL*, 1:47–49, Suppl. 78–83. See also Régis Blachère, "Problème de la transfiguration du poetè tribal en héros de roman 'courtois' chez les 'logographes' arabes du IIIe/IXe siècle," *Arabica* 8 (1961): 131–36; J. C. Vadet, *L'Esprit courtois en Orient dans les premiers siècles de l'Hégire*; and Rudi Paret, *Früharabische Liebesgeschichten: Ein Beitrag zur vergleichenden Literaturgeschichte.* For a survey of *adab* works related to love and lovers, see Lois A. Giffin, *Theory of Profane Love among the Arabs: The Development of the Genre.*

24. For Ḥātim aṭ-Ṭayyi', see *EI*[2], 3:274–75; Brockelmann, *GAL* 1:26, Suppl. 1:55; Sezgin, *GAS*, 2:208–9; as well as the introductory study (9–129) by Adel Sulaiman Gamal attached to the edition of Ḥātim's poetic *Diwān* prepared by Yaḥyā ibn Mudrik aṭ-Ṭayyi' and Hishām Muḥammad al-Kalbī. Parts of his story are incorporated into *Sīrat ʻAntar* (see appendix I, 36). For Abū Nuwās, see *EI*[2], 1:143–44; Brockelmann, *GAL*, 1:75–77, Suppl. 1:114–18; and Sezgin, *GAS*, 543–50, esp. 544–46. Chapbooks on Abū Nuwās, Ḥātim, Majnūn and Laylā, and so on are still regularly printed in the Arab world.

25. See the translation of Ibn Isḥāq by A. Guillaume, *The Life of Muḥammad.* Also useful is the chapter on the "Historical Novel" in Rosenthal, *Muslim Historiography.* Cf. R. Sellheim, "Prophet, Chalif und Geshichte: die Muḥammad-Biographie des Ibn Isḥāq," *Oriens* 18–19 (1967): 33–91.

26. For the Iranian epic tradition, see Jan Rypka, *History of Iranian Literature*, 44–45, 151–66, and 617–48; and William L. Hanaway, Jr., "The Iranian Epic," in *Heroic Epic and Saga*, ed. F. J. Oinas, 76–98, both of which provide basic bibliography. For *sīras*, see the introduction above.

27. See *EI*[2], 4:503–7; and Chauvin, *Bibliographie*, vol. 2.

28. For *Bilauhar wa-Yūdāsaf*, see *EI*[2], 1:1215–17. For *Sindbād*, see B. E. Perry, "The Origin of the *Book of Sindbad*," *Fabula* 3 (1960): 1–94, who convincingly argues for the Iranian origin of the frame story concept. For references to the *Nights*, see note 40 below.

29. Ibn an-Nadīm devotes sections to "Books of the Indians" and "Books of the Byzantines" in his discussion of stories in *al-Fihrist*, but the books of Indian origin he cites came to Arabic through Pahlavi, while most of the Byzantine books are Iranian versions of Greek material. Even the Alexander romance came to Arabic through Pahlavi: see *EI*[2], 4:127.

30. For Ibn an-Nadīm and Arabic editions of his work, see *EI*[2], 3:895–96. Bayard

Dodge has translated it into English as *The Fihrist of al-Nadīm: A Tenth-Century Survey of Muslim Culture.* For stories and storytellers, see 2:712–44 of the translation.

31. Dodge, ed., *The Fihrist*, 2:714.

32. For popular preachers, see *EI*^{2}, 4:733–35; Johannes Pedersen, "The Criticism of the Islamic Preacher," *Die Welt des Islams* 2 (1953): 215–31: and Ibn al-Jauzī, *Kitāb al-quṣṣāṣ wa-'l-mudhakkirīn*, ed. and trans. Merlin L. Swartz. The article "Ḥikāya," in *EI*^{2}, 3:367–72, has references on storytellers; see also Edward W. Lane, *Manners and Customs of the Modern Egyptians*, 397–430. For al-Hamadānī, see *EI*^{2}, 3:106–7; for al-Ḥarīrī, *EI*^{2}, 3:221–22; I should add to this class of works that of Muḥammad ibn Aḥmad Abu 'l-Muṭahhar al-Azdī, edited by A. Mez under the title *Abulkāsim, ein bagdāder Sittenbild.* Also of relevance is Clifford Edmund Bosworth, *The Medieval Islamic Underworld: The Banū Sāsān in Arabic Society and Literature.*

33. The formulation Standard Written Middle Arabic is my own. For the general concept of Middle Arabic, however, see the many works on the subject by Yehoshua Blau, such as "The Importance of Middle Arabic Dialects for the History of Arabic," in *Studies in Islamic History and Civilization*, 206–28, and *A Grammar of Christian Arabic: Based Mainly on South Palestinian Texts from the First Millennium*, Corpus Scriptorum Christianorum Orientalium, vols. 267, 276, 279, subsidiary vol. 29.

34. See "Kiṣaṣ al-anbiyā'" by T. Nagel, in *EI*^{2} 5:180–81; for ath-Tha'labī, *EI*^{1}, 4:735–36; and for al-Kisā'ī, *EI*^{2}, 4:176; for an English translation of the latter, see W. M. Thackston, Jr., trans., *The Tales of the Prophets of al-Kisā'ī.*

35. For al-Wāqidī and pseudo-al-Wāqidī, see Brockelmann, *GAL*, 1:135 and Sezgin, *GAS*, 1:295–97, for al-Bakrī, *EI*^{2}, 1:946–47; Brockelmann, *GAL*, 1:362, Suppl. 1:616; and Shoshan, *Popular Culture in Medieval Cairo*, 23–39. Useful for Muḥammad's biography in general is the article "Sīra" by G. Levi della Vida, in *EI*^{1}, 4:439–43; Brockelmann, *GAL*, 1:134–37, Suppl. 1:205–9; and Sezgin, *GAS*, 1:275–302. More work is needed on the popular literature concerning this subject; but useful as a general introduction is Annemarie Schimmel, *And Muhammad Is His Messenger: The Veneration of the Prophet in Islamic Piety.*

36. For Tamīm ad-Dārī, see *EI*^{1}, 4:646–48; for Abū Yazīd, *EI*^{2}, 1:162–63. A good place to obtain an idea of the nature and range of such religious stories is Ahlwardt, *Verzeichnis*, vol. 8, part 15: "Legenden und Bekehrungsgeschichten," 1–52.

37. See Rudi Paret, *Die legendäre Maghāzī-Literatur.*

38. See references in note 19 above; also Rudi Paret, "Die legendäre Futūḥ-Literatur, ein arabische Volksepos?" in *La poesia epica e la sua formazione*, 735–47. Also useful as an overview of *maghāzī*, *futūḥ*, and *sīra* narratives as a whole is the same author's *Die Geschichte des Islams im Spiegel der arabischen Volksliteratur.*

39. Prominent examples of this genre are enumerated and discussed in the introduction (and note 5).

40. See the article "Alf Layla wa-Layla" by E. Littmann, in *EI*^{2}, 1:358–64; and Chauvin, *Bibliographie*, vols. 4–7 and 11. Also important are Mia I. Gerhardt, *The Art of Story-telling*; Muhsin Mahdi's introduction to his edition of *The Thousand and One Nights*; Ferial J. Ghazoul, *The Arabian Nights: A Structural Analysis*; Suhair al-Qalamāwī, *Alf laila wa-laila*; André Miquel, *Sept contes de Mille et une Nuits*; Peter Heath, "Romance as Genre in *The Thousand and One Nights*," 2 pts., *Journal of Arabic Literature* 18 (1987): 1–21; 19 (1988): 1–26; the numerous essays by Andras Hamori, such as the two studies in *On the Art of Arabic Medieval Literature*, "Notes on Two Love Stories from the Thousand and One

Nights," *Studia Islamica* (1976): 65–80, and "A Comic Romance from the Thousand and One Nights: The Tale of the Two Vezirs," *Arabica* (1983): 38–56; Sandra Naddaff, *Arabesque: Narrative Structure and the Aesthetics of Repetition in* 1001 Nights; and David Pinault, *Story-telling Techniques in the* Arabian Nights. A recent work on *'Ajīb wa-Gharīb* is André Miquel, *Un conte des Milles et une Nuit: Ajīb et Gharīb*; a useful recent introduction is Robert Irwin, *The Arabian Nights: A Companion.*

41. The *Kitāb al-ḥikāyāt al-'ajība* has been edited by Hans Wehr under the title *Das Buch der wunderbaren Erzählungen und seltsamen Geschichte*; for Azād-Bakht, see *EI*², 1:955 (under "Bakhtiyār-nāma"); for the others, see Ahlwardt, *Verzeichnis*, vol. 8.

42. For anthologies of *nawādir*, both polite and popular, see Brockelmann, *GAL*, 2:55–60; 2:302–4; and Suppl. 2:53–58. For Abū Nuwās, see note 24 above; for Barmacides, see *EI*², 1:1053; for Juḥā, see *EI*², 2:590–92; for Qarāqūsh, see *EI*², 4:613–14.

43. Ibn Sanā' al-Mulk, *Dār aṭ-ṭirāz fī 'amal al-muwashshaḥāt*, ed. J. al-Rikābī. See also *EI*², 3:929.

44. Ṣafī 'd-Dīn al-Ḥillī, *al-'Āṭil al-ḥālī wa-'l-murakhkhaṣ al-ghālī*, ed. W. Hoenerbach, 7–8, for the quote and the typology that follows. Examples of these forms can be found in translation in G. Rat's translation of al-Ibshīhī's *al-Mustaṭraf*: *Al-Mostatraf: Recueil de morceaux choisis çà et là dans toutes les branches des connaissances réputées attrayantes.*

45. On the *muwashshaḥ* and the *zajal*, see *EI*², 7:809–12; and James T. Monroe, "*Zajal* and *Muwashshaḥa*: Hispano-Arabic Poetry and the Romance Tradition," in Salma Khadra Jayyusi, *The Legacy of Muslim Spain*, 398–419. The whole subject of religious poetry, elite and popular, is ignored in this analysis, even though this was an important and widespread genre. For a recent study of the important genre of poetic praise of the Prophet, see Earle H. Waugh, *The Munshidīn of Egypt: Their World and Their Song.*

46. For Ibn Dāniyāl, see *EI*², 3:742.

5. THE HEROIC CYCLE

1. This episode encompasses 20:478–22:187. The kings of the Banī Harīqa, the Banī Sa'd, and the Banī Kalb all successively fall in love with 'Abla.

2. In formulating this description of *Sīrat 'Antar*'s Heroic Cycle I keep specifically to the evidence contained in the narrative itself and make no claims for its validity for other stories, of Arab or other provenance. I have been helped by studies that have taken more general viewpoints, however, such as Cedric M. Bowra's *Heroic Poetry*. Several scholars have also deduced narrative templates underlying heroic stories similar to the one outlined in this chapter: cf. Lord Raglan, *The Hero: A Study in Ritual, Tradition, and Drama*; see also his article "The Hero in Tradition," *Folklore* 45 (1934): 212–31; and Jan de Vries, *Heroic Song and Heroic Legend.* For more psychoanalytic perspectives, see Joseph Campbell, *The Hero with a Thousand Faces*; and Otto Rank, *The Myth of the Birth of the Hero: A Psychological Interpretation of Mythology.* Also important are Vladimir Propp's *Morphology of the Folktale*, trans. Laurence Scott; and Albert B. Lord's *The Singer of Tales.* Robert Scholes and Robert Kellog's *The Nature of Narrative*, Northrop Frye's *The Secular Scripture: A Study of the Structure of Romance*, and Eugene Vinaver's *The Rise of Romance* are helpful for understanding narrative themes, patterns, and devices common in heroic cycles and romances in Western medieval literature.

3. The elements of the story patterns also often constitute individual folk motifs. My

discussion does not focus on this aspect of the narrative, but I note its correlation to the story patterns by referring to Hasan M. El-Shamy's excellent new motif index, *Folk Traditions of the Arab World: A Guide to Motif Classification* (hereafter *GMC-A*). El-Shamy's work both subsumes the relevant motifs from Stith Thompson's *Motif Index of Folk-Literature* and adds new motifs (designated here as new by the addition of §). Hence, for example, El-Shamy has new entries for heroes and heroines of *sīras*, *GMC-A* Z203§ and *GMC-A* Z205§, respectively. Volume 2 of Malcolm C. Lyons, *The Arabian Epic*, also consists of a useful motif index. Lyons, for some reason, does not rely on the Thompson motif index framework, which limits the universal applicability of his efforts; hence, I do not cite him point by point as I do El-Shamy. Nevertheless, students of *sīra* should make use of the enormous efforts that Lyons's undertaking represents.

4. *GMC-A* F611.3.2 and F612.2.

5. *GMC-A* L113.1.7 and L113.1.8. Other black heroes of the *Sīra* are Ghaṣūb, Maisara, al-Ghaḍbān, ʿUnaitira, al-Ghaḍanfar, and al-Jufrān, all children of ʿAntar. Khufāf ibn Nadba (26:88–27:166) is also black, as are the fierce brigands Ṭāriqat az-Zamān (6:3–19) and Sulaika ibn Sulaka (26:21–29). (ʿAntar, Khufāf, and Sulaika were accounted three of the *Aghribat al-Arab* [Ravens of the Arabs] of pre-Islamic times.) Heroes with mixed blood are by no means unusual in heroic literature (cf. Hercules, Digenis Akritas, and Achilles); but the Arabic *sīra* seems to have become infatuated with the idea of the black hero. The Indian king ʿAbd Hayyāf in *Sīrat ʿAntar* is black even though both of his parents were white (42:171)! The same is true of Abū Zaid of *Sīrat Banī Hilāl* and al-Baṭṭāl of *Sīrat Dhāt al-Himma*. In *Sīrat Saif ibn Dhī Yazan* the situation is reversed: the white hero Saif is discriminated against by black Abyssinian society.

6. *GMC-A* L114.1 and F632. Heroes such as Bisṭām ibn Qais (8:234ff.), Muqri ʾl-Waḥsh (19:347ff.), ʿAmr ibn Maʿdīkarib (25:471ff.), and Hānī ibn Masʿūd (30:475ff.) typify this tendency.

7. *GMC-A* Z205§. Dhāt al-Himma is an Amazon-like figure to whom a complete Arabic *sīra* is devoted. Such figures also exist in the premodern Persian tradition of popular epic and romance: see William L. Hanaway, Jr., "Persian Popular Romances before the Safavid Period," 25–54.

8. ʿUnaitira is the daughter of ʿAntar and ʿAmr Dhu ʾl-Kalb's sister, al-Haifāʾ. ʿAntar and al-Haifāʾ, who is a close friend of ʿAbla's, keep their marriage a secret, and after ʿAntar's death ʿUnaitira grows up believing that she is ʿAmr's daughter (56:53–57:103). Al-Jufrān is the result of ʿAntar's liaison with the Byzantine maiden Maryam. ʿAntar plans to kill Maryam but is thwarted when she runs off with the Frankish prince Kūbart (52:189ff.). Later all three become friends (53:257); nevertheless, al-Jufrān remains ignorant of his true parentage until he meets and captures ʿAntar's children and friends (57:175ff.). Al-Ghaḍanfar is the son of ʿAntar and Maryam, princess of Rome, whom Antar married and then left in Byzantium, fearing that desert life would be too difficult for her. Al-Ghaḍanfar grows up in the Byzantine court, and he too remains unaware of his true lineage until he meets and fights ʿUnaitira (57:131–64). A final example: Mājid ibn Mālik is conceived on his parents' wedding night. The next morning his father is assassinated by the Banī Fazāra (18:213). On the theme of the birth of the hero in general, see Alan Dundes, "The Hero Pattern and the Life of Jesus," in Dundes, *Interpreting Folklore*, 223–61. On the same theme in Arabic popular epics, see Aḥmad Shams ad-Dīn al-Ḥajjājī (el-Heggagi), *Maulid al-baṭal fi ʾs-sīra ʾsh-shaʿbiyya*, esp. 85–94.

9. Although the *Sīra*'s heroes are interested in changing society so that it accepts them, they do not necessarily want to transform it by fomenting social change. 'Antar is often insulted about his black skin and feels an affinity for other blacks—he saves a black slave whom Shaibūb is about to kill (8:282–83), he is unhappy about helping King Qais attack the black King Yaksūm, although he does it (45:388–89), and he is more than willing to help young black heroes like Khufāf ibn Nadba (26:88–27:166). Nevertheless, he shows little interest in altering the stratified framework of the social order in which he lives. He bristles if others call him a slave but calls himself a slave when he talks to rulers (16:8, 19:309); at one point he even upholds the divine right of kingship when al-Ghaḍbān asks him why he does not make himself a king (44:367).

10. *GMC-A* F611.3.3.5§, F611.3.3, F833.

11. *GMC-A* F628.1.1. The lion is an important associative symbol for the hero in *Sīrat 'Antar*. By defeating the lion, the hero overcomes his or her own equivalent in the animal kingdom. Fighting lions is thus one proof of heroism. Jealous Persian nobles convince the shah to test 'Antar by making him fight a lion (5:456). And when al-Ghaḍbān accuses 'Antar of having become old and feeble, 'Antar goes into the desert and kills some lions (44:347–51). For his wedding 'Antar kills 700 lions and 500 leopards for his guests to eat (20:408). Other heroes whose stories include a lion fight are 'Amr ibn Ma'dīkarib (26:18), Duraid ibn aṣ-Ṣimma's foster-son Daththār ibn Rizq (27:101), Māzin ibn Shaddād (29:349–50), Hānī ibn Mas'ūd (31:16–7), al-Ghaḍbān (twice: 40:5, 40:24), 'Unaitira (56:54–55), and al-Ghaḍanfar (57:137–38). Too frequent association with lions can be dangerous. The brigand al-Yaqẓān ibn Jayyāsh ate lion meat so much that he became more lion than human. He trained lion cubs to fight for him and developed a taste for the flesh of humans (especially young women), until 'Antar killed him and his cubs (9:323–30). Another hero of the Arabic *sīra* genre, az-Zīr Sālim, lived alone in the desert with lions too; in folk prints he is usually portrayed riding a lion.

12. Besides having a king, individual tribes of *Sīrat 'Antar* often have a single hero who is known as the tibe's *ḥāmī* or protector, a combination warlord and champion. He advises the king in the counsels of war and is his tribe's representative in the bouts of single combat that fill the *Sīra*'s battles. 'Antar, needless to say, becomes *ḥāmī* of the Banī 'Abs, just as Bisṭām becomes *ḥāmī* of his section of the Banī Shaibān. Not all tribes have such protectors; the Banī Fazāra, for example, do not. The position of *ḥāmī* is not really a formal one; nor is king, for that matter. Duraid ibn aṣ-Ṣimma is portrayed as the greatest leader of the Banī Jusham (a subgroup of the Banī Hawāzin). He is their *ḥāmī* and, de facto, their king, but he is never given the latter title. The same is true of 'Āmir ibn aṭ-Ṭufail. He fights for and leads the Banī 'Āmir, but he does not rule them. Often, especially when 'Antar travels and meets tribes who appear only once in the *Sīra*, the king himself is portrayed as the mightiest warrior, the one who finally appears on the field of battle after his generals, sons, nephews, brothers, and vassals have been defeated (20:478–22:187, 36:71–39:305, 41:63–42:153, 42:153–44:375, etc.).

13. *GMC-A* F628. Notice that in the process he gains his extraordinary arms and accouterments.

14. When 'Antar deals outside his tribe, he has no compunctions about imposing his will by force, as the two episodes about hanging his *mu'allaqa* poem demonstrate (34:306–35:443, 46:52–47:123).

15. *GMC-A* L113.7, L113.1.8§. The issue of long-term acceptance does not usually

arise for the other lowborn heroes of the *Sīra* because they tend to become friends with 'Antar and join his group of companions.

16. *GMC-A* N731.2. The main father-son confrontations of the *Sīra* are the fights between 'Antar and Maisara (30:472–74), Ghaṣūb (34:381–35:400), and al-Ghaḍbān (41:35–44). Social acceptance can also be a repeated motif in the story of a single hero. 'Antar wins the acceptance of his father, on the lowest level, King Zuhair at the next, then King al-Mundhir, Shah Anūshirwān, and other kings, heroes, and rulers who test and challenge him. Father-son confrontations are common in Persian popular epics as well. The most famous example is that between Rustam and Suhrāb in the popular Rustam cycle (as well as in Abu 'l-Qāsim Manṣūr al-Firdousī's *Shāhnāma*).

17. *GMC-A* P295.1.1§, T106§. 'Antar is the main example of this cousin motif, but compare the stories of Ḥiṣn (3:254–71), Mahriyya and her lover (25:423–27), and Muqri 'l-Waḥsh, who is not lowborn but is poor (19:347–20:400). In Muqrī's story, although he is a prince, his rival stems from an even higher political level: he is Prince Badr, son of the mighty king of the Banī Ghassān, overlord of the Syrian Arabs. Thus the distinction between lower-born lover and higher-born rival is maintained (20:457–78).

18. *GMC-A* P92.11. Ironically, 'Antar sometimes becomes the unattractive rival in such situations. When warriors such as Bisṭām ibn Qais (8:234ff.), Wāqid ibn Mas'ara (5:463ff.), or Mufarrij ibn Hammām (6:30ff.) fall in love with 'Abla they are, from their point of view and from the point of view of 'Abla's father, rescuing her from the clutches of an arrogant and unattractive rival who is the cousin of the beloved—'Antar. See also al-Ḥārith/Lubnā (13:273ff.). In general the difference between lover and rival perhaps has less to do with exact blood ties than with appearances. Superficially, the rival always appears to have a better claim to the beloved than the lover. If the lover is poor, the rival is rich ('Antar/'Umāra); if the lover is a prince, the rival is a greater prince (Muqrī/Badr); if the lover comes from outside the tribe, the rival comes from the same tribe as the beloved (Mājid/Maisara); if the lover is black, the rival is white (Khufāf/al-'Abbās), and so on. The charge of the Love Story is to show that it is the interior force of love that unites people, not such external considerations as wealth, family or tribal ties, social status, or race.

19. *GMC-A* T10, T11.1. 'Antar, Ḥiṣn (3:254–71), and Muqri 'l-Waḥsh (19:347ff.) are examples of lovers who fall in love with their cousins. But many lovers fall in love through daily contact with the beloved, such as Nāziḥ (14:315–81), Khufāf ibn Nadba (27:121ff.), Maisara (30:407–74), and al-Ghaḍbān (40:463–41:63). Love at first sight is common with those who fall in love with 'Abla: for example, Bisṭām (9:299ff.), Mufarrij ibn Hammām (6:30–73), Musaḥḥil ibn Ṭarrāq (9:335–62), Mu'āwiya ibn an-Nazzāl (21:19-44), but it occurs in other lovers' stories as well, such as Mājid/Asmā' (30:407–74), Ḥāṭim/Marya (29:299–331), al-Ḥārith/Lubnā (13:273–14:315). Examples of the third motif, love by hearsay, include Wāqid ibn Mas'ara (5:463–6:5), Rauḍa ibn Manī' (7:139–52), King an-Nu'mān (10:445ff.), al-Laqīṭ ibn Zurāra (17:103–74—if not love, then at least intention of marriage), and Shah Khudāwand (31:9ff.).

20. *GMC-A* R161.

21. *GMC-A* T97.

22. *GMC-A* T52.0.2§, T52.0.3§.

23. *GMC-A* T52.0.2§. For examples of lovers who amass material goods for their dowries, see 3:254–71, 19:347ff., 30:449ff., 34:389ff., 39:338ff., 47:179ff. For examples of lovers who capture people as part of their dowries, see 7:152ff., 8:234ff., 9:335ff., 10:398ff., 14:367ff., 27:121ff.

24. On their way to Iraq to find the 'Aṣāfīr camels, 'Antar and Shaibūb meet on old man in the desert. He gives them lodging for a night and, when he learns their plans, informs them how dangerous their project is. Since the old man and Shaibūb realize that Mālik has sent 'Antar on a suicide mission, they urge him to stop; but 'Antar replies: "Woe to you, Shaibūb! What kind of talk is this? I won't listen to it lest my uncle look upon me with the eye of deficiency. I am not saying 'Yes' yesterday and 'No' afterward, even if I become food for the beasts of the desert. I would not do this even if the mountains opposed me in the shapes of men" (4:358). 'Antar and Shaibūb have a similar conversation when they set out to capture al-Jaidā' (7:167–68).

25. *GMC-A* H332.1. Al-Jaidā' and Khālid are cousins who grow up in different tribes because al-Jaidā's father emigrated after he quarreled with his brother, Khālid's father. Al-Jaidā' is raised as a warrior; but when Khālid appears in her tribe, she falls in love with him. Khālid is only interested in fighting, not love, so to attract his attention she challenges him to single combat. When she defeats him, she falls out of love with him. But when she reveals her face to him, he falls in love. He proposes marriage, and after he successfully performs several dowry missions that she sets she marries him (7:169–87). For other examples of this Amazon pattern, see Ghamra and Sabī' ibn al-Ḥārith (27:131ff.) and 'Abd al-Hayyāf's parents (42:166–70).

26. *GMC-A* T100, T132, 160. 'Antar and 'Abla's wedding is by far the most elaborate and sumptuous of the *Sīra* (see 20:405–54). The other descriptions of wedding ceremonies in the *Sīra* take up at most a page or two: thus al-Jaidā'/Khālid (7:185–88), Prince al-Ḥārith/Lubnā (14:380), al-Laqīṭ/Badr ad-Dīn (17:111), 'Amr ibn Ma'dīkarib/Lamīs (26:12–13), Ḥātim aṭ-Ṭayyi'/Marya (29:328), Mājid/Asmā' (31:75), Ṣafwān/U'jūbat al-Anām (38:261), Rabī'a ibn al-Mukaddam/Ḥind (39:357–58), al-Ghaḍbān/Da'da (41:62), Wizr ibn Jābir/Kabsha (47:182), Zaid ibn 'Urwa/Rabāba (52:111).

27. *GMC-A* N838. This motif is labeled "hero (culture hero) as helper." It has no subcategories, however, which suggests one way that folk story motifs, which form the basis for most motif index classifications, differ from long epic narrative motifs.

28. The basis for the hero's overweening bravery is an essentially fatalistic view of life. Fate appoints an inescapable time of death for each person, so there is little point worrying about when it will come. More important is to meet one's appointed time with courage and honor intact. Thus at one point in their battle with the Persians and Arabs of al-Ḥīra (12:231), when 'Abs is heavily outnumbered, King Zuhair says to 'Antar, "O Father of Knights, the multitude against us is great, the number profuse." 'Antar turns to him and says, "What kind of talk is this, O King of the Age? I swear to you by the Lord, the Judge, the Merciful, the Compassionate, Who created man and jinn, that I will show you war and combat that will be remembered the rest of time."

Similarly, when 'Antar and his forty companions are overtaken by five thousand enemy pursuers (3:235):

> The warriors of the Banī 'Abs looked at this calamity [the large number of pursuers], and it terrified them and broke their backs [spirits]. They said to each other, "By God! These warriors of the Banī Qaḥṭān have come to seize our souls. Today lives will be sold freely."
>
> Then they turned to 'Antar and saw that he was smiling. They wondered at his slight concern for the horsemen, and they said to him: "O Father of the Brave, today our spoils will be taken and our skulls will fly from their bodies."

> Then 'Antar said to them, "Lifespans do not decrease or exceed [their appointed times]. The skin of he whose time of death is delayed will not be harmed by iron. He is safe from the wiles of freemen and slaves." [Then he attacks the pursuers.]
>
> In 'Abs's battle with the Banī Zubaid (3:220) King Zuhair turns to 'Antar and says:
>
> "O Father of Knights, this is a dismal day, stained by the sadness and concern that will come in it." Then 'Antar said to him, "By your dear life, my Lord, appointed times of death do not decrease or exceed [their times]. I have wished and hoped for something like this [being faced with overwhelming odds]. If a man's time has not come, iron swords cannot cut him off. Sire, what use is the sword my shoulder bears if I do not strike my enemy with it; or the lance that I thrust with if I do not kill men with it; or the horse that I ride if I do not charge against warriors with it?"

Such sentiments occur extremely frequently in the battles of the *Sīra.* For a study of similar ideas of heroic fatalism in pre-Islamic poetry, see Helmer Ringgren, *Studies in Arabic Fatalism.*

29. 'Antar's rivalry with ar-Rabī ibn Ziyād and with 'Abs's nominal allies the Banī Fazāra at times strains his relations with 'Abs's rulers and disrupts the tribe (10:420–11:40, 11:41–90, 26:55–76, 55:433–62). He also defies King Qais to help a complete stranger against the king of India's men and thus brings down the ruler's wrath upon 'Abs and Arabia (42:153–44:375). Moreover, he is willing to befriend 'Āmir ibn aṭ-Ṭufail (23:233–88) even though 'Abs and the Banī 'Āmir have been engaging in a feud (14:381–17:102, 17:125–30) and to help the Byzantine emperor against the Persian shah, 'Abs's traditional overlord (32:138–33:205).

30. Note that 'Antar is frequently referred to as *Abu 'l-Fawāris* (Father of Knights) throughout the *Sīra.*

31. Kings and rulers are, everything considered, the only ones who are allowed nonviolent deaths: King al-Mundhir (8:248), Shah Anūshirwān (31:7, although he miraculously revives later, 51:34), and Queen Ghamra, who succumbs to illness (39:302).

32. *GMC-A* Z292. There are literally hundreds of examples of this idea in the *Sīra*: see, for example, 53:230–31, 53:232, 55:392–93, 55:397, 55:398, 55:400.

33. In general, the group of heroes who constitute 'Antar's band of companions becomes more vulnerable toward the *Sīra*'s end. Here the deaths of long-term friends and major relatives—Bisṭām ibn Qais (51:82–84), 'Urwa ibn al-Ward (52:110–15), Māzin ibn Shaddād (52:131), Prince al-Ḥārith (55:391–93), Maisara (55:397–98), al-Hiṭāl (55:399–400), and Shaibūb (55:419–23)—are signs that the world that 'Antar holds together by his heroic force is declining, foreshadowings of the death of 'Antar himself. Thus toward the end of the *Sīra,* after he has killed Maisara and al-Hiṭāl and is about to fight 'Antar, al-Muhalhil ibn Masrūq taunts:

> O lowly black! Your time is set to pass away, and your span of time, to depart. Do you think that Time will always be on your side? Do you not know that just as it makes you laugh, it makes you cry; and just as it pleases you, it hurts you? And just as it has sweetened your pride and strengthened you with sons, it will burn your heart with them [i.e., with their deaths] in your old age? Today, this is the

last of your days, and I will take revenge for the Arabs upon you and lift Disgrace from them.

ʿAntar, however, is not one to weaken during difficulties or let himself be paralyzed by grief. He replies, "Woe unto you and your father! May God curse your people and descendants! Do you think that your killing my nephew and son will make you safe from my hand, or are you delaying looking for a weak point?" Then ʿAntar charges and kills him (55:401). Al-Muhalhil was right about one thing, though: ʿAntar's death is not far off.

34. The most effective and carefully constructed death stories (as opposed to death scenes) are, apart from ʿAntar's, those of Prince Shāsh and King Zuhair (14:381–15:411), Rabīʿa ibn al-Mukaddam (39:306–40:462), and King an-Nuʿmān (30:475–31:73, 32:100–132). These three stories, it should be noted, stem from the *Ayyām al-ʿArab.*

35. *GMC-A* P681. Examples of funerals are King Zuhair (15:408–12), Prince Mālik ibn Zuhair (18:212–15), Shaddād (35:55–59), Rabīʿa ibn al-Mukaddam (40:429–31), al-Ghaḍbān (47:157–63), ʿUrwa ibn al-Ward (52:115–16), and ʿAntar (twice: 56:34–36, 58:264–74).

36. *GMC-A* P681.0.2.1§. Revenge is the single guiding theme of a shorter *sīra* work, *Sīrat az-Zīr Sālim.*

37. Thus the raiders of the Banī Riyān are happy when they capture Prince Shāsh because his father killed the father of one of them (7:128). ʿAntar fights the Franks when they demand that Caesar send him to them in chains so that they can avenge their king's death at his hands (53:197–201).

6. USE OF THE HEROIC CYCLE: COMPOSITIONAL PRINCIPLES

1. Modern narratology has tended to rely on single novels as a basis of theoretical paradigms (see, for example, Mieke Bal, *Narratology: Introduction to the Theory of Narrative,* trans. Christine van Boheemen; and Gérard Genette, *Narrative Discourse: An Essay in Method,* trans. Jane E. Lewin) or has focused on short narratives, such as the folktale (see Vladimir Propp's *Morphology of the Folktale* and Heda Jason, *Whom Does God Favor: The Wicked or the Righteous?*). The narrative elements stemming from a long epic cycle, such as those surveyed in this chapter, have received little individual attention, although a useful foray into this subject is Eugene Vinaver's *The Rise of Romance.* For a somewhat different approach to principles of narrative structure in *sīras*, see Malcolm Lyons, *The Arabian Epic,* 1:73–76.

2. The *Sīra*'s use of stylistic and compositional repetition is addressed in the next chapter. For a discussion of structural repetition in *The Thousand and One Nights,* see Sandra Naddaff, *Arabesque,* esp. 59–121.

3. We must also remember that the *Sīra* appears to have been created for the purpose of public storytelling. Read or recited in this context, in relatively small amounts at any one time, the epic's many repetitions would have been less obvious. In such situations, repetition would often have the positive affect of maintaining and reinforcing a unified narrative context. A modern analogue would be the many plot repetitions in and among contemporary television series.

4. *GMC-A* F611.3.3. For a discussion of the idea of motifs, narrative patterns, or

themes becoming reduced until they exist as associative vestiges within successive storytelling traditions, see Albert B. Lord, "The Traditional Song," in *Oral Literature and the Formula*, ed. Benjamin A. Stolz and Richard S. Shannon III, 1–15.

5. In fact, the *Sīra*'s account of 'Antar, Muqri 'l-Waḥsh, and Maisara's encounter is a very good example of how it uses the combined possibilities of its story pattern to good dramatic effect (38:3–4).

While 'Antar, Mājid, Muqrī, et al. follow Asmā' and her family, 'Antar has a disturbing dream. Seeing the moon rising on his left, he seizes it to push it back where it came from, but its rays burn him. When he switches it to his right hand, however, it becomes a sword of light that splits the darkness. He awakens and relates this dream to Muqrī, who is unsure how to interpret it but guesses that the symbols "moon" and "sword" indicate that the dream has something to do with a son (30:447–48).

The next morning they continue their pursuit and finally overtake Maisara, who has met and captured Asmā' and al-Minhāl, and here the *Sīra* pauses to give us the story of Maisara's early life and experiences (30:448–62). Then Maisara fights and captures 'Urwa and Māzin. 'Antar plans to meet him in single combat, but Muqrī asks to be allowed to fight this stranger. 'Antar agrees, but asks him not to kill Maisara, for he feels a strange affection for him (30:463–64). Muqrī and Maisara fight all day without either gaining an advantage. 'Antar again plans to fight Maisara the next day, but again Muqrī asks to fight him and 'Antar agrees. That night, however, Muqrī has a disturbing dream in which he sees himself alone in the desert surrounded by wild beasts. He awakens certain that his death is at hand. But he remains firm in his desire to fight Maisara that day, if only to prove his dream wrong (30:468–71). 'Antar spends the night waiting for morning so that he can avenge Muqrī's defeat, and after a hard fight he captures Maisara. When Shaibūb asks 'Antar why he has not killed Maisara, 'Antar replies that he does not know, but that he cannot bring himself to do it (30:471–74).

Thus we see how elements of Muqri 'l-Waḥsh's Death of the Hero, Maisara's Rise of the Hero, and 'Antar's Heroic Service and the revenge part of the Death of the Hero patterns are combined, all within the frame of Mājid, Asmā', and Maisara's Love Stories (Muqrī later dics of his wound: 39.4).

7. COMPOSITIONAL MODELS AND DESCRIPTION

1. The lines of this and other long quotes from the *Sīra* (cf. appendix IV) are divided and numbered according to rhyme for two reasons. First, it allows the nonreader of Arabic to perceive more easily aspects of rhyme and rhythm in the epic's rhymed prose. Second, it facilitates discussion and comparison of rhyme, rhythm, and formulaic uniformity and variety in its style. Short quotes, friendlier to the eye, have been left in their original form. The hero's encounter with the lion is motif *GMC-A* F628; see also Malcolm Lyons, *The Arabian Epic* 2:297.

2. Dictionaries (Hans Wehr, J. G. Hava) cite *yatamakhtar* as *yatamakhṭar* (with *ṭ* instead of *t*). The *Sīra* uses both forms: cf. appendix IV, lion descriptions 1/12 and 3/3.

3. Appendix IV contains all eleven lion descriptions found in the *Sīra.* The first and last examples of these descriptions, numbers 1 and 11 in the appendix, are quoted.

4. Lines 2/5, 10 are exactly the same as lines 1/4, 7; lines 2/6, 7, 8, 12, 13 only differ from 1/5, 15, 16, 8, 9, respectively, by a word or two; and lines 2/9, 11 are synonymous

with lines 1/6, 14. Even the remaining two lines have close (compare 2/4 to 1/13) or metaphoric (compare 2/14 to 1/19 or 20) equivalents.

5. Albert B. Lord (*The Singer of Tales*, 35–36) refers to the homology between the general grammar of a language and the grammar of the linguistic subunit that a tradition of oral composition represents as follows: "In studying the patterns and systems of oral narrative verse we are in reality observing the 'grammar' of poetry, a grammar superimposed, as it were, on the grammar of the language concerned. Or, to alter the image, we find a special grammar within the grammar of the language."

6. Especially Lord's *The Singer of Tales* and Milman Parry's writings, conveniently collected and edited by his son Adam Parry in one volume entitled *The Making of Homeric Verse: The Collected Papers of Milman Parry*. The number of articles and books using or discussing the theory is quite large and rapidly growing. A clear and useful overview of the theory, along with a review of current trends, is John Miles Foley, *The Theory of Oral Composition: History and Methodology*. Useful bibliographies of this corpus are Edward R. Haymes, *A Bibliography of Studies Relating to Parry's and Lord's Oral Theory*; and John Miles Foley, ed., *Oral-Formulaic Theory and Research: An Introduction and Annotated Bibliography*.

Several students of Arabic literature have attempted to apply this theory to the study of pre-Islamic Arabic poetry; see James T. Monroe, "Oral Composition in Pre-Islamic Poetry," *Journal of Arabic Literature* 3 (1972): 1–53; and Michael Zwettler, *The Oral Tradition of Classical Arabic Poetry: Its Character and Implications*. Bridget Connelly applied the theory to *Sīra Banī Hilāl* in "The Oral-Formulaic Tradition of *Sīrat Bani Hilāl*: Prolegomena to the Study of *Sīra* Literature."

7. Lord, *Singer of Tales*, 30 and 69, respectively. Parry's definition of the formula originally appeared in his monograph "Studies in the Epic Technique of Oral Verse-Making I: Homer and Homeric Style," *Harvard Studies in Classical Philology* 41 (1930): 80 (in *The Making of Homeric Verse*, 272).

8. The problem of how exactly to conceive of and define the formula has been one of the main points of controversy and discussion regarding the Lord-Parry theory. In general, two points have concerned scholars. First, along which linguistic level should the formula primarily be conceived as working? Is it primarily a matter of repeated lexicon, repeated linguistic structures, or repeated deep-structural forms? Second, how much formulaic repetition must be present in a narrative before we may justifiably consider its style to be a result of formulaic composition? Obviously, the first question must be settled before the second can be, but this has not prevented scholars from discussing it. A good impression of the disagreement and confusion that have reigned regarding these questions and the theory in general may be obtained from the papers assembled in Benjamin A. Stolz and Richard S. Shannon III, eds., *Oral Literature and the Formula*. In general these papers, drawn from a 1974 conference on the subject, share faults typical of much "oral-formulaic" scholarship: instead of basing their analyses on narratives that they can easily demonstrate to be formulaic, the great majority of scholars examine works they think (or hope) might prove to be formulaic; moreover, scholars almost always base their studies on materials too limited in size to produce conclusive results; finally (perhaps because of the first two faults), scholars work on highly theoretical (speculative?) planes. For comments on such fallacies and suggestions on how to remedy them, see Foley, *The Theory of Oral Composition*, 102–3 and 109–11.

9. Lord, *Singer of Tales*, 69.

10. In formulating the distinction between the formula and the traditional phrase, I have profited from several conversations with Professor Lord. In fact, he suggested the term "traditional phrase" to me. Its creator, according to Professor Lord, is Dr. Marius Cantalina of the University of Venice, Italy, who uses it, apparently, in the same sense that I do here.

Theoretically, any repeated phrase in a traditional narrative may be considered a traditional phrase. A distinction should be made, however, between narrative traditions whose style reveals occasional recurrence and those in which it is pervasive. For example, phrasal repetition exists in *The Thousand and One Nights* storytelling tradition. Story beginnings, descriptions, portrayal of certain events, and frame elements may all be composed of recurrent phrases. In general terms, however, phrasal recurrence is not great. *Sīrat ʿAntar*, in contrast, is composed entirely of recurrent phrases.

11. This elaboration of Lord and Parry's terminology is my own, developed out of the necessity of adequately describing *Sīrat ʿAntar*'s composition and style.

12. This is a point that Lord has repeatedly made in *The Singer of Tales*: "The ideal [of a tradition of formulaic composition] is a true story well and truly told" (29); and "Formulas and groups of formulas, both large and small, serve only one purpose. They provide a means for telling a story in song and verse. The tale's the thing" (69).

13. For more on the functions of verse in the *Sīra*, see Compositional Structure and Narrative Invention in chapter 8.

14. We may note here that *Sīrat ʿAntar*'s construction of this scene, and of its narrative in general, conforms to many of Axil Olrik's epic laws—in this case, the Law of Two to a Scene and the Law of Tableaux Scenes. See Axel Olrik, "Epic Laws of Folk Narrative," in *The Study of Folklore*, ed. Alan Dundes, 131–41; also in Olrik's *Nogle Grundsætninger for Sagnforskning*, 66–82.

15. The "other" in panic and the "other" who praises the hero need not be the same individual or group, as long as fear is expressed at the lion's appearance and congratulations and relief at its death.

16. For other attempts to ambush ʿAntar, see appendix I, 7.1–2 and 8.5.

17. *Fitna* is a common topos of late Arabic (and Persian and Ottoman) love poetry. It combines the idea of something very desirable with the tumult (both inner and exterior) that the sight of such a thing can cause. Beloveds are *fitna*s because they tempt the lover to such an extent that a riot ensues, either in the lover's soul or in the streets that the beloved walks through.

8. COMPOSITIONAL MODELS AND NARRATIVE GENERATION: THE BATTLE SCENE

1. Properly, *khuwadh*. Again, I have arranged this passage in short lines to demonstrate its reliance on rhyme. I have also added punctuation to facilitate reading.

2. The usual plural for *junna* (shield) is *junān*. The *Sīra* has apparently co-opted the plural form *ajinna* to create rhyme with *asinna* in line 37.

3. The *Sīra* frequently uses *rūh* as a reflexive pronoun instead of *nafs* (compare also line 21). For similar usage in a *maghāzī* work, see Martin Abel, *Die arabische Vorlage des Suaheli-Epos Chuo Cha Herkal: Ein Beitrag zur Kenntnis des legendären Magāzī-Literatur*, 16.

4. The vestigial presence of traditional phrases, thematic units, or themes is one telltale sign that a narrative stems from a tradition of oral composition. They are instances

when the ideational and linguistic models and matrixes of the tradition overwhelm the particular narrative necessities of the moment, when the singer momentarily loses the song within the larger tradition of singing. As Albert B. Lord says (*Singer of Tales*, 94):

> In a traditional poem, therefore, there is a pull in two directions: one is towards the song being sung and the other is towards the previous uses of the same theme. The result is that characteristic of oral poetry which literary scholars have found hardest to understand and accept, namely, an occasional inconsistency, the famous nod of Homer.

5. The use of the "dust cloud" theme to portray arriving armies is not confined to popular *sīra*s. Compare Lord Thomas Babington Macaulay's description of the same phenomenon in his poem *Horatius* (*Lays of Ancient Rome: Essays and Poems*, 423–24):

XX. Just then a scout came flying,
All wild with haste and fear:
"To arms! to arms! Sir Consul:
Lars Porsena is here."
On the low hills to westward
The Consul fixed his eye,
And saw the swarthy storm of dust
Rise fast along the sky.

XXI. And nearer fast and nearer
Doth the red whirlwind come;
And louder still and still more loud,
From underneath that rolling cloud,
Is heard the trumpet's war-note proud,
The trampling, and the hum.
And plainly and more plainly
Now though the gloom appears,
Far to left and far to right,
In broken gleams of dark-blue light,
The long array of helmets bright,
The long array of spears.

XXII. And plainly and more plainly,
Above that glimmering line,
Now might ye see the banners
Of twelve fair cities shine;
But the banner of proud Clusium
Was highest of them all,
The terror of the Umbrian,
The terror of the Gaul.

6. This thematic unit is extremely common in *Sīrat 'Antar*; the more examples one examines, the stronger the conviction of its essential linguistic unity; compare, for example, 2/172, 2/184, 3/234–235, 3/254, 4/365, 6/4, 6/30, 6/77, 6/80, 7/104, 7/132, 8/196,

8/207, 8/265, 8/270, 9/315, 14/302, 15/415, 15/431, 16/81, 17/128, 17/131, 17/135, 17/172, 20/454, 21/12, 21/34, 21/93, 22/100, 22/153, 22/177, 23/219, 23/250, 23/269, 25/442, to mention only a few examples.

7. See the section Compositional Structure and Narrative Invention below.

8. This type of cycling of conflicts into a series of steadily escalating battles is an essential device of narrative construction in the *Sīra.* Thus the feud between ʿAntar and Ziyād clan (15) expands to become a war between ʿAbs and King an-Nuʿmān (16), which then expands into a war between the ʿAbs and ʿĀmir (20), consisting of a series of battles, as does ʿAbs's journey to Yemen (25). ʿAntar's conflict with the king of India's warriors ends as an international war (52), and ʿAntar's campaign against the Frankish king al-Lailamān ends as an invasion of North Africa, Spain, and Egypt (62–64), to mention only several prominent examples. On battle and war, see also Malcolm Lyons, *The Arabian Epic,* 1:54–60.

9. There are times when narrative habit, instead of clarifying our sympathies, creates a conflict of sympathies. For instance, ʿAntar's son Maisara enters the narrative by fatally wounding ʿAntar's best friend. In this case, though, blood is thicker than friendship; the idea of revenge is never brought up. By allowing one protagonist to kill another, however, the *Sīra* is breaking one of its self-imposed narrative conventions: killers of protagonists should become antagonists, not protagonists. Because of narrative habit, our sympathy lies with Muqrī during his single combat with Maisara, and seeing Muqrī lose the fight produces an emotional jolt—even if he is killed by a son of ʿAntar. The *Sīra* attempts to soften this jolt by having Muqrī foresee his own death in a dream (30/467–68) and by having him die offstage (39.4).

10. For an account of the legend that the pre-Islamic Arabs hung certain poems on the Kaʿba in Mecca, see the introduction of A. J. Arberry's *The Seven Odes.*

11. For examples of descriptive poems, see 2/122, 4/310, 7/115 (women); 3/217 (a horse); 3/265 (a sword); 4/357 (an old man); 5/428 (a palace); 5/468 (a garden); 8/229 and 8/249 (battle). For examples of poems expressing gnomic sentiments, see 4/345, 4/377 (envy); 4/382, 5/435 (tact); 7/114 (the usefulness of money); 3/288, 5/540 (love); 9/322 (the duplicity of uncles); and 11/16 (dissension). On some occasions the *Sīra* attributes such lines to famous Arab poets, as when it quotes Majnūn (Qais ibn al-Mulawwaḥ) on love, 24/363, 36/41; or ʿAmr ibn Hilāl on the beauty of women, 38/358. Such direct attribution is, however, relatively rare.

12. William Wordsworth, "Preface to the Second Edition of the *Lyrical Ballads,*" in *Criticism: The Major Texts,* ed. Walter Jackson Bate (New York: Harcourt, Brace, and World, 1952), 344.

13. All four types of poems occur too frequently to necessitate detailed reference; as a beginning the reader may compare the love poems, 1/145–46, 2/147, 2/178, 3/208, 3/210, and 2/236–37; the battle poems, 2/130, 2/143, 2/150, 2/162, 2/169–70, 2/174; the panegyrics, 3/253–54, 3/283, 5/429–30, 5/461, 8/303; and the group of elegies recited at Zuhair's death, 14/419–21 and 14/458–61.

The poetry of Arabic popular narratives has been little studied. Udo Steinbach briefly describes verse's function in *Sīrat Dhāt al-Himma* (*Ḏāt al-Himma,* 121–26), as does Rudi Paret in the pseudo-*maghāzī* literature (*Die legendäre Maghāzī-Literatur,* 164–67). In both cases, the function of verse is generally similar to that in *Sīrat ʿAntar* (both these scholars make the same objective/subjective division that I make here). Verse also appears to play similar roles in *The Thousand and One Nights.* Joseph Horowitz initiated the study of the origins of the verse of the *Nights* in his article "Poetische Zitate in Tausend und eine Nacht," in *Festschrift E. Sachau gewidmet* (375–79), but no one has followed up this study. Karel Petràcek has raised the question of the extent to which one might use this poetry as a generic "Volksroman" in "Die Poesie als Kriterium des arabischen 'Volksroman,' " *Oriens* 23–24 (1970–71): 301–5, but his remarks are introductory rather than conclusive.

14. This situation is not totally typical of the *sīra* genre. Verse does play a more active narrative role in the other *sīras*, notably *Sīrat Zīr Sālim* and *Sīrat Banī Hilāl.* One gets the general impression that these narratives' written tradition is more recent and that they more closely reflect the oral narrative tradition that created them. At any rate, in these two epics, verse is almost totally used to express conversations and thus naturally becomes an integral part of narrative action.

15. The division of tribes into North Arabians and South Arabians is based on genealogical, not geographical (at least in terms of sixth-century geography), criteria. Northern Arab tribes traced their genealogy back to 'Adnān, while southern Arab tribes (some of whom lived in North Arabia–southern Mesopotamia) traced their genealogy back to Qaḥṭān. However important this division was in pre-Islamic Arabia, it assumed enormous importance in Umayyad times and affected political divisions in places as far from Arabia as Sapin and Central Asia. The best account of Arab genealogical traditions in a Western language is Werner Caskel's redaction of *Gamharat al-nasab: Das genealogische Werk des Hisām ibn Muḥammad al-Kalbī.*

16. Space prevents a detailed examination of the single combat scene's traditional phrases, thematic units, and themes here; those who wish to gain an impression of them may consult the single combat scenes in 14/310–12, 14/347, 14/348, 14/350, 14/357, 14/365–67, 14/370–73, 19/337, 19/351–55, 22/148, 22/147, 22/168, 23/212–13, and 23/255–62, to suggest only a few of many possible examples.

9. THE USES OF HISTORY

1. Most versions of *sīras* and the *Nights* introduce their texts by claiming that the events they portray are true and that they are compiled to instruct and admonish their audiences with the lessons of the past. See Franz Rosenthal, *A History of Muslim Historiography,* 186–93; and Peter Heath, "Romance as Genre in *The Thousand and One Nights,*" part 2, *Journal of Arabic Literature* 19 (1988): 17–19.

2. See Rosenthal, *Muslim Historiography,* 186–93; and Rudi Paret, *Die Geschichte des Islams im Spiegel der arabischen Volksliteratur.* Both acknowledge that although these narratives are, in Rosenthal's words, "greatly inferior to the best products of Muslim literature, both in their artistic form and in the intellectual level of their contents" (186), they are nevertheless "invaluable sources for the understanding of the psychology and aspirations of the common man in Islam" (186*n*1)

3. See chapter 1 and note 50 there; and Peter Heath, "A Critical Review of Scholarship," 37–40; also my review of Bridget Connelly's *Arab Folk Epic and Identity* in *Journal of the American Oriental Society* 108, no. 2 (1988): 315–17, esp. 317.

4. Raymond Williams, *The Long Revolution,* esp. 41–71.

5. Raymond Williams, *Keywords: A Vocabulary of Culture and Society,* 146–48. Of course, questions regarding the exact meaning of such terms as "qualified authority" and "real past events" as well as approaches as to how such inquiries should be "organized" are on the one hand culturally and historically determined and on the other subjects for detailed

debate. Cf. Rosenthal's definition: "History [i.e., Western history] . . . should be defined as the literary description of any sustained human activity either of groups or individuals which is reflected in, or has influence upon the development of a given group or individual" (*Muslim Historiography*, 10).

6. For the term "horizon of expectations," see Hans Robert Jauss, *Toward an Aesthetic of Reception*, trans. Timothy Bahti.

7. On Muslim historiography's methods and hermeneutical stance, see Rosenthal, *Muslim Historiography*, which contains translations of methodological passages from diverse works; see also A. A. Duri, *The Rise of Historical Writing among the Arabs*, ed. and trans. Lawrence I. Conrad; and B. Lewis and P. M. Holt, eds., *Historians of the Middle East.*

8. Abū ʿUbaida (d. circa 207/824) and Ḥammād ar-Rāwī (d. 155–56/772–73) are well-known early transmitters of *akhbār* and poetry. I have been unable to identify the other names as belonging to historical figures.

9. The *rāwī* often does this by invoking the name and blessings of the Prophet Muḥammad: for example, "So let us return to the course of the story and the account, after blessing and benediction on the Lord of Mankind, may God save him, his family, and his companions, and bless what the ear has heard and the eye has beheld, O noble sirs" (2:135). See also Susan Slyomovics, *The Merchant of Art*, 13 and 36–37; and Bridget Connelly, *Arab Folk Epic and Identity*, 225–74.

10. Cf. Heath, "Romance as Genre in *The Thousand and One Nights*," 16–21.

11. For an overview of this period of compilation, see Régis Blachère, *Histoire de la littérature arabe, des origines à la fin de XVe siècle de J.-C.*, 1:85–166; and Shauqī Ḍaif, *Tārīkh al-adab al-ʿarabī: al-ʿasr al-jāhilī*, 138–82.

12. On rare occasions, the *Sīra* also cites histories as a source; see 51:67 and 52:177, where a history called *ʿArf* (*ʿUrf*?) *al-murūr* (or *al-maurūd*) is cited.

13. See, for example, 2:147, where al-Aṣmaʿī affirms ʿAbla's beauty; or 13:22, where he is an eyewitness to a battle between the Arabs and the Persians; he also enters the text at 7:169, 10:443, 13:232, 13:233–35, 22:133–34, 27:183, and 54:311. On several occasions the unidentified *rāwī* enters the story, such as 43:232, 43:255, 43:266, 53:196, 54:315, 57:135. Only once is a narrator besides al-Aṣmaʿī specifically named: at 34:358–59, Abū ʿUbaida enters the text.

14. Hayden White, *Tropics of Discourse: Essays in Cultural Criticism*, 121–34. He argues this position throughout this book, as well as in his *Metahistory: The Historical Imagination in Nineteenth-Century Europe.*

15. This tribal antipathy existed in pre-Islamic times but intensified greatly in the early Islamic and Umayyad periods, when the conquest created new tribal alliances that held throughout the far-flung empire. See J. Welhausen, *The Arab Kingdom and Its Fall*, trans. Margaret G. Weir, for the east; and Reinhart Dozy, *Histoire des musulmans d'Espagne* (English trans. of the 1st ed., *Spanish Islam: A History of the Moslems in Spain*, trans. and intro. Francis G. Stokes) for the west. Much of the action in *Sīrat Dhāt al-Himma* revolves around the rivalry of northern and southern tribal confederations in the Umayyad period. Compare also Malcolm Lyons, *The Arabian Epic*, 1:8–35.

16. See the preceding chapter. For an English translation of this part of the *Sīra*, see H. T. Norris, *The Adventures of Antar.*

17. On the correlation of names mentioned in *Sīrat ʿAntar* with those of historical figures, see Norris, *Antar*, 239–48; and B. Heller's article on *Sīrat ʿAntar* in EI^2, 1:518–21.

18. This idea is reiterated in 10:413, 20:43, 43:209, 43:266, and 46:91. On the conception of religion in the *sīra* genre, see also Lyons, *The Arabian Epic*, 1:42–48.

19. See, for example, the Muslim historian Ibn Khaldūn's criticism of al-Mas'ūdī and others for their lack of concern for such accuracy: *al-Muqadimma*, 13–35; English trans. by Franz Rosenthal, *The Muqaddimah: An Introduction to History*, 1:6–77. See also the materials translated by Rosenthal in *Muslim Historiography*. On Mas'ūdī, see Tarif Khalidi, *Islamic Historiography: The Histories of Mas'ūdī*.

20. On the *Ayyām al-'Arab*, see *EI*[2], 1:793–79, which cites the relevant sources; Werner Caskel, "Aijām al-'Arab: Studien zur altarabischen Epik," *Islamica* 3, supplement (1931): 1–99; and Egbert Meyer, *Der historische Gehalt der Aiyām al-'Arab*. *Ayyām* accounts are scattered in different renditions in such works as Ibn 'Abd ar-Rabbih's *al-'Iqd al-farīd* and al-Iṣfahānī's *Kitāb al-aghānī*; for a useful modern collection, see M. A. Ibrāhīm, A. M. al-Bijāwī, and M. A. al-Maulā Bey, *Ayyām al-'Arab fi 'l-Jāhiliyya*.

21. Michel Foucault, *The Discourse on Language*, 224.

22. Rosenthal, *Muslim Historiography*, 186.

23. For an extended analysis of the concept of emplotment, see Paul Ricoeur, *Time and Narrative*, trans. K. McLaughlin and D. Pelleur.

24. Thus we have the extranarrative context of storyteller and audience, the narrative context of the narrator (*rāwī*), and the pseudo-historical authority of historians and sources. Within this structure, the story occurs on two planes, earthly and cosmic:

Prologue	Main Story	Epilogue
Earthly Plane		
Early Arab History	Life of 'Antar	Muḥammad & Islam
Cosmic Plane		
Story of Abraham	Life of 'Antar	Muḥammad & Islam

25. Hayden White would describe *Sīrat 'Antar*'s main trope as "metaphoric" due to its concern with synthesis and patterns; he would consider its viewpoint "romantic" because of its focus on the individual as the shaper of history.

26. Northop Frye, *Anatomy of Criticism: Four Essays*, 33.

27. Ibid., 33–34.

28. Cf aṭ-Ṭabarī, *The History of al-Ṭabarī, Volume 1: General Introduction and the Creation to the Flood*, trans. Franz Rosenthal, 168 (Leiden Arabic edition, 1:5):

> In this book of mine, I shall mention whatever information has reached us about kings throughout the ages from when our Lord began the creation of His creation to its annihilation. There were messengers sent by God, kings placed in authority, or caliphs established in the caliphal succession. God had early on bestowed His benefits and favors upon some of them. They were grateful for His favors, and He thus gave them more favors and bounty in addition to those He bestowed upon them in their fleeting life, or He postponed the increase and stored it up for them with Himself. There were others who were not grateful for His favors, and so He deprived them of the favors He had bestowed upon them early on and hastened for them His revenge. There were also others who were not grateful for His favors; He let them enjoy them until the time of their death and perdition.

29. White would consider their operational trope to be metonymy and their historical outlook "radical." Compare Aristotle's comment that "poetry tends rather to express the universal, history rather the particular fact" (*Aristotle's Poetics*, trans. and intro. James Hutton, 54 [1451^{b}]).

30. It is interesting, if beyond the purview of this discussion, to compare modern Western historiography with elite Muslim historiography and to inquire as to why the former has so embraced individualism and narrative synthesis as principles of composition.

31. M. M. Bakhtin, *The Dialogic Imagination: Four Essays*, ed. and trans. Caryl Emerson and Michael Holquist, 15–16.

10. DIRECTIONS FOR FUTURE RESEARCH

1. Malcolm Lyons, *The Arabian Epic*, 1:77–132, and on the *ʿayyār* esp. 118–27. See also the introduction above and the sources cited in note 10 there. In addition, see Marina Gaillard, *Le livre de Samak-e ʿAyyār: Structure et idéologie du roman persan médieval*, 17–53.

2. Remke Kruk, "Warrior Women in the Arabic Popular Romance: Qannāṣa bint Muzāhīm and Other Valiant Ladies," part 1, *Journal of Arabic Literature* 24, no. 3 (1993): 213–30; part 2, "The Story of Qannāṣa bint Muzāhīm," *Journal of Arabic Literature* 25, no. 1 (1994): 16–33; William L. Hanaway, Jr., "Persian Popular Romances," 25–54; Nabīla Ibrāhīm, *Sīrat al-Amīra Dhāt al-Himma*; and Lyons, *The Arabic Epic*, 1:109–18.

3. W. T. H. Jackson, *The Hero and the King: An Epic Theme*. See also Gaillard, *Le livre de Samak-e ʿAyyār*, 123–60.

APPENDIX III. INTRODUCTION TO THE TOPKAPı MANUSCRIPT (NO. 1145)

1. The following prolegomenon is in Arabic.

2. Qur'ān 17:70.

3. Qur'ān 49:13.

4. *al-Ḥatīm*, literally, the wall of the Ka'ba, or the interdicted spot near the wall or thereabouts. S.v. in Edward W. Lane, *Arabic-English Lexicon*, 1:595.

5. Qur'ān 68:4.

6. Asia and Europe.

7. The language here changes to Ottoman Turkish.

Bibliography

SĪRAS

Sīrat ʿAntar

ʿAntar-nāma. 3 vols. (Karatay, Turkish nos. 2805–7.) Topkapı Sarayı Müzesi Kütüphanesi, Istanbul.

Kitāb ʿAntara ibn Shaddād. 6 vols. Beirut: al-Maṭbaʿa 'l-adabiyya, 1883–88.

Qiṣṣat ʿAntara ibn Shaddād al-ʿAbsī. 8 vols. Cairo: Maktabat Muṣṭafa 'l-Bābi 'l-Ḥalabī, 1961.

Sīrat ʿAntara ibn Shaddād. 8 vols. Cairo: Maktabat al-Mashhad al-Ḥusainī, 1971.

Sīrat ʿAntar ibn Shaddād. 7 vols. (Flügel no. 783.) Austrian National Library, Vienna.

Sīrat ʿAlī Zaibaq

As-Sīra 'l-kubrā li-'l-ʿāʾiq ash-shāṭir al-muqaddam ʿAlī az-Zaibaq al-Miṣrī. Cairo: al-Maktaba 'l-mamlūkiyya, n.d.

Sīrat al-Amīr Ḥamza

Qiṣṣat al-Amīr Ḥamza 'sh-shahīr bi-Ḥamzat al-ʿArab. 4 vols. Cairo: Maktabat Muṣṭafa 'l-Bābi 'l-Ḥalabī, 1962.

Qiṣṣat al-Amīr Ḥamza al-Bahlawān al-maʿrūf bi-Ḥamzat al-ʿArab. 4 vols. Beirut: al-Maktaba 'th-thaqafiyya, n.d.

Sīrat Banī Hilāl

Sīrat al-'Arab al-Ḥijāziyya. Cairo: Maktabat al-Jumhūriyya 'l-'Arabiyya, n.d.
Sīrat al-'Arab al-Ḥijāziyya: ad-Durra 'l-munīfa. Cairo: Maktabat al-Jumhūriyya 'l-'Arabiyya, n.d.
Sīrat Banī Hilāl. Beirut: al-Maktaba 'th-thaqafiyya, n.d.
Taghrībat Banī Hilāl. Cairo: Maktaba wa-maṭba'at Muḥammad 'Alī Ṣubaiḥ, n.d.

Sīrat Dhāt al-Himma

Qiṣṣat al-Amīra Dhāt al-Himma. 8 vols. Cairo: Maktabat Muṣṭafa 'l-Bābi 'l-Ḥalabī, 1963.
Qiṣṣat al-Amīra Dhāt al-Himma. 8 vols. Beirut: al-Maktaba 'th-thaqafiyya, n.d.

Sīrat Fīrūz Shāh

Qiṣṣat Fīrūz Shāh ibn al-Malik Ḍābāb. N.p.: al-Maktaba 'l-'ilmiyya 'l-ḥadītha, n.d.
Sīrat Fīrūz Shāh. 4 vols. Cairo: Maktabat al-Mashhad al-Ḥusainī, 1971.

Sīrat al-Malik Saif ibn Dhī Yazan

Sīrat fāris al-Yaman al-Malik Saif ibn Dhi 'l-Yazan. 4 vols. Cairo: Maktabat al-Mashhad al-Ḥusainī, 1971.
Sīrat al-Malik Saif ibn Dhī Yazan. Beirut: al-Maktaba 'th-thaqafiyya, n.d.

Sīrat al-Malik aẓ-Ẓāhir Baibars

Sīrat al-Malik aẓ-Ẓāhir Baibars. 5 vols. Cairo: 'Abd al-Ḥamīd Ḥanafī, 1902.
Sīrat al-Malik aẓ-Ẓāhir Baibars. Beirut: al-Maktaba 'th-thaqafiyya, n.d.

Sīrat az-Zīr Sālim

Qiṣṣat az-Zīr Sālim al-kubrā Abū Laila l-Muhalhil. Jidda: As'ad Muḥammad Sa'īd al-Ḥabbāl, n.d.
Sīrat az-Zīr Abū Laila l-Muhalhil. Beirut: Mu'assasat al-ma'ārif, n.d.

CATALOGUES OF MANUSCRIPTS AND BOOKS

Ahlwardt, Wilhelm. *Verzeichnis der arabischen Handschriften der Königlichen Bibliothek zu Berlin.* Vol. 8: *Die Grossen Romane.* Berlin: A. Asher, 1896.

Arberry, Arthur J. *A Second Supplementary Hand-List of the Muḥammadan Manuscripts in the University and Colleges of Cambridge.* Cambridge: Cambridge University Press, 1957.

Aumer, Joseph. *Die arabischen Handschriften der K. Hof- und Staatsbibliothek in München.* Munich: Palmische Hofbuchhandlung, 1866.

Blochet, E. *Bibliothèque Nationale: Catalogue des manuscrits arabes des nouvelles acquisitions (1884–1924).* Paris: Editions Ernest Leroux, 1925.

———. *Catalogue des manuscrits Turcs.* 2 vols. Paris: Bibliothèque Nationale, 1932.

Browne, Edward G. *A Hand-List of the Muḥammadan Manuscripts including All Those Written in the Arabic Character, Preserved in the Library of the University of Cambridge.* Cambridge: Cambridge University Press, 1900.

———. *A Supplementary Hand-List of the Muḥammadan Manuscripts including All Those Written in the Arabic Character, Preserved in the Libraries of the University and Colleges of Cambridge.* Cambridge: Cambridge University Press, 1922.

Catalogus codicum manuscriptorum orientalium qui in Museo Britannico asservantur, 3 parts: *Syriac, Arabic, Aethiopic.* London: British Museum, 1838–79.

Dictionary Catalogue of the Oriental Collection, The New York Public Library Reference Department. 16 vols., 8 suppl. vols. Boston: G. K. Hall, 1960.

Dozy, R. *Catalogus codicum orientalium Bibliothecae Academiae Lugduno Batavae* (Leiden). 6 vols. Leiden: E. J. Brill, 1851.

Ellis, A. G. *Catalogue of Arabic Books in the British Museum.* 2 vols. London: British Museum, 1894.

Fihris al-kutub al-ʿarabiyya ʾl-maujūda bi-Dār al-Kutub li-ghāyat sanat 1936. 6 parts in 3 vols. Cairo: Dār al-Kutub, 1924–33.

Fihrist al-kutub al-ʿarabiyya ʾl-maḥfūẓa bi-ʾl-Kutubkhāna ʾl-Khidīwiyya. 7 vols. Cairo: Dār al-Kutub, 1887–90.

Fleisher, Henricus Orthobius. *Catalogus codicum manuscriptorum orientalium Bibliothecae Regiae Dresdensis.* Leipzig: Chr. Guil. Vogel, 1831.

Flügel, Gustav. *Die arabischen, persischen und türkischen Handschriften der Kaiserlich-Königlichen Hofbibliothek zu Wien.* 3 vols. Vienna: K. K. Hof- und Staatsdruckerei, 1865–67.

Fulton, Alexander S., and A. G Ellis. *Supplementary Catalogue of Arabic Printed Books in the British Museum, 1901–1926.* London: British Museum, 1926.

Goeje, M. J. de, and Th. Houtsma. *Catalogus codicum arabicum Bibliothecae Academiae Lugduno Batavae* (Leiden). 2nd ed. Leiden: E. J. Brill, 1888.

Hitti, Phillip K., Nabih Amin Faris, and Buṭrus ʿAbdul-Malik. *Descriptive Catalogue of the Garrett Collection of the Arabic Manuscripts in the Princeton University Library.* Princeton: Princeton University Press, 1939.

Ḥusain, Shams-ul-ʿUlamāʾ M. Hidayat. *Catalogue Raisonné of the Būhār Library.* Vol. 2: *Catalogue of the Arabic Manuscripts in the Būhār Library.* Calcutta: Imperial Library, 1923.

Karatay, Fehmi Edhem. *Topkapı Sarayı Müzesi Kütüphanesi Arapça Yazmalar Kataloğu.* 3 vols. Topkapı Sarayı Müzesi yayinları, no. 5. Istanbul: Topkapı Sarayı Müzesi, 1963–66.

———. *Topkapı Sarayı Müzesi Kütüphanesi Türkçe Yazmalar Kataloğu.* 2 vols. Topkapı Sarayı Müzesi yayinları 11. Istanbul: Topkapı Sarayı Müzesi, 1961.

Mach, Rudolf. *Catalogue of Arabic Manuscripts (Yahuda Section) in the Garrett Collection, Princeton University Library.* Princeton: Princeton University Press, 1977.

Mehren, August F. *Codices orientales bibliothecae Regiae Hafniensis enumerati et descripti.* Copenhagen: ex officina Schultziana, 1851.

Mingana, A. *Catalogue of the Arabic Manuscripts in the John Rylands Library, Manchester.* Manchester: Manchester Library Press, 1934.

Nadwi, Maulavi Muinuddin. *Catalogue of the Arabic and Persian Manuscripts in the Oriental Public Library at Bankipore.* Vol. 15: *History.* Calcutta: Baptist Mission Press; Patna: Government Printing, 1929.

Nicoll, Alexander. *Catalogi codicum manuscriptorum orientalium Bibliothecae.* 2 parts. Oxford: E Typographeo Academia, 1885.

Pertsch, Wilhelm. *Die arabischen Handschriften der Herzoglichen Bibliothek zu Gotha.* 5 vols. Gotha: Frier. Andr. Perthes, 1892.

Rieu, Charles. *Catalogue of the Turkish Manuscripts in the British Museum.* London: British Museum, 1888.

———. *Supplement to the Catalogue of the Arabic Manuscripts in the British Museum.* London: British Museum, 1894.

Sayyid, Fuʾād. *Fihrist al-makhṭūṭāt: Nashra bi-ʾl-makhṭūṭāt allati ʾqtanat-hā ad-Dār min sanat 1936–1953.* 3 vols. Cairo: Dār al-Kutub, 1961–63.

———. *Jāmiʿat ad-Duwal al-ʿArabiyya, Maʿhad al-Makhṭūṭāt al-ʿArabiyya: Fihris al-makhṭūṭāt al-muṣawwara.* 3 vols. Cairo: Dār ar-riyāḍ; Maṭbaʿat as-Sunna ʾl-Muḥammadiyya, 1954-60.

Slane, William Mac-Guckin, Baron de. *Catalogue des manuscrits arabes de la Bibliothèque Nationale.* Paris: Imprimerie Nationale, 1883–95.

Voigt, Wolfgang, gen. ed. *Verzeichnis der orientalischen Handschriften in Deutschland.* Wiesbaden: Franz Steiner, 1963–. Vol. 13, 1: *Türkische Handschriften,* by Barbara Flemming.

GENERAL

Aarne, Antti, and Stith Thompson. *The Types of the Folktale: A Classification and Bibliography.* 2nd rev. ed. Folklore Fellows Communications 2. Helsinki: Suomalainen Tiedakatemia, 1961.

Abbott, Nabia. "A Ninth-Century Fragment of the *Thousand Nights*: New Light on the Early History of the *Arabian Nights*." *Journal of Near Eastern Studies* 8 (1949): 129–64.

———. *Studies in Arabic Literary Papyri 1: Historical Texts*. Chicago: University of Chicago Press, 1957.

'Abd al-Laṭīf, Muḥammad Farīd. *Alwān min al-fann ash-sha'bī*. Cairo: al-Maktaba 'th-thaqafiyya, 1964.

'Abdel-Meguid, 'Abdel-'Aziz. "A Survey of Story Literature in Arabic from before Islam to the Middle of the Nineteenth Century." *Islamic Quarterly* 1 (1954): 104–13.

Abel, Armand. "Formation et constitution de roman d'Antar." In *La poesia epica e la sua formazione*, 717–30. Roma: Accademia nazionale dei Lincei, 1970.

Abel, Martin. *Die arabische Vorlage des Suaheli-Epos Chuo Cha Herkal: Ein Beitrag zur Kenntnis des legendären Magāzī-Literatur*. Beihefte zur Zeitschrift für Eingeborenen-Sprachen 18. Berlin: Dietrich Reimer, 1938.

Abkāriūs, Iskandar Bey. *Minyat al-nafs fī ash'ār 'Antar al-'Abs*. 2nd ed. Beirut: al-Maṭba'a 'l-adabiyya, 1881.

Abrahams, Roger D. "The Complex Relations of Single Forms." *Genre* 2 (1969): 104–28.

———. "Folklore and Literature as Performance." *Journal of the Folklore Institute* 19 (1972): 75–94.

———. "Introductory Remarks to a Rhetorical Theory of Folklore." *Journal of American Folklore* 81 (1968): 143–58.

Ahlwardt, Wilhelm. *The Divans of Six Ancient Arabic Poets*. Reprint of 1870 edition. Osnabrück: Biblio Verlag, 1972.

Albright, Charlotte F. "The Azerbaijānī 'Āshiq and His Performance of a Dastān." *Iranian Studies* 9 (1976): 220–47.

Alf laila wa-laila. 4 vols. Cairo: Maṭba'at Muḥammad 'Alī Ṣubaiḥ, n.d.

'Alī, Fu'ād Ḥasanain. *Qiṣaṣ-na 'sh-sha'bī*. Cairo: Dār al-fikr al-'arabī, 1947.

Ali, Muhsin Jassim. *Scheherazade in England: A Study of Nineteenth-Century English Criticism of the Arabian Nights*. Washington, D.C.: Three Continents Press, 1981.

"'Antara al-'Absī." *al-Hilāl* 5 (Cairo, 1896–97): 723–30.

'Antara ibn Shaddād. *Dīwān*. Edited by 'Abd al-Mun'im 'Abd ar-Ra'ūf Shalabī. Cairo: Maktabat at-tijāriyya l-kubrā, n.d.

Arberry, A. J. *Oriental Essays: Portraits of Seven Scholars*. London: George Allen and Unwin, 1960.

———. *The Seven Odes: The First Chapter in Arabic Literature*. London: George Allen and Unwin, 1957.

Aristotle. *Aristotle's Poetics*. Trans. and intro. James Hutton. New York and London: W. W. Norton, 1982.

Arnold, Matthew. "The Function of Criticism at the Present Time." In *The Portable Matthew Arnold*, ed. and intro. Lionel Trilling. New York: Viking Press, 1949.

Ashley, Bob. *The Study of Popular Fiction: A Source Book.* Philadelphia: University of Pennsylvania Press, 1989.

Auerbach, Eric. *Mimesis: The Representation of Reality in Western Literature.* Trans. Williard R. Trask. Princeton: Princeton University Press, 1953.

Ayoub, Abderrahmann, and Bridget Connelly. "A propos des manuscrits de la geste des Banū Hilāl conservés à Berlin." In *Association internationale d'étude de civilizations méditerranéennes: Actes du IIième congrès*, ed. M. Galley, 347–63. Algiers: Société National d'Edition et Diffusion, 1978.

———. "An Experiment on the Metrics of Arabic Oral Poetry," *Arabica* 32 (1985): 323–59.

al-Azdī, Muḥammad ibn Aḥmad Abu 'l-Muṭahhar. *Abulkāsim, ein bagdāder Sittenbild.* Ed. A. Mez. Heidelberg: n. p., 1902.

Bachelard, Gaston. *The Poetics of Space.* Boston: Beacon Press, 1969.

———. *The Psychoanalysis of Fire.* Boston: Beacon Press, 1968.

Baer, Gabriel. *Egyptian Guilds in Modern Times.* Oriental Notes and Studies 8. Jerusalem: Israel Oriental Society, 1964.

Baghdādī, 'Abd al-Qādir ibn 'Amr al-. *Khizānat al-adab wa-lubb lubāb lisān al-'Arab.* 4 vols. Būlāq: al-Amīriyya 'l-kubra, 1881–82.

Baker, Cathryn Anita. "The Hilālī Saga in the Tunisian South." Ph.D. dissertation, Indiana University, 1978.

Bakhtin, M. M. *The Dialogic Imagination: Four Essays.* Ed. Michael Holquist. Trans. Caryl Emerson and Michael Holquist. Slavic Series 1. Austin: University of Texas Press, 1981.

Bal, Mieke. *Narratology: Introduction to the Theory of Narrative.* Trans. Christine van Boheemen. Toronto, Buffalo, and London: University of Toronto Press, 1985.

Barth, John. *Chimera.* New York: Random House, 1972.

———. *The Last Voyage of Somebody the Sailor.* Boston: Little, Brown, 1991.

Barthes, Roland. *Image, Music, Text.* Trans. Stephen Heath. New York: Hill and Wang, 1977.

Basgöz, Ilhan. "Turkish *Hikaye*-Telling Tradition in Azerbaijan, Iran." *Journal of American Folklore* 83 (1970): 391–405.

Basset, René. "Un épisode d'une chanson de geste arabe." *Bulletin de Correspondance Africaine* 3 (1885): 136–48.

———. *Mille et une contes: Récits et legendes arabes.* 3 vols. Paris: Maisonneuve Frères, 1924–26.

Bel, A. "La Djāzya, chanson arabe précedée d'observations sur quelques légendes arabes et sur gestes des Banū Hilāl." *Journal Asiatique* (1902): 289–347, (1903): 169–236, 311–66.

Ben-Amos, Dan. "Analytical Categories and Ethnic Genres." *Genre* 3 (1969): 275–301.

Benjamin, Walter. *Illuminations: Essays and Reflections.* Trans. Harry Zohn. Ed. and intro. Hannah Arendt. New York: Schocken Books, 1968.

Bennet, Tony, ed. *Popular Fiction: Technology, Ideology, Production, Reading.* Popular Fiction Series. London and New York: Routledge, 1990.

Bettelheim, Bruno. *The Uses of Enchantment: The Meaning and Importance of Fairy Tales.* New York: Random House, Vintage Books, 1977.

Blachère, Régis. *Histoire de la littérature arabe, des origines à la fin de XVe siècle de J.-C.* 3 vols. Paris: Librairie Adrien Maisonneuve, 1952–66.

———. "Problème de la transfiguration du poète tribal en héros de roman 'courtois' chez les 'logographes' arabes du IIIe/IXe siècle." *Arabica* 8 (1961): 131–36.

———. "Regards sur la littérature narrative en arabe au Ier siècle de l'hégire (VIIIe s. J.-C.)." *Semitica* 6 (1956): 75–86.

Blau, Yehoshua. *A Grammar of Christian Arabic: Based Mainly on South Palestinian Texts from the First Millennium.* Corpus Scriptorum Christianorum Orientalium, vols. 267, 276, 279, subsidiary vol. 29. Paris: Louvain, 1966–67.

———. "The Importance of Middle Arabic Dialects for the History of Arabic." In *Studies in Islamic History and Civilization,* 206–28. Scripta Hierosolymitana 9. Jerusalem: Hebrew University, 1961.

Bohas, Georges, and Jean-Patrick Guillame, trans. *Roman de Baibars.* 8 vols. Bibliothèque Arabe. Collection Les Classiques. Paris: Sindbad, 1985–92.

Booth, Wayne C. *The Rhetoric of Fiction.* Chicago: University of Chicago Press, 1961.

Boratav, Pertev Naili. "L'Epopée et la 'hikaye.' " In *Philologiae Turcicae Fundamenta,* ed. Jean Deny et al., 2:44–66. Wiesbaden: Franz Steiner, 1965.

———. *Halk hikayeleri ve halk hikayeciliği.* Ankara: Milli Egitim Basımevı, 1946.

Bosworth, Clifford Edmund. *The Medieval Islamic Underworld: The Banū Sāsān in Arabic Society and Literature.* 2 parts. Leiden: E. J. Brill, 1976.

Bourdieu, Pierre. *Distinction: A Social Critique of the Judgement of Taste.* Trans. R. Nice. Cambridge, Mass.: Harvard University Press, 1984.

———. *Language and Symbolic Power.* Intro. John B. Thompson. Trans. G. Raymond and M. Adamson. Cambridge, Mass.: Harvard University Press, 1991.

———. *Outline of a Theory of Practice.* Trans. Richard Nice. Studies in Social and Culture Anthropology 16. Cambridge: Cambridge University Press, 1977.

Bowra, Cedric M. *Heroic Poetry.* London: Macmillan, 1952; rpt. 1966.

Bravman, Meir M. "Heroic Motives in Early Arabic Literature." *Der Islam* 33 (1958): 256–79; 35 (1960): 4–36.

Brockelmann, Carl. *Geschichte der arabischen Litteratur.* 2nd ed. 2 vols. 3 supplements. Leiden: E. J. Brill, 1937–49.

Brooks, Peter. *Reading for the Plot: Design and Intention in Narrative.* Cambridge, Mass., and London: Harvard University Press, 1984.

Burke, Peter. "*From Pioneers to Settlers: Recent Studies of the History of Popular Culture*: A Review Article." *Comparative Studies in Society and History* 25, no. 1 (1983): 181–87.

Bustānī, Fu'ād Ifrām al-. "'Antarat at-ta'rīkh wa-'Antarat al-usṭūra." *al-Mashriq* 28 (1930): 534–40, 631–47.

Bynum, David E. "The Generic Nature of Oral Epic Poetry." *Genre* 2 (1969): 236–58.

Cachia, Pierre. "The Egyptian Mawwāl." *Journal of Arabic Literature* 8 (1977): 77–103.

———. *Popular Narrative Ballads of Modern Egypt.* Oxford: Clarendon Press, 1989.

Campbell, Joseph. *The Hero with a Thousand Faces.* Bollingen Series 17. 2nd ed. Princeton: Princeton University Press, 1968.

Canard, Marius. "*Delhemma*, épopée arabe des guerres arabo-byzantines." *Byzantion* 10 (1935): 283–300.

———. "Delhemma, Sayyid Baṭṭāl, et Omar al-No'mān." *Byzantion* 12 (1937): 183–33.

———. "Les principaux personnages du roman du chevalerie arabe Dāt al-Himma wa-l-Baṭṭāl." *Arabica* 8 (1961): 158–73.

Canova, Giovanni. "Gli studi sull'epica popolare araba." *Oriente Moderno* 57 (1977): 211–26.

———. "Testimonianze Hilaliane nello Yemen orientale." *Studi Yemeniti* 1, no. 14 (1985): 161–96.

Caskel, Werner. "Aijām al-'Arab: Studien zur altarabischen Epik." *Islamica* 3, supplement (1931): 1–99.

———. "Die einheimischen Quellen zur Geschichte Nord-Arabiens vor dem Islam." *Islamica* 4, no. 3 (1927): 331–41.

———, ed. *Gamharat al-nasab: Das genealogische Werk des Hisām ibn Muḥammad al-Kalbī.* 2 vols. Leiden: E. J. Brill, 1966.

Caussin de Perceval, A. "Notice et extrait du Roman d'Antar." *Journal Asiatique* (August 1833): 97–123.

Cawelti, John G. *Adventure, Mystery, and Romance: Formula Stories as Art and Popular Culture.* Chicago: University of Chicago Press, 1976.

Chadwick, H. M., and K. M. Chadwick. *The Growth of Literature.* 3 vols. Cambridge: Cambridge University Press, 1932, rpt. 1968.

Chadwick, Nora K., and Victor Zhirmunsky. *Oral Epics of Central Asia.* Cambridge: Cambridge University Press, 1969.

Chauvin, Victor. *Bibliographie des ouvrages arabes ou relatifs aux Arabes, publiés dans l'Europe chrétienne de 1810 à 1885.* 12 vols. Liège: H. Vaillant-Carmanne, 1892–1922.

Chaytor, H. J. *From Script to Print: An Introduction to Medieval Vernacular Literature.* Cambridge: W. Heffer and Sons, 1945.

Cheikho, Louis. *Kitāb shu'arā' an-naṣrāniyya.* Beirut: Matba'at al-Ābā' al-Mursilīn al-Yasū'iyīn, 1890.

Christides, Vassilios. "An Arabo-Byzantine Novel '*Umar b. al-Nu'mān* Compared with *Digenis Akritas.*" *Byzantion* 32 (1962): 549–604.

Connelly, Bridget Ann. *Arab Folk Epic and Identity.* Berkeley and Los Angeles: University of California Press, 1986.

———. "The Oral-Formulaic Tradition of *Sīrat Banī Hilāl*: Prolegomena to the Study of *Sīra* Literature." Ph.D. dissertation, University of California, Berkeley, 1974.

———. "The Structure of Four Banī Hilāl Tales: Prolegomena to the Study of *Sīra* Literature." *Journal of Arabic Literature* 4 (1973): 18–47.

———. "Three Egyptian Rebāb-Poets: Individual Craft and Poetic Design in *Sīrat Banī Hilāl.*" *Edebiyāt* 2, nos. 1–2 (1988): 117–47.

Ḍaif, Shauqī. *Tārīkh al-adab al-'arabī: al-'asr al-jāhilī.* Cairo: Dār al-ma'ārif, 1976.

Dégh, Linda. *Folktales and Society: Story-telling in a Hungarian Peasant Community.* Bloomington: Indiana University Press, 1969.

Devic, L. U., trans. *Les aventures d'Antar, fils de Cheddad: Roman arabe des temps antéislamiques.* Vol. 1: *Depuis la naissance d'Antar jusqu'à la captivité et la délivrance de Chas.* Paris: Hetzel, 1864.

Dictionary of Scientific Biography. S.v. "al-Samaw'al ibn Yaḥyā al-Maghrībī," by Adel Anbouba. New York: Scribner, 1970–.

Djaït, Hichem. *Europe and Islam: Cultures and Modernity.* Trans. Peter Heinegg. Berkeley, Los Angeles, London: University of California Press, 1985.

Dodge, Bayard, trans. *The Fihrist of al-Nadīm: A Tenth-Century Survey of Muslim Culture.* 2 vols. New York: Columbia University Press, 1970.

Dorson, Richard M., ed. *Folklore and Folklife: An Introduction.* Chicago: University of Chicago Press, 1972.

Dover, Cedric. "The Black Knight." *Phylon: Atlanta University Review of Race and Culture* (1954): 41–57, 177–89.

———. "Terrick Hamilton: A Forgotten Orientalist." *Calcutta Review* (1954): 199–211.

Dozy, Reinhart. *Histoire des musulmans d'Espagne.* 4 vols. Leiden, 1861; 2nd rev. ed., E. Lévi-Provençal, Leiden, 1932. Eng. trans. of 1st ed. *Spanish Islam: A History of the Moslems in Spain.* Trans. and intro. Francis G. Stokes. London: Chatto and Windus, 1913.

Dundes, Alan. "The Hero Pattern and the Life of Jesus." In Dundes, *Interpreting Folklore*, 223–61.

———. *Interpreting Folklore.* Bloomington and Indianapolis: Indiana University Press, 1980.

———. *The Morphology of North American Indian Folktales.* Folklore Fellows Communications 195. Helsinki: Suomalainen Tiedakatemia, 1964.

———, ed. *The Study of Folklore.* Englewood Cliffs, N.J.: Prentice-Hall, 1965.

———. "Texture, Text, and Context." In Dundes, *Interpreting Folklore*, 1–19.

Duri, A. A. *The Rise of Historical Writing among the Arabs.* Ed. and trans. Lawrence I. Conrad. Modern Classics in Near Eastern Studies. Princeton: Princeton University Press, 1983.

During, Simon, ed. *The Cultural Studies Reader.* London and New York: Routledge, 1993.

Eberhard, Wolfham. *Minstrel Tales from Southern Turkey.* Berkeley and Los Angeles: University of California Press, 1955.

Edebiyāt: A Journal of Middle East and Comparative Literature n.s. 2, nos. 1 and 2 (1988). Special issue on Middle Eastern Folklore.

Elisséef, Nikita. *Thèmes et motifs des Mille et une Nuits: Essai de classification.* Beirut: Institut Française de Damas, 1949.

El-Shamy, Hasan M. *Folk Traditions of the Arab World: A Guide to Motif Classification.* 2 vols. Bloomington and Indianapolis: Indiana University Press, 1995.

Encyclopedia of Islam. 1st ed. 4 vols. Leiden and Leipzig: E. J. Brill and Otto Harrassowitz, 1913–36. S.v.:
"Saif b. Dhī Yazan," by R. Paret, 4:71–72.
"Sīra," by G. Levi della Vida, 4:439–43.
"Tamīm ad-Dārī," by G. Levi della Vida, 4:646–48.
"Tā'rīkh," by H. A. R. Gibb, supplement 233–45.
"al-Tha'labī," by C. Brockelmann, 4:435–36.
"Wahb ibn Munabbih," by J. Horowitz, 4:1084–85.

Encyclopedia of Islam. 2nd ed. Leiden: E. J. Brill, 1960–. S.v.:
"Abū Nuwās," by E. Wagner, 1:143–44.
"Abū Yazid al-Bisṭamī," by H. Ritter, 1:162–63.
"Alf Layla wa-Layla," by E. Littmann, 1:358–64.
"'Antara," by R. Blachère, 1:521–22.
"'Arabiyya," by Ch. Rabin et al., 1:561–603.
"al-Aṣma'ī," by B. Lewin, 1:717–19.
"Ayyām al-'Arab," by E. Mittwoch, 1:793–94.
"Ayyār," by Fr. Taeschner, 1:794.
"Bakhtiyār-nāma," by J. Horowitz and H. Masse, 1:955.

"al-Bakrī," by F. Rosenthal, 1:946–47.
"Banī Hilāl": see below, "Hilāl."
"al-Barāmika," by D. Sourdel, 1:1033–36.
"al-Baṭṭāl (Sayyid Baṭṭāl Ghāzī)," by I. Mélikoff, 1:1103–4.
"Bilawhar wa-Yūdāsaf," by D. M. Lang, 1:1215–17.
"Dhu 'l-Himma," by M. Canard, 2:233–39.
"Djūḥā'," by Ch. Pellat, 2:590–92.
"al-Hamadānī, Badī' az-Zamān," by R. Blachère, 3:106–7.
"Ḥamāsa," by Ch. Pellat et al., 3:110–19.
"Ḥamza b. 'Abd al-Muṭṭalib," by G. M. Meredith-Owens, 3:152–54.
"al-Ḥarīrī," by L. Massignon, 3:221–22.
"Ḥātim aṭ-Ṭayyi'," by C. van Arendonk, 3:274–75.
"Ḥikāya," by Ch. Pellat et al., 3:367–77.
"Hilāl: The Saga of the Banū Hilāl," by J. Schleifer, 3:387.
"Ibn 'Arabshāh," by J. Pedersen, 2:711–12.
"Ibn Dāniyāl," by J. M. Landau, 3:742.
"Ibn Hishām," by W. M. Watt, 3:800–801.
"Ibn al-Muqaffa'," by F. Gabrieli, 3:883–85.
"Ibn al-Nadīm," by J. W. Fück, 3:895–96.
"Ka'b al-Aḥbār," by M. Schmitz, 4:316–17.
"al-Kisā'ī," by R. Sellheim, 5:175–76.
"Kiṣaṣ al-anbiyā'," by T. Nagel, 5:180–81.
"Luqmān," by B. Heller, N. A. Stillman, 5:810–13.
"al-Ma'mūn," by M. Rekaya, 6:331–39.
"al-Mathal," by R. Sellheim et al., 6:815–28.
"Muwashshaḥ" by G. Schoeler, 7:809–12.
"Qarāqūsh," by M. Sobernheim, 4:613–14.
"Sīrat 'Antar," by B. Heller, 1:518–21.
"Sīrat Baybars," by R. Paret, 1:1126–27.

Evliya Çelebi. *Seyahatnamesi.* Vol. 10: *Misir, Sudan, Habeş.* Istanbul: Devlet Basimevi, 1938.

Finnegan, Ruth. "How Oral Is Oral Literature?" *Bulletin of the School of Oriental and African Studies* 37 (1974): 52–64.

———. *Oral Poetry: Its Nature, Significance and Social Context.* Cambridge, London, New York: Cambridge University Press, 1977.

Fischer, Wolfdietrich, and Helmut Gätje. *Grundriss der Arabischen Philologie,* Part 1: *Sprachwissenschaft.* Wiesbaden: Reichert, 1982.

Foley, John Miles, ed. *Oral-Formulaic Theory and Research: An Introduction and Annotated Bibliography.* New York: Garland, 1986.

———, ed. *Oral Traditional Literature: A Festschrift for Albert Bates Lord.* Columbus, Ohio: Slavica, 1983.

———. *Oral Tradition in Literature.* Columbia: University of Missouri Press, 1986.

———. *The Theory of Oral Composition: History and Methodology.* Bloomington and Indianapolis: Indiana University Press, 1988.

Forster, E. M. *Aspects of the Novel.* Ed. Oliver Stallybrass. Harmondsworth, Middlesex: Penguin Books, 1977.

Foucault, Michel. *The Archeology of Knowledge and the Discourse on Language.* Trans. A. M. Sheridan Smith. New York, Hagerstown, San Francisco, London: Harper Torchbooks, 1972.

———. *The Order of Things: An Archeology of the Human Sciences.* New York: Vintage Books, 1970.

Fresnel, Fulgence. *Lettres sur l'histoire des Arabes avant l'islamisme.* Paris: T. Barrois and B. Duprat, 1836.

———. "Quatrième lettre sur l'histoire des Arabes avant l'islamisme." *Journal Asiatique* (1838): 497–544.

Frye, Northrop. *Anatomy of Criticism: Four Essays.* Princeton: Princeton University Press/Atheneum Paperback, 1970.

———. *The Secular Scripture: A Study of the Structure of Romance.* Cambridge, Mass.: Harvard University Press, 1976.

Fück, Johann. *Die arabische Studien in Europa, bis in der Anfang den 20. Jahrhunderts.* Leipzig: Otto Harrassowitz, 1955.

———. *'Arabiya: Recherches sur l'histoire de la langue et du style arabe.* Trans. Claude Denizeau. Publications de l'Institut des Hautes Etudes Marocaines, notes et documents 16. Paris: Librairie Marcel Didier, 1955.

Gaillard, Marina. *Le livre de Samak-e 'Ayyār: Structure et idéologie du roman persan mediéval.* Travaux de l'Institut d'Etudes Iraniennes de l'Université de la Sorbonne Nouvelle 12. Paris: C. Klincksieck, 1987.

Galley, Micheline, ed. "Manuscrits et documents relatifs à la geste hilalienne dans les bibliothèques anglaises." *Littérature oral arabo-berbère* 12 (1981): 183–92.

———, ed. *Proceedings of the Second International Congress of Studies on Cultures of the Western Mediterranean* II. International Association of Studies on Mediterranean Civilizations, Algiers (1978).

Gamal, Adel Sulaiman. Introduction to *Diwān Ḥātim aṭ-Ṭayyi'.* Ed. Yaḥyā ibn Mudrik aṭ-Ṭayyi' and Hishām Muḥammad al-Kalbī. Cairo: Maktabat al-Khānjī, 1990.

Genette, Gérard. *Narrative Discourse: An Essay in Method.* Trans. Jane E. Lewin. Ithaca, N.Y.: Cornell University Press, 1980.

Gerhardt, Mia I. *The Art of Story-telling: A Literary Study of the Thousand and One Nights.* Leiden: E. J. Brill, 1963.

———. "La technique du récit à cadre dans les *1001 Nuits.*" *Arabica* 8 (1961): 137–57.

Ghanem, Chekri. *Antar, pièce en cinq actes.* Paris: n.p., 1910.
Ghazi, Mohammed Ferid. "La littérature d'imagination en arabe du IIe/VIIIe au Ve/XIe siècles." *Arabica* 4 (1957): 164–78.
Ghazoul, Ferial J. *The Arabian Nights: A Structural Analysis.* Cairo: Cairo Associated Institution for the Study and Presentation of Arab Cultural Values, 1980.
Gibb, Hamilton A. R. *Studies on the Civilization of Islam.* Ed. Stanford J. Shaw and William Polk. Boston: Beacon Press, 1962.
Giffin, Lois A. *Theory of Profane Love among the Arabs: The Development of the Genre.* New York University Studies in Near Eastern Civilization 3. New York: New York University Press, 1971.
Goldziher, Ignaz. *Muhammedanische Studien.* 2 vols. Hildesheim: George Olms, 1961. Eng. trans. *Muslim Studies.* 2 vols. London: George Allen and Unwin, 1967–71.
———. "Ein orientalischer Ritteroman." In *Jubilee Volume in Honor of Bernhard Heller on the Occasion of His Seventieth Birthday,* ed. Alexander Scheiber, 7–13. Budapest: n.p., 1941. Originally in *Pester Lloyd* 64 (1918), Morgenblatt no. 17.
Goody, Jack. *The Interface between the Written and the Oral.* Studies in Literacy, Family, Culture and the State. Cambridge, New York, Melbourne: Cambridge University Press, 1987.
Grégoire, Henri. "Comment Seyyid Baṭṭāl, martyr musulman du VIIIe siècle, est-il devenu dans la légende le contemporain d'Amer (+863)?" *Byzantion* 11 (1936): 571–75.
Greimas, Algirdas J. *On Meaning: Selected Writings in Semiotic Theory.* Trans. Paul J. Perron and Frank H. Collins. Theory and History of Literature 38. Minneapolis: University of Minneapolis Press, 1987.
Grunebaum, Gustav E. von. "Firdausi's Concept of History." In *Fuad Köprülü Armağanı,* 177–93. Istanbul: Osman Yalçın Matbaası, 1953.
———. "The Hero in Medieval Arabic Prose." In *Concepts of the Hero in the Middle Ages and the Renaissance,* ed. Norman T. Burns and Christopher J. Reagan, 83–100. Albany: State University of New York Press, 1975.
Guillaume, A. *The Life of Muḥammad.* Oxford: Oxford University Press, 1955.
al-Ḥajjājī [el-Hegaggi], Aḥmad Shams ad-Dīn. *Maulid al-baṭal fī 's-sīra 'sh-sha'biyya.* Cairo: Dār Hilāl, 1991.
Hall, Stuart. "Encoding, Decoding." In Simon During, ed., *The Cultural Studies Reader,* 90–103.
Hamdānī, Abū Muḥammad al-Ḥasan al-. *al-Iklīl min akhbār al-Yaman wa-ansāb Ḥimyar: al-Kitāb al-'āshir fī ma'ārif Hamdān wa-'uyūn akhbār-hā.* Ed. Muḥibb al-Dīn al-Khaṭīb. Cairo: al-Maṭba'a 's-salafiyya, 1948.

Hamilton, Terrick, trans. *Antar: A Bedoueen Romance.* 4 vols. London: John Murray, 1820.

Hammer-Purgstall, Joseph von. *Fundgruben der Orients* 2 (Vienna, 1802): 304–6.

———. "On Arabian Poetry, Especially the Romance of Antar." *New Monthly Magazine* (London, January/February 1820): 12–18; 115–61. Translation of a German article in *Jahrbücher der Literatur* (Vienna, 1802).

———. "Sur l'auteur de roman de chevalerie arabe Antar." *Journal Asiatique* (April 1838): 383–88.

Hamori, Andras. "A Comic Romance from the Thousand and One Nights: The Tale of the Two Vezirs." *Arabica* (1983): 38–56.

———. "Notes on Two Love Stories from the Thousand and One Nights." *Studia Islamica* (1976): 65–80.

———. *On the Art of Medieval Arabic Literature.* Princeton: Princeton University Press, 1974.

Ḥanafī, Maḥmūd al-. *Sīrat ʿAntara.* Cairo: Dār al-qauma, n.d.

Hanaway, William L., Jr. "The Iranian Epics." In *Heroic Epic and Saga: An Introduction to the World's Great Folk Epics,* ed. F. J. Oinas, 76–98. Bloomington and London: Indiana University Press, 1978.

———. *Love and War: Adventures from the "Fīrūz Shāh Nāma" of Sheikh Bīghamī.* Persian Heritage Series 19. New York: Delmar, 1974.

———. "Persian Popular Romances before the Safavid Period." Ph.D. dissertation, Columbia University, 1970.

Hanna, Sami A. "ʿAntarah: A Model of Arabic Folk Biography." *Southern Folklore Quarterly* 32 (1968): 295–303.

Hartman, Martin. "Die Benī-Hilāl Geschichten." *Zeitschrift für afrikanische und oceanische Sprachen* 4 (1898): 289–315.

Hatto, A. T., ed. *Traditions of Heroic and Epic Poetry.* 2 vols. London: Modern Humanities Research Association, 1980.

Hava, J. G. *al-Farāʾid Arabic-English Dictionary.* Beirut: Dār al-Mashriq, 1986.

Haymes, Edward R. *A Bibliography of Studies Relating to Parry's and Lord's Oral Theory.* Publications of the Milman Parry Collection, no. 1. Albert B. Lord, gen. ed. Cambridge, Mass.: Harvard University Press, 1973.

Heath, Peter. "Arabische Volksliteratur im Mittelalter." In *Neues Handbuch der Literaturwissenschaft,* vol. 5: *Orientalisches Mittelalter,* ed. Wolfhart P. Heinrichs, 423–39. Wiesbaden: AULA-Verlag, 1990.

———. "A Critical Review of Scholarship on *Sīrat ʿAntar ibn Shaddād* and the Popular *Sīra,*" *Journal of Arabic Literature* 15 (1984): 19–44.

———. "Lord and Parry, *Sīrat ʿAntar,* Lions." *Edebiyat* n.s. 2, nos. 1 and 2 (1988): 149–66.

———. Review of Bridget Connelly, *Arabic Folk Epic and Identity. Journal of the American Oriental Society* 108, no. 2 (1988): 315–17.

———. Review of David Pinault, *Story-telling Techniques in the* Arabian Nights. *International Journal of Middle East Studies* 26, no. 2 (1994): 358–60.

———. Review of Heda Jason, *Whom Does God Favor: The Wicked or the Righteous? Journal of the American Oriental Society* 113, no. 2 (1993): 303.

———. Review of Ibrahim Muhawi and Sharif Kanaana, *Speak Bird, Speak Again: Palestinian Arab Folktales. Journal of the American Oriental Society* 110, no. 4 (1990): 784.

———. Review of Jan Knappert, *Islamic Legends: Histories of the Heroes, Saints, and Prophets of Islam. Journal of the American Oriental Society* 110, no. 1 (1990): 138–39.

——— . Review of María Rosa Menocal, *The Arabic Role in Medieval Literary History: A Forgotten Heritage. La Crónica* 18, no. 1 (1989–90): 114–17.

———. Review of Shmuel Moreh, *Live Theatre and Dramatic Literature in the Medieval Arabic World. International Journal of Middle East Studies* 26, no. 3 (1994): 516–18.

———. Review of Susan Slyomovics, *The Merchant of Art: An Egyptian Hilali Oral Epic Poet in Performance. Journal of the American Oriental Society* 110, no. 4 (1990): 784–85.

———. "Romance as Genre in *The Thousand and One Nights*," part 1, *Journal of Arabic Literature* 18 (1987): 1–21; part 2, *Journal of Arabic Literature* 19 (1988): 1–26.

———. Translation from *Sīrat ʿAntar* (1:9–15) in Lowell Edmunds, *Oedipus: The Ancient Legend and Its Later Analogies*, 69–73. Baltimore: Johns Hopkins University Press, 1985.

Hegel, Robert E. "Distinguishing Levels of Audiences for Min-Ch'ing Vernacular Literature." In David Johnson, Andrew J. Nathan, and Evelyn S. Rawski, eds., *Popular Culture in Late Imperial China*, 112–42.

Heller, Bernhard. "Der arabische ʿAntarroman." *Ungarische Rundschau* 5 (1916): 83–107.

———. *Der arabische ʿAntarroman: Ein Beitrag zur vergleichenden Literaturgeschichte.* Hannover: n.p., 1927.

———. *Die Bedeutung des arabischen ʿAntarroman für die vergleichende Literaturkunde.* Leipzig: Herman Eichblatt, 1931.

al-Ḥillī, Safi'a-Dīn. Die vulgärarabische Poetik: al-Kitāb al-ātil al-hālī wa'l-murakhkhas al-ghālī der Safiyaddin al-Hilli, ed. Wilhelm Hoenerbach. Veröffentlichungen der Orientalischer Komission 10. Wiesbaden: F. Steiner, 1956.

Horowitz, Joseph. "The Earliest Biographies of the Prophet and Their Authors." *Islamic Culture* 1 (1927): 535–59; 2 (1927): 22–50, 164–82, 495–526.

———. "The Origins of The Arabian Nights." *Islamic Culture* 1 (1927): 36–57.

———. "Poetische Zitate in Tausend und eine Nacht." In *Festschrift E. Sachau gewidmet.* Berlin: Georg Reimer, 1915.

Hourani, Albert. *Islam in European Thought.* Cambridge: Cambridge University Press, 1991.

Hull, Dennison B., trans. *Digenis Akritas, The Two-Blood Border Lord: The Grottoferrata Version.* Athens: Ohio University Press, 1972.

Ḥusain, Ṭāḥā. *al-Aiyām.* 2 vols. Cairo: Dār al-ma'ārif, 1929–39.

Ibn Abī Uṣaibi'a. *'Uyūn al-anbā' fī ṭabaqāt al-aṭibbā'.* Ed. A. Müller. 2 vols. Königsberg, 1884.

Ibn Ḥazm, Abū Muḥammad 'Alī ibn Aḥmad. *Jamharat ansāb al-'Arab.* Cairo: Dār al-ma'ārif, n.d.

Ibn Hishām, Abū Muḥammad 'Abd al-Malik. *Kitāb at-tījān fī mulūk Ḥimyar.* (*Akhbār 'Ubaid ['Abīd] ibn Sharya* is also printed in this volume.) Hyderabad: Dā'irat al-ma'ārif al-'uthmāniyya, 1928.

Ibn Isḥāq, Muḥammad. *The Life of Muhammad.* Trans. Alfred Guillaume. Lahore and Karachi: Oxford University Press, Pakistan Branch, 1974.

Ibn al-Jauzī, 'Abd ar-Raḥmān ibn 'Alī. *Kitāb al-quṣṣāṣ wa-l-mudhakkirīn.* Ed., trans., intro. Merlin L. Swartz. Recherches publiées sous la direction de l'Institut de Lettres Orientales de Beyrouth. Serie 1: Pensées arabe et musulmane 47. Beirut: Dār al-Mashreq, 1971.

Ibn Khaldūn, 'Abd ar-Raḥmān. *Kitāb al-'ibar.* 7 vols. Vol. 1: *al-Muqaddima.* Beirut: Dār maktabat al-hilāl, 1983.

———. *The Muqaddimah: An Introduction to History.* Trans. Franz Rosenthal. 3 vols. Bollingen Series 43. New York: Pantheon Books, 1958.

Ibn Manẓūr, Muḥammad ibn Mukarram. *Lisān al-'Arab.* 15 vols. Beirut: Dār Ṣādir, 1955.

Ibn al-Muqaffa', 'Abdullāh. *Kalīla wa Dimna.* Ed. Louis Cheikho. Beirut: Dār el-Mashreq, 1969.

Ibn an-Nadīm, Muḥammad ibn Isḥāq. *The Fihrist of an-Nadīm: A Tenth-Century Survey of Muslim Culture.* Ed. and trans. Bayard Dodge. 2 vols. New York: Columbia University Press, 1970.

———. *Kitāb al-Fihrist.* Ed. Gustav Flügel. 2 vols. Leipzig, 1871–72; rpt. Beirut: Khayyat, 1967.

Ibn Qutaiba, Abū Muḥammad 'Abdullāh ibn Muslim. *Kitāb ash-shi'r wa-'sh-shu'arā'.* 2 vols. Ed. Muḥammad Shākir. Cairo: Dār al-ma'ārif, 1966.

Ibn Sallām al-Jumaḥī, Muḥammad. *Ṭabaqāt fuḥūl ash-shu'arā'.* Ed. Joseph Hell. Leiden: E. J. Brill, 1916.

Ibn Sanā' al-Mulk. *Dār aṭ-ṭirāz fī 'amal al-muwashshaḥāt.* Ed. J. al-Rikābī. Damascus: Dār al-fikr, 1977.

Ibrāhīm, Muḥammad Abu l-Faḍl, and 'Alī Muḥammad al-Bijāwī. *Ayyām al-'Arab fī 'l-Islām.* Cairo: Dār iḥyā' al-kutub al-'arabiyya, 1974.

Ibrāhīm, Muḥammad Abu l-Faḍl, 'Alī Muḥammad al-Bijāwī, and Muḥammad Aḥmad al-Maulā Bey. *Ayyām al-'Arab fī 'l-Jāhiliyya.* Cairo: Dār iḥyā al-kutub al-'arabiyya, 1961.

Ibrāhīm, Nabīla. *Ashkāl at-ta'bīr fī l-adab ash-sha'bī.* Cairo: Dār nahḍat Miṣr, n.d.

———. *Sīrat al-Amīra Dhāt al-Himma.* Cairo: Dār al-kitāb al-'arabī, n.d.

Ibshīhī. See Rat, G.

Irwin, Robert. *The Arabian Nights: A Companion.* London: Allen Lane/Penguin Press, 1994.

Iṣfahānī, Abu 'l-Faraj al-. *Kitāb al-aghānī.* Vols. 1–16. Cairo: Dār al-Kutub, 1927–34. Vols. 17–24 (and beginning from vol. 1 again). Cairo: al-Hai'a l-miṣriyya l-'āmma, 1970–.

Ismā'īl, 'Izz ad-Dīn. *al-Qiṣaṣ ash-sha'bī fī s-Sūdān.* Cairo: al-Hai'a l-miṣriyya l-'āmma, 1971.

Jackson, W. T. H. *The Hero and the King: An Epic Theme.* New York: Columbia University Press, 1982.

Jakobson, Roman. "Closing Statement: Linguistics and Poetics." In *Style in Language,* ed. T. A. Sebeok, 350–77. Cambridge, Mass.: MIT Press, 1960.

Jamāl, Aḥmad Ṣādiq al-. *al-Adab al-'āmmī fī Miṣr fī 'aṣr al-Mamlūkī.* 2 vols. Cairo: ad-Dār al-qaumiyya, 1966.

Jameson, Fredric. *The Prison-House of Language: A Critical Account of Structuralism and Russian Formalism.* Princeton: Princeton University Press, 1972.

Jason, Heda. "Genre in Folk Literature." *Fabula* 27, no. 3/4 (1986): 67–94.

———. *Whom Does God Favor: The Wicked or the Righteous?* Folklore Fellows Communications 240. Helsinki: Suomalainen Tiedakatemia, Academia Scientarum Fennica, 1988.

Jauss, Hans Robert. *Toward an Aesthetic of Reception.* Trans. Timothy Bahti. Theory and History of Literature 2. Minneapolis: University of Minnesota Press, 1982.

Jayyusi, Salma Khadra. *The Legacy of Muslim Spain.* Handbuch der Orientalistik 12. Leiden, New York, Cologne: E. J. Brill, 1992.

Johnson, David. "Communication, Class, and Consciousness in Late Imperial China. In *Popular Culture in Late Imperial China,* ed. David Johnson, Andrew J. Nathan, and Evelyn S. Rawski, 34–72.

Johnson, David, Andrew J. Nathan, and Evelyn S. Rawski, eds. *Popular Culture in Late Imperial China.* Berkeley, Los Angeles, London: University of California Press, 1985.

Ker, W. P. *Epic and Romance.* New York: Dover, 1957.

Khalidi, Tarif. *Islamic Historiography: The Histories of Mas'ūdī.* Albany: State University of New York Press, 1975.

Khūrshīd, Fārūq. *Aḍwā' 'ala 's-siyar ash-sha'biyya.* Cairo: al-Maktaba 'th-thaqafiyya, 1974.

Khūrshīd, Fārūq, and Maḥmūd Dhihnī. *Fann kitābat as-sīra 'sh-sha'biyya.* 2nd ed. Beirut: Iqrā', 1980 (1st ed. 1961).

Kitāb Bakr wa-Taghlib; Kitāb Ḥarb Banī Shaibān ma'a Kisrā Anūshirwān (2 works published in 1 volume). Bombay: Muḥammad Rashīd ibn Da'ūd as-Sa'dī, 1887.

Kitāb Rustam-nāma. [Ed.] Muḥammad Ḥasan 'Alamī. Tehran: Bāzār Bain al-Ḥaramain, n.d.

Knappert, Jan. *Islamic Legends: Histories of the Heroes, Saints, and Prophets of Islam.* 2 vols. Leiden: E. J. Brill, 1985.

Köroğlu Destani. Ed. Pertev Naili Boratav. Istanbul: Evkaf Matbaası, 1939.

Kremer, Alfred von. *Aegypten: Forschungen über Land und Volk während eines Zehnjährigen Aufenthalts.* 2 vols. Leipzig: F. A. Brockhaus, 1863.

Krenkow, F. "The Two Oldest Books on Arabic Folklore." *Islamic Culture* 2 (1928): 55–89, 204–36.

Kruk, Remke. "Warrior Women in the Arabic Popular Romance: Qannāṣa bint Muzāhīm and Other Valiant Ladies." Part 1. *Journal of Arabic Literature* 24, no. 3 (1993): 213–30. Part 2: "The Story of Qannāṣa bint Muzāḥim." *Journal of Arabic Literature* 25, no. 1 (1994): 16–33.

Kyriakides, Stilpon P. "Eléments historiques byzantins dans le roman épique turc de Sayyid Baṭṭāl." *Byzantion* 11 (1936): 563–70.

Lamartine, Alphonse de. *Vie des grands hommes.* 2 vols. Paris, 1856.

———. *Voyage en Orient.* 2 vols. Paris, 1875.

Lane, Edward W. *Arabian Society in the Middle Ages: Studies from a Thousand and One Nights.* Ed. Stanley Lane-Poole. London: Curzon Press; New York: Humanities Press, 1987 (originally published 1883).

———. *Arabic-English Lexicon.* 2 vols. London: Islamic Texts Society, 1984.

———. *Manners and Customs of the Modern Egyptians.* London: Dent, Everyman's Library, 1966.

Larkin, Margaret. "A Brigand Hero of Egyptian Colloquial Literature." *Journal of Arabic Literature* 23, no. 1 (1992): 49–64.

Leavis, F. R. *Mass Civilization and Minority Culture.* Minority Pamphlets 1. Cambridge: Gordon Fraser, 1930.

Lemon, Lee T., and Marion J. Reis, trans. *Russian Formalist Criticism: Four Essays.* Regents Critics Series. Lincoln: University of Nebraska Press, 1965.

Le Tourneau, Roger. *Fès avant le protectorat: Etude économique et sociale d'une ville de l'occident musulman.* Publications de l'Institut des Hautes Etudes Marocaines, no. 4. Casablanca: Société marocaine de libraire et d'édition, 1949.

Levend, Agāh Sırrı. *Türk edebiyatı tarihi.* Vol. 1. Ankara: Türk Tarih Kurumu Basımevi, 1973.

Levi della Vida, G. "Pre-Islamic Arabia." In *The Arab Heritage*, ed. Nabih Faris. Princeton: Princeton University Press, 1944.

Lewis, B., and P. M. Holt, eds. *Historians of the Middle East.* Historical Writing on the Peoples of Asia. London, New York, Toronto: Oxford University Press, 1962.

Lewis, Geoffrey, trans. *The Book of Dede Korkut.* Harmondsworth, Middlesex: Penguin Books, 1974.

Littmann, Enno. "Zur Entsehung und Geschichte von Tausendundeiner Nacht." In vol. 6 of Littman's translation of the *Thousand and One Nights: Die Erzählungen aus den Tausendundein Nächten*, 649–738. 6 vols. Wiesbaden: Insel, 1953.

Lord, Albert B. *Epic Singers and Oral Tradition.* Ithaca and London: Cornell University Press, 1991.

———. "Memory, Meaning, and Myth in Homer and Other Oral Traditions." Paper delivered at the University of Urbino, Italy, July 1980.

———. "Perspectives on Recent Work on Oral Literature." *Forum for Modern Language Studies* 103 (1974): 187–210.

———. *The Singer of Tales.* Cambridge, Mass.: Harvard University Press, 1960; New York: Atheneum, 1973.

———. "The Traditional Song." In *Oral Literature and the Formula*, ed. Benjamin A. Stolz and Richard S. Shannon III, 1–15. Ann Arbor: Center for the Coordination of Ancient and Modern Studies, University of Michigan, 1976.

———. "Tradition and the Oral Poet: Homer, Huso and Avdo Medjedovic." In *La poesia epica e la sua formazione*, 13–30. Rome: Accademia nazionale dei Lincei, 1970.

Lüthi, Max. *The Fairytale as Art Form and Portrait of Man.* Trans. Jon Erickson. Bloomington: University of Indiana Press/Midland Books, 1987.

———. *Once upon a Time: On the Nature of Fairy Tales.* Bloomington and London: University of Indiana Press/Midland Books, 1976.

Lyons, Malcolm C. *The Arabian Epic: Heroic and Oral Story-telling.* 3 vols. Cambridge: Cambridge University Press, 1995.

———. "The Crusading Stratum in the Arabic Hero Cycles." In *Crusaders and Muslims in the Twelfth-Century*, ed. Maya Shatzmiller, 147–51. The Medieval Mediterranean: Peoples, Economies and Cultures, 400–1453, 1. Leiden, New York, Cologne: E. J. Brill, 1993.

Macaulay, Lord Thomas Babington. *Lays of Ancient Rome: Essays and Poems.* Everyman's Library 439. London: Dent; New York: Dutton, 1968.

Macdonald, Duncan B. "The Earlier History of the *Arabian Nights.*" *Journal of the Royal Asiatic Society* (1924): 353–97.

———. "A Preliminary Classification of Some Mss. of the *Arabian Nights.*" In *A Volume of Oriental Studies: Presented to E. G. Browne,* 305–21. Cambridge: Cambridge University Press, 1922.

Machiavelli, Niccolò. *The Letters of Machiavelli.* Ed. and trans. Allan H. Gilbert. New York: Capricorn Books, 1961.

Mahdi, Muhsin. *The Thousand and One Nights (Alf Layla wa-Layla), From the Earliest Known Sources.* 3 parts. Leiden: E. J. Brill, 1984–94.

Mahfouz, Naguib. *Midaq Alley.* Translated by Trevor Le Gassick. Rev. 2nd ed. London: Heineman, 1975.

———. *Zuqāq al-midaq* (*Midaq Alley*). Cairo: Dār al-kitāb al-ʿarabī, n.d.

Maranda, Pierre, and Elli Kongas Maranda, eds. *Structural Analysis of Oral Tradition.* Philadelphia: University of Pennsylvania Press, 1971.

Martin, Richard C., ed. *Approaches to Islam in Religious Studies.* Tucson: University of Arizona Press, 1985.

Mason, Eugene, trans. *Aucassin and Nicolette and Other Medieval Romances and Legends.* London: Dent, Everyman's Library, 1910.

Massé, Henri. *Firdausi et l'épopée nationale.* Paris: Librairie Académique, 1935.

Matejka, Ladislav, and Krystyna Pomorska, eds. *Readings in Russian Poetics: Formalist and Structuralist Views.* Cambridge, Mass.: MIT Press, 1971.

Mavrogordato, John, ed. and trans. *Digenis Akritas.* Oxford: Oxford University Press, 1956.

McPherson, Joseph W. *The Moulids of Egypt.* Cairo: Ptd. N. M. Press, 1941.

Meeker, Michael. "Heroic Poems and Anti-Heroic Stories in North Arabia; Literary Genres and the Relationship of Center and Periphery in Arabia." *Journal of Middle Eastern and Comparative Literature* 2, nos. 1 and 2 (1988): 1–40.

———. *Literature and Violence in North Arabia.* Cambridge Studies in Cultural Systems. Cambridge, London, New York: Cambridge University Press, 1979.

Mélikoff, Irène. *Abū Muslim: Le "Porte-Hache" du Khorassan.* Paris: Adrien Maisonneuve, 1962.

———. *Le Geste de Malik Dānishmend.* 2 vols. Bibliothèque Archéologique et Historique de l'Institut Français d'Archéologie d'Istanbul, no. 10. Paris: Adrien Maisonneuve, 1960.

Meyer, Egbert. *Der historische Gehalt der Aiyām al-ʿArab.* Wiesbaden: Otto Harrassowitz, 1970.

Mez, Adam. *The Renaissance of Islam.* Trans. S. Khuda Bakhsh and D. S. Margoliouth. Patna: Jubilee Printing and Pub. House, 1937.

Miller, J. Hillis. *Ariadne's Thread.* New Haven: Yale University Press, 1992.

Miquel, André. *Un conte des Mille et une Nuits: Ajīb et Gharīb.* Paris: Flammarion, 1977.

———. *Sept contes des Mille et une Nuits.* Paris: Sindbad, 1981.

Molé, Marian. "L'Epopée iranienne après Firdosi." *La Nouvelle Clio* 5 (1953): 377–93.

Monroe, James T. "Oral Composition in Pre-Islamic Poetry." *Journal of Arabic Literature* 3 (1972): 1–53.

———. "*Zajal* and *Muwashshaḥa*: Hispano-Arabic Poetry and the Romance Tradition." In Salma Khadra Jayyusi, *The Legacy of Muslim Spain,* 398–419.

Moreh, Shmuel. *Live Theatre and Dramatic Literature in the Medieval Arabic World.* New York University Studies in Near Eastern Civilization 17. New York: New York University Press, 1992.

Muhawi, Ibrahim, and Sharif Kanaana. *Speak Bird, Speak Again: Palestinian Arab Folktales.* Berkeley and Los Angeles: University of California Press, 1989.

Mukerji, Chandra, and Michael Schudson, eds. *Rethinking Popular Culture: Contemporary Perspectives in Cultural Studies.* Berkeley, Los Angeles, Oxford: University of California Press, 1991.

Mukhlis, Faiq Amin. "Studies and Comparison of the Cycles of the Banū Hilāl Romance." Ph.D. dissertation, School of African and Oriental Studies, University of London, 1964.

Musil, Alois. *The Manners and Customs of the Rwala Bedouins.* American Geographical Society of Oriental Explorations and Studies, no. 6. New York: Czech Academy of Sciences and Arts and Charles R. Crane, 1927.

Naddaff, Sandra. *Arabesque: Narrative Structure and the Aesthetics of Repetition in* 1001 Nights. Evanston, Ill.: Northwestern University Press, 1991.

Nadīm, 'Abdullāh, ed. *At-Tankīt wa-'tabkīt* 1 (1881).

Nagler, Micahel N. "Towards a Generative View of the Oral Formula." *Translations and Proceedings of the American Philological Association* 98 (1967): 269–311.

Najjār, Muḥammad Rajab an-. *Ḥikayāt ash-shuṭṭār wa 'l-'ayyārīn fi 't-turāth al-'arabī.* Kuwait: al-Majlis al-waṭanī li-'th-thaqāfa wa-'l-funūn al-'arabī, 1981.

Neuberg, Victor E. *Popular Literature: A History and Guide.* Harmondsworth, Middlesex: Penguin Books, 1977.

New Literary History: A Journal of Theory and Interpretation 18, no. 2 (1987). Issue on Literacy, Popular Culture, and the Writing of History.

Nöldeke, Theodor. *The Iranian National Epic, or The Shahnamah.* Trans. L. Bogdanov. Philadelphia: Porcupine Press, 1979. Originally in *Grundriss der iranischen Philologie,* ed. Ch. Bartholomae et al. 2 vols. Strassburg:

K. J. Trübner, 1895–1904. Bogdanov's translation first appeared in *Journal of the K. R. Cama Oriental Institute* 6 (1960): 1–161.

Norris, H. T. *The Adventures of Antar.* Approaches to Arabic Literature 3. Warminster, Wilts: Aris and Phillips, 1980.

———. *Saharan Myth and Saga.* Oxford Library of African Literature. Oxford: Clarendon Press, 1972.

Oestrup, J. *Studier over Tusind og en Nat.* Copenhagen: Gyldendalske Boghandels, 1891.

O'Flinn, P. "Production and Reproduction: The Case of *Frankenstein.*" *Literature and History* 9, no. 2 (1983): 194–213. Partially repr. in Bob Ashley, *The Study of Popular Fiction,* 23–39.

Oinas, F. J., ed. *Heroic Epic and Saga: An Introduction to the World's Great Folk Epics.* Bloomington and London: Indiana University Press, 1978.

O'leary, DeLacey E. *Arabia before Muhammad.* London: K. Paul Trench, Trübner, 1927.

Oliverius, Jaroslav. "Aufzeichnungen über den Basūs-Krieg in der Kunstliteratur und deren Weiterentwicklung im arabischen Volksbuch über Zīr Sālim." *Archiv Orientalni* 33 (1965): 44–64.

———. "Themen und Motiv im arabischen Volksbuch Zīr Sālim." *Archiv Orientalni* 39 (1971): 129–45.

Olrik, Axel. "Epic Laws of Folk Narrative." In Alan Dundes, ed., *The Study of Folklore,* 131–41.

———. *Nogle Grundsætninger for Sagnforskning.* Danmarks Folkeminder 23. Copenhagen: Schoenbergske Forlag, 1921.

Ong, Walter J. *Orality and Literacy: The Technologizing of the Word.* New Accents Series. London and New York: Routledge, 1982.

Oral Tradition 4, nos. 1–2 (1989). Special issue on Arabic Oral Traditions.

Page, Mary Ellen. "Naqqālī and Ferdowsi: Creativity in the Iranian National Tradition." Ph.D. dissertation, University of Pennsylvania, 1977.

Pantke, Mechthild. *Der arabische Bahrām-Roman: Untersuchungen zur Quellen- und Stoffgeschichte.* Studien zur Sprache, Geschichte und Kultur des islamische Orients, n.s. 6. Berlin and New York: Walter de Gruyter, 1974.

Pantůček, Svetozár. *Das Epos über den Westzug der Banū Hilāl.* Prague: Academia, 1970.

Paret, Rudi. *Früharabische Liebesgeschichten: Ein Beitrag zur vergleichenden Literaturgeschichte.* Bern: P. Haupt, 1927.

———. *Die Geschichte des Islams im Spiegel der arabischen Volksliteratur.* Philosophie und Geschichte, no. 13. Tübingen: J. C. B. Mohr, 1927.

———. "Die legendäre Futūḥ-Literatur, ein arabische Volksepos?" In *La poesia epica e la sua formazione,* 735–47. Rome: Accademia nazionale dei Lincei, 1970.

———. *Die legendäre Maghāzī-Literatur.* Tübingen: J. C. B. Mohr, 1930.

———. *Der Ritter-Roman von 'Umar an-Nu'mān und seine Stellung zur Sammlung von Tausendundeiner Nacht.* Tübingen: J. C. B. Mohr, 1930.

———. *Sīrat Saif ibn Dhī Jazan: Ein arabischer Volksroman.* Hannover: Heinz Lafaire, 1924.

Parry, Milman. *The Making of Homeric Verse: The Collected Papers of Milman Parry.* Edited by Adam Parry. Oxford: Clarendon Press, 1971.

Pedersen, Johannes. "The Criticism of the Islamic Preacher." *Die Welt des Islams* 2 (1953): 215–31.

———. "The Islamic Preacher: *Wā'iẓ, mudhakkir, qāṣṣ.*" In *Ignaz Goldziher Memorial Volume,* ed. S. Löwenger and J. Somogyi, part 1, 226–51. Budapest: n.p., 1948.

Pérès, Henri. "Le roman dans la littérature arabe des origines à la fin du Moyen Age." *Annales de l'Institut d'Etudes Orientales* (Algiers) 16 (1958): 5–40.

———. "Le roman historique dans la littérature arabe." *Annales de l'Institut d'Etudes Orientales* (Algiers): 15 (1975): 5–39.

Perron, A. "Lettre sur Antar." *Journal Asiatique* (December 1840): 481–526.

Perry, B. E. "The Origin of the *Book of Sinbad.*" *Fabula* 3 (1960): 1–94.

Petràcek, Karel. "Die Poesie als Kriterium des arabischen 'Volksroman.' " *Oriens* 23–24 (1970–71): 301–5.

———. "Quellen und Anfänge der arabischen Literatur." *Archiv Orientalni* 36 (1968): 381–406.

Pinault, David. *Story-telling Techniques in the* Arabian Nights. Leiden, New York, Cologne: E. J. Brill, 1992.

Propp, Vladimir. *Morphology of the Folktale.* Trans. Laurence Scott, rev. Louis A. Wagner. Bloomington: Research Center in the Language Sciences, 1968. 2nd ed. rev. and ed. with a preface by Louis A. Wagner. Austin: University of Texas Press, 1975.

Qalamāwī, Suhair al-. *Alf laila wa-laila.* Cairo: Dār al-ma'ārif, 1966.

Quraishī, Ḥasan 'Abdullāh al-. *Fāris Banī 'Abs.* Cairo: Dār al-ma'ārif, 1969.

Quraishī, Riḍā Muḥsin al-. *al-Funūn ash-shi'riyya as-saba'.* Baghdad: Dār al-ḥurriya, 1975.

Rabkin, Eric S. *The Fantastic in Literature.* Princeton: Princeton University Press, 1976.

———. *Narrative Suspense: "When Slim Turned Sideways . . ."* Ann Arbor: University of Michigan Press, 1973.

Radlov, Vasili V. *Proben der Volkslitteratur der nördlichen türkischen Stämme,* vol. 5: *Der dialect der Kara-Kirgisen.* St. Petersburg: Commissionäre der Kaiserlichen Akademie der Wissenschaften, 1885.

Raglan, Fitzroy R. A., Lord. *The Hero: A Study in Tradition, Ritual, and Drama.* London: Methuen, 1936.

———. "The Hero in Tradition." In Alan Dundes, ed., *The Study of Folklore*, 142–57.

Rank, Otto. *The Myth of the Birth of the Hero: A Psychological Interpretation of Mythology.* New York: Vintage Books, 1959.

Rat, G., trans. Al-Ibshīhī, *Al-Mostatraf: Recueil de morceaux choisis çà et là dans toutes les branches des connaissances réputées attrayantes.* Toulon: n.p., 1889–1902.

Raymond, André. "Une liste des corporations de métiers au Caire en 1801." *Arabica* 4 (1957): 150–63.

Redfield, Robert. *Peasant Society and Culture.* Chicago and London: University of Chicago, 1956; rpt. 1967.

Renard, John. *Islam and the Heroic Image: Themes in Literature and the Visual Arts.* Studies in Comparative Religion. Columbia: University of South Carolina, 1993.

Reynolds, Dwight Fletcher. "Heroic Poets, Poetic Heroes: Composition and Performance in an Arabic Oral Epic Tradition in Northern Egypt." Ph.D. dissertation, University of Pennsylvania, 1991.

———. *Heroic Poets, Poetic Heroes: Composition and Performance in an Arabic Oral Epic Tradition in Northern Egypt.* Myth and Poetics. Ithaca and London: Cornell University Press, 1995.

Ricoeur, Paul. *Time and Narrative.* 3 vols. Trans. K. McLaughlin and D. Pelleur. Chicago: University of Chicago Press, 1984.

Ringgren, Helmer. *Fatalism in Persian Epics.* Uppsala Universitets Aarskrift, no. 6. Uppsala: Lundequistska Bokhandeln, 1952.

———. *Studies in Arabic Fatalism.* Uppsala Universitets Aarskrift, no. 3. Uppsala: Lundequistska Bokhandeln, 1955.

Rodinson, Maxime. *Europe and the Mystique of Islam.* Trans. Roger Veinus. Near Eastern Studies 4. Seattle and London: University of Washington Press, 1987.

"The Romance of Antar." *Asiatic Journal* n.s. 27 (September 1838): 57–61.

Rosenthal, Franz. *A History of Muslim Historiography.* Leiden: E. J. Brill, 1968.

Ross, Andrew. *No Respect: Intellectuals and Popular Culture.* New York and London: Routledge, 1989.

Rypka, Jan. *History of Iranian Literature.* Dordrecht: D. Reidel, 1968.

Said, Edward W. *Orientalism.* New York: Pantheon, 1978.

Sakhāwī, Muḥammad ibn 'Abd ar-Raḥmān as-. *Tuḥfat al-aḥbāb wa-bughyat aṭ-ṭullāb.* Cairo: Maṭba'at al-'ulūm wa-'l-adab, 1937.

Sale, Roger. *Fairy Tales and After: From Snow White to E. B. White.* Cambridge, Mass., and London: Harvard University Press, 1978.

Ṣaliḥ, Rushdī. *al-Adab ash-sha'bī.* Cairo: Maktabat an-nahḍa 'l-miṣriyya, 1971.

———. *al-Funūn ash-sha'biyya.* Cairo: al-Maktaba th-thaqāfiyya, 1961.

Sallām, Muḥammad Zaghlūl. *al-Adab fī 'l-'aṣr al-mamlūkī.* 2 vols. Cairo: Dār al-ma'ārif, 1971.

Schimmel, Annemarie. *And Muhammad Is His Messenger: The Veneration of the Prophet in Islamic Piety.* Chapel Hill and London: University of North Carolina Press, 1985.

Scholes, Robert. *Structuralism in Literature: An Introduction.* New Haven and London: Yale University Press, 1974.

Scholes, Robert, and Robert Kellog. *The Nature of Narrative.* Oxford: Oxford University Press, 1966.

Schreiner, Martin. "Samaw'al b. Jaḥya al-Magribī und seine Schrift *Ifḥām al-Jahūd.*" *Monatsschrift für Geschichte und Wissenschaft des Judenthums* n.s. (1898): 123–33, 170–80, 214–23, 253–61, 407–18.

Schwab, Raymond. *The Oriental Renaissance: Europe's Rediscovery of India and the East 1680–1880.* Trans. Gene Patterson-Black and Victor Reinking. New York: Columbia University Press, 1984.

Sebeok, Thomas A., ed. *Myth: A Symposium.* Bloomington: University of Indiana Press/Midland Books, 1974.

———, ed. *Style in Language.* Cambridge, Mass.: MIT Press, 1960.

Seetzen, Ulrich Jasper. *Reisen durch Syrien, Palästina, Phönicien, die Transjordan-länden, Arabia Petraea und Unter-Aegypten.* 4 vols. Berlin: Georg Reimer, 1859.

Sellheim, R. "Prophet, Chalif und Geshichte: die Muḥammad-Biographie des Ibn Isḥāq." *Oriens* 18–19 (1967): 33–91.

Sezgin, Fuat. *Geschichte des arabischen Schrifttums.* Leiden: E. J. Brill, 1967–.

Shauqī, Aḥmad. *'Antara.* Cairo: Dār al-kutub al-miṣriyya, 1932.

Shoshan, Boaz. "High Culture and Popular Culture in Medieval Islam." *Studia Islamica* 83 (1991): 67–107.

———. "On Popular Literature in Medieval Cairo." *Poetics Today* 14, no. 2 (1993): 349–69.

———. *Popular Culture in Medieval Cairo.* Cambridge Studies in Islamic Civilization. Cambridge: Cambridge University Press, 1993.

Sīrat Imām 'Ali 'bn Abī Ṭālib (Futūḥ al-Yaman). Cairo: Maktabat al-Jumhūriyya 'l-'Arabiyya, n.d.

Slyomovics, Susan. "The Death-Song of 'Āmir Khafājī: Puns in an Oral and Printed Episode of Sīrat Banī Hilāl." *Journal of Arabic Literature* 18 (1987): 62–78.

———. *The Merchant of Art: An Egyptian Hilali Oral Epic Poet in Performance.* Modern Philology 120. Berkeley and Los Angeles: University of California Press, 1987.

Sowayan, Saad Abdullah. *Nabaṭi Poetry: The Oral Poetry of Arabia.* Berkeley, Los Angeles, London: University of California Press, 1985.

Steinbach, Udo. *Dāt al-Himma: Kulturgeschichtliche Untersuchungen zu einem arabischen Volksroman.* Freiburger Islamstudien, no. 4. Wiesbaden: Franz Steiner, 1972.

Stolz, Benjamin A., and Richard S. Shannon III, eds. *Oral Literature and the Formula.* Ann Arbor: Center for the Coordination of Ancient and Modern Studies, University of Michigan, 1976.

as-Subkī, Tāj ad-Dīn. *Mu'īd an-ni'am wa-mubīd an-niqam.* Ed. D. W. Myhrman. Semitic Text and Translation Series 18. London: Luzac, 1908.

Sulaimān, Mūsā. *al-Adab al-qaṣaṣī 'ind al-'Arab.* 4th ed. Beirut: Dār al-kitāb al-lubnānī, 1969.

Surmelian, Léon, trans. *Daredevils of Sassoun: The Armenian National Epic.* Denver: Alan Swallow, 1964.

Suyūṭī, Jalāl ad-Dīn as-. *Sharḥ maqāmāt Jalāl ad-Dīn as-Suyūṭī.* Ed. Samīr Maḥmūd ad-Durūbī. 2 vols. Beirut: Mu'assasat ar-risāla, 1989.

Ṭabarī, Abū Jarīr Muḥammad Aṭ-. *The History of al-Ṭabarī, Volume 1: General Introduction and the Creation to the Flood.* Trans. Franz Rosenthal. Bibliotheca Persica. Albany: State University of New York Press, 1989.

———. *Kitāb jāmi' al-bayān fī tafsīr al-qur'ān.* 30 vols. Cairo: Būlāq, 1905–12.

Taimūr, Maḥmūd. *Ḥawwā' al-khālida.* Cairo: Maṭba'at al-istiqāma, 1945.

———. "Übertragungen aus der neuarabischen Literatur." *Die Welt des Islams* 13 (1932): 1–103.

Taine, Hippolyte. *Philosophie de l'art.* 3rd ed. 2 vols. Paris: Hachette, 1881.

Thackston, W. M., Jr., trans. *The Tales of the Prophets of al-Kisā'ī.* Library of Classical Arabic Literature. Boston: Twayne Publishers, 1978.

Tha'labī, Abū Isḥāq Aḥmad ibn Muḥammad, ath-. *Qiṣaṣ al-anbiyā'* (also called *'Arā'is al-majālis*). Cairo: Dār iḥyā' al-kutub al-'arabiyya, n.d.

Thompson, John B. "Editor's Introduction." In Pierre Bourdieu, *Language and Symbolic Power,* 1–31.

Thompson, Stith. *The Folktale.* New York: Holt, Rinehart and Winston, 1946.

———. *Motif Index of Folk-Literature.* 6 vols. Revised and enlarged. Bloomington: Indiana University Press, 1955–58.

Thorbecke, Heinrich. *Antarah: Des vorislamischen Dichters Leben.* Heidelberg: Fr. Basserman, 1868.

Todorov, Tzvetan. *The Fantastic: A Structural Approach to a Literary Genre.* Trans. Richard Howard. Ithaca, N.Y.: Cornell University Press, Cornell Paperbacks, 1975.

———. *Introduction to Poetics.* Trans. R. Howard. Theory and History of Literature 1. Minneapolis: University of Minnesota Press, 1981.

Türkmen, Fikret. *Aşık Garıp hikâyesi üzerinde mukayeseli bir arastırma.* Atatürk Üniversitesi Yayın, no. 357. Edebiyet Fakültesi Yayın 70. Arastırma Yayın 59. Ankara: Baylan Matbaası, 1974.

Vadet, J. C. *L'Esprit courtois en Orient dans les premiers siècles de l'Hégire.* Paris: Maisonneuve et Larose, 1968.

Vermeulen, Urbain. "'Antar en al-Andalus." In *Proceedings of the XIIIth Congress of the Union Européenne des Arabisants et Islamisants,* 741–57. Venice: Casa Editrices Armena, 1986.

———. "'Antar et la Ville Blanche." *Orientalia Lovaniensia Periodica* 18 (1987): 163–76.

———. "L'Apparition de prophète dans la *Sīrat 'Antar.*" *Quaderni di Studi Arabi* 7 (1989): 153–61.

———. "Une apparition 'prématuré' du prophète dans la *Sīrat 'Antar.*" *Orientalia Lovaniensia Periodica* 21 (1990): 177–85.

Vinaver, Eugene. *The Rise of Romance.* Oxford: Oxford University Press, 1971.

Virolleaud, Charles. "Le roman de l'Emir Hamza, oncle de Mahomet." *L'Ethnographie* 53 (1958–59): 3–10.

Vollers, K. "Das Religionsgespräch von Jerusalem (um 800 A.D.): aus dem Arabischen übersetzt." *Zeitschrift für Kirchengeschichte* 29 (1908): 29–70.

Vries, Jan de. *Heroic Song and Heroic Legend.* Trans. B. J. Timmer. Oxford: Oxford University Press, 1963.

Waldman, Marilyn R. "Primitive Mind/Modern Mind: New Approaches to an Old Problem Applied in Islam." In *Approaches to Islam in Religious Studies,* ed. Richard C. Martin, 90–105. Tucson: University of Arizona Press, 1985.

Wangelin, Helmut. *Das arabische Volksbuch von König eẓẒāhir Baibars.* Stuttgart: W. Kohlhammer, 1936.

Wāqidī, al- [pseudonym]. *Futūḥ ash-Shām.* 2 vols. Cairo: Dār al-jīl, n.d.

Waugh, Earle H. *The Munshidīn of Egypt: Their World and Their Song.* Columbia: University of South Carolina Press, 1989.

Wehr, Hans, ed. *Das Buch der wunderbaren Erzählungen und seltsamen Geschichte.* Bibliotheca Islamica 18. Wiesbaden: Franz Steiner, 1956.

Welhausen, J. *The Arab Kingdom and Its Fall.* Trans. Margaret G. Weir. Khayyats Oriental Reprints 6. Beirut: Khayyats, 1963.

Wetzstein, J. G. "Der Markt in Damaskus." *Zeitschrift der Deutschen Morgenländischen Gesellschaft* 11 (1857): 493–525.

White, Hayden. *Metahistory: The Historical Imagination in Nineteenth-Century Europe.* Baltimore and London: Johns Hopkins University Press, 1973.

———. *Tropics of Discourse: Essays in Cultural Criticism.* Baltimore and London: Johns Hopkins University Press, 1978.

Widengren, Geo. "Oral Tradition and Written Literature among the Hebrews in the Light of Arabic Evidence, with Special Regard to Prose Narratives." *Acta Orientalia* 23 (1956): 201–62.

Williams. Raymond. *Keywords: A Vocabulary of Culture and Society.* Rev. ed. New York: Oxford University Press, 1983.

———. *The Long Revolution.* London: Chatto and Windus, 1961.

———. *The Sociology of Culture.* New York: Schocken Books, 1981.

Yūnis, 'Abd al-Ḥamīd. *Difā' 'an al-fūlklūr.* Cairo: al-Hai'a 'l-miṣriyya 'l-'āmma, 1973.

———. *al-Ḥikāya 'l-sha'biyya.* Cairo: al-Maktaba 'th-thaqāfiyya, 1968.

———. *al-Hilāliyya fī 't-ta'rīkh wa-'l-adab ash-sha'bī.* Cairo: Maṭba'at Jāmi'at al-Qāhira, 1956.

Zipes, Jack. *Fairy Tales and the Art of Subversion: The Classical Genre for Children and the Process of Civilization.* New York: Methuen, 1983.

Zumthor, Paul. *Oral Poetry: An Introduction.* Trans. K. Murphy-Judy. Theory and History of Literature 70. Minneapolis: University of Minnesota Press, 1990.

Zwettler, Michael. "Classical Arabic Poetry between Folk and Oral Tradition." *Journal of the American Oriental Society* 96, no. 2 (1976): 198–212.

———. *The Oral Tradition of Classical Arabic Poetry: Its Character and Implications.* Columbus: Ohio University Press, 1978.

Index